Anaïs Nin's Narratives

Florida A&M University, Tallahassee
Florida Atlantic University, Boca Raton
Florida Gulf Coast University, Ft. Myers
Florida International University, Miami
Florida State University, Tallahassee

University of Central Florida, Orlando
University of Florida, Gainesville
University of North Florida, Jacksonville
University of South Florida, Tampa
University of West Florida, Pensacola

Anaïs Nin's Narratives

Edited by Anne T. Salvatore

University Press of Florida
Gainesville/Tallahassee/Tampa/Boca Raton
Pensacola/Orlando/Miami/Jacksonville/Ft. Myers

Permissions to quote from copyrighted material appear in the acknowledgments section, which begins on page xvii.

Library of Congress Cataloging-in-Publication Data
Anaïs Nin's narratives / edited by Anne T. Salvatore.
    p. cm.
  Includes bibliographical references and index.
  ISBN 0-8130-2113-8
  1. Nin, Anaïs, 1903–1977—Technique. 2. Women and literature—United
States—History—20th century. 3. Narration (Rhetoric). I. Salvatore, Anne T., 1941–
PS3527.I865 Z545 2001   00-069066
818'.5209–dc21

The University Press of Florida is the scholarly publishing agency for the State University System of Florida, comprising Florida A&M University, Florida Atlantic University, Florida Gulf Coast University, Florida International University, Florida State University, University of Central Florida, University of Florida, University of North Florida, University of South Florida, and University of West Florida.

University Press of Florida
15 Northwest 15th Street
Gainesville, FL 32611–2079
http://www.upf.com

for Megan Elizabeth

That wisdom and grace shall be her companions;
that love shall inhabit her soul.

I write . . . and I am changed; it seems as though all the darkness has vanished like a cloud.

Anaïs Nin, *Linotte*

Contents

The debate over canonical representation in the academy has prompted many feminist scholars to explore reasons for the study of women writers, both in the classroom and as a scholarly pursuit. While some female writers may have been initially chosen for study mainly on the basis of their historical importance, considerations of aesthetic value and literary merit began to fuel the controversy as criteria for selection were examined and argued. Anaïs Nin's place in the canon was, for many decades, assumed to be nearly nonexistent. Yet, her image as a popular cult figure seemed to remain undiminished, perhaps even reinforced by what many reviewers of her books apparently considered her exaggerated narcissism, a claim based on the personal focus of her *Diary*. During the most recent decade, however, a steady increase in scholarly attention to Nin's work has given rise to a number of books and articles dealing with her fiction as well as her diaries. With this book, I intend to build upon this scholarly base by presenting essays with explicit or implied theoretical underpinnings. Approaches include a focus on one or more of the currently prominent critical theories—narratological, feminist, psychoanalytical, semiological, Barthesian, reader response—as well as the traditional New Critical or close-reading analyses. To counteract popular notions of Nin as cult figure, and to better understand the complexity and implications of her literary initiatives, the importance of connecting her works to these theories cannot be overstated. Since several of the articles use more than one theoretical base, and since all deal in some way with narrative strategy, I have chosen to organize the essays thematically, rather than theoretically or methodologically.

Two articles focus on sociological concerns. Diane Richard-Allerdyce's essay on Nin's erotica, "Anaïs Nin's 'Poetic Porn': Problematizing the Gaze," demonstrates through close readings of several erotica how the desiring male gaze perpetuates society's acceptance of sexual exploitation. She proposes that Nin, as author, subverts the objectivizing gaze that manifests her patron's desire by finding narrative strategies to make the gaze look ridiculous and by revealing the estrangement and the social tragedy that follow the sexual exploitation. Examining such stories as "The Hungarian Adventurer," "Mathilde," "Marianne," "The Veiled Woman," "Little Birds," and "Runaway" in the collections *Delta of Venus* and *Little Birds*, Richard-Allerdyce suggests that these texts prompt a self-questioning by readers, who are encouraged to notice the manner in which they themselves have been manipulated both by such pornography and by the general patriarchal culture. In demonstrating that love is possible only between two subjectively realized human beings, the stories imply the need for a substantive cultural shift that includes a recognition and tolerance for the Other. Nin thus indicates that a connection is possible between literature and social action, a theme that she often promoted in her lectures as well as in her other fictional works.

Some critics have denied Nin's implied interest in social action, however. Accusing her of narcissism, they claim that her writings ignore the horrors surrounding her and demonstrate a lack of care and concern for public welfare. Marion Fay defends Nin from these accusations in "Anaïs Nin's Narrative Dilemma: The Artist and Social Conscience." By examining the ideology in the *Diary* and in some of Nin's theoretical writings, Fay reveals Nin's conflicting thoughts regarding the artist's role in the public sphere. Fay also clarifies Nin's reasons for eschewing social realism in her work, yet shows how in the stories from *Under a Glass Bell* Nin dramatically suggests a very real care and concern for those who feel the brutal effects of social injustice. The narration in "The Mouse," "Birth," "The Child Born Out of the Fog," and "Houseboat" implies, both directly and indirectly, a great humanitarian sensitivity. The article also demonstrates that Nin's emphasis on self-exploration and emotional integrity indicates her belief in the importance of the inner life as a starting point in any reform effort. In addition, Fay asserts, Nin's works suggest that the primary responsibility of the artist is to create an aesthetic alternative to the tragedies taking place in the social world.

Four essays study the personal responses of the wounded female psyche victimized by some form of patriarchal exploitation, as personified or symbolized by one or more father figures. Examing Nin's use of Freudian psychoanalytic principles, Suzette Henke offers an in-depth look at one of Nin's most intriguing female characters in "Psychoanalyzing Sabina: Anaïs Nin's *A Spy in the House of Love* as Freudian Fable." Of Freud's famous libidinal types (ego, superego, and id), the instinctual, erotic character of the id seems best suited for an investigation of Sabina's personality, which struggles continually with the Freudian superego as personified by the Lie Detector, the symbol of the law and the Word of the Father. Showing how Nin exploits narrative strategies to undermine some of Freud's assumptions, Henke presents Sabina as an "artist of life" who seeks through her multitudinous affairs with father figures to recover the comforting joys of childhood, but suffers from the same objectivizing noticeable in the erotica as she yields her subjectivity. Unconsciously responding to this discomforting situation, she fabricates a fantasy life even while she experiences the guilt of sensing her own deception and the fear of the Lie Detector's discovery of it. As Henke traces the effects of Sabina's illusory strategies, it becomes clear that the character suffers from a serious disparity between her actual vulnerable ego and the apparently confident player of roles that she manifests to the world at large. The deleterious effects of this disparity include a series of transient relationships with men unable or unwilling to construct a meaningful relationship with Sabina's fragmented personality. Henke concludes that while the novel's ending seems ambiguous, the narrative may be suggesting that a coherent identity proves, at least in this case, to be impossible to grasp, rendering the Freudian assumption of potential integrity itself a psychological fantasy.

In "Sex with Father: The Incest Metaphor in Anaïs Nin," Ellen G. Friedman studies the ways in which incest as a trope suggests the tensions and paralysis that patriarchal authority may cause for women artists. Surveying samples of a variety of Nin's fictional works from *House of Incest* to *Winter of Artifice* to *Under a Glass Bell* to *Ladders to Fire*, Friedman considers the paralyzing relationship between the woman and the father, viewed against the background of destructive and suffocating social and artistic patriarchal forms. The essay suggests that Nin's biographical experiences with male authority figures who tried to control her development as an artist—Rank, Durrell, Miller—form an analogue with the tortured experiences of her fictional women who try to escape from the artistic house of incest by writing as women, from the womb, or out of the woman's body.

Diane Richard-Allerdyce's "Transference, Mourning, and Narrative Recovery in *House of Incest*" features an analysis both of the author's and of the fictional narrator's struggles through an ultimately therapeutic process of facing a past in which the Father figure violated his expected function of upholding the law and protecting his offspring. The "hysterical" discourse that results from his perpetration of sexual exploitation is the linguistic equivalent of the daughter's overwhelming sense of fragmentation. Using Lacanian theory to help reveal the narrator's progress backward to relive the wound and forward to mourn its presence, Richard-Allerdyce traces the imaginary fusions and the actual disconnections from reality experienced by the narrator's psyche. The essay suggests, however, that finding a voice to articulate their stories reflects both the author's and the narrator's movements toward leave-taking, in itself a creative process with power to heal the psychic wounds and offer an Otherness separate from the father's incestuous domain.

Writing against the patriarchy takes a personal and dramatic form in Sharon Spencer's "'Musique Ancienne': The Ultimate Seduction in 'Winter of Artifice.'" Focusing on the mutual attraction of father and daughter in the text, Spencer traces the complex seductions that lead from the daughter's traditional idealization of the father as a god, through her later disillusionment as she awakens to his artificiality, to her ultimate rejection of him as her self-awareness increases after the encounter. Nin's own seduction of the reader into a romanticization of the incestuous affair is artfully achieved, Spencer asserts, through the "musicalization" of the prose. Stylistic devices such as repetition and inversion, along with figurative language including assonance and alliteration, heighten the intensity of the poetic text. But like the narrator in *House of Incest*, the daughter in "Winter" senses that the "musique ancienne" must be rejected for the woman to hear her own music and to discover her own unity and subjectivity as a separate being from the father.

Two essays explore some of the less explicit forms of patriarchy together with the varying mechanisms people use to deal with the resulting difficulty of achieving their own subjectivity in such prescribed contexts. My essay "Trying to Tell Her Story: Mothering Scripts and the Counternarrative in Nin's *Diary* and *Cities of the Interior*" demonstrates women's reliance on external, authoritarian blueprints or "scripts" to create a pseudo-identity rather than an authentic self-narrative. Both the persona in the diaries and the three central women characters in *Cities* struggle against the patriarchal motherhood script, which prescribes a sacrificial, passive, nonsubjective role for women. I trace in these works the nature and implications of a psychoanalytic counternarrative voice that exposes the damaging effects of these maternal scripts on various female characters. The psychoanalytic voice demonstrates women's complicity in the scripts, but it also offers a way for these women to discover their complex subjectivity by articulating their own stories. Thus, Nin highlights the importance both of the psychoanalytic process and of the articulation and dissemination of women's narratives to counteract the insistent presence of sociological scripts that dominate women's lives.

In "The Artist as Character (or the Character as Artist): Narrative and Consciousness in Anaïs Nin's *Collages*," on the other hand, Thomas M. March shows how the characters in *Collages* rely, not on the externally established authority of a single, static narrative voice, but rather on their own mythmaking mechanism in an attempt to achieve "diverse (and ostensibly independent) represented consciousnesses." March uses Freudian and Barthesian theories to examine the process of mythmaking itself both as a narrative technique and as a way of reading oneself. Confronted by experience, the characters either embrace or reject objects according to the objects' relevance to their own previously constructed internal myths or readings. According to March, the narrator's role in *Collages* is then to reveal the mythological nature of experience through a representation of these various consciousnesses. Because the narrator allows these consciousnesses primacy in the text, however, the former's own authority is, in effect, greatly reduced. The text itself, no longer a static reality, is subject to the interpretation or "reading" of the individual consciousnesses. March then applies his theory of mythmaking to various elements in *Collages*, including the old man and the seal, Renate's dreams and subsequent disillusionment with her myth of "Bruce," and the relationship at the end between Dr. Mann and Judith Sands.

Two writers with historical concerns suggest ways of fitting Nin's writing into the modernist period, despite the apparent tension between traditional modernism and Nin's characteristically feminist writing. In her essay "'Dismaying the Balance': Anaïs Nin's Narrative Modernity," Philippa Christmass examines women writers' creation of "another modernism" based on techniques that differ significantly from those used by many canonized male modernists. Noting the predominantly negative reaction by patriarchal modernist critics and writers to Nin's writing, Christmass considers some of the narrative qualities found objectionable by these critics. Ironically, many of the same characteristics—alleged impenetrability, impressionism, introspection—criticized in Nin's work were not only present but often celebrated in the works of such male writers as James Joyce. The essay asserts that in her rejection of social realism and her focus on subjectivity, fluidity, ambiguity, rhythm, and corporeality, Nin anticipated *écriture féminine*. Illustrating the use of imagery and other techniques in *House of Incest* and in "Birth" from *Under a Glass Bell*, Christmass proposes that Nin's works also suggest her modernist proclivities through techniques that parallel surrealist strategies. The essay argues that Nin's modernism deserves to be considered in new, feminist contexts that are not based solely on criteria established by patriarchal assumptions. Moreover, the essay points out that Nin's work may be viewed as representative of the works of other female modernists: all experiment with literary means of awarding to gender a role of central importance.

Like Philippa Christmass, Maxie Wells proposes to situate Nin's work within the framework of modernist poetics in "Writing the Mind in the Body: Modernism and Écriture Féminine in Anaïs Nin's *A Spy in the House of Love* and *Seduction of the Minotaur*." Analyzing these two novels from *Cities of the Interior*, Wells specifies as modernist a host of narrative techniques, some that Nin shares with canonized male practitioners and many others that she practices in ways analogous to the artistry of certain female, marginalized writers. The techniques Wells examines include subject matter, especially issues related to gender and human relationships; linguistic form; interest in marginalized genres such as the poetic novel, the prose poem, the diary, the essay, and the short story; fragmented, episodic chronology; surrealism; and symbolism. As Wells interprets the two novels, she demonstrates that beyond these affinities with male and female artists, Nin offers her own distinctive brand of modernism. She replaces the artist-as-priest characters who seek to rise above the horrors of the modern world with artist-as-healer figures who search for integrity within the painful reality of their world, and who attempt to forge a union of body, emotion, and mind. Thus, Wells reveals how Nin uses *écriture féminine* to reconstitute certain archetypal symbols and myths and to assert the fluid nature of human experience.

The final essay situates Nin's writing politically. In "Anaïs Nin's Rhizomatic *Diary*," Mai Al-Nakib examines the nature of the *Diary's* appeal to feminists. Arguing against viewing the *Diary* as the narcissistic, subjective form that many of Nin's earlier critics had labeled it, Al-Nakib uses Gilles Deleuze and Félix Guattari's term "rhizome" to demonstrate both the continual multiplicity and the intentionally political nature of Nin's diary narratives. This essay, in fact, sometimes agrees with, but more often disputes, ideas in several other essays in this book. While Al-Nakib confirms, for instance, the idea of other critics that Nin aims to escape the limitations imposed by traditional forms, this critic asserts that Nin's method of doing so often includes a refusal to espouse the aims and assumptions of traditional psychoanalysis. In opposition to the views of some other feminist critics, Al-Nakib views the incest that Nin describes in her unexpurgated diary[1] not as an illustration of female victimhood but as Nin's narrative/political statement against hierarchical assumptions about taboos and gender. Central to this essay is its suggestion that the *Diary's* paradoxical nature, as a statement at once imperceptible and public, allows readers to experience the narrative as Nin's move toward the creation of an alternative collective common sense.

The variety of theoretical investigations and the substantive controversy among Nin's critics may help to indicate the depth and complexity of her work. Our hope for this book, then, is that the scholarly attention we devote to her narratives will strengthen further the communal reception for the vital insights these works contain.

NOTE

1. In discussing Nin's diaries, critics like Al-Nakib, as well as other contributors to this collection, typically assume at least two types of editing processes: Nin's own heavy-handed editing by which she removed material from the originals that she wanted to remain confidential, and the less manipulative later editing, usually undertaken by a publisher or family member after Nin's death, that left some or most of the inflammatory material intact. The term "unexpurgated," as used in this anthology, is applied to the latter type of editing. The term is not meant to suggest that no editing took place.

Acknowledgments

I wish to thank Rider University for the research leave that enabled me to begin work on this book. I am grateful to the University Press of Florida's acquisitions editor Susan Fernandez for her wise and knowledgeable counsel and her enthusiastic support; to project editor Judy Goffman for her informative, practical suggestions; to copyeditor Ann Marlowe for her astute commentary on textual and stylistic matters; and to my husband, Nicholas Salvatore, whose continued encouragement has been indispensable to this project.

I thank all those who have granted us permission to reprint material that was published previously. Portions of several essays appeared earlier in *Anaïs: An International Journal*, of which Gunther Stuhlmann is the editor and copyright holder on the overall issues. Parts of chapter 2 by Marion Fay first appeared as "Selfhood and Social Conscience: On Reading Some Stories in *Under a Glass Bell*," 13 (1995): 100–108. Parts of chapter 4 by Ellen G. Friedman were originally published as "Escaping from the House of Incest: On Anaïs Nin's Efforts to Overcome Patriarchal Constraints," 10 (1992): 39–45. Parts of chapter 11 by Mai Al-Nakib appeared as "A Secret Proliferation: Anaïs Nin's 'Diary' as Deleuzian Rhizome," 17 (1999): 78–86.

Some material in chapter 5 appeared in *Anaïs Nin and the Remaking of Self* by Diane Richard-Allerdyce, copyright © 1998 by Northern Illinois University Press; used by permission of the publisher. Parts of chapter 8 were included in a doctoral dissertation, "Sympathetic Narration: The Party and the Collage in Virginia Woolf, Anaïs Nin, and Jeanette Winterson," by Thomas M. March. Some material in chapter 9 was originally part of a doctoral dissertation, "The 'Double-Voiced Discourse' and Performing Persona in the

Early Works of Anaïs Nin: A Feminist Re-Evaluation," by Philippa Lyn Christmass.

I am grateful to all those who granted us permission to quote passages from primary sources. Chapter 6 includes quotations from *Winter of Artifice* by Anaïs Nin, copyright © 1946, 1974 by Anaïs Nin, copyright © 1977, 1991 by The Anaïs Nin Trust, reprinted by permission of the author's representative, Gunther Stuhlmann, all rights reserved. Chapter 8 contains passages from *Collages* by Anaïs Nin, copyright © 1964 by Anaïs Nin, copyright © 1992 by The Anaïs Nin Trust, reprinted by permission of the author's representative, Gunther Stuhlmann, all rights reserved. Quotation of passages reprinted in chapter 9 is authorized by (1) the author's representative, Gunther Stuhlmann, for *Under a Glass Bell and Other Stories* by Anaïs Nin, with a foreword by Gunther Stuhlmann, copyright © 1948, 1976 by Anaïs Nin, copyright © 1995 by The Anaïs Nin Trust, all rights reserved; and (2) Peter Owen Ltd., London, for *Under a Glass Bell* by Anaïs Nin. Chapter 10 incorporates passages from (1) *Seduction of the Minotaur* by Anaïs Nin, copyright © 1961 by Anaïs Nin, copyright © renewed 1989 by The Anaïs Nin Trust, reprinted by permission of the author's representative, Gunther Stuhlmann, all rights reserved; (2) *A Spy in the House of Love* by Anaïs Nin, copyright © 1954 by Anaïs Nin, copyright © 1982, 1987 by The Anaïs Nin Trust, reprinted by permission of the author's representative, Gunther Stuhlmann, all rights reserved; and (3) "Talking About Proust," an interview with Anaïs Nin by Frank S. Alberti, in *Anaïs: An International Journal,* volume 2 (1984), copyright © 1984 by the Anaïs Nin Foundation and Gunther Stuhlmann, reprinted by permission of the editor, all rights reserved. Quotation of passages reprinted in chapter 11 is granted by (1) Harcourt, Inc., for *The Diary of Anaïs Nin,* volume 1, *1931–1934,* copyright © 1966 by Anaïs Nin, copyright © renewed 1994 by Rupert Pole and Gunther Stuhlmann, and for *Incest: From "A Journal of Love"* by Anaïs Nin, copyright © 1992 by Rupert Pole, as trustee under the last Will and Testament of Anaïs Nin; and by (2) the author's representative, Gunther Stuhlmann, for *The Diary of Anaïs Nin,* volume 1, *1931–1934,* edited and with an introduction by Gunther Stuhlmann, copyright © 1966 by Anaïs Nin, copyright © 1977 by The Anaïs Nin Trust, all rights reserved, and for *Incest: From "A Journal of Love," The Unexpurgated Diary of Anaïs Nin, 1932–1934,* copyright ©1992 by The Anaïs Nin Trust, all rights reserved.

Introduction

Nin's Narrativity: An Overview

Anne T. Salvatore

In recent decades, the theoretical field of narratology has gained steadily in popularity among literary critics. While in the days of so-called pure formalism we might have been content with describing theme, character, point of view, structure, and use of time in particular stories, more recent critics often focus on the meta-narrative; they generate and respond to questions that link the primary work with theoretical concerns: What does plot linearity or the omission of it imply (Homans)? What does an unresolved ending suggest (Booth)? How does repetition relate to the order and/or duration of events (Genette)? How do the theories of Freud, Lacan, Gilligan, and other psychoanalysts illuminate methods of characterization? What issues of power and authority emerge from the manner in which the narrator is represented (Knutson)? What is the relation between the "primary story time" and other designations of time in the narrative (Bal)? How is narrative "truth" judged (Bruner)? What, if any, features of tone, structure, style can we expect to find in a "feminist" narrative (Freedman, S. Friedman, Lanser)? These and similar questions, as well as the formalist issues, need to be applied to Anaïs Nin's works—to her diaries and fiction. Obviously, no one book can resolve such questions. Indeed, they are probably never "resolvable" because, like all literary criticism, they are based on interpretable situations.

This book aims to advance the task of examining Nin's work through the complex lens of contemporary narratology. In so doing, we proclaim the worthiness of her narratives to be subjects of exacting scholarly study. At the same time, in describing various

parts of her canon, we wish to avoid the temptation toward essen-
tialism. Her narratives shifted in nature and grew in sophistication
from her charming childhood diary to her later, mature diaries and
her fictional tales that challenge established techniques as well as
conventional assumptions about the definition of "narrative." Ultimately, Nin stretches that definition to include unexpected elements and transfigure traditional ones. Her resulting text becomes
a hybrid that has puzzled many critics and perhaps alienated some.
But in the process of growth, she has revolutionized the concept of
narrative itself and raised important issues that need serious investigation in the burgeoning domain of feminist narrative.

In a typical "handbook" definition, Frye, Baker, and Perkins
defined narrative in 1985 as "an account of real or imagined
events, a story" (302). Their definition of "story" includes its ety-
mology from the Latin *historia,* or history, and refers to a "sequence
of events" (442). These definitions highlight events occurring in a
time structure. Similarly, Paul Ricoeur takes narrativity to be "the
language structure that has temporality as its ultimate referent"
(165). Susan Stanford Friedman understands narrative to be "a
mode that foregrounds a sequence of events that move dynamical-
ly in space and time" (164). In a less typical context, psychologist
Jerome Bruner explains narrative as "an account of events occurring over time. It is irreducibly durative" (6). While these critics
ascribe a linear progression to narrative in their definitions, others
have begun to consider sequence a convention rather than an
inherent element in narration. For example, Rimmon-Kenan calls
linear chronology "a conventional 'norm'" (17). W.J.T. Mitchell
asserts that "conflict, and not mere sequence, connexity, or a central subject, is one of the essentials of narrative" (viii). More
recently, in a discussion of Kenneth Burke's views on narrative,
Anneliese Watt suggests that in his fictional works, Burke wrestled
with "the dialectical tension between the temporal and the eternal,
between the successive and the simultaneous—between, for
example fiction, that makes plot central versus fiction that emphasizes atemporal modes of expression" (50).

To discuss the concept of temporal sequence[1] simply on the basis
of its presence or absence in a narrative may be too facile an
approach to Nin's total body of work, however. Her narratives do
incorporate linearity in varying degrees, yet long passages in some
works advert temporality so infrequently or so subtly that readers
can easily lose track of "real" time. Nin's diaries, of course, are the
most obvious examples of a linear progression; they contain spe-

cific labels of months and years in the earlier volumes, or seasons
and years in the later ones. In addition, the text of the diary entries
refers often to time: "It is exactly a month and a half since I have
news from you" (*Linotte* 164); "a day and a night" (*Diary* 2:109);
"Lecture Monday at City College" (*Diary* 6:202).

This traditional emphasis on the passage of time conforms to
what Julia Kristeva has called the "conception of time as project,
teleology"; this type of temporality includes "linear and prospec-
tive unfolding; time as departure, progression, and arrival—in
other words, the time of history" (17). Kristeva asserts that women
have had three types of reactions to the teleological notion of time.
First, in earlier years of the women's movement, they "aspired
to gain a place in linear time" (18). Second, in later years of
the movement—which Kristeva specifies as subsequent to May
1968—linear temporality was "almost totally refused" by women,
especially those interested "in the specificity of female psychology
and its symbolic realizations" (19). These women sought to "give a
language to the intra-subjective and corporeal experiences left
mute by culture in the past" (19). Third, Kristeva states, in the
later seventies in France and Italy, some women began to mix the
first two attitudes; that is, they combined an "insertion into history" with a "radical refusal of the subjective limitations imposed
by this history's time on an experiment carried out in the name of
the irreducible difference" (20). By writing a diary, Nin herself
may have experienced the first reaction, aspiring to gain a place in
history for a woman's own story. Certainly, life writing by its
nature incorporates a progression, at least in age and experience if
not ultimately in wisdom and grace. But the concept of temporality implied by many of Nin's fictional works is more wide-ranging
and complex. Her fictional methods demonstrate not so much the
second reactive phase in which women refuse temporality but
rather Kristeva's third-stage attitude: Nin takes from the teleological construct whatever she finds suitable, while simultaneously
stretching beyond its boundaries to experiment for sometimes
lengthy passages with a "monumental" temporality that includes
"repetition" as well as "eternity" (Kristeva 16). In brief, although
most of the fiction and many of the diaries were written prior to
the periods of the women's movement that Kristeva describes,
Nin's narratological methods suggest and anticipate Kristeva's conception of "women's time."

In *Under a Glass Bell*, on the simplest level, a narrator may deal
with historical time through grammatical references similar to

those in the diaries, such as these in "Houseboat": "The houseboat must have traveled during the night" (16); "the same day" (17); "during the night" (19); "one morning" (21). Other types of references deal with time through tropes. In the same story, a barge pulling the houseboat along suggests movement through a metaphorical journey into conflict, as noted by the spatial allusion "The barge was traversing a dissonant climate" (16). "The Child Born Out of the Fog" also suggests time figuratively, as in this example, in which progression applies to a shifting mental state but the linguistic cues again refer to the close relation of time and space in narration: "She had traveled from a land of cold words to a land of warm words, from a land of detachment to a land of tenderness, from shallowness to richness" (84). Adding another layer to the element of progression, several stories in this volume thematize the concept of time. In "Ragtime," for instance, the narrator, a ragpicker, finds broken fragments of past lives—a faceless clock, a basket without a bottom, last year's holy palm leaves— which cause sadness, but which will somehow be reused in a continual, if conventional, blending of the old and the new, suggesting that time progression causes not so much death but shifting forms and states of being. In most of these stories in *Under a Glass Bell*, then, Nin uses linguistic cues and figurative references as well as external physical or spatial details to imply sequence. But in some stories, the established sequence stops abruptly without closure. In "The Mouse," when the narrator's servant girl induces her own abortion and then needs urgent medical attention, the story ends suddenly, and readers are never told the ultimate consequences. Thus, in this early anthology of her stories, Nin generally follows conventional narrative methods to convey a series of events that we may wish to call plots, but she also experiments with the linear structure by deliberately breaching traditional norms for plot development toward a conclusion.

Winter of Artifice contains similar methods of suggesting a linear structure through grammatical or figurative allusions, but in this collection of novellas Nin often manipulates time by significantly extending what Gerard Genette terms narrative stasis, which is a subdivision of his concept of duration ("Order" 135–37) in a story. He defines stasis as a pause that occurs "when the narrative discourse continues while historical time is at a standstill" (137). Obviously, Nin did not invent stasis; most fictional authors make use of it to describe or explain characters, scenes, or situations. But in *Winter* Nin begins to allocate large portions of text to it. Since other conventional references to linearity remain frequent in this volume, however, readers can generally maintain their sense of progression.

For example, in the title story of an abandoned daughter finally meeting her father after his twenty-year absence, the third-person narrator spends many pages evaluating the father psychologically through the daughter's perception. Such passages are interrupted only sporadically by a dramatic miniscene, during which conversation passes briefly between the two characters or at least one of the characters speaks about an idea which then sparks another long stasis in the narrative flow. The passage in which the father calls his daughter an Amazon (80) is a case in point. Not until more than a page later does he resume speaking on the same topic, and because overt time references are omitted here, readers cannot be sure even that the two sets of remarks were articulated in direct sequence; linearity seems disrupted, at least minimally. After several similar instances of prolonged stasis in the novella, chronological movement is recovered in the text when the daughter announces that she must leave on a trip—an event in time (112). Because of the still relatively strong presence of these conventional signs of temporality, the effect of the oft-repeated stasis on the reader is mitigated.

Time sequence in *Winter*'s last story, "The Voice," becomes somewhat more problematic, though still discernable. The "events" themselves are presented in the form of characters' emotional states, but sequence, which by definition assumes links among events, may seem at first to be completely disrupted as the narrator switches without warning from one focalization[2] point to another. For instance, readers must move through the consciousness of Djuna musing in an elevator (124–26) to the perceptions of a new character (Lillian) who talks to the Voice or analyst, then on to Mischa, back to Djuna, to Lilith, back to Djuna, and so on. An ellipsis,[3] apparently connoting the passage of time, often separates the emotional experiences of the various characters. But the time itself is unspecified, perhaps even irrelevant. Moreover, the characters' experiences seem unconnected to one another for much of the novella, until some links are eventually established in their relationships. Although one pervasive link does emerge in that all characters interact with the Voice/analyst, the frequency of the ellipses, together with readers' difficulty in designating precise time, still undermines the strength of a sequential structure. The resulting sense of indeterminacy attains thematic status, suggesting that "progress" may emerge not from the external events common to traditional linear plot movement but rather from psychological flux which is not necessarily definable in "real" time.

This enhanced value placed on psychological engagement becomes one of the most strongly emphasized narratological methods in *Cities of the Interior*. The second novel in this series, *Children of the Albatross*, illustrates the manner in which some portions of the text again seem traditional while other parts of the narrative prompt us to question our definition of the genre or, conversely, to challenge our assumptions that Nin's "novels" are in fact narratives. The novel is divided into two chapters, "The Sealed Room" and "The Cafe." In the first chapter, expanded stories unfold concerning Djuna's artistic experience at the dancing school and her response to the ballet master, her emotional struggle with the powerful Watchman at the orphanage, her dreamlike encounter with various rooms in the house she has taken, and her relationship with Michael, then Paul. Threads of time are often linguistically stated or figuratively implied during these stories, as the experiences do seem to follow one another consecutively, even if time jumps quickly from childhood to adulthood. But in the second chapter, Nin sometimes jolts readers by moving abruptly from one experience to another, with no explicit connection between the passing time and the following experience, and with no intervening ellipsis as warning: "City and cafes became intimate like a room that was carpeted, quilted for the easy intermingling of man's inner landscapes, his multiple secret wishes vibrating from table to table as elbows and the *garçon* not only carried brimming glasses but endless messages and signals as the servants did in the old Arabian tales. / Day and night were colliding gently at twilight, throwing off erotic sparks. / Day and night met on the boulevards. / Sabina was always breaking the molds which life formed around her" (200–201).

The apparent and deliberate incoherency between the description of the cafe, the generalizations about time, and the behavior of Sabina explodes the assumption of linearity, at least temporarily, since the concept of sequence suggests some sort of logical connectivity. Moreover, following the above sentence on Sabina are three full pages of stasis in the text with actual time almost completely erased. Instead the narrator's voice generalizes about Sabina's patterns of behavior and her psychological state: "She lived entirely by a kind of opportunism" (201); "She wanted desperately to answer man's most impossible wishes" (202); "When someone asked her:

where are you going now? whom are you going to meet? she lied"
(202); "She was the firebug who was never detected" (203). At the
end of these generalizations, a larger space indicates another sudden switch of focalization, this time to Lillian: "At dawn Jay turned
towards Lillian lying beside him and his first kiss reached her
through the net of her hair" (204). Which dawn? Have only days
passed? Have months or even years passed? Specifics of time seem
irrelevant here, as they often are in "The Voice." So the narrative
method combining expanded stasis, which includes comprehensively stated psychological generalizations, with very sudden
switches in focalization, and with the dropping away of linguistic
references to time, contributes to many readers' disorientation, and
perhaps to the assumption by some critics that Nin's novels are not
narratives at all.

The absence of place or spatial references for long passages may
also contribute indirectly to readers' sense of sequential lack. During the psychological generalizations, places are hardly named at
all. Occasionally a city—Bombay, Budapest, Paris—is mentioned in
context, or a room, or the café: "Faustin . . . awakened in a room
he thought he had selected blindly" (221); "they sat in circles in
the café" (232). But except for the café, which becomes both a
"real" and a symbolic meeting place, the place references exist
mainly as externalizations of the characters' personalities. Since
we seldom see the characters moving from one place to another,
few conventional anchors exist to establish traditional sequence of
any kind in these passages.

While these atemporal techniques occur sporadically through all
five novels in *Cities of the Interior,* the impression of sequence, never
wholly lost, is more decidedly recaptured in *Seduction of the Minotaur.* Though obviously a symbolic voyage, Lillian's journey to Golconda suggests movement from one place to another—the places
being, of course, psychological states. The journey incorporates
definable events, such as the death of Dr. Hernandez, that lead
sequentially to an identifiable shift in Lillian's ability to discover
her repressed past, and to resurrect the existence and importance
to her of her husband and children. A final event—the birth of two
subjectivities, Lillian's and Larry's—returns the reader to an
impression of stability. Thematically, while traditional unbreached
and unexamined linearity suggests only the illusion of progress,[4]
Nin's discourse indicates that an authentic and comforting return
to a linear structure is possible only after the individual breaks out
of society's superficial appearance of progress to examine deeply

and comprehensively the nonlinear, often chaotic portions of his or her own being. Narratologically, such investigations provide what Kristeva suggests: an attempt not simply to grasp the social code or to subvert it but rather to "explore the constitution and functioning of this contract, starting less from the knowledge accumulated about it (anthropology, psychoanalysis, linguistics) than from the very personal affect experienced when facing it as subject and as a woman" (24).

In *Collages* Nin examines in depth not only the formal properties of the existing social contract but also its constitution. The title itself signals a separation from that contract through a breakage in cohesion, but, interestingly, the concept of collage also includes a reassemblage. Gregory L. Ulmer refers to a philosophical explanation of collage: "Each cited element breaks the continuity or the linearity of the discourse and leads necessarily to a double reading: that of the fragment perceived in relation to its text of origin; that of the same fragment as incorporated into a new whole, a different totality. The trick of collage consists in never entirely suppressing the alterity of these elements reunited in a temporary composition" (Group Mu 34–35, quoted in Ulmer). Through the use of collage as both topic and narrative device in her last novel,[5] Nin manages to have it both ways. On the one hand, the linearity of the discourse is internally sustained through the continual appearance and reappearance of the central consciousness, Renate. As in the earlier works, moreover, linguistic signs and descriptions of events signal time passing: "While driving along Pacific Palisades" (44); "When she came on holiday" (63); "The Consul was opening the champagne" (84); "She remembered a day in Morocco" (90).

But on the other hand, the text manifests continual breakages through narrative techniques mentioned earlier such as significant periods of stasis or, more prominently in this novel, through sudden shifts in focalization from one apparently bizarre character to another. With the exception of Renate and Bruce, the characters establish few or mainly superficial relationships with one another; collectively, they do not advance a definable plot. The individuality of text fragments is crucially important, however, in Nin's construction of a narrative that refuses to be swept into a slavish patriarchal progression. In fact, the eccentric characters—Raven who bought a raven to express her dark side, Count Laundromat, Henri the chef who served "Gargantuan" dinners, the old man who lived with seals, John Wilkes the fraudulent millionaire, the stylized Colonel Tishnar, Lisa who makes her shabby New York apartment into an Acapulco set, and Doctor Mann who pursues the author Judith Sands—seem a humorous call for attention to Nin's patchwork text. By exaggerating their unconventionality, she emphasizes their rebellion against their social contract. Their personal aberrations metaphorically suggest her narrative aberration; she celebrates both—with some reservations.

As Ulmer points out, a collage forces us to do a double reading. In *Collages* we become aware of these textual fragments in relation to their narrative "text of origin"—that is, we recall other, conventional characters in other, more conventional narratives. But simultaneously we view them in a new whole—Nin's hybrid text. In the novel, the painter Varda makes collages that replicate this process. With scissors and glue, he cuts, pastes, and transforms his cutouts of women. He uses his art to make something new: "he was always mixing a new brew, a new woman"; his women "bore the names of new brands of sainthood" (60). But even while Nin commends the formal artistic process of making collages by highlighting the aesthetic beauty and mythologizing implications of the resulting images, she also undercuts Varda's particular approach to collage-making by repeatedly suggesting that his art creates an illusory view of women as canonized saints. Their human reality is ignored, just as it had been in many traditional novels for over two centuries: "He never painted homely women, jealous women, or women with colds"; "He never depicted the death of a love, fatigue or boredom. Every collage was rich with a new harem, the constancy of illusion, fidelity to euphorias born of woman" (60). Changing the formal properties of discourse alone will not significantly alter the existing social contract, the narrative hints.

For Nin, a real alterity consists of *both* selective formal disruption *and* substantive textual evidence of the artist's revisionary philosophy, in this case concerning the portrayal of certain characters—in particular, women. In Varda's artistic process, patriarchal authority remains unchallenged: he cuts out women "in the shape of circles, triangles, cubes, to suit the changing forms *of his desires*" (66, italics added). Thus, in his world, true individuality—and therefore subjectivity—is sacrificed when the same forms are repeated for many women. A truly revisionist philosophy would, among other things, likely unsettle the tendency to objectify women, by presenting them not merely as the cutouts that a patriarchy may desire them to be but rather as what they are in their wholeness and complexity. Nin's own narratives, unlike Varda's paintings, portray women in all their humanity: a child-woman bored with domestic tasks and burdened by her mother with the care of siblings (*Linotte*); a woman emotionally if not physically abused by her father ("Winter of Artifice"); the women paralyzed by guilt and role-playing they fail to understand (*Cities of the Interior*); a woman adrift with ephemeral goals whose relationships with others remain distant and superficial (*Collages*). These portrayals constitute a difference in the way character is envisioned. I am not arguing about verisimilitude here. The question of whether Nin's women are more real than those of previous artists is a philosophical miasma because the notion of what is "real" can be endlessly debated without resolution. At issue, rather, is a view of narrative: these subjectively rendered characters, and the indeterminacy with which Nin often endows them, may be less likely to emerge from the more streamlined, sequential narrative that one expects as part of the prevailing social contract in mid-twentieth century, when Nin wrote much of her fiction.

Another essential element of her narrative that distracts from the narrative "flow"—albeit more gently than other structural features I have been discussing—is her use of poetic language, which affects both substance and style. Critics have frequently noticed this lyricism in her prose. For instance, Sharon Spencer calls Nin's writing "musical" because it "achieves its experiential impact through carefully constructed lyrical passages built up of textured, interrelated images" ("Music" 161). Spencer mentions also the "rhythmical organization of all literary units" (162). Anna Balakian notes similar features of Nin's poetic prose: "In every subsequent so-called novel [after *House of Incest*, Nin's prose poem] and meandering through the diaries we find the poetic presence as the dominant imprint of Nin's work, whether it is through the repetition of what she calls 'key words' in association with that presence or the rhythms of the various forms of music that accompany her words, or the special illumination, which is neither of sun nor of electricity, which surrounds her characters at some time or other in the process of her narrative" (74).

Holistic features of Nin's poetic narrative have also interested critics. Using Roman Jakobson's definition of poetic language as language that refers back to itself, Lajos Elkan labels Nin's texts poetic because they are "self-referential" and because they contain "the authentic voice of the author mixed with the characters' words" (153). Both Balakian and Elkan suggest a significant similarity between Nin's language and the methods and thought of the symbolist poet Rimbaud. And taking the poetry to a thematic level, Balakian comments further that for a number of nineteenth- and twentieth-century writers, including Nin, "efforts at self-recognition become part of the poetic process" (65).

Less interruptive than diverting—a more positive term—Nin's poetry sporadically leads readers away from a perceived progression in the discourse. Instead the focus rests on the aesthetic pleasure arising, as in a lyric poem, from a host of techniques including the rhetorical repetition of clauses, phrases, interrogatives, nouns, adjectives, and the use of sentence fragments that, lacking a predicate, accent the images, as in the following passage from *Diary* 2: "Everything seems miraculous, that the summer should be so soft, that fountains should play on the Champs-Élysées, that men and women are walking. A city never entirely known, yet which gives you the feeling of intimacy, of possessing it intimately. A sky which changes every day and yet keeps its opaline tones. Can life continue to unroll this way with a freshness never withered, new faces, new marvels? Can one arrive so many times at fullness without touching bottom, every year new leaves, new skins, new loves, new words" (226). At times, an extended metaphor breaks the progression of an event, as illustrated by the following passage in "Stella," which directly follows the narrator's report of a ringing telephone: "The music alone was capable of climbing those stairways of detachment, of breaking like the waves of disturbed ocean at her feet, breaking there and foaming but without the power to suck her back into the life with Bruno and into the undertows of suffering" (*Winter* 26). Lists of sensuous images draw the reader's attention, even as an actual event is taking place; here the copulative act becomes simultaneously metaphoric, and the repetitive diction imposes rhythm and emphasis that will heighten the drama and perhaps prompt readers to repeat the act of reading the passage rather than go forward: "They fled from the eyes of the world, the singer's prophetic, harsh, ovarian prologues. Down the rusty bars of ladders to the undergrounds of the night propitious to the first man and woman at the beginning of the world, where there were no words by which to possess each other, no music for serenades, no presents to court with, no tournaments to impress and force a yielding, no secondary instruments, no adornments, necklaces, crowns to subdue, but only one ritual, a joyous, joyous, joyous, joyous impaling of woman on man's sensual mast" (*Spy* 386).

Strategically positioned within discernable elements of sequential flow in Nin's works, these poetic flights from traditional progression, along with the other textual "breakages" I have discussed, demonstrate that her narrative discourse fluctuates between traditional and nontraditional methodologies. While in

The Novel of the Future she asserts that, like Henry Miller, she is con-cerned in her novels with "freedom from old forms" (68), her works show that this freedom for the new is nevertheless based on a knowledge of and respect for the old. Like the third generation of (European) feminists that Kristeva describes, Nin embraces history even while she uses an original composite of discourse strategies that constitute a "radical refusal" to accept the patriarchal limita-tions of a sequential narrative mode. To clarify further our under-standing of Nin's hybrid method, we can consider Frank Kermode's useful distinction between sequential events in a text, which collectively present the *fabula* or fable, and what he calls the text's "secrets," or "the less manifest portions of . . . text" (82, 84), by which he means, very broadly, those that are interpretable, that challenge readers to give the text "abnormally attentive scrutiny" (84). He points out that many readers look for the "comfort" they derive from sequence, as being closest to their notion of life (83). In these readers' perceptions, the text's "secrets" then take on neg-ative implications because they disrupt the sequence; such inter-ferences are viewed as "treacherous"; they are "displacements," "debauched significances," "disposable noise" (83). The negative diction Kermode uses to describe such readers' reactions is not sur-prising. As he points out, many such passages in novels may even go unread by these readers. To avoid this outcome, one might "'foreground' sequence and message," Kermode continues (84).[6]

But Nin refuses. Instead she foregrounds the "secrets," drama-tizes them, celebrates them; her text bulges with them. Without entirely dismissing sequence, she relaxes its stranglehold, takes from it what she finds helpful, while maintaining her right to diverge from it. Thus, if she has not entirely changed the classical definition of narrative, her works show that she has questioned seriously its essential elements. With the exception of the diaries, most of her texts have no "primary story time" as Bal envisions it (57). Rather she establishes her own sense of "women's time," the simultaneity of women's subjective experience made real and val-ued for its own sake. I believe that J. Hillis Miller is right in saying that we are powerfully attracted to reading novels because of the "intimate access [they provide] to the mind and heart of another person" (31). Nin's unique blend of traditional and divergent strategies invites both male and female readers to experience the most private and personal recesses of women's minds and hearts. With her emotionally charged discourse, she challenges us to ig-

nore boundaries and to shift our perspectives on the ways narratives are conceived.

NOTES

1. I am referring here to the temporal order of events in what might be loosely termed the plot or story, as opposed to the temporal order of events as they are presented in the text or narrative itself. I base this distinction on Gerard Genette's explanation of the difference between story and narrative (35).
2. Nilli Diengott and other narratologists distinguish between the mind who "sees" and the voice that "tells" (45). Focalization applies to the former, or to the character whose perception is presented in the text.
3. According to Genette, ellipsis consists of a "certain amount of historical time covered in a zero amount of narrative" ("Order" 137).
4. See Margaret Homans's article in which she refers to the "illusion of progress powerfully suggested by sequence" (5).
5. In *Collage of Dreams: The Writings of Anaïs Nin,* Sharon Spencer argues that Nin's fiction and diaries are themselves collages, in which "components belonging to separate intellectual or perceptual categories are combined, regardless of the nature of the materials" (5).
6. Of course, Kermode is not suggesting here that an author *should* necessarily foreground sequence, but only that many authors do so to accommodate the demands of some readers.

WORKS CITED

Bal, Mieke. *Narratology: Introduction to the Theory of Narrative.* Trans. Christine van Boheemen. Toronto: University of Toronto Press, 1985.

Balakian, Anna. "Anaïs Nin, the Poet." *Anaïs Nin: Literary Perspectives.* Ed. Suzanne Nalbantian, 63–78. New York: St. Martin's Press, 1997.

Bruner, Jerome. "The Narrative Construction of Reality." *Critical Inquiry* 18 (1991): 1–21.

Booth, Alison, ed. *Famous Last Words: Changes in Gender and Narrative Closure.* Charlottesville: University Press of Virginia, 1993.

Diengott, Nilli. "Narratology and Feminism." *Style* 22 (1988): 45–51.

Elkan, Lajos. "Birth and the Linguistics of Gender: Masculine/Feminine." *Anaïs Nin: Literary Perspectives.* Ed. Suzanne Nalbantian, 151–63. New York: St. Martin's Press, 1997.

Freedman, Diane P. "Discourse as Power: Renouncing Denial." *Anxious Power: Reading, Writing, and Ambivalence in Narrative by Women.* Ed. Carol J. Singley and Susan Elizabeth Sweeney, 363–78. Albany: State University of New York Press, 1993.

Friedman, Susan Stanford. "Lyric Subversion of Narrative in Women's Writing: Virginia Woolf and the Tyranny of Plot." *Reading Narrative:*

Form, Ethics, Ideology. Ed. James Phelan, 162–85. Columbus: Ohio State University Press, 1989.

Frye, Northrup, Sheridan Baker, and George Perkins. *The Harper Handbook to Literature.* New York: Harper & Row, 1985.

Genette, Gerard. *Narrative Discourse: An Essay in Method.* Trans. Jane E. Lewin. Ithaca: Cornell University Press, 1980.

———. "Order, Duration, Frequency." *Narrative/Theory.* Ed. David H. Richter, 132–39. White Plains, N.Y.: Longman, 1996.

Group Mu, eds. *Collages.* Paris: Union Générale, 1978.

Homans, Margaret. "Feminist Fictions and Feminist Theories of Narrative." *Narrative* 2 (1994): 3–16.

Kermode, Frank. "Secrets and Narrative Sequence." *On Narrative.* Ed. W.J.T. Mitchell. Chicago: University of Chicago Press, 1981.

Knutson, Susan. "For Feminist Narratology." *Tessera* 7 (1989): 10–14.

Kristeva, Julia. "Women's Time." Trans. Alice Jardine and Harry Blake. *Signs: Journal of Women in Culture and Society* 7 (1981): 13–35.

Lanser, Susan. "Toward a Feminist Narratology." *Style* 20 (1986): 341–63.

Miller, J. Hillis. *Ariadne's Thread: Story Lines.* New Haven: Yale University Press, 1992.

Mitchell, W.J.T. *On Narrative.* Chicago: University of Chicago Press, 1981.

Nin, Anaïs. *Children of the Albatross. Cities of the Interior,* 128–238. Chicago: Swallow Press, 1959.

———. *Collages.* Athens: Swallow Press/Ohio University Press, 1964.

———. *The Diary of Anaïs Nin* (1931–74). Ed. Gunther Stuhlman. 7 vols. San Diego: Harcourt Brace Jovanovich, 1966–80.

———. *Linotte: The Early Diary of Anaïs Nin, 1914–1920.* Trans. Jean L. Sherman. New York: Harcourt Brace Jovanovich, 1978.

———. *The Novel of the Future.* Athens: Swallow Press/Ohio University Press, 1986.

———. *Seduction of the Minotaur. Cities of the Interior,* 465–589. Chicago: Swallow Press, 1959.

———. *A Spy in the House of Love. Cities of the Interior,* 360–462. Chicago: Swallow Press, 1959.

———. "Stella." 1945. *Winter of Artifice: Three Novelettes,* 7–54. Chicago: Swallow Press, 1961.

———. *Under a Glass Bell and Other Stories.* Chicago: Swallow Press, 1948.

———. "The Voice." 1939. *Winter of Artifice: Three Novelettes,* 120–75. Chicago: Swallow Press, 1961.

———. "Winter of Artifice." 1939. *Winter of Artifice: Three Novelettes,* 55–119. Chicago: Swallow Press, 1961.

Ricoeur, Paul. "Narrative Time." *On Narrative.* Ed. W.J.T. Mitchell. Chicago: University of Chicago Press, 1981.

Rimmon-Kenan, Shlomith. *Narrative Fiction: Comtemporary Poetics.* London: Methuen, 1983.

Spencer, Sharon. *Collage of Dreams: The Writings of Anaïs Nin.* Expanded ed.
     New York: Harcourt Brace Jovanovich, 1981.
———. "The Music of the Womb: Anaïs Nin's 'Feminine' Writing." *Breaking
     the Sequence: Women's Experimental Fiction.* Ed. Ellen G. Friedman and
     Miriam Fuchs, 161–73. Princeton: Princeton University Press, 1989.
Ulmer, Gregory L. "The Object of Post-Criticism." *The Anti-Aesthetic: Essays
     on Postmodern Culture.* Ed. Hal Foster, 83–110. Port Townsend, Wash.:
     Bay Press, 1983.
Watt, Anneliese. "The Dialectic of Temporal Embodiment and Eternal
     Essence." *Narrative* 6 (1998): 49–71.

CHAPTER I

Anaïs Nin's "Poetic Porn"

Problematizing the Gaze

Diane Richard-Allerdyce

Although Anaïs Nin had estab-
lished herself as a published writer by the mid-1930s, her first best-
seller was not published until after her death. Ironically, as Deirdre
Bair points out, her most successful books were comprised of work
Nin both scorned and, at times, felt ashamed of: *Delta of Venus*
(1977) and the companion collection that soon followed, *Little
Birds* (1979). Initially, it had been against Nin's judgment to allow
publication of the material she had written to order in the early
1940s for a "patron" of Henry Miller's.[1] She was particularly concerned that the reputation of *The Diary of Anaïs Nin*, six volumes of
which had by then been published by Harcourt Brace Jovanovich,
could be tainted by her erotic stories. In a sense, she was right, at
least in terms of her popular image in the decade or so following
her death. In the long run, however, the erotica have only added
to Nin's reputation as a writer ahead of her time. According to Bair,
"critics have agreed that her erotica represents one of the most
striking expressions of the feminine sensibility and especially of
female sexuality" (516). Karen Brennan takes feminist admiration
of Nin's erotica a step further, asserting that Nin's ability to resist
narrative closure and to shift between subject and object positions
makes possible a feminist reading of the erotica.

In this essay, I shall employ close readings of several stories from
Delta of Venus and *Little Birds* to show that, by calling into question
the attitudes and positions conducive to the responses much of

erotica evokes, Nin's erotica perform not only a literary but also an analytic function. In particular, the self-questioning perspectives of Nin's texts encourage readers to notice the ways in which their responses have been manipulated by the text and by the culture at large and, ideally, to begin to analyze their complicity in that manipulation. The erotica thus participate in the aims of what Mark Bracher has called a socially relevant literary theory. In *Lacan, Discourse, and Social Change* (1993) Bracher asserts that literary theory has the potential to bring about shifts in social realities by calling attention to the ways readers are manipulated by and respond to texts and other cultural artifacts—an idea that supports Nin's own sense that political change occurs one individual at a time. Self-questioning and analysis provoked by a text can result in a greater tolerance for otherness displacing the desire to dominate it.[2] When readers begin "to work through [rather than deny, repress, or insist on eradicating without analysis] some of their more debilitating and destructive conflicts of identification and desire, . . . such working through can open the way not only to greater jouissance for these subjects but also, through the resulting changes in their attitudes and behavior, to beneficial social change" (Bracher 191–92).[3] That one writer's erotic stories can bring about social change is debatable, of course. But whether her intention was unconscious or conscious at that point, Nin created in the erotica both a literature and a performative model of socially relevant theory.[4]

Delta of Venus and *Little Birds* call into question men's and women's responses to situations that might reflect their complicity in oppression—such as their finding pleasure in scenes of masochism—and in the process mirror the responses that Nin went through herself in seeking new signifiers for her identity as she tried to work out her own relation to suffering.[5] Through writing, together with years of psychoanalysis, Nin was able to achieve some distance from her tendency to act out her need for approval in the gaze of numerous "fathers" and to loosen herself, at least somewhat, from her tendency to remain complicit in her subjugation through attachment to an unconscious masochism. In the erotica, she parodies that tendency.

The distinction Nin's work makes between positions that reinforce oppression and those that encourage each person to recognize and tolerate otherness is echoed by Janet Barron. In an essay on female responses to D. H. Lawrence—whose work provided Nin a springboard into her own lifelong attempt to understand sexuality from a novelist's perspective—Barron writes: "We simply do not as yet have an adequate vocabulary for comment on female response to erotica. . . . pornography, for example, is for the most part produced wholly in accordance with male criteria, with women as its material. In many less glaringly obvious ways, too, society is still so unequal in its treatment of men and women that it is remarkably difficult to distinguish between women's actual reactions and the potentially discriminatory consequences" (21). Barron's comments point out the complexity inherent in the feminist goal of creating a bridge between literature and social action. I believe, however, that through engaging a multiplicity of perspectives through which readers can analyze their own responses to her texts and recognize their own relation to patterns of behavior and attitude represented there, Nin suggests that such a bridge is possible.

II

It is specifically by engaging the oscillation identified by Brennan as a doubleness of perspective that the erotica allow the reader to occupy multiple positions along a line of vision between spectator and object and thus to call into question the relationship between socially constructed positions and sexual desire. Brennan argues that Nin's narrative perspective goes beyond, and allows the reader/critic to go beyond, what Freud considered the feminine position and what Teresa de Lauretis has described as the female spectator's position: the double identification or vacillation between subject/object positions and between perspectives traditionally considered masculine (identifying with the gaze) and those traditionally considered more feminine (identifying with the image). Nin's point of view, because it alternates between these positions, allows for multiple identifications among reader, narrator, voyeur, object, author, and critic. Brennan insists that Nin avoids the trap of reinforcing the systematic oppression of women through her complicity in the process of her representation as object because her work also calls such representation into question and leaves Nin in a position "closer to the one occupied by the feminist theorist . . . than [to] the female spectator de Lauretis describes. The feminist theorist (de Lauretis herself, for example) adds another layer of vision to the already doubled vision of the less-theoretically aware female spectator" (Brennan 69).

Nin's erotica also use the multiplicity of perspective to thematize "looking." Both collections are replete with characters unconscious of, or all too conscious of, being looked at as objects. Nin's looking motif in the erotica echoes a Lacanian interpretation of the gaze, where the term refers not so much to the act of looking or being looked at in return but to seeking, in the eyes of others, their approval and recognition. An example of Nin's playful subversion of "looking" roles operates through a recurring scenario in the erotica: An untrustworthy male authority figure takes advantage of his strength, social position, and power in order to take his pleasure, often minimalizing the female "object" in the process. As Nin uses visual imagery to expose the way this happens, the vantage point—and thus the position of advantage—shifts so that it is the reader (male or female) who is looking at both the action of the narrative and the structure of domination held in place by the invisible but implicated voyeuristic "patron" who can be seen—even through his invisibility—watching the drama.

During the shift in perspective, the process of gaze-seeking occurs on several levels: not only between Nin's persona and her patron, but also on the level where reader as would-be voyeur identifies with narrative object and realizes, through that identification, the intended object's position as desiring subject. In this process, if Nin is successful, readers participate in the kind of recognition Bracher describes, a recognition of the ways in which a reader has been manipulated by the text. By extension, the process as Nin provides for it in her erotica leads to a rejection of that manipulation, much in the way that she, as a wounded daughter, had to learn to recognize and reject the ways she continued to be manipulated by her father's desire. The following readings of Nin's erotic stories illustrate how Nin's erotica operate as both fiction and theory to call into question the exclusionary, objectivizing perspective that perpetuates exploitation and sexual injustice.

III

The idea of a man using his advantage over a weaker female and then being made to look ridiculous occurs in the first selection of *Delta of Venus*, a story called "The Hungarian Adventurer." The adventurer is described in many of the same terms Nin uses for her own father in both diary and fiction: he is charismatic, charming, handsome, and aristocratic. He travels extensively, and everywhere he goes he seduces women, only to leave them and flee to another country after they have fallen in love with him. Once, he almost falls into "a trap of human love" (2), with a woman named Anita.

Anita is a Peruvian dancer whose eyes close differently than other women's eyes. Nin's appreciation for her character's beauty leads into her implicit warning that such beauty is a liability: Anita's eyes, Nin writes, close like "the eyes of tigers, pumas, and leopards, the two lids meeting lazily and slowly . . . with a lascivious, oblique glance falling from them like the glance of a woman who does not want to see what is being done to her body" (2).

The adventurer actually comes to love Anita and her submissive air. He stays with her longer than with other women, long enough that she bears him two daughters. But soon after they are born, he is off again. At his next stop, he stays in a hotel next to an aristocratic family whose two daughters of about ten and twelve years of age come to visit in his room each morning. They tease, laugh, and play as they wake him up in his bed, tumbling over him as he joins in the game, pretending innocent fun himself and caressing them by tickling. Most overt among his abusive behaviors is a catch-the-finger game. The girls chase his upright finger from on top of the blanket while he moves it around underneath, sometimes substituting his erect penis for the finger while the girls remain unaware. "They never suspected," Nin writes, that the adventurer, watching the girls' panties and thighs whenever their childish skirts flew up during their play, would reach orgasm under the thick quilt while they happily played "horsey" on top.

This passage is troubling on more than one level. It mirrors the way that significances of events can be retroactively understood, lying buried in unconscious memory until they are brought to consciousness (*if* they are brought to consciousness) but often causing psychological disruption in the meantime.[6] The girls, Nin implies, must certainly be affected by the game being played at their expense, for even if they are not consciously and presently aware that they are involved in a sexual act, the effects of their exploitation must register in their psyches. And just as certainly, the narrative statement that they never suspect what is going on is doubly ironic, for in it Nin implicates her own position. That is, Nin's narrator is similarly involved in a "game" with her patron, pretending to operate straightforwardly to provide him what he has commissioned while guiding him toward an understated denouement that—she might hope—will retrospectively "prick" his conscience. Unlike the adventurer who takes his pleasure at the girls' future expense, however, the narrator participates in a purpose that aims beyond a limited personal satisfaction. It aims, from beneath the text's surface—as the adventurer moved his penis under the blanket—toward the kind of pleasure one might enjoy at seeing attitudes toward exploitation change.

But first the adventurer must continue his exploits. He moves on to marry a woman in New York and to settle down with her to raise a son. Then, when the boy is about fourteen years old, the adventurer receives word that Anita, the Peruvian dancer, has died. His daughters by her, now aged fifteen and sixteen, are to come to live with him. Soon after their arrival he rapes them—an event called seduction rather than rape in the story. The narrator, thematizing the taking of pleasure through another's "voluntary" submission, indicates that although they resist and weep at first, the girls comply with their father's desires. This arrangement continues for some time.

Eventually the adventurer's wife discovers his abuse and leaves him, providing no intervention on the children's behalf. That the wife's inaction remains implicit is also an undercurrent in the narration; her silence speaks to the systems by which a woman's position within family and social structures may be internalized to such a degree that she defines herself only in terms of her desirability to her male other and remains in competition, rather than in solidarity, with others who fill the role of man's desired object.

While the purported "patron" would ostensibly remain oblivious to this ironic undercurrent, its resonance is discernable to readers for whom the silencing of subordinated members within extant power structures is affectively real—and increasingly intolerable. The results of such silencing affect not only the individual victim but others who might otherwise be given a voice by that person's refusal to be silent. In "The Hungarian Adventurer," for instance, the wife's mute departure leaves her husband more room for abuse—and echoes the narrator's silent scream in Nin's prose poem *House of Incest* as well as Nin's need to find a voice with which to express her victimization, whatever its specific form, at the hands of her own father during childhood.

That the Hungarian adventurer exhausts his daughters with his demands but is still never satiated underlines the nature and scope of objectivizing desire and the traditionally male "right" to move toward satisfaction—that which, in the *Diary,* Nin ironizes as *le droit du seigneur.*[7] Through the adventurer's unenlightened jouissance Nin's narrator also provides a metonymy for the actual and social tragedy his action represents—the abuse of less powerful members of families and societies by others who are stronger in one way or another.

In this story, it is through the adventurer's becoming "blinded by. . . desire" (8) that he is defeated. The defeat itself is mild in proportion to his crime—a narrative move necessitated by the conditions for Nin's erotic writing and the genre in which Nin is writing itself, since an overt punishment of the adventurer would be rejected by the patron. As it is, the story's ending is not even unquestionably subversive, in that one can imagine a protagonist-identified reader taking some pleasure in the voracity of the adventurer's sexual appetite and accepting his small slap on the hand, as it were, with a patronizing amusement. Yet the very possibility of such identification remains thematized by the narrative: While masturbating by his son's bedside one night, the obsessed man puts his penis in the mouth of the sleeping boy, who awakens and strikes his father. The girls then awaken also, and the three children escape their abuser for good.

The story ends here as the "folly" of the "now frenzied, aging Baron" is exposed. That the word "folly" may be a dangerous euphemism only emphasizes the distance between the point of view represented by the "patron" of this story and the needed transformation of the exploitive gaze. For although the tone is light and detached, the real effect of such behavior on actual people—as well as within the "as if" world of the fiction in which at least five children have been perhaps irrevocably wounded—is emphasized by wounded victims' frequent inability to achieve detachment at all. Nin herself is an example, one who strove all her life with only intermittent success to distance herself from the effects of early abuse. Whether that abuse was technically sexual, as Fitch argues and Nin later believed, there is no doubt that Nin suffered from it as both child and adult.

As for the story, Nin's narrator has "pricked" her commissioner with his own weapon by setting him up to gaze upon the suffering caused by his position even while the narrative tone and style belie and thereby leave as potentially unconscious their agenda. A further troubling point—that a male's intervention (the brother's) was the one effecting rescue—is thematized as well: whether he was unaware of his sisters' dilemma or simply remained uninvolved until it affected him personally is not clear. The author's message is somewhat more transparent: exploitation is dangerous for all members of a society in which it is allowed to exist, and change is the responsibility of even those who are not overtly affected by it.

One of Nin's chief goals, throughout her lifelong writings, was to attain a cooperation between male and female so that qualities of both might be appreciated, neither at the expense of the other.

Although the abuse of power is often gender specific, it is ultimately an objectivization of a human subject, a greed that, in principle, is negating of all humanness and all otherness. The male and
female together must rebel, Nin implies, against sexual exploitation in any form.

IV

The second story of *Delta of Venus*, "Mathilde," is equally assertive.
Mathilde is a hatmaker in Paris who engages in group sex while all
involved take opium. She lies nude on the floor while groups of
young men lie around on pillows lazily fingering her genitals. Just
when the rhythm of the prose and the pleasant string of surreal
images promises at least a poetic pleasure, Nin's resistance to the
fragmenting perspectives of those who see women—or anyone—
as objects appears in her description of Martinez, one of the men
involved in the orgies.

Martinez has erotic images of fragmented women, fantasies of
legs spread so impossibly far apart as to seem "severed from the
woman" (13), breasts floating in air, bellies unconnected to an
intact body. It is as if, we are told by the suddenly intruding narrator, "one had taken a tulip in the hand and opened it completely
by force" (14). No reader could miss the editorial attitude toward
Martinez's objectivizing obsession with women as collections of
body parts.

Yet Mathilde seems unaware of the way she has been rendered
fantasy and robbed of her subjectivity; only from the reader's perspective does one "see" her, and Nin makes it impossible, it seems,
for one in the patron's position to enjoy the show. Each time the
description becomes potentially alluring, a sober undercurrent of
what-is-really-happening-here exposures becomes evident in the
text. In one scene Mathilde, alone in the room after an episode of
group sex, has not had an orgasm, and sits naked in front of a mirror admiring her own belly and pubic hair as she looks down at
her spread legs. To her, the vulva looks "flawless." Nin continues in
a passage characteristic of her portrayal of women: "The sight [is]
enchanting." The next two paragraphs are a poetic celebration of
the female sex, in which the "odorous moisture" of Mathilde's
excitement is compared to the glistening of sea shells, the "kernel
of salt honey in her" to the birthing of Venus from the sea.

Mathilde's own appreciation of her sexual beauty is held within
the boundaries of the male gaze. She wonders how she would look
to Martinez. Her fingers, as they explore, become linked in her

imagination with Martinez and a second lover both stroking her simultaneously. When she lies down on the floor and "see[s] her sex from the other side" (15), she seems to be trying to put herself in her male partner's position, regarding herself as an object of male pleasure.

Yet after she reaches orgasm, she suddenly understands a story a sailor has told her about how he and several shipbound friends once made a rubber woman-doll to satisfy their sexual longings for the six or seven months at sea. The sailors all loved this doll, adored her, slept with her, and shared her. They found her "untiring and yielding—truly a marvelous companion. There were no jealousies, no fights" (16–17).

Again, Nin makes it difficult to miss her point. Here it is unlikely that a reader will miss the connection between the nonhuman woman who makes no demands, this "perfect" woman adored for her complicity, and the objectivizing force of Mathilde's use by her so-called friends. Nin's version of poetic justice does reign, however, for a short span in this part of the story, as it does at the end, and Mathilde laughs aloud thinking of how, despite the rubber woman's friendly pliability, she gave all the sailors syphilis.

At this point Mathilde sees the link between the using of her body by others (and herself) and the using of a thing for sexual satisfaction. But she actually likes the "feeling of utter abandon" (17) it gives her to take opium and lie with men who do not see the danger in divorcing sex from human subjectivity. Her only concern, the next line continues, is "to count the money that her friends left her" (17)—an obvious allusion to Nin's own relation to her literary patron.

Herein lies Nin's narrative complexity: at the same time that one sees Nin behind the text counting the money earned from her erotica and laughing in the face of the system she has used to her advantage, her narrator also reveals how unjustified it is to put any human being in the position to do so. For Mathilde's acceptance of her own desubjectification is not convincing, and Nin has exposed the weakness of Mathilde's defense, the falsity of her rationalization.

As if to warn against the abandonment of responsibility for dehumanizing sexuality that Mathilde may represent, Nin's narrator informs us next that one of Mathilde's friends, Antonio, is not content to stay in Mathilde's room. In his restlessness, he persuades her to go to a rented apartment with him. Antonio cannot take her to his home, for he lives with someone. We learn that he is obsessed with his mistress's breasts but will not have genital intercourse with her, and that she is always left aching for fulfillment. The one-sidedness of Antonio's sexuality is portrayed in his eyes, which seem to communicate, according to the narrator, a lack of any acceptance of responsibility to fulfill the desires he arouses.

At the story's end, we find the reason Antonio avoids his mistress's genitals. Before the narrator reveals this reason, though, Antonio's seduction of Mathilde is interrupted by the image of a sick, scabbed drug addict lying on the floor of the apartment to which he has taken her. Full of infected needle holes but begging for further injection by another's hand, this character, a cocaine thief, reminds the reader of Mathilde's implicit masochism. The story climaxes with Mathilde lying in another room, paralyzed by opium, while Antonio moves a knife toward her genitals until, in the nick of time, the police enter to apprehend the cocaine thief and end up saving Mathilde from Antonio's attack against "what he called 'woman's little wound,' which he was so violently tempted to enlarge" (22).

Whether the narrator's implication is one of fantasy that women will be saved from violent subjugation in which they have participated, or of ironic comment that heroic measures are required to reverse the trend toward perverse dehumanizing forces of one-sided, exclusive, and fragmenting sexuality, the final image leaves little room for doubt or for the patron's voyeuristic pleasure. Rather, Nin's disquieting sabotage of erotic expectation with exposure of exploitation once again subverts the structure of voyeuristic privilege. By negating the exclusion of anyone's personhood, even that which takes place with that person's consent, Nin's erotica subvert not sexual pleasure in general but sexual pleasure achieved through the devaluation of subjectivity.

V

In the stories that follow "The Hungarian Adventurer" and "Mathilde," Nin continues to thematize the assigning of value within economic and sexual relationships. Posing as the compliant literary prostitute (her own comparison), she accepts the patron's money in lieu of the legitimate approval she had hoped for from the American reading public. Yet all the while, she turns this pimp-prostitute relation on its head, taking her artistic pleasure at her patron's expense. While his mute presence behind the work gives little clue about his real level of understanding, Nin's mockery of him gives her at least imagined control over the desired object—his gaze—which she manipulates in order to subvert the terms of their relationship. She gives him what he demands, but she withholds what he wants. Like the woman pictured on the cover of *Delta of Venus*, who averts her eyes from the camera and seems to be looking at her own body, Nin takes literary pleasure in the female body, as her loving depictions of women characters' features attest. According to Bair, Nin had to be persuaded to accept the image on the cover; however, Nin's "feminine" perspective actually finds expression in the girl's subtle, shadowed smile—the smile of a woman who leaves her regarder unsure of her intentions as she averts her eyes from his to assume a relation to her own femininity that excludes objectification and mocks anyone who enjoys a voyeur's advantage. As in "Mathilde," Nin affirms female subjectivity in general and her own validity as a writer and as a woman by drawing situations in which the reader cannot fail to recognize the danger in any enterprise that, as she puts it in the preface, encourages the separation of love (or of recognition of a partner's otherness) from sex.

The feminine point of view she portrays, however, is clearly more than a singular position. The oscillation between points of view that Brennan highlights as a particular strength of Nin's work—her doubleness of perspective—finds particular expression within the stories that follow as she thematizes the spectator's or voyeur's position vis-à-vis her characters' desire to become the spectacle and their taking pleasure in seeing themselves being seen. Both collections of Nin's erotica, for example, contain stories ("Artists and Models" in *Delta of Venus*, "A Model," "The Queen," "Hilda and Rango" in *Little Birds*, to name a few) in which an artist's model comes to represent the subject's reduction to physical object—a detail significant in light of Nin's father's tendency to reduce his children to visual images by photographing them unexpectedly, often when they were naked and in the process of bathing or changing (Bair 18).[8]

In most of these stories, the relation between artist and model serves as a springboard and background for other spectator-object relationships. In fact, "Artists and Models"—really a long, rambling collection of vignettes about various experiences related by both artists and the models who pose for them—explores only superficially the relationship between sexual desire and being looked at. Similarly, "A Model" deals mainly with a young, inexperienced girl's encounters with the people who hire her to model and her quest to achieve true sexual experience—though it does contain a scene in which a man derives pleasure from watching the narrator reach orgasm while she poses on a leather "model" horse for a painting that is to depict a woman riding horseback. Other stories, however, deal directly with the connections among looking, being looked at, and sexual relationships.

In "Marianne," a story in *Delta of Venus,* the narrator tells of the experiences her typist has with a man who is addicted to being looked at; she also thematizes the economics of erotica writing which Nin discusses in the prefaces to both collections. Several layers of narration in "Marianne" draw attention to the structure of the text as a "veil" over Nin's own relation to her writing arrangement; like Nin, the narrator announces that she will call herself "the madam of a house of literary prostitution" (68). Already a story within the larger story about Nin's career as erotica writer, "Marianne" contains two additional layers: the typist, Marianne, leaves an account of her own experience for the narrator to read, and to narrate; and Marianne finds herself assigned to the task of typing a manuscript that her boyfriend, Fred, has submitted to the collector. By this point in the story, we are reading the narrator's account of Marianne's account of Fred's account of his fetish.

We also see, from the beginning, a variation on Nin's oscillation between subject and object, between male and female positions, and between employer and employee. As a model, Fred has reversed the traditional financial arrangements between artist and model by hiring Marianne to draw his nude portrait. At first, Marianne thinks the financial aspect is the only unusual part of the deal. She does not find anything strange in Fred's request despite the reversal of role between artist and model. She tells Fred as much, and "with the right to observe that is given to painters" she studies his eyes, attracted to a certain femininity in him and to an evasiveness she notices (71). This passage both establishes the importance of looking and calls into question the relationship between traditional gender roles (as in feminine evasiveness) and their corresponding positions as object or viewer. Marianne learns that the young man's evasiveness is a particularly cruel kind of passivity that causes him to erase her sexuality: when Marianne has worked herself into a frenzy over the man who poses naked with an erection but is "only interested in [her] *looking* at him" (74) rather than in her as a potential lover, she tries to no avail to arouse his desire. Eventually she enacts a ritual of kneeling and worshiping Fred's erect penis, which the narrator tells with great parody of larger meaning: "Again she kneeled and prayed to this strange phallus which demanded only admiration" (75). Although Fred moves in with Marianne, he never consummates their relationship: "Fred acted as if she had no sex at all" (75); by extension, he erases her as a desiring subject, rendering her gaze the object he desires.

Similarly, when Fred becomes interested in Marianne's painting class, it is not because he is interested in her involvement there but because he sees that he could become a model for the class. When he is hired, Marianne feels as if he is giving himself sexually to others, for his way of making love is to seek being looked at. Marianne tears up her drawings of him in an effort to remove his remembered image. Her effort is most likely in vain since the story makes clear that she loves him and has not equated his image with his subjectivity or with her desire of him. The story ends with Fred and Marianne's complete estrangment—an illustration of what Bracher calls the alienating quality of passive narcissistic desire (20). In the last sentence, the narrative gaze zooms back to the original frame: "And Marianne was left alone again to type our erotica" (78).

The theme of estrangement is furthered in the story that follows "Marianne" in the collection, "The Veiled Woman." As Brennan has pointed out, this story represents the arrangement Nin saw between her role as writer of the erotica and that of the collector who paid her to write it. In "The Veiled Woman" a man named George accepts an arrangement an acquaintance has set up to become a paid participant in a one-night stand with a veiled woman who wants only a stranger whom she will never see again. George is paid fifty dollars, blindfolded, sworn to secrecy, and taken to a lavish, mirrored apartment where he encounters a woman he recognizes as the same woman that, earlier, he had admired in a bar. They make ecstatic love for a long time, then George is sent off to be haunted by the images of that night.

Eventually, George meets a friend who tells him the story of an adventure he has had, for which he paid one hundred dollars—a sum he considers well spent for the pleasure. He was taken to watch from behind a mirrored wall the exploits of a woman having wild sex. George is horrified to recognize in his friend's description the very woman with whom he had *his* adventure, and to realize someone was most likely watching him that night. He feels betrayed, and afterward is haunted by the suspicion that any woman with whom he has sex is hiding someone behind a curtain.

With this story Nin explores the nature of voyeurism and its relation to the literary enterprise in which she has become involved. Brennan argues that because Nin can oscillate between spectator and object positions, she does not feel castrated by the arrangement she has with the collector and thus can write erotica successfully. (By contrast, argues Brennan, Henry Miller could not carry on with the erotica collector's deal because he, like George, was bothered by the sense that there was a voyeur at the keyhole looking in on his writing, and felt castrated by the arrangement.) In particular, in this story, Nin once again pokes fun at the arrangement, implying that she as writer stands both inside and outside the text, profiting from it on her own terms as she both explores her own sexuality and plays the part of the veiled woman who commands a financial return proportional to the profit wrought in the deal. If the spectator (George's friend) paid one hundred dollars and the hired lover (George) is paid fifty, someone behind the scenes has also made fifty. The voyeur behind the scenes of Nin's erotica project is paying her, she implies, to have fun at his expense.

On a more serious note, Nin points in this story to the structuring of human desire itself through the gaze—the seeking of others' approval and love. The social implications of this recognition involve not a rejection of this arrangement—since it is quite likely that there is no escaping the human reality of the other's desire—but an extension of the recognition to include an acknowledgment of the subjectivities structured by desire. "The Veiled Woman" seems playful on the surface, but it throws the moral of "Marianne" into the light: Making of another's gaze an object leaves one—everyone—vulnerable to the isolating tendencies of narcissistic desire. Anyone can be played as an object in his or her own game. If there is hope of love, Nin implies when she is outside the role as veiled woman, it lies in recognizing the terms of the game and the status of all players, ultimately, as subjective human beings whose desire cannot be reduced to a role—at least not without betraying their trust and their humanity.

VI

All of Nin's writing coheres with its individual elements and the work as a whole. An internal logic, comparable to that of the unconscious ordering systems that structure consciousness, governs not only the shape of each story or novel but also its relationship to all of the others. Of course, much of the arrangement of Nin's erotica can be attributed to its editor. But because the coherence Nin wrote into her works is organic (following the logic of the unconscious) rather than linear, the arrangement of the works only enhances the thematic connections among various stories and other components of the text.

An important motif in all the erotica is bringing something into the light so that it can be looked at more objectively. In *Little Birds,* it is the specific theme of the introduction as well as of the first selection, the title story. There we meet again a character— Manuel, an exhibitionist and voyeur—whom we first encounter in *Delta of Venus* in the story named for him.

In both stories, Manuel's exhibitionism leads to isolation. In the story "Manuel," we learn that he is in love with the sight of his own erect penis as well as with others' appreciation of it. Nin sets him up as she did Fred in "Marianne" as a symbol of phallocentric egoism and implies that as erotica writer she must play the role of worshipful admirer. Her position is occupied within the story by a housewife with whom Manuel has struck a deal, a kind of alternative to prostitution but employing its devices. He will perform her household tasks; she is to pay him afterward with her fully attentive admiration as he shows himself. The parody comes into full view when he becomes so excited at being admired that he rolls himself into a ball on the floor and ejaculates onto his own face.

Manuel likes the traditional raincoat routine as well, but he does not take the risk often, as "the police punished such behavior rather severely" (229). In his effort to find a "safe" place for his behavior, Manuel takes to boarding trains and ends up meeting his match and future wife, a prostitute who is equally turned on by the sight of herself being seen. The story ends with the statement that she, at least, will never try to "possess him in the way of other women" (230). In this case, we can conclude that for Manuel and his wife, each is only a means to an end. Love is precluded because otherness is excluded—or at least reduced to a mirror image.

When Manuel appears in "Little Birds," his wife now has a name, Thérèse, and works during the day. He exhibits the same characteristics as in the earlier story, but in "Little Birds" his obsession to become the object of others' gazes takes the form of a more troubling obsession, for Manuel turns to attracting the attention of prepubescent schoolgirls. The birds of the title are his bait. Manuel rents an apartment for himself and Thérèse above a schoolyard that he can see from the apartment's balcony. Thérèse at first rejects the idea of living there. But Manuel is so taken with the sight of the little girls' short skirts, thighs, developing breasts, and long hair that he redecorates the apartment in her absence and persuades her to live there. By putting all kinds of tropical birds on the balcony he eventually attracts the attention of the girls at recess and they accept an invitation to come up to his apartment after school. Upon their second visit, he exposes himself fully and the girls, frightened, run away. Again, one must question the effect of his behavior upon a reader. The question itself is clearly one of Nin's points as Manuel's young guests run from his view.

"Runaway" is the title of the last story in the collection, a story in which several of Nin's themes culminate in a way that highlights not only John Ferrone's arrangement of the material but also Nin's repetition of theme and character. While such repetition sometimes grows tiresome in her nonerotic works, here it provides a strong sense of unity and frames both collections with a sense of purpose. "Runaway" gestures toward the collector with at least an illusion that the key to women's sexuality lies in men's hands and, in particular, in an oedipal competition between men. (The competition among male lovers for the attention of a female also replicates—from one of Nin's many perspectives—the arrangement among the female author/spectator/object she represents and the other players in the erotica game: Miller, Ruder, the anonymous and fictional "collector.")

Jeanette is the sixteen-year-old runaway protagonist of the story. A virgin, she is initiated into the world of sex by a man twice her age, Jean (whose name plays on hers in the way the mirror motif operates in "Manuel"). Initially Jean holds only innocent intentions of rescuing Jeanette and providing her a place to stay and food to eat in order to get her off the street. His intentions change when it becomes clear that Jeanette is in competition with her protective but sexually active mother and wants to become sexually experienced. In this, Jean eventually obliges.[9] Her insatiability belies her inexperience, however, and Jean soon tires of her, wishing he could return her to her mother. His fear of being possessed by the "clutching" hospitality of women echoes the fear of commitment shared by Manuel, Fred, and other characters who appear in Nin's erotica as representing fear of relationship and otherness.

At first resistant and indifferent, Jean's roommate Pierre later takes over. Although he is intimidated by the record Jean has set with Jeanette, Pierre is attracted to the idea of her smallness, which evokes in him a desire to "do violence to her" (156). This too, of course, is one of Nin's familiar themes, with which she oscillates between prurience and critique; the relationship between vulnerability (or its pretense) and a sexual desire based on the show of greater power is once again called into question. In truth, the only violence Pierre does to Jeanette is to ensure her desiring him by denying her needs until she is psychologically in his power. Only then, the story and stories conclude, she "bloomed under his caresses, no longer the girl but the woman already being born" (162).

VII

By provoking a response such as desire or anger in order to call into question the process by which the production of such response rests on the repression of otherness—and thus potentially one's own and all subjectivity—Nin's erotica call upon readers, male and female both, to examine their own attitudinal positions and to determine what adjustments in subjective positionings may be in order. As I have shown, Nin's work in this genre, by "operating precisely with the forces that construct the desiring . . . body" (Bracher 102),[10] functions as both cultural critique and provocative challenge to the kind of self-analysis that Bracher advocates when he argues for the revolutionary potential of an analytical rather than a polemic approach to pornography (101–2). In taking advantage of the opportunity Nin's erotica provide to notice the ways in which responses are manipulated by the text, readers can participate in a process analogous to Nin's rebellion against the very genre within which she works. This kind of questioning can open the way to authentic love (Bracher 10)—an idea that finds expression in Nin's preface to *Little Birds,* where she argues that psychological need, like economic deprivation among artists, obliterates what is truly erotic in human nature. In the same preface, Nin also insists that behind numerous layers of veils lies a natural or true human sexuality as yet only "half-dreamed." Whether or not such a state is truly possible, it is clear that Nin attempts through her erotica to make it so.

AUTHOR'S NOTE

This essay grew out of my paper "Anaïs Nin's 'Poetic Porn': Subverting the Male Gaze," which I first presented at the Popular Culture Association/American Culture Association annual meeting in March 1990 in Toronto.

NOTES

1. According to the third volume of Nin's (expurgated) *Diary*—excerpts from which are included in the preface to *Delta of Venus*—she accepted the offer to write erotica for Miller's "patron," for one dollar per page, shortly after arriving in America from war-threatened France. She soon involved a group of her friends and fellow artists in the erotica project.

   According to Bair, the "patron" was most likely the book collector who pretended to be merely arranging the deal, Barnett Ruder (261).

2. "This accommodation of otherness—of alien jouissance—which culminates in the emergence in the ego ideal of new signifiers bearing one's identity, makes subjects more capable of accepting and nurturing otherness not only in themselves but also in other subjects" (Bracher 100).

3. As Bracher points out, pornography may well have the positive effect of "exercis[ing] a salutary effect on jouissance, desire, and even identity" and making possible a "greater jouissance" (97). On the other hand, he acknowledges that pornography may reinforce the degradation of women and others, and he proposes that the reinforcement process be analyzed in order to bring about social change; see his chapter "Pornography" (83–104).

4. One way Nin invokes the analytic function—and invites readers to add their own responses to the layers of awareness her erotica evoke—is to thematize the economics of producing the very genre through which she calls it into question. Nin reports in her *Diary*, for example, and in the preface to *Delta of Venus*, that she created the erotica by mixing her sense of sensual and poetic appreciation with a rebellion against the exploitation inherent in her patron's demands for pornography. By teasing the patron—or the voyeuristic reader he represents—with titillating details interspersed among pages of the kind of poetic description he supposedly asked her to leave out, by reversing gender roles among her characters, and by embedding in her narratives a subtle editorial voice sometimes satirizing the production and consumption of erotica writings themselves, Nin patronizes her patron.

5. As part of Nin's working through her own overwhelming need for approval, Nin's erotica speak to the devastating effects of early childhood abuse, an implication only fully understandable within the context of Nin's "unexpurgated" diaries, which, along with Bair's biography, help to clarify the nature of her relationship with her father.

6. See, for instance, Jane Caputi's *Gossips, Gorgons, and Crones: The Fates of the Earth* (1993) for discussion of the long-term effects of incest and other forms of early sexual abuse. Caputi cites Ellen Bass and Laura Davis, *The Courage to Heal: A Guide for Women Survivors of Child Sexual Abuse* (New York: Harper & Row 1988); Gail Elizabeth Wyatt and Gloria Johnson Powell, eds., *Lasting Effects of Child Sexual Abuse* (Newbury Park, Calif.: Sage Publications, 1988); and E. Sue Blume, *Secret Survivors: Uncovering Incest and its Aftereffects in Women* (New York: Wiley, 1990).

7. In the fourth volume of the *Diary*, for instance, Nin uses the phrase "droit du seigneur" (traditionally, the right of the master to have sexual relations with his female servants) to critique Edmund Wilson's and Otto Rank's power over her: "At first I would at times be elated by power. . . . But at some point or other, HE asserted his prerogative. Le

droit du seigneur . . . made his claim. And then I used my charm to enslave and abandon first" (4:143).

8. Nin's experiences as a teenage model in New York were also fraught with anxiety; her use of the artist's model highlights her process of coming to terms with that anxiety.

9. The recurring theme of an innocent, just developing girl is enhanced through repeated references to Jeanette's "little breasts" (152), her "firm and pointed little breasts" that are also described as "fresh breasts" (153), her "tiny white panties" and "the smallness of the sex" (156), her "little rosy sex" (157), and her "little ass" (157).

10. Out of respect for otherness, Bracher quite appropriately specifies his scope as pertaining to the "heterosexual male." With the same respect, in this essay I have included within the categories of desiring bodies in Nin's erotica those who have been "othered" by the symbolic status of male heterosexual identity.

WORKS CITED

Bair, Deirdre. *Anaïs Nin: A Biography*. New York: Putnam, 1995.

Barron, Janet. "Equality Puzzle: Lawrence and Feminism." *Rethinking Lawrence*. Ed. Keith Brown, 12–22. Milton Keynes, Bucks., and Philadelphia: Open University Press, 1990.

Bracher, Mark. *Lacan, Discourse, and Social Change: A Psychoanalytic Cultural Criticism*. Ithaca: Cornell University Press, 1993.

Brennan, Karen. "Anaïs Nin: Author(iz)ing the Erotic Body." *Genders* 14 (1992): 66–86.

Caputi, Jane. *Gossips, Gorgons, and Crones: The Fates of the Earth*. Santa Fe: Bear, 1993.

de Lauretis, Teresa. "Desire in Narrative." *Alice Doesn't: Feminism, Semiotics, Cinema*. Bloomington: Indiana University Press, 1984.

Felski, Rita. *Beyond Feminist Aesthetics: Feminist Literature and Social Change*. Cambridge: Harvard University Press, 1989.

Fitch, Noël Riley. *Anaïs: The Erotic Life of Anaïs Nin*. Boston: Little, Brown, 1993.

Jong, Erica. "A Story Never Told Before." *Anaïs: An International Journal* 12 (1994): 15–25.

Kamboureli, Smaro. "Discourse and Intercourse, Design and Desire in the Erotica of Anaïs Nin." *Journal of Modern Literature* 11.1 (1984): 143–58.

Lacan, Jacques. *Écrits: A Selection*. Trans. Alan Sheridan. New York: Norton, 1977.

———. *Feminine Sexuality: Jacques Lacan and the école freudienne*. Ed. Juliet Mitchell and Jacqueline Rose. Trans. Jacqueline Rose. New York: Norton, 1982.

Nin, Anaïs. *Delta of Venus: Erotica*. New York: Harcourt Brace Jovanovich, 1977.

————. *The Diary of Anaïs Nin,* vol. 3, *1939–1944.* Ed. Gunther Stuhlmann. New York: Harcourt, Brace & World, 1969.

————. *House of Incest.* Chicago: Swallow Press, 1958.

————. *Incest: From "A Journal of Love": The Unexpurgated Diary of Anaïs Nin, 1932–1934.* New York: Harcourt Brace Jovanovich, 1992.

————. *Little Birds: Erotica.* New York: Harcourt Brace Jovanovich, 1979.

————. *The Novel of the Future.* New York: Macmillan, 1968.

————. *A Woman Speaks: The Lectures, Seminars, and Interviews of Anaïs Nin.* Ed. Evelyn J. Hinz. Chicago: Swallow Press, 1975.

CHAPTER 2

Anaïs Nin's Narrative Dilemma

The Artist as Social Conscience

Marion N. Fay

An inner life, cultivated, nourished, is a well of strength. To confuse this with the much persecuted ivory tower is to lack understanding of the inner structure we need to resist outer catastrophes and errors and injustices.

Anaïs Nin, *The Novel of the Future*

Anaïs Nin's work unquestionably focuses on the inner life, her own as well as that of others. For some critics, this emphasis on subjectivity reveals not only Nin's self-absorption, even narcissism, but a lack of social conscience. Put in more contemporary terms, subjectivity negates concern for "the other." It is this charge, most recently voiced by Deirdre Bair in a 1995 biography of Anaïs Nin, that I intend to examine and respond to here.

Bair portrays Nin as unconcerned about the rise of fascism prior to World War II and, following the declaration of war, "seemingly oblivious to the political drama playing out around her" (252). When the war was over, "to read . . . Nin's diary," Bair claims, "one would hardly know there had been one" (308). Claudia Roth Pierpont, in a 1993 *New Yorker* article, suggests that Nin concealed her own indifference to the war by calling attention to Henry Miller's indifference. In the late 1960s feminists accused Nin of ignoring social injustice in favor of luxuriating in a private world. Nin herself tells about working with a group of women artists in Los Angeles when suddenly two women challenged her, demanding a reply to their question "What about the ghetto?" (Williams, Clark, and Reyes 77).

Complaints about Nin's alleged lack of social conscience were set forth most strongly, perhaps, by Alice Walker in a *Ms.* magazine article published in April 1977, shortly after Nin's death. Walker commended Nin's erotic writing on the grounds that the core experiences "were not imagined" and thus were "useful" to others, and she praised Nin for urging women toward self-exploration. But she objected to the "decadence and insularity" of her work overall, and concluded: "Anaïs' apolitical nature was self-indulgent and escapist; her analysis of poverty, struggle, and political realities, mere romantic constructions useful to very few" (46).[1]

Walker's charge seems almost a recast of Nin's self-criticism amidst the rumblings of impending war. Nin realizes that "my own Christian remedies were ineffectual, my individual charity powerless except in a small radius, and my individual sacrifices useful to only a few. . . . I brought nothing to the great suffering of the world except palliatives, the drug of poetry, the individual loves which change nothing in the great currents of cruelty" (*Diary* 2:344–45).

This passage, dated September 1939, reveals Nin's concern for the fate of others, but also her underlying conflict about how to express it. Before taking a closer look at these and similar revelations, some concessions to her critics need to be made. Although, as Alice Walker pointed out, Nin's erotica contained a "useful" message—that a woman has the right to enjoy sex without shame or fear—Nin was certainly not a political writer. She rejected social realism in literature, and she refrained from presenting social reform programs or urging revolution. Occasionally she wrote about social activists, claiming that they tended to ignore important aspects of self-development in favor of collective action. As she saw it, such behavior was self-deceptive and potentially ineffectual in the larger world. When Nin did write about public affairs, some of her statements—if taken out of context—suggest superficiality of thought.

Consider the following from "Notes on Feminism": "Poverty and injustice and prejudice are not solved by any man-made system. I want them solved by a higher quality of human being who, by his own law of valuation upon human life, will not permit such inequalities" (30). This notion, looked at apart from Nin's belief in the primary importance of psychological self-integration, seems to imply a willingness to rest in the lap of a benign dictator. Also, some of her comments, such as "In the old days, things like war hurt so much, I didn't want to look at them" (Stocking 103), set Nin up for the "escapist" charge made by Alice Walker. Then, too, her preface to the 1968 British edition of *Under a Glass Bell* suggests a "small radius" indeed. Referring to the earlier, 1944 edition, Nin says that the story collection was first published "at an inauspicious time." She is not speaking about the tragedy of war; she is talking about the practical problems spawned by war—insufficient paper, reviewers, and readers—that caused her career to suffer.

Personal views and lapses notwithstanding, the charge that Anaïs Nin's work reveals a lack of social conscience deserves scrutiny. For one thing, such a charge leads to complex questions about the purpose of art, questions that cannot be resolved here, but cannot be ignored either. Is art an end in itself? If not, is it a tool—or should it be—in the service of social or political belief systems? Would Nin's work be praiseworthy if she had employed it in an effort to change or save the world? Should she have infused her writing with ideological messages? If so, then which ideology?

The lack-of-social-conscience charge comes primarily from political liberals who seem to believe that Nin should have both adopted their moral outrage and promoted their prescriptions for saving the world.[2] And thus another question arises here: Had Nin espoused a rightist ideology, might her work have been attacked on the basis of its "wrong" politics? Pulitzer Prize winner Alice Walker, in a twist of irony, has been criticized by right-wing religious fundamentalists for broaching the topic of racism in her fiction. In a polar opposite case, the groundbreaking films made by Leni Riefenstahl (born, incidentally, the same year as Anaïs Nin) have been deprecated by scholars and others because of Riefenstahl's apparent artistic collaboration with Hitler. Among other things, these examples illuminate the problems associated with using ideologically based political criteria to determine the value and/or purpose of art.

In Nin's case, we might ask, is limited commitment to social action sufficient grounds to devalue her work? Her person? Does her decision to de-emphasize public issues indicate submission to an ideological status quo? To larger world forces of oppression? If she had overridden her own creative vision in favor of social/political messages, would the world be better off? And how accurate, in fact, is the charge that she lacked a social conscience?

Many of Nin's critics, I would argue, fall into an either-or trap, illogically concluding that an emphasis on personal experience necessarily implies disregard for the public welfare. Yes, Anaïs Nin sometimes slipped into either/or postures herself. She had a propensity for romanticism, too. And she tended to distance herself from public events. But she was not, in my view, bereft of social conscience or totally detached from outer-world ills.

To help defuse the charge of social irresponsibility, I plan to look at several of Nin's chief literary and life concerns, concerns that, while certainly distinct, are inevitably conjoined. This will include tracing the development of her literary theory, examining her conflict about political activism, and discussing the social/political ramifications of specific literary works. What will become clear is that, despite the above-mentioned conflict, Nin's literary theory—and the social convictions from which it cannot be separated—evolved in a fundamentally consistent direction over a forty-five-year period.

Beginning with the first words she penned in her diary, Nin favored "subjective writing," which, as she explained it, meant that she was more interested in recounting the emotional experiences of the perceiving subject than in analyzing the nature of the external world. Nin's reasons for choosing a "subjective" approach to writing, and her negative view of social realism in literature, date back at least to 1932 when she published her first book, *D. H. Lawrence: An Unprofessional Study.* Her reluctance to depend on collective action in the solution of personal and social problems is rooted both in her early childhood and in her cultural milieu. But social conscience is not precluded by these views and beliefs. Social conscience entails an awareness of injustice imbued with empathy for its victims; it may or may not entail social action.

Nin's awareness of social injustice emerges in debates with herself recorded in the *Diary,* particularly volumes 2 (1934–1939) and 3 (1939–1944). Empathetic yet conflicted, she struggled "to make clear the relationship of our individual dramas to the larger one, and our responsibility" (2:348). At the same time, she questioned the value of her own work in the face of public chaos, she expressed support for Republican Spain, and she revealed her anguish about World War II. Nin wrote about these concerns in the 1944 foreword to *Under a Glass Bell,* which is entirely different, as I will demonstrate later, from the 1968 British version quoted above. The 1944 foreword shows her still wrestling with questions about private and public life commitments, yet the stories themselves—more than any of Nin's other works—bespeak her resolutions. And they reveal an indubitable social conscience.

Although Nin focused on fiction after *Under a Glass Bell* appeared, she published three critical essays, "Realism and Reality" (1946), "On Writing" (1947), and "The Writer and the Symbols" (1959), that further explained her reasons, initially set forth in the Lawrence book, for objecting to social realism. These essays also shed light on the philosophical premises for her literary and social theories. Nin's last theoretical work, *The Novel of the Future* (1968), provides a coherent elucidation of her views on the artist's public responsibilities. Taken together, these writings show that while Nin's literary and social conviction clarified over the years, she steadfastly adhered to her most fundamental views. The basic premise for these views is best summarized by Nin herself in "On Writing": "Only when the inner lens of our vision is clear can we act toward a larger order and creation. That is why I believe subjective writing is valuable and necessary" (53).

In the last decade of her life, it should be noted, Nin acknowledged that she had learned from feminists about the value of collective social action. Moreover, she participated in several civil rights campaigns.

Personal Background and Cultural Milieu

Anaïs Nin used the term "cultural restrictions" to help account for her early resistance to collective social action. Nin was raised to become like her prototypically feminine Spanish grandmother, Angela: she was "encouraged to please the man and influence indirectly, not directly" ("Interview for Sweden" 20). Sheltered from economic hardships and permitted to read and dance as a child, the adult Nin recalled messages from her mother discounting the pursuit of outer-world objectives. She explained, too, that her thinking was molded by the Catholic religion, with its requirement that women submit to a hierarchy of male authority within and outside the home (Loeb 27–28).

Reflecting on her young adulthood—the decade following her move to France in 1924 with husband Hugh (Hugo) Parker Guiler—the mature Nin observed that she and Henry Miller and Lawrence Durrel "were not committed politically" ("Sweden" 18). Like many other people after the Great War, she continued, they thought they "had finished with war. There was a certain sense of freedom. . . . All of our energies went into our work. We believed in this work, and we were very serious about it" ("Sweden" 18). As she saw it, the cultural climate in France at that time promoted introspection: "all the writers there kept diaries . . . and there is no diary without an 'I'" (Bailey 243).

Nin's earliest diary entries—childhood reflections on loss and betrayal, laced with hope for reunification with a missing father— make it clear that, from the outset, she wrote both in response to her own sense of otherness (a child deprived of her native country, language, culture and father) and as a means of self-exploration. Instead of seeking answers from outside sources, she endeavored over decades in the solitary practice of journal-keeping to "peel off" early conditioning and traumas and to construct an identity. The mature Anaïs Nin divulged retrospectively that she "used to feel that the inner journey was selfish, egocentric, and narcissistic" (Williams, Clark, and Reyes 78). But guiding her from the start was the realization that, step by step, "I had to find myself through that before I faced the world's problems" (Loeb 28).

The search for self was a long-term project. Writing at the age of twenty-nine, Nin admits she had not overcome a sense that there were at least two women within her, one "desperate and bewil-dered, who felt she was drowning, and another who would . . . conceal her true emotions because they were weaknesses, help-lessness, despair, and present to the world only a smile" (*Diary* 1:ix). However long, the search for self is a prerequisite, according to Nin, in one's own life as well as in preparation for political engagement. Self-integration must precede communal action, or, as Nin puts it, "You cannot be a valuable member of universal life unless you first become a complete, unified and balanced entity" ("Sweden" 20). This key theme in the *Diary*—self-exploration rest-ing on a belief in its ultimate "usefulness" to others—spilled over into Nin's other works and came to underlie her literary theory.

Literary Theory: Early Writings

D. H. Lawrence: An Unprofessional Study (1932), Nin's first foray into criticism, praises Lawrence's subjective impressionism—his preoc-cupation with interior life—while simultaneously outlining the approach she would take in her own future novels. Lawrence gives evidence "that revolutions are better fought inwardly in our-selves than en masse," she argues (95). Dubbing his style "interlin-ear," Nin cites his effort to make conscious "the silent subconscious communication between human beings" (16). This is why she finds *Lady Chatterly's Lover* a remarkably complete love story, commending not its graphic sexual detail but its "consistently double point of view. . . . every moment of the relationship reveals the woman's feelings as well as the man's" (58).

The seeds for Nin's rejection of social realism, that is, a quasi-scientific focus on external world events, were planted in the Lawrence book. People who "want a sane, static, measurable world" or who cling to initial impressions of events or other people, she asserts, are limited in their imaginations (31–32). Although Lawrence's novel *Kangaroo* does in fact deal realistically with wartime issues, Nin interprets it as a deeply retrospective "story of the individual's struggle to remain sane in spite of the madness of the mob when it accepts war" (28). This depiction aptly applies to the struggle she herself would go through a few years hence when faced with the horror of World War II. And in a claim compatible with her lifelong insistence on the priority of self-integration, Nin says that Lawrence, prefiguring his character Sommers in *Kangaroo*, opted for a more courageous act than risking death in war: he confronted his own "isolated soul."

Soon after publication of the Lawrence book, Nin, along with Henry Miller, joined the editorial staff of a Paris literary magazine, the *Booster* (later named *Delta*). In September 1937 the *Booster* announced its refusal to endorse "political line-ups," "social panaceas," and "economic nostrums." Nin's voice (as well as Miller's) seems to echo in the succeeding portion of the statement, which reads: "We leave the dirty work of making the world over to the quacks who specialize in such matters. For us things are all right just as they are" (5).

Both mocking and glossy, this assessment is disturbing in view of the concurrent war in Spain. Yet Nin's apparent hesitation to publicly condemn that bloody horror does not impugn her compassion for its individual victims, expressed simultaneously in her *Diary*.

The Diaries: On Life, Writing, and Responsibility

Nin examined all of her commitments, private and public, in the *Diary*. Volume 1 (1931–1934) begins just after she finished the Lawrence book. Primarily concerned with her relationships with Henry and June Miller, Dr. René Allendy, and Dr. Otto Rank, volume 1 also concerns Nin's early attempts to elude her traditional upbringing and to develop her subjective approach to writing. Daydreaming during a psychoanalytic session with Rank in the fall of 1933, Nin reflected, as the *Diary* records it, on the "difficulties with writing, my struggles to articulate feelings not easily expressed. Of my struggles to find a language for intuition, feelings, instincts which are, in themselves, elusive, subtle, and wordless" (276).

Volume 1 also records her responses to external world chaos. In June 1934 Nin describes "the monstrous reality outside, out in the world, the cause of D. H. Lawrence's and Henry's ravings and railings on the disintegration of the world. Doom! Historical and Political. Pessimism. Suicides. The concrete anxieties of men losing power and money. . . . I saw families broken apart by economic dramas. . . . Individual lives shaken, poisoned, altered" (331).

Overwhelmed, she decides that she cannot become a political activist or try to reform social conditions: "With greater, more furious, more desperate stubbornness I continued to build my individual life, as if it were a Noah's Ark for the drowning" (332).

Nin continued to reexamine her position vis-à-vis social/political action, yet almost always retreated from "monstrous reality," determined to create a private sanctuary. But contrary to the views of some critics, a personal commitment does not necessarily imply selfishness or escapism. The *Booster* proclamation and Nin's earlier expressed reluctance to join group causes notwithstanding, she anguished in volume 2 of the *Diary* (1934–1939) over the nature of her social responsibility. As Nin herself explains, volume 2 "opens into the world and brings out the conflict of the artist, whether or not he will commit himself to what is happening in the world; in this case it was the Spanish War . . . and the breakdown of the feeling we had at the beginning of 1930 that there were not to be any more wars" ("Sweden" 23).

Nin's compassion for Spanish Civil War victims literally punctuates volume 2. And, as historian Robert Zaller observes, her notation of outer-world events is expressed "in a brief staccato totally at variance with her normal style" (178). "The death of the Republicans in Spain wounds me like the death of flesh I love," a 1936 entry begins. "We buy a newspaper. Blood. Massacres. Blood. Torture. Cruelty. Fanaticism. People burned with gasoline. Stomachs ripped open in the shape of a cross" (120). Exclamations, potent silences, and single cries of pain and outrage are "more eloquent than any analysis," Zaller writes, astutely concluding that Nin resisted the lure of mass solutions not because of selfishness but because she recognized "the responsibility of protecting her own humanity in order to extend it to others" (179).

The desire for self-protection, however, did not forestall Nin's continuing struggle—most pronounced during the period bounded

by the Spanish War and World War II—to define her responsibility to the larger world. In June 1936 she confided to the *Diary:* "I have not been unaware of the political drama going on, but I have not taken any side because politics . . . seemed rotten to the core and all based on economics and not humanitarianism" (92). And: "I feel tempted to engage my allegiance. But I must find a leader I trust. . . . if I met a revolutionary who was a great man . . . I could serve, fight, die. But meanwhile I help in a small radius, and I wait" (93).

In August she wonders if writing is as important as serving others: "The two pulls are there. Selflessness and work" (103). Nin does carry on with her work, writing the *Under a Glass Bell* stories, intermittently socializing and visiting the beach. She also attends political meetings with Gonzalo More, the Peruvian revolutionary, and she persists in documenting her inner discord, noting in January 1937 that Gonzalo "tore me from tradition, he awakened me politically. Let him put my name down" on a list of people working for Republican Spain (152).

Later that month, she fears that she cannot help reconstruct the world: "I know too well that man can only change himself psychologically. . . . with each revolution, just a change of men in power . . . The evil remains (154–55).

Nin agrees to work for pacifists and to collect signatures on behalf of the Spanish Loyalists, but asks herself, does this represent "Duality? No," she answers in a *Diary* monologue. "I believe in philosophical detachment from violence . . . and I also believe . . . in rebellion" (155). Still conflicted, she writes at the end of 1937: "Every time there is talk of Spain there is a tornado in me of emotion and desire to participate"; persuaded, however, that she would be of no use, she is "thrown back to writing" (270).

In September 1939, when World War II is declared, Nin responds in the *Diary,* "Nothing left but to share humanely in the error, and the suffering of the world" (338). Shortly thereafter, she begins to study Marx. Seeking "to understand the new world," she wants "to evolve and change with it" (342). Nin criticized all political ideologies but had professed Marxist sympathies since the late 1930s, when she also participated in letter-writing campaigns on behalf of the Loyalist cause in Spain. Yet a key question continued to haunt her: whether "the artist who creates a world of beauty to sustain and transcend and transmute suffering is wiser than those who believe in revolution" (346).

Pulled both toward and away from the larger world, she writes on the last pages of volume 2: "Before the war . . . I set up individual creativity against the decomposition of our historical world . . .

but now nothing is left but to recognize my connection with it and to participate humanely in the error. . . . I knew I could not separate myself from the world's death" (348). Note the change in wording from "share in the error" in the *Diary* entry ten pages earlier and, quoted here, to "participate."

Coming to terms—inconsistently, paradoxically even—Nin concludes this paragraph that began with a recognition of her "connection" with the larger world by emphasizing her separateness: "the artist is not here to be at one with the world, he is here to transform it" (348). Having described Henry Miller's wartime departure for Greece as an "escape," Nin attributes her own departure to her husband's being "ordered back to the U.S. . . . Alone I might have chosen to stay and share the war with France," she writes. "I was not glad to escape tragedy" (349).[3]

Although Nin ended volume 2 of the *Diary* in the fall of 1939 emphasizing the artist's separation from the public realm, her position had not fully hardened. Volume 3 (1939–1944), which details her readjustment to life in the United States, reveals Nin's inability to divorce herself from world affairs. She continued, however, to criticize social realism in literature, arguing that "the general obsession with observing only historical or sociological movements, not a particular human being . . . is as mistaken as a doctor who does not take an interest in a particular case" (44). Social realists are "confused about their role [because they] seek to convert, philosophize or moralize" (13) and because, as Nin would further elucidate in her critical essays, they ignore the most authentic reality—individual emotional life—and thus they fail to offer counterexamples that might actually "convert" the abusers and nurture the wounded.

Reiterating her central theme in volume 3, Nin writes that "any experience carried out deeply to its ultimate leads you beyond yourself into a larger relation to the experience of others" (299). And she likens social realists to political activists: the former seek meaning in the external world and the latter seek personal identity outside themselves. As she had in the Lawrence study, Nin suggests that realists and reformers tend to mask inner conflicts and to skirt internal wars. Referring to her friend Olga, for instance, who "gave her life to politics," Nin asserts that "she had run away from a confrontation with herself, from the task of training, nurturing, maturing it before giving it away" (225).

Political reformers, she goes on, are "escapists from another world, escaping from insights which blinded them in their very own political work, insights into human beings" (225). As in earlier diaries, Nin does not totally condemn political reform activities; instead she calls for a priori self-reform, personal "training, nurturing, maturing." But Nin, having described Olga as "a prisoner of duty," is a prisoner of sorts too, caught in an either-or trap. She seems to rule out the possibility of multiple reasons for "giving one's life to politics"; for example, she ignores motivations that might stem from empathy, rational commitment, and/or a principled value system. A similar narrowness appears in a passage in volume 2 of the *Diary* when Nin deduces that those who worry about hunger in India and China disclose a "personal starvation" (25), as if such concern could only be psychologically based and self-deceptive.

For all her reservations about social action, Nin cannot put the issue to rest. Writing in the midst of World War II, when "Every bomb falls on a house we lived in, on a human being we love," she asks, "What can one do? Are we needed in this new world, can we create a new world here?" (*Diary* 3:125) Then in May 1943 come the disarmingly honest utterances of a woman grasping for a thread that will bind us as a species. Nin wonders if her personal anxiety, "this illness of the soul," unites her in "brotherhood with others." Continuing this inquiry in the second person—signifying her actual sense of detachment, Nin's critics might say—she concedes that she has not suffered in a concentration camp, has not been jailed or tortured in Spain: "None of that. But as you cross the street . . . you feel as if all these horrors had happened to you, you feel the nameless anxiety, the shrinking of the heart, the asphyxiation, the suffocation of pain. . . . Anxiety is a woman screaming without a voice, out of a nightmare. Could it come from participation, an empathy with what is happening to others: Is it the only link we have with the fate of other human beings?" (276).

Social Conscience in *Under a Glass Bell*

Still debating the artist's relation to the larger world, Nin nevertheless gave full attention, in the spring of 1943, to the printing of *Under a Glass Bell*. She had acknowledged in the *Diary* the poet's anxiety and guilt "for working out his individual patterns and pleasures separately from the rest of the world," a theme also expressed in her story about Antonin Artaud, "Je Suis le Plus Malade des Surréalistes." These feelings "drove him mad," she concluded in volume 3 (299). Yet she tried to justify the separation, writing, "Because the outer reality was monstrous, the poet turned to the construction of a fantasy world" (299), a *Diary* entry that prefigures the 1944 *Under a Glass Bell* foreword.

"Stories," she reminds us as she prepares to give hers to the public, "are the only enchantment possible, for when we begin to see our own suffering as a story, we are saved" (296). Nin realizes, too, that stories and dreams "do not create a human relationship by themselves. . . . similarities of human experience, war, birth, death, suffering, draw people together" (299). These realizations belie the depiction of Nin as a selfish isolationist. Along with other *Diary* entries, they unveil an empathetic yet conflicted human being, pondering alternatives, then returning to her own vision, then reaching again and again for answers to disturbing questions about what can and cannot be shared.

Under a Glass Bell, written for the most part in the late 1930s, leaves little doubt about Anaïs Nin's compassion for the dispossessed. A distinguished story collection, according to critic Oliver Evans, who compares it to Joyce's *Dubliners,* it was presented at a time when Nin "was strongly preoccupied with ideas of social justice" (64). Hand set and printed over a four-month period by Nin herself with the help of Gonzalo, the publication was truly a labor of love undergirded by intense commitment to her own vision. The first edition, three hundred copies issued by Nin's Gemor Press in February 1944, was followed by a second printing of eight hundred copies in June. These editions contained the foreword drafted in volume 3 of the *Diary.* At extreme variance from the 1968 preface quoted earlier, with its seemingly self-indulgent worries about the scarcity of writing paper and reviewers, the 1944 foreword addresses the question of the artist's responsibility to others, combining apology—as both regret and defense—with soul-searching.

Not always easy to follow, the foreword begins with Nin's admission that she considered destroying the stories because they seemed to be fantasies unrelated to the horrors of war. Then it offers a justification for these fantasies: "These stories represent the moment when many like myself had found only one answer to the suffering of the world: to dream, to tell fairy tales, to elaborate and to follow the labyrinth of fantasy. All of this I see now was the passive poet's only answer to the torment he witnessed. Being ignorant of the causes and therefore of the possibility of change, he sought merely a balm art, the drug."

"I did not stay in the world of the isolated dream or become permanently identified with it," Nin goes on to explain. "The Spanish

War awakened me. I passed out of romanticism, mysticism and neurosis into reality." She decided not "to destroy the art which was produced under an evil social structure," but realizes it is necessary to "understand, to be aware of what caused the suffering which made such an opium essential and what this fantasy world concealed. And to this task I will devote the rest of my writing. I am in the difficult position of presenting stories which are dreams and of having to say: but now, although I give you these, I am awake!"

She continues, "It is in 'The Mouse' that first appears the thread of humanity that was to lead me out of the dream," and the story reflects this. Set on Nin's houseboat, the story tells of a maid abandoned by other employers, by her family, then by her lover after she becomes pregnant. So bound to her social station that she scurries and cowers like a mouse, the maid is an uneducated woman rejected in the end by hospital officials worried about who would pay for treatment of an unmarried servant's sin-tainted, abortion-related infection. "The woman bleeding there on the bench meant nothing to them" (34), Nin writes, her words ladened with sadness for the plight of another. They reverberate, too, her cry "Spain is bleeding," a *Diary* entry in 1936 (2:93). Some critics say that Spain bleeding "meant nothing" to Anaïs Nin. And yet these two "bleeding" lines suggest her intuitive grasp of a link between cruelty to one and cruelty to the many.

In fact, war and its fallout pervade "The Mouse," a story that manifests Nin's central tenet: Attending to the individual—in this instance, a distraught pregnant woman—leads "into a larger relation to the experience of others" (*Diary* 3:299). Deserted by her soldier lover, ridiculed by a bitter war-wounded doctor, the mouse is a war victim. "The bleeding little mouse spurned by society," as British poet Hugo Manning portrays her, belongs to "the time of the bewildered, adolescent girls in the blackout, or the lonely demoralized wife, or even those near soldiers' camps who gave themselves up to an unsatisfactory ritual of love for a bar of soap or a tin of corned beef. These things are done in a 'gesture of panic'" (123).

Social responsibility in art, to borrow from Carlos Fuentes, involves imagination that "forces us to see what we don't see"; cruelty comes from "a failure of the imagination, the inability to assign the same feelings and values to another person that you harbor in yourself" (quoted in Smith). In "The Mouse," Nin has brought a female discard into emotional visibility; she has given us, too, a character, the doctor reluctantly on board the houseboat to give cursory medical treatment, who "fails to imagine the other." Sardonically identifying him as the *grand blessé de guerre*, Nin unveils a great war hero unable to cope with the personal pain of a maid. Kill for his country he could, but, repeatedly washing his hands—of responsibility and sin and lower-class grime—he "did not look at the mouse as if she were a human being. Everything about him said clearly: you are only a servant, just a little servant, and like all of them, you get into trouble, and it's your own fault" (31).

Disapproval born of classism, "a failure of imagination" in its social form, undermines the confidence and perpetuates the vulnerability of the "other." This is what the story reveals. Deprived, oppressed, frightened, "the mouse" resorts to stealing because she is, in Nin's analysis, without hope of ever getting what she needs. Her sense of hopelessness is reconfirmed at the hospital, for "they refuse to take her in" (33). In a tone both matter-of-fact and empathetic, Nin delineates a full-fledged victim of social injustice, "someone who has taken abuse so often that he/she comes to expect it from everyone" (Terkel 162).

A consequence of her own early experience, Nin's sense of the outsider's vulnerability infuses, indeed sears through, the story "Birth." In this autobiographical narrative, Anaïs—hardly a drab, mousy servant, but a woman tainted nevertheless by apparent sin—undergoes brutal treatment in the circumstances of an abortion. At the zenith of her pain, the "doctor paced up and down angrily, impatiently," and the nurses "were laughing." At the very moment when Anaïs cannot remember why she should want to live, the doctor thrusts a long instrument into her, making her "cry out. A long animal howl. That will make her push, he says to the nurses" (99).

Are Nin's depictions of hostile medical care, the burdens of the womb, and the lot of servant women in 1930s Paris "mere romantic constructions," to use Alice Walker's phrase? On the contrary. Though not sociological analyses, "The Mouse" and "Birth" ask readers to contemplate inequities they might otherwise have ignored. Moreover, these stories deal with harsh realities that persist today—the battle over abortion and the unavailability of adequate medical care for certain segments of the population.

It cannot be argued that Nin completely led herself out of the dream, as the 1944 *Under a Glass Bell* foreword predicted, or that she centered attention on what the "fantasy world concealed," war horrors, for instance. On the other hand, as Edmund Wilson concluded in his 1944 review of the story collection, Nin had no reason to apologize for entering "the Labyrinth of fantasy" because her stories "reflect the torment" of the times (74). This fact is illuminated by a comparison of her "The Child Born Out of the Fog" with a contemporaneous story by an indisputable political writer, Kay Boyle, who also lived in Paris between the world wars.[4]

Boyle maintained that a writer "must bear the full weight of moral responsibility" (quoted in Gilbert and Gubar 1965) and took the suffering wrought by World War II as an overt theme for much of her work. Her story "Winter Night," for instance, explores psychological wounds attributable to Nazism. Published in 1946, it tells of a Jewish child orphaned in a concentration camp and another child figuratively orphaned in New York City. The American girl's mother leaves her affection-starved daughter in the care of a babysitter—herself a grieving war victim—to seek relief in "night life" from her own loneliness. What will this mother learn, Boyle nudges readers to ask, when she finds her child and the "sitting parent" in mutual solace, asleep in each other's arms?

Anaïs Nin's story "The Child Born Out of the Fog" focuses, not unlike "Winter Night," on an innocent girl trapped by larger world social antagonisms involving her parents. In "Fog" the child Pony, desperate for affection but denied it, is the daughter of an interracial couple condemned because of their union: "Stones were thrown at them, and [her father's] life was in danger . . . from strangers . . . so they never walked together, and [her mother, Sarah] could not carry Pony safely through the streets" (83). Despite differences in narrative line, Nin's and Boyle's concerns resonate. Both writers contemplate the pain of private loss and the deepest personal yearnings for love in times of public uncertainty.

As in "Winter Night," the suffering of the child in "Fog" embodies social cruelty, but also transmutes into hope, into Nin's vision of the possibility for love, understanding, and equality between blacks and whites: "Two tears had frozen on [Pony's] cheeks, tears at having been deserted by both parents, but halfway down her face they had stopped flowing because she had found them again. Soft dark brown curls and two hands stretch towards the white mother and the dark father for equal consolation" (83).

An innocent child groping for love and security also appears in "Houseboat." Fearful of being sent to an orphanage, the boy runs away instead of accepting Nin's invitation to come aboard. "Voyage of Despair" (17) is Nin's minimalist response, but one whose subtext is compassion for the abandoned boy. And her response echoes a line in "Fog," where Nin has said of Sarah, "Everyone who is hurt takes a long voyage" (83). Certainly she is musing on an individual journey, but "Fog" has a subtext, too, one that embraces the larger world. The "hurt," as Nin conceives it, has prompted Sarah to travel far from the coldness of an Aryan to the warmth of a dark "other." Though she resorts here to either-or stereotyping, equating "white" with cold and "black" with warm, it seems fair to acknowledge Nin's effort, through illumination of what the fog blurs and hides and protects, to break through the ignorance, hostility, and fear regarding mixed-race couples and dark-skinned people.[5] The story is a gesture toward love in the face of bigotry—and a reiteration of hope for the coming together of the races.

Dispossessed herself as a child, Nin has not forgotten other dispossessed children, or adults, for that matter, such as the tramps in the autobiographical story "Houseboat," where Nin too is one of the dispossessed. Early on here, she divulges a wish to break away from "the current of the crowd," from social chaos as well as from the rules on land. Her wish could, of course, be labeled escapist, but what would this mean? Where exactly is the demarcation between self-indulgent escape and the right to choose one's own way of life? The story itself ponders these questions as they pertain to Nin and to the tramps who live under the Seine bridges. "Like me," she observes, they had "fallen out of crowd life" and "refused to obey. . . . they had abandoned time, possessions, labor, slavery" (110). Nin hasn't given up all her possessions, and, unlike the tramps, she rejects alcohol, finding dream-inspiration in the flow of the river. But she neither criticizes them nor enters their lives as a social worker. At bottom, she shares with them a hunger for individual freedom.

Nin's vision tarnishes, though, when she is ordered by city officials to leave the river that lulled and transported her internally. Attuned to the forlorn fate of the tramps as well, she writes of the oldest one with sadness and affection; when "he was lifted by alcohol wings and ready for flight, the wings collapsed into nausea. This gangplank of drunkenness led nowhere" (17). Yet it is by way of the tramps' alcohol-induced hyperbole that she reveals her own skepticism about social change: "They gave me the news of the day, of the approach of war, of the hope for revolution. . . . An aurora borealis and all men out of prison" (16). This skepticism, however, does not detract from Nin's empathy—for the tramps, the young boy, and a drowning woman in "Houseboat," or for the mulatto child Pony, the "bleeding mouse," and the other characters in *Under a Glass Bell*. As Studs Terkel rightly points out, Nin's concern in these stories is a humanitarian one for the displaced and marginalized, "for people who seem outside what is in the norm" (154).

Literary Theory: Later Writings

Nin elaborated on the twin themes first expressed in the Lawrence study—the priority of subjectivity over realism and the necessity of self-integration—in several essays published after *Under a Glass Bell:* "Realism and Reality" (1946), "On Writing" (1947), and "The Writer and the Symbols" (1959). Sounding a "delicate battle cry," in the words of Nin scholar Philip K. Jason (34), she disparages social realism—though without naming specific writers—while simultaneously refining her own approach. "Reportage," work that focuses on external events, evades the "disturbing deeper world . . . the essential inner drama," Nin asserts in "Realism and Reality" (26), a claim that reappears in "On Writing." All three essays suggest that we are being "cheated of reality" by so-called realistic writers. Here we get a glimpse of the philosophical orientation underlying her literary theory and worldview. Realists "cheat" us because they neglect what Nin considers the most basic reality, namely, the nonmaterial world that is directly, immediately perceivable in emotional life. This view, supplemented by her decision to give priority to the impingement of characters' inner worlds, represents a variant of philosophical idealism.

Evelyn Hinz, whose *Mirror and the Garden* (1971) is one of the first critical studies of Nin, labels her a transcendentalist because she found reality in the unconscious (11) and because, in Nin's own words, she believed in "the spiritual content of every act and of every object" ("The Writer and the Symbols" 49). Whatever we call it, Nin's philosophical orientation does not entail a denial of the empirical world. Nor does it disallow action on behalf of those suffering from empirical world ills. For her, the individual psyche is the domain of authenticity, of unadulterated truth; only what "we discover emotionally has the power to alter our vision" ("On

Writing" 35). In that sense, the interior world is more real than the external world.

But Nin is talking about a continuum of reality, the whole of which she chose to embrace. In an introduction to the first published edition of "On Writing," William Burford, an Amherst student who later became a professor of literature, offers a practical interpretation of her position. Burford recognizes the import of the material and/or cultural context in which a work is produced but explains what some of Nin's critics seem to forget, that understanding our culture begins with "understanding the individuals who both made and are made by that culture" (42).[6]

As it happens, the stories in *Under a Glass Bell* that most directly reveal Nin's social conscience, "Birth," "The Mouse," and "The Child Born Out of the Fog," though poetic in style, follow a realistic narrative line. Most of her work, of course—in contrast to social realism—eschews conventional plots and themes. Nin explores dreams, feelings, and unconscious images—or the subterranean, to use one of her preferred terms—shining laser light on the personal journey of self-discovery. Unconscious content, it should be said, has uses in addition to the therapeutic. Nin delves into a wellspring of creativity that ultimately gives meaning to externally lived life, one's own and that of others.[7] Her subjective vision does not merely "produce a hothouse plant; it is projected into the outer world, there to combine with other beings" (Balakian 123).

This vision accounts for the poetic, intensely introspective quality of the story "Houseboat," where Nin writes, "The river and I united in a long, winding, never-ending dream, with its deep undercurrents, its deeper undertows of dark activity, the river and I rejoicing at teeming obscure mysteries of river-bottom lives" (20). Yet this probing into a "disturbing deeper world" was not for private reasons alone. The houseboat has a meaning beyond itself; it signifies a quest for independence, "the need to imagine one's self as traveling, moving" (*Diary* 3:300). Neither insular nor unique, this dream/myth no doubt rises to consciousness in many of us, regardless of our station, class, or political ideology.

To separate such dreams from our lives is dangerous, Nin insists, for when we refuse to address the needs "within us we will never have an objective understanding of what is happening outside. We will not be able to relate to it, to choose sides, to evaluate historically, and consequently we will be incapacitated for action" ("Realism and Reality" 30). Continually urging us to build bridges and to forge relationships, Nin calls for a synthesis of private and public world concerns. In her 1959 essay "The Writer and the Symbols," she once again champions a ripple effect that begins at home: "Even in a world of conflict and war, there is the possibility of harmony in personal relationships, which will in turn infect the relations between nations" (53). Romanticism may well flourish in these words; they offer hope as well.

What, then, would be a fair assessment of Nin's effort to work out the relationship between private and public concerns? Claudia Roth Pierpont snidely devalued Nin's support for Republican Spain, portraying her removing "nail polish and stashing her jewelry away in order to attend [political] meetings" (79). Alice Walker characterized Nin's writing as insular, as self-indulgently detached from the harsh realities of the external world. Deirdre Bair suggested that Nin's protection of her own way of life, especially in time of war, revealed her as indifferent to the fate of others. I read Nin differently, finding in her words a true-to-life mix of thought and emotion that conjoins self-probing honesty with basic—and also worthy—commitments. Over the years, these commitments were tested, sometimes redefined, and occasionally tinged by excuse-making and romanticism.

Nin was doubtful about grand schemes to transform the human condition and reluctant to immerse herself in the blood and guts of social change. These attitudes seem to me not so much evidence of Nin's insularity as tendencies consistent both with her early questioning of the artist's relationship to the larger world and with her later thinking articulated in texts on literary theory. Nin veered from the original foreword to *Under a Glass Bell:* she did not devote the rest of her writing to exposing social ills. Nevertheless, seminal ideas from the 1944 foreword can be found in the essays discussed here earlier and in her last theoretical work, *The Novel of the Future* (1968). There Nin repeats that it was never her intention to permanently reside within the world of dreams, but to explore them; she underscores the public value of dreams, too, asserting, "Man has to live outside and beyond history as well as in it or he will be swept like hysterical sheep into its errors (such as the horrors of Nazism)" (12).

The details of Nin's position on the communal responsibility of the artist are further clarified in *The Novel of the Future*. Summarized only briefly here, they reveal the evolving yet fundamentally consistent direction of Nin's thinking in her later life:

- Human cruelty is the work of psychologically damaged individuals.
- The cause of social injustice is human cruelty, not political systems.
- Neither political systems nor social realism in literature will change the world for the better.
- Individual psychological integration best prepares one to contribute to the community.
- The artist's primary responsibility involves a refusal to add to social chaos and a commitment to create a world of beauty, a counter example to destruction and hatred.

Although Nin's emphasis on individual experience is undeniable, I see her as continuously moving between, and sometimes living within, two worlds, the personal and the public. Her intention was not to escape from reality but, as Evelyn J. Hinz explains it, to "escape from the nightmare of the Western world" (112). With the rise of feminism in the early 1970s, Nin began to recognize the value of group action, saying she had learned from the women's movement that some problems "could be socially and politically dealt with . . . by unity between women" (Chicago 109). More specifically, Nin noted the limits of individual effort and admitted that she could not do anything by herself to help, for instance, "the mouse." But "working together" in the women's movement, she averred, we might have changed the abortion laws, and "the mouse's problems could have been solved" (Terkel 168).

Although Nin always returned to her basic theme—the priority of personal experience—she never emphasized it simply for itself. "When you go deeply into the personal," she reminds us, "you really go deeply into the collective. You have something to contribute to the collective" (Chicago 113). In the last decade of her life, Nin demonstratively lived out these words. She participated in a vigil for Martin Luther King Jr., signed petitions for Another Mother for Peace, and gave readings on behalf of Poets for Peace. Also, she advocated abortion rights and gave public support to the politically liberal presidential candidate George McGovern.

But Nin did not claim to be an agent of social/political change. Her agency was primarily aesthetic. The *Under a Glass Bell* stories discussed here beckon readers to reflect upon the tragedies of others, yet leave all decisions about responsive actions to us. Not engaged in social analysis, Nin chose to explore the psychological causes of cruelty and the effects of social injustice on individuals. Thus she bore witness to the "severity of the world," as in "The Mouse" (26), and she imagined possibilities for hope, as in "The Child Born Out of the Fog." We may disagree with her rather tradition-bound views on the nature of femininity. We may find reason to question her reliance on psychological approaches to the solution of world problems. But Nin's determination to be free from social authority was her right, and her decision to reject political writing a valid personal choice. Compassion for others and commitment to one's own vision are not mutually exclusive. Indeed, Anaïs Nin long held to a vision—as does Alice Walker today—of a living relationship between all things, a vision symbolized in her work by the flowing ocean that unites everyone.

AUTHOR'S NOTE

This essay is a revised and expanded version of "Selfhood and Social Conscience: On reading some stories in *Under a Glass Bell*" originally published in *Anaïs: An International Journal* 13 (1995): 100–108.

NOTES

1. Ironically, Walker indulged in the very type of writing for which she criticized Nin. Forgoing analysis, she gave a first-person account of a meeting with Anaïs Nin that emphasized Walker's subjective responses to the life and work of the deceased.
2. I cannot exclude myself from the political liberal category. Nor can I deny an ambivalence about carrying on with private work in the shadow of larger-world ills and turmoil. I nevertheless intend to show in this essay that Anaïs Nin's life and work choices were meaningful—and in many instances founded on compassion.
3. Biographer Deirdre Bair, citing unpublished diary number 61, located in the Anaïs Nin archive at UCLA, claims that Nin—devoid of moral concern about the war—left France in 1939 because of a romantic liaison with Gonzalo More. Nin "persuaded herself that she was racked with conflict," Bair concludes, "when in truth it was a choice she made easily" (252).
4. Interestingly, both women eschewed overt feminism in their later years and were similar in their evaluation of femininity as more of an asset than not. Boyle remained a social activist until her death in 1993; Nin's limited social activism, supporting Martin Luther King, Jr., for instance, occurred primarily during the last part of her life.
5. In the novel *Seduction of the Minotaur*, Nin falls into a similar either-or trap. Here the white man looking through cameras, glasses, and other vision-enhancing equipment distances himself from the pulse of life, whereas the dark-skinned native immediately apprehends the warmth and texture of life with his naked eye. Racial stereotypes

notwithstanding, Nin's apparent intention is to laud the people of color with whom she favorably identifies. Also, the either-or categorization in *Seduction* is meant to call attention to the distinctions Nin makes between social realists, obsessed by the measurement and ordering of external events, and the intuitive, poetic writers such as herself, whose approach she likens to the dark-skinned natives'.

6. Citing unpublished letters and her interview with William Burford on 27 October 1993, biographer Deirdre Bair writes that Nin revised Burford's introductory essay to satisfy herself but without informing Burford (316).

7. Nin is not talking about nighttime figments and/or fantasies. As she defines it in *The Novel of the Future,* a dream is an idea or image in the mind *"not under the command of reason.* It is not necessarily an image or an idea that we have during sleep. It is merely an idea or image which escapes the control of reasoning or logical or rational mind" (5).

WORKS CITED

Bair, Deirdre. *Anaïs Nin: A Biography.* New York: Putnam, 1995.

Balakian, Anna. "The Poetic Reality of Anaïs Nin." *A Casebook on Anaïs Nin.* Ed. Robert Zaller, 113–31. New York: New American Library, 1974.

Bailey, Jeffrey. "Link in the Chain of Feeling: An Interview with Anaïs Nin." *Conversations with Anaïs Nin.* Ed. Wendy M. DuBow, 235–49. Jackson: University Press of Mississippi, 1994.

Boyle, Kay. "Winter Night." *The Norton Anthology of Literature by Women.* Ed. Sandra M. Gilbert and Susan Gubar, 1695–1703. New York: Norton, 1985.

Burford, William. "The Art of Anaïs Nin: Introduction to 'On Writing.'" *Anaïs: An International Journal* 8 (1990): 40–44.

Chicago, Judy. "Women in the Arts: Diarist Anaïs and Judy Chicago." *Conversations with Anaïs Nin.* Ed. Wendy M. DuBow, 104–15. Jackson: University Press of Mississippi, 1994.

DuBow, Wendy M., ed. *Conversations with Anaïs Nin.* Jackson: University Press of Mississippi, 1994.

Editorial. *Booster* 2.7 (1937): 5.

Evans, Oliver. *Anaïs Nin.* Carbondale: Southern Illinois University Press. 1968.

Gilbert, Sandra M., and Susan Gubar. *The Norton Anthology of Literature by Women: The Tradition in English.* New York: Norton, 1985.

Hinz, Evelyn J. *The Mirror and the Garden: Realism and Reality in the Writings of Anaïs Nin.* New York: Harcourt Brace Jovanovich, 1973.

"Interview for Sweden." *Conversations with Anaïs Nin.* Ed. Wendy M. DuBow, 15–26. Jackson: University Press of Mississippi, 1994.

Jason, Philip K. "A Delicate Battle Cry." *Anaïs* 89 (1990): 30–34.

Loeb, Clare. "Anaïs Nin on Women's Liberation." *Conversations with Anaïs Nin*. Ed. Wendy M. DuBow, 27–39. Jackson: University Press of Mississippi, 1944.

Manning, Hugo. "An Open Letter from England, 1944."*Anaïs: An International Journal* 8 (1990): 121–24.

Metzger, Deena. *"The Diary:* The Ceremony of Knowing." *A Casebook on Anaïs Nin*. Ed. Robert Zaller, 133–43. New York: New American Library, 1974.

Nin, Anaïs. "Birth." *Under a Glass Bell,* 96–101. Chicago: Swallow Press, 1948.

———. "The Child Born Out of the Fog." *Under a Glass Bell*, 82–85. Chicago: Swallow Press, 1948.

———. *D.H. Lawrence: An Unprofessional Study.* 1932. Chicago: Swallow Press, 1964.

———. *The Diary of Anaïs Nin* (1931–74). New York: Swallow Press/Harcourt Brace Jovanovich, 1966–80.

———. Foreword to *Under a Glass Bell*. New York: Gemor Press, 1944.

———. "Houseboat." *Under a Glass Bell*, 11–25. Chicago: Swallow Press, 1948.

———. "The Mouse." *Under a Glass Bell*, 26–34. Chicago: Swallow Press, 1948.

———. "Notes on Feminism." *In Favor of the Sensitive Man and Other Essays*, 27–32. New York: Harcourt Brace Jovanovich, 1976.

———. *The Novel of the Future.* New York: Macmillan, 1968.

———. "On Writing." *The Mystic of Sex and Other Writings*, 32–44. Santa Barbara, Calif.: Capra Press, 1995.

———. Preface to *Under a Glass Bell*. London: Peter Owen, 1968.

———. "Realism and Reality." *The Mystic of Sex and Other Writings*, 23–31. Santa Barbara, Calif,: Capra Press, 1995.

———. *Seduction of the Minotaur.* Denver: Swallow Press. 1961.

———. "Winter of Artifice." 1939. *Winter of Artifice: Three Novelettes*, 55–119. Chicago: Swallow Press, 1961.

———. "The Writer and the Symbols." *The Mystic of Sex and Other Writings*, 45–58. Santa Barbara, Calif.: Capra Press, 1995.

Pierpont, Claudia Roth. "Sex, Lies, and Thirty-five Thousand Pages." *New Yorker,* 1 March 1993, 74–80, 82–90.

Smith, Joan. "Carlos Fuentes, Literature is History in the Making." *San Francisco Examiner,* 24 April 1994, B13.

Stocking, Susan. "Personas Unmasked in Visit with Anaïs Nin." *Conversations with Anaïs Nin*. Ed. Wendy M. DuBow, 98–103. Jackson: University Press of Mississippi, 1994.

Terkel, Studs. "Interview with Anaïs Nin." *Conversations with Anaïs Nin*. Ed. Wendy M. DuBow, 152–71. Jackson: University Press of Mississippi, 1994.

Walker, Alice. "Anaïs Nin: 1903–1977." *Ms.,* April 1977, 46.

Williams, Nancy, Evelyn Clark, and Barbara Reyes. "A Conversation with
    Anaïs Nin." *Conversations with Anaïs Nin.* Ed. Wendy M. DuBow,
    75–91. Jackson: University Press of Mississippi, 1994.
Wilson, Edmund. "Books." *New Yorker,* 1 April 1944, 73–74.
Zaller, Robert. "Anaïs Nin and the Truth of Feeling." *A Casebook on Anaïs Nin.*
    Ed. Robert Zaller, 177–83. New York: New American Library, 1974.

CHAPTER 3

Psychoanalyzing Sabina

Anaïs Nin's A Spy in the House of Love *as Freudian Fable*

Suzette Henke

Anaïs Nin's novels have never enjoyed the popularity of her *Diary,* nor have they been widely read. Her Proustian magnum opus, *Cities of the Interior,* falls between the cracks of modernist fiction and postmodern experimentation. The five novellas in this series exfoliate as Freudian fables—on the surface, glittering relics of realistic exposition, but held together by improbable psychic journeys, surrealistic interior dreamscapes, and a fiercely focused avant-garde exercise in psychoanalytic characterization. Nin attempts to offer something rare in American fiction—a meticulous and intimate portrait of the artist as a mature woman. The three protagonists of *Cities of the Interior* strike the reader as tripartite replications of a single female persona unable to reconstruct woman's subject position in twentieth-century society without first deconstructing its ideological determinants.

Anaïs Nin was writing women's liberation novels long before the second wave of the feminist movement rendered them stylish. But without politically contextualizing her efforts, she struggled toward unique and isolated victories. Nin appears to have been initially committed to a modernist belief in the unified, rational, integrated self that faces perpetual confusion, assault, fragmentation, and social vertigo. Her fictional world pivots on a vision of the solitary female subject, buttressed by an infrangible faith in Renaissance notions of the Cartesian ego and in Freudian models of psychological mastery. This implicitly humanist paradigm posits the ideal of a "seamlessly unified self," which proves to be a phallic model of the universal subject—"self-contained, powerful," univocal, and authoritative (Moi 8). Originally impelled by a modernist belief in the possibility of coherent identity and integrated self-presence, Nin paradoxically proceeds to deconstruct this illusion by boldly exploring the gaps, fissures, cracks, and interstices in her fallible Freudian landscape.[1] Because she initially envisaged women's liberation in terms of a reverse sexual discourse, a Janus image of male domination and erotic freedom, her early novels unfold as female versions of an Oedipal quest that seeks to conquer and displace the spectral and indifferent father/lover/god.

In the fifth volume of her *Diary* Nin declared: "This should have been the era of deep probings in the novel, the era of Freud" (*D* 5:187). First analyzed by Dr. René Allendy, she was later trained in psychoanalytic practice, albeit somewhat haphazardly, by another analyst and lover, Otto Rank. At the behest of both these disciples of the master, she read Freud, Jung, and Adler extensively (Fitch 96), then spent the majority of her adult life in therapy with various psychoanalysts. It is no wonder that the novellas in *Cities of the Interior* seem, in some sense, to be structured like Freudian fables of female psychological development.[2]

The three protagonists of *Cities,* for instance, might correspond to the libidinal types described and analyzed by Freud: Lillian Beye to the Freudian ego perpetually in search of creative mastery; Djuna to Freud's "obsessional type," distinguished by the predominance of the superego; and Sabina, the protagonist of *A Spy in the House of Love,* to Freud's "erotic type," driven by the instinctual demands of the id. Erotic personalities, Freud explains, "are those whose main interest . . . is turned towards love. Loving, but above all being loved, is the most important thing for them. They are dominated by the fear of loss of love and therefore especially dependent on others" (*SE* 21:218).[3]

Sabina's psyche is a veritable battleground, a mental landscape ravaged by the "irremediable antagonism between the demands of instinct and the restrictions of civilization" (*SE* 21:60). Like a confused child, she clings frantically to what Freud termed the "pleasure-ego" (*SE* 21:67) in relentless pursuit of the satisfactions of Eros. Defining herself as a maverick and a social outcast, Sabina desperately tries to enact the contradictory personalities invented by her fertile imagination. Because she transforms the tapestry of her life into the sexual/textual medium of artistic expression, she feels like a criminal, an "international spy in the house of love" (*Cities* 410).[4]

In *A Spy in the House of Love*, Sabina acts out a dazzling array of iridescent personalities based on the magical deceptions of childhood fairytale. "What I corrupted was what is called the truth in favor of a more marvelous world" (457). Dressed in fiery colors of red and silver, she sounds a "long cry of alarm to the poet who survives in all human beings" (362). Sabina tempts her auditors to ascend the ladders of the imagination that lead to the fires of art and love. Her prolific inventions evoke a world of aesthetic wonder, a chaotic and surrealistic landscape.[5]

A female Rimbaud, Sabina acts as poet and seer, a *voyante* whose imaginary worlds manifest the startling originality of artistic creation. Driven by a childlike need to embellish reality, to fulfill every wish instantaneously, Sabina enacts Freud's description of the imaginative writer as "one who dreams in broad daylight" (*SE* 9:149). Freud explains that "the opposite of play is not what is serious but what is real" (*SE* 9:144). "Might we not say that every child at play behaves like a creative writer, in that he creates a world of his own, or, rather, re-arranges the things of his world in a new way which pleases him?" (*SE* 9:143–44). As the child grows up, he or she substitutes mental fantasy for play. But the motivating forces of fantasy in adult life continue to be the unsatisfied wishes of childhood, and "every single phantasy is the fulfillment of a wish" (*SE* 9:145–46). It is the role of the artist to give communal voice to the repressed desires of the mature psyche in aesthetic productions that prove "analogous variations of the day-dream" (*SE* 9:151).

According to Freud, both dreams and art evoke a world of primary process in touch with the archaic heritage of the unconscious. Poetry recalls a "childhood that has since become prehistoric" (*SE* 4:247). Exploring the deepest recesses of the psyche, art conjures a secondary world balanced in critical tension between manifest and latent content. It "constitutes a region halfway between a reality which frustrates wishes and the wish-fulfilling world of the imagination" (*SE* 13:188). Art involves an elaborate rhetoric of concealment, through which symbolic iterations may disguise a panoply of latent meanings offensive to the censor of the adult mind.

Sabina has long trained herself as an artist of life seeking to recover the euphoria of childhood omnipotence. An autodidact, self-schooled in a complex rhetoric of concealment, she carefully

balances her richly woven stories between reality and fantasy, fac-
tual truth and fabulative deception. She lives out a perpetual fairy-
tale in which "His majesty the Ego" plays all the roles of heroism
and deceit. In a fascinating life of literary masquerade, Sabina
becomes both artist and objet d'art, creator and the thing created.
She projects her mythmaking talents into the intensity of immediate experience and captures her illusions through exuberant dramatic role-playing.

Sabina has plunged into the chaos of dream to explore the intuitive, instinctual, and uninhibited possibilities of the imagination.
There is a surrealistic quality about her discourse, as she talks "a
broken dream" (363). Her tales are protean and elusive, full of
metamorphoses and contradictions; her characters are androgy-
nous and intangible; her stories refuse to obey comprehensible
laws of linear chronology. History becomes a confused puzzle of
faces, names, dates, and implausible events that fit together in the
fragmented form of a cubist mosaic or a postmodern panoply of
contradictory, self-reflexive diegetic worlds. The past is constantly
erased and recreated, as the present gives way to marvels of invention. Sabina, in some sense, resembles a postmodern artist continually painting a nonrepresentational, recursive portrait of herself.
As in cubist art, angles of vision are disparate and misaligned in
such a way that the emergent representation is rich and multidimensional, but palimpsestic and expressionistic rather than recog-
nizably mimetic.[6]

Like her prototype June Miller, Sabina is a Bacchic figure who
yields to Dionysiac frenzy. Nin tells June in the first volume of the
Diary: "I always endowed madness with a sacred, poetic value, a
mystical value" (*D* 1:40). Liberated into a world of creative fantasy,
Sabina is free to lie, to fabricate numerous identities, and to adopt
all the personae rife in her imagination.[7] But like June Miller, she
eventually finds herself trapped in the chimera of an uncontrolled
nightmare and becomes a prisoner of her own imaginings,
ensconced in a web of tightly woven deceptions. Like the prover-
bial spy or criminal, she must remain ever vigilant, always afraid of
catastrophic exposure.[8]

Driven by a confessional fever, Sabina projects her guilt onto the
enigmatic figure of a Lie Detector, a protean emblem of the father,
priest, psychiatrist, and judge produced by her tortured imagination. The Lie Detector, apparently based on Otto Rank, embodies
the Freudian superego, "a materialization of . . . an Eye watching
and following her throughout her life" (367).[9] He is evidently an

introjected authority figure, a symbol of the law and the word of the Father who will serve as a catalyst in Sabina's psychological rite of atonement.

Like all Nin's protagonists, Sabina harbors a schizoid sense of her own identity, born of a radical disjunction between her ego—the frightened, vulnerable, timid, and shrunken self she recognizes as "I" (the Lacanian *je*)—and the confident persona (or socially constructed *moi*) she presents to the world. Overwhelmed by fear, she cannot identify with her mirror reflection as a "tall, strong, mature woman of thirty, equal to her surroundings" (368). Similarly, Nin confesses in her *Diary:* "There were always, in me, two women at least, one woman desperate and bewildered, who felt she was drowning, and another who . . . would leap into a scene, as upon a stage, [and] conceal her true emotions [with] a smile" (*D* 1:270).[10]

Like a wounded warrior returning from battle, Sabina finds refuge in her husband, Alan, who offers sanctuary from a turbulent, hostile world and willingly connives in the social construction of a strong, coherent personality. In Alan's presence, Sabina feels enormous security: "I am safe. . . . I will no longer have to struggle" (370). This smiling paternal figure is the rocklike center of her existence, the one individual who holds a fixed position in her erratic, fluctuating emotional life. Sabina feels overwhelmed with guilt because of the radical discrepancy between her confused, fragmented subject position and the idealized image that Alan blindly imposes on her: "His love is for something I am not. . . . I do not deserve it" (373). Like the moon, Sabina displays only a single luminous aspect of her personality to her husband. She hides from him a secret, darker self that exults in illicit passion and thrives on the vertiginious pleasures of sexual infidelity.[11]

For Alan's benefit, Sabina pretends to be a successful actress cast in the role of Flaubert's Madame Bovary. In a psychological house of mirrors, she distorts her bold adulterous practices by translating her socially constructed role to the stage of theatrical illusion. Protected by a professional mask, she is free to enact implausible, contradictory parts: "Wherever I am, I am in many pieces, not daring to bring them all together" (374). Unlike the stage actress, however, Sabina can never divest herself of the dramatis personae she embraces. Adapting roles from the theater of her own life, she is bound to the fascinating array of multiple personalities she dramatically invents for an ingenuous audience so skillfully deceived.

Sabina's most challenging role is that of the secure and integrated self generated by Alan's implicit adoration. Sabina longs to fulfill her husband's expectations, but she realizes, in panic, that "only half of [her] is being sheltered" (375). Compelled to embody this idealized projection, Sabina paradoxically becomes an art object fashioned by a uxorious spouse, who molds her imaginary portrait to suit his private emotional needs. He (re)constructs Sabina as a loving, faithful, childlike, and dependent partner; she, in turn, relegates him to the static, unchanging role of father/lover/protector. Their marriage is based on the "laborious weaving of life-giving lies" (375). The two collude in mutual deception to create an unreal atmosphere of perpetual wish fulfillment—a sustained illusion of conjugal bliss.

Although Sabina has never been to Provincetown, she fabricates a convincing tale of eight days spent on Cape Cod with a local acting company. Later she reenacts the same phantasmic trip for the benefit of the reader: "In the darkness she relived entirely the eight days spent in Provincetown" (377). At this point, the narrative moves in the direction of self-reflexive, recursive strategies associated with metafiction. Are Sabina's experiences on Cape Cod real or invented? Is Nin's character becoming the author of her own fictional history and luring the reader into a seductive labyrinth of contradictory stories? Or does the reader simply accept such fabulation as part of Nin's experimental framework? Once Sabina's fantastic tales have been imbricated into an ongoing narrative, they take on an artistically valid, nonrepresentational life of their own. And Sabina, as the protagonist of her own embedded novel, gains the freedom of Duchamp's *Nude Descending a Staircase,* liberated into a cubist world that recognizes the value of multiple personalities depicted on intersecting diegetic planes.

From an artistic perspective, Sabina becomes an emblem of the modern woman who, in an ostensibly liberated society, adopts a facade of strength and self-assurance to protect herself from the possibility of rejection. On the surface, she displays an aggressive attitude of sexual conquest, the formidable persona of a contemporary Don Juan. Tormented by perpetual self-doubt, however, she hysterically plunges into a maelstrom of passion that proves little more than a self-destructive whirlwind. Sabina has apparently constructed her own "sex-identity" on male-defined models. As Luce Irigaray observes in *This Sex Which Is Not One,* the obsessive "attention paid to erection in Western sexuality proves to what extent the imaginary that governs it is foreign to the feminine. . . . Woman, in this sexual imaginary, is only a more or less obliging prop for the enactment of man's fantasies. That she may find pleasure there in that role, by proxy, is possible, even certain. But such pleasure is above all a masochistic prostitution of her body to a desire that is not her own, and it leaves her in a familiar state of dependency upon man" (24–25).

In Provincetown, Sabina meets Philip, an opera singer who calls to her like a merman crooning an enchanting aria from *Tristan und Isolde*. He emerges from the environment of sun and sand like a mythic Adonis, a voluptuous incarnation of the sea's sensuality. Like a Wagnerian hero from the Black Forest, he appears to Sabina as an admirable trophy of male beauty and physical strength. Yet Philip proceeds to scrutinize Sabina with the kind of scopophilic *regard* that obviates individuality and reduces her to an impersonal object of the masculine gaze. "It was the alchemy of desire fixing itself upon the incarnation of all women into Sabina" (380). Sabina understandably perceives Philip's desire as a threat to her unique (self-)identity. She imagines their affair orchestrated by Ravel's *Bolero*, a "waltz leading to catastrophe" (382).[12]

The love affair between Sabina and Philip leads back to a primordial world of sensual passion, shrouded in disturbing metaphors of masochistic pain and erotic violence. Isolated on a volcanic island of sexual desire, the couple explore an incandescent landscape of "joyous epilepsies." Like amorous adventurers, they respond to the animal "cry of pleasure . . . danger . . . fear . . . childbirth . . . pain" issuing "from the same hoarse delta of nature's pits" (385). They metaphorically resemble Adam and Eve enacting an ancient ritual, the "joyous impaling of woman on man's sensual mast" (386).[13]

Because this erotic/sacrificial rite is not climactic for Sabina, she rises from Philip's embrace angry and restless, feeling like a "love addict" enslaved to obsessive-compulsive patterns of behavior: the "same irresistible impulse, tension, compulsion and then depression," followed by "revulsion, bitterness" (387). When Sabina does finally achieve orgasm with Philip, she revels in the triumphant illusion of her own liberation into the male-identified freedom "to enjoy without love" (394). Ironically, she defines sexual *jouissance* in terms that resemble Erica Jong's "zipless fuck"—the ability to enjoy physical intimacy with a stranger, to pursue sexual gratification without emotional commitment, and to love without "warmth of the heart, as man could" (394). Terrified of sexual rejection, Sabina finally succeeds in defining herself as an uncaring and supposedly invulnerable lover. Her partner, in turn, cherishes the fantasy of "taking a woman whose arms were bound behind her back" (394). In this sadistic reverie of sexual bondage, Philip reveals an obsessive fear of emotional commitment. Secretly he desires a position of total mastery that would allow him to violate a helpless partner stripped of agency and subjectivity, a woman unable to cling to him in suffocating embraces. Like Sabina herself, he wants to be "free of attachment, dependency, and the capacity for pain" (395).[14]

Philip evidently suffers from an unresolved Oedipal complex that leads him to perceive women as either virgins or whores, temptresses or madonnas. Trapped in a childish distinction between maternal and profligate love, he cannot fuse the affectionate and sensual dimensions of Eros. As Freud explains, "the whole sphere of love in such people remains divided in the two directions personified in art as sacred and profane (or animal) love. Where they love they do not desire and where they desire they cannot love" (*SE* 11:183). Although Philip demands of Sabina the fiery passion of sensual pleasure, he reserves his true affection for a pale and ethereal singer, a mother/madonna on whom he can lavish filial adoration.

In her own narcissistic imagination, Sabina resembles Diana, the virgin goddess repudiating man and shining alone in Amazonian splendor. Through symbolic moon-baths, she aspires to the mythic position of Cybele or Kali—a figure of woman as seductress and sexual destroyer, "homeless, childless, free" (389). Her moon-baths allow her to explore the lunatic regions of the unconscious and to discover "myriad lives" within herself (390). Hence the musical enchantment of Debussy's *Clair de Lune*, an intoxicating celebration that illumines "many Îles Joyeuses" (392).[15]

In the company of her black lover Mambo, Sabina tastes the explosive joy of Caribbean passion, which she experiences as "a silken voluptuousness without harshness or violence" (406).[16] Immersed in postcolonial fantasy, she explores the tropics through Mambo's glistening body and imbibes what she takes to be the exotic "blood-consciousness" of his race, pulsating with primitive sensuality. Mambo is justifiably offended by the subaltern position Sabina implicitly assigns him, without regard for the artist-self he so passionately values. This Afro-Caribbean lover is, for her, a racial stereotype, the composer of hypnotic rhythms that evince "barbaric themes of his origin" (406). Mambo feels threatened, as well, by the dazzling presence of a volatile woman whose musical autobiography is recorded in Stravinsky's *Firebird* by the "phosphorescent tracks" of her passion, by emotional fireworks reminiscent of the "purple tongues of the Holy Ghost" (408–9).[17]

Another lover, John, a grounded British aviator, shares Sabina's hatred of middle-class monogamy and her disdain for bourgeois life. His cynicism makes him a spiritual comrade, but he too proves incapable of climbing Sabina's perilous ladders to fire—of submitting, like the phoenix, to flames of consuming *jouissance*. While Sabina is soaring on the wings of "prolonged, deep-thrusting ecstasy," her lover plunges back to earth, a captive of "his own venomous guilt" (421). Like Philip, he is bound by puritanical mores that reduce lovemaking to surreptitious naughtiness, a shameful act of "being bad." Through the character of John, Nin makes a sardonic comment on the Nietzschean warrior-hero. His macho ethic of conquest and sexual mastery leaves him in a sociopathic state of arrested development. Intent on military pursuits, he fosters an infantile view of woman either as a reflection of the mother, "the child's primary object-choice" (*SE* 11:180), or as a degraded prostitute. As Freud observes, the "main protective measure . . . which men have recourse to in this split in their love consists in a psychical *debasement* of the sexual object, the overvaluation that normally attaches to the sexual object being reserved for the incestuous object and its representatives" (*SE* 11:183).[18]

In still another abortive relationship, Sabina consents to serve as an idealized mother figure for the homosexual Donald, who relates to women as "wax figures of puerility and treachery" (428). Though adept at the sex-stereotyped role of attentive and nurturant female, Sabina can never defeat the maternal specter haunting Donald's Oedipal imagination and binding her to a "third woman forever present in a perpetual triangle, a *ménage à trois*" (429). Because he cannot break the ultimate taboo of touching the forbidden territory of the maternal body, Donald relates to Sabina only through fetishes— shoes, silken clothing, satin, feathers, and trinkets. As Freud explains, the "fetish is a substitute for the woman's (the mother's) penis that the little boy once believed in and . . . does not want to give up" (*SE* 21:152–53). Touching Sabina's foot, Donald experiences an erotic transport evocative of embryonic bliss. This tantalizing sensation, however, strikes a chord of residual horror at the prospect of oceanic engulfment. Donald evidently fears symbolic absorption by the physicality of the mother, "drowning as within the sea itself, her body a chalice" (430).

Donald identifies Sabina metaphorically as the illusory firebird of his dreams—the magical witch/woman capable of filling the empty cages of his hungry imagination. And Sabina responds to his filial fantasies through altruistic subservience as "dispenser of food, of solace—soft, warm and fecund" (433). For the admiring and dependent surrogate son, "there is only BEING" in the "mystery of total love" (434). "Her breasts were no longer tipped with fire, they were the breasts of the mother, from which flowed nourishment" (432).

In a movement toward psychoanalytic self-discovery, Sabina begins to realize that her personality has not been modeled on that of the nurturant mother but has developed in tacit emulation of the Don Juan daddy who earlier abandoned her. Through the alchemy of mimetic love, Sabina has *become* the absent parent, his passionate blood guiding her in a series of compulsive infidelities. She has assumed the aggressive role of sexual predator in imitation of the narcissistic father who betrayed her at a vulnerable stage of Oedipal development. Sabina has spent her life desperately searching for the kind of emotional security and paternal commitment that might, in fantasy, fuse her psychically dispersed selves into a single integrated and coterminous identity. She feels lost in an attitude of mental chaos: "not ONE, but a multitude of Sabinas . . . constellating in all directions and breaking" (439).[19]

Sabina recognizes in the artist Jay's wild, expressionistic paintings a surrealistic replica of her own interior landscape—the psychological remnants of an atomic explosion. For the first time, she acknowledges herself as the victim of her own insincerities, fabrications, and personal betrayals. Her life has been devoted to a protracted quest for a love relationship that will weld together the disparate fragments of her shattered personality. This frantic search has, nonetheless, been continually undermined by elaborate disguises that defend her against the unbearable pain of emotional rejection. "For Sabina, to be becalmed meant to die" (441).

A Spy in the House of Love resembles a postmodern fictional construction that circles back upon itself in the manner of an elusive Möbius strip. The earlier narrative description of Sabina's invitation to climb perilous "ladders to fire" is now sardonically reiterated by her old acquaintance Jay, who portrayed her in one of his paintings in the guise of a tropical flower—solitary, sensuous, mysterious, and enigmatic. He despises Sabina because he cannot possess her. Only once, in a meteoric elevator ride, did he "taste the mystery" of her elusive attraction, which he now represents in the ambiguous image of a female mandrake.[20]

Sabina's true portrait is captured not by Jay but by Duchamp's *Nude Descending a Staircase:* "Eight or ten outlines of the same woman, like many multiple exposures of a woman's personality, neatly divided into many layers, walking down the stairs in unison" (452). She feels that each of these personalities replicates a detached "cut-out" of the self, a "mere outline of a woman" divided into "numberless silhouettes" (453). Her husband, Alan, fell in love with her initial image and preserved it in a static photographic frame. He now seems self-deluded in his stubborn refusal to acknowledge the "complex and extended series of Sabinas which had been born later" (453). Each figure has split from its original self and has embarked on a separate life characterized by a frenzied search for its idealized romantic partner. Sabina has been engaged in a lifelong project to transform her own experiences into marvelous fabulations, but she fails to give this postmodern epic the kind of aesthetic coherence demanded by convincing narrative. Although she distrusts Alan's uxorious devotion, she unwittingly casts her husband in a similar static configuration as the all-forgiving "idealized father . . . invented by a needy child" (458–59).[21]

At the end of *A Spy in the House of Love,* Sabina seems to undergo either mental breakdown or ritual purgation. Moved by the emotional resonance of a Beethoven quartet, she sinks onto the floor of Djuna's apartment and dissolves in a flood of tears. Begging the Lie Detector to free her from a long history of deception, she soon discovers that no one else is capable of implementing such psychological transformation. Sabina alone can liberate the repressed spiritual potential residual in her troubled psyche. The Lie Detector, like an omniscient father/god, utters an inscrutable benediction: "In homeopathy there is a remedy called pulsatile for those who weep at music" (462).[22] Citing the homeopathic cure for contradictory individuals, he seems to imply that Sabina's breakdown will lead through catharsis to a climactic reintegration of disparate selves—a fusion of her multiple personalities into a single coherent identity. In a moment of watery dissolution, Sabina experiences ritual death and purgation, and her tears might, indeed, signify the baptismal waters of psychological rebirth.[23]

Nin has evidently refused to offer her readers a satisfying sense of closure at the end of this intriguing novella. Whether Sabina sinks into beatitude or perdition, one does not know.[24] She has, at least, achieved a new image of herself—a vision that might possibly lead to psychological transformation, if the Lie Detector is intended to function as the text's deus ex machina. On the other hand, Nin may deliberately be experimenting with an avant-garde gesture of undecidability. Flirting as she does with postmodern reflexivity, she might have constructed an ending that intentionally mimics Sabina's own art of illusion by placing the entire novella *sous rature.* "Modernist form," says Marianne DeKoven, "continually puts itself, including its own self-consciousness, under erasure" and "*constitutes itself* as self-contradictory, though not incoherent" (23–24).

It is possible that Nin cunningly tantalizes her readers by deploying avant-garde strategies of "self-cancellation, unresolved contradiction, unsynthesized dialectic" (DeKoven 22). If so, she has made the scene of writing into an experimental stage for cultural, aesthetic, and ideological conflict that remains, in postmodern fashion, imaginatively unresolved. Like a metafictional text, Nin's multidimensional, palimpsestic narrative "systematically draws attention to its status as an artifact in order to pose questions about the relationship between fiction and reality" (Waugh 2). The center of Sabina's life history is everywhere and nowhere. A decentered ur-narrative perpetually eludes our grasp, just as the humanist fantasy of stable identity proves, from the point of view of poststructuralist subjectivity, ultimately unattainable. If the hyposthesis of postmodern recursive play is indeed applicable to *A Spy in the House of Love*, then Nin's experimental fiction, while demystifying the demands of narrative realism, simultaneously unmasks and destabilizes the Freudian paradigm of a unified, coterminous subject fully endowed by psychoanalysis with agency, mastery, and integrated self-presence.

NOTES

1. As Chris Weedon explains, humanist discourses "presuppose an essence at the heart of the individual which is unique, fixed and coherent. . . . Against this irreducible humanist essence of subjectivity, poststructuralism proposes a subjectivity which is precarious, contradictory and in process, constantly being reconstituted in discourse each time we think or speak" (32–33).
2. Anaïs explains in a letter to Frances Keene: "The distortions in our present-day world are not caused by self-absorption but by lack of self, lack of centrality. . . . I belong to the age of Freud" (*D* 6:280–81).
3. Sabina's story, Anaïs insists, is "universal. . . . Sabina is a phenomenon of our time" (*D* 6:288). In the process of composing *Cities of the Interior*, the author remarks in her *Diary*: "Composites are false. Sabina, the woman of passion; Lillian, the woman of instinct but inhibited; Djuna, the woman of the psyche" (*D* 4:70).
4. In her journal *Nearer the Moon* Anaïs confesses: "I live the life of a spy. Spies do not live *with* their fear. The risk and danger *is* their climate. They live in tension, of course, alertness, wakefulness. Not trembling. That is how I live. I am aware of the danger but not afraid" (*NM* 239). Later she complains: "I wish for peace, a life without *angoisse* and danger, secrets, lies" (*NM* 295). "Nin's continuous novel," says Bettina Knapp, "allowed her to probe her characters in various situations and milieus. These beings, which she labeled 'faulty cellular structures,' are always in search of wholeness and completion" (97). In *Spy,* "Nin used the new shattering-of-the-

personality technique with felicity. By perpetually altering situations and events in Sabina's life, she succeeded in giving the impression of a woman whose psyche is truly dispersed" (132). In a fascinating comparison of Nin's novel with Hawthorne's *Scarlet Letter,* Anna Balakian points out that, ironically, Sabina retains a religious "sense of guilt and the need for a confessional" (167). Oliver Evans, too, defends Sabina against charges of nymphomania and sees her as "a woman of considerable dignity" who "possesses a very keen ethical sense" (146).

5. In her *Diary* Anaïs tells Henry Miller: "I have always believed in Bergson's *'mensonge vital.'.* . . . I decided to be the fairy godmother who made things come true" (D 1:246–47). *"Lying is the only way I have found to be true to myself. . . .* To sustain illusion I have to lie" (F 58).

6. Oliver Evans identifies *Spy* as Nin's most experimental novella: "Its arrangement is spatial rather than chronological, consisting of a series of episodes which are not related by any causal connection" (145). Bettina Knapp illuminates Nin's stylistic experimentation in terms of innovative techniques similar to those of the French New Novelists: "an attempt at further depersonalization of the main character; greater emphasis on cyclical time; . . . repetitions of entire scenes" (131). "In the style of the New Novelists, time and space are *dechronologized,* feelings and sensations are expressed through 'undefinable inner movements'" (133).

7. In the first volume of her *Diary* Anaïs declares: "June and I have paid with our souls for taking fantasies seriously" (D 1:22). Later she observes that June "does what others only do in their dreams" (D 1:45).

8. Evelyn Hinz has suggested intriguing analogies between Nin's characters and the *"dramatis personae* of the *Psychomachia* of Prudentius and its offshoot, the Christian morality plays. . . . In the modern *psychomachia* of Nin personifications of the basic passions battle for supremacy in the female psyche" (63). Sabina, she tells us, might be considered a "modern choleric character" (64). Hinz judges her a "female Raskolnikov," a Dostoevskian "schizophrenic with a conflicting will to crime and punishment" (65). In a letter to Maxwell Geismar, Anaïs explains that Sabina "sought man's liberation in separating the pleasures of sensuality from the pains of love *but failed to do so"* (D 5:159). In response to Frances Keene's scathing review of *Spy,* Nin defends the psychological seriousness of her novel: "Sabina is the story of the dissociation of the personality . . . which motivates Don Juanism" (D 6:279).

9. In her biography *Anaïs,* Noël Riley Fitch identifies the Lie Detector as Otto Rank (184), and Anaïs observes in *Fire* that Rank is able to elucidate her "deceptive games, because he can be more accurate and more realistic, and because he says the woman in me always leaves a clue, wants to be discovered, mastered, wants to lose" (F 6). In her *Diary* Anaïs explains to Victor Weybright that the "lie detector was a

personification of conscience dressed in modern clothes" (*D* 5:78). Franklin and Schneider similarly interpret this character as realistic, a shrewd and megalomanic psychiatrist whose avatar earlier appeared in "The Voice" (113–14). Bettina Knapp calls him a "fantasy image that takes on reality, . . . a kind of superego or father figure . . . like the Greek Fates" (131). Deirdre Bair ascribes the genesis of Nin's Lie Detector to the practice of "dédoublement," a "double-state through fantasy" and self-projection (228). Bair explains that although the figure of the Lie Detector was originally envisioned by Nin as a "'fantasy personage,' a projection of one of the many different emotions that engulf Sabina," and a "subjective identification with what one feels," Anaïs later attempted to simplify the novel by reconfiguring this character: "As she revised, the Lie Detector finally became a real (as opposed to imaginary) person whose only purpose is to enhance Sabina's increasing frustration, her frantic search for resolution and contentment, and her inability to achieve stasis either alone or within a relationship" (366).

10. Franklin and Schneider diagnose Sabina's problem as "one of self-perception, a sense of unwarranted selfworthlessness that leads her to confront life with excessive gusto to compensate for her supposed inadequacies" (114). Yet Sabina also recognizes in her mirror image an acute sense of psychic fragmentation similar to the Lacanian *corps morcelé*, that "morsellized body" experienced by the subject prior to inscription into the symbolic register. Closely in touch with the world of primary process, Sabina suffers from an uncanny awareness that the Lacanian *moi*, or subject of utterance, emerges from the subject's *méconnaissance*, misrecognition, of the mirror image as a figure of wholeness and plenitude—a coterminous, self-present ego contingent on a socially valorized *mensonge vital*. It is, says Chris Weedon, precisely the "imaginary quality of the individual's identification with a subject position which gives it so much psychological and emotional force" (31).

11. Analogies between Alan and Anaïs Nin's own long-suffering husband Hugh Guiler are fairly obvious. In *Fire* Anaïs declares: "With a religious attitude, I love Hugh, all that he lets me be, do, feel, think. My true ideal father is Hugh" (*F* 153). In *Nearer the Moon* she testifies that "Hugh, because he is the man without defects, because he protects and forgives all things, is God-the-father" (*NM* 145). She later invokes a litany of Hugo's multiple roles in her life: "My guardian angel, my young father, my fixed stability, my protector, my brother, and my child" (*NM* 197). Deirdre Bair notes that, like Hugo, Sabina's Alan "is more father than husband, thus both frustrating and complicating Sabina's feelings for him" (366).

12. In her *Diary* Anaïs describes meeting a singer preparing to debut at the New York Metropolitan Opera in the role of Siegfried (*D* 3:130).

"The resemblance between his love life and my father's struck me," she confesses, as she sees in this troubled Lothario a "more Nordic duplicate of my father" (D 3:132). Anaïs would later insist that Sabina was not meant to be perceived as "sexually aggressive and masculine in the scene with Philip," but was merely experimenting with a female "impersonation of the father" (D 6:316).

13. This passage has always struck me as awkward in its erotic evocations of primordial instincts, but Evelyn Hinz finds the prose captivating in its lyrical replication of the basic rhythms of "pulse and copulation," as it moves from a "low heavy chant," through increased discursive urgency, to a climactic and orgasmic explosion (78).

14. One might compare Sabina to the character Beth, described in the third volume of Nin's *Diary* as a promiscuous young woman whose nonchalant life of casual sex involves "sleeping around with everyone." Anaïs is dumbfounded to learn that Beth "had never known an orgasm" (D 3:24) and finds such promiscuity baffling because, she tells us, "I could only enjoy sexuality when I was in love" (D 3:24).

15. Sharon Spencer points out in *Collage of Dreams* that Nin was strongly influenced by M. Esther Harding's books *The Way of All Women* and *Woman's Mysteries*. "Harding shows how the archetype of mother is related to the many moon goddesses that were worshipped in the ancient world. . . . The goddesses of the moon (Diana, or Artemis, Ishtar, Hecate, Shakti, and the Celtic Anu or Annis) were the givers of life and the protectors of fertility, but they were also attributed with the destructive powers of nature (particularly floods)" (88).

16. Mambo, says Bettina Knapp, "seems to encompass all the Louis Armstrongs, Buddy Boldens, Duke Ellingtons, Fats Wallers. Although an individual, Mambo is an archetypal figure, a black divinity whose powerful harmonies and cacophonies, beats and syncopations, capture her entire being" (138).

17. Nin's purple prose apparently takes its inspiration from a number of literary sources: from D. H. Lawrence's celebration of blood consciousness, Rousseau's idealization of the noble savage, a symbolist appropriation of sacramental imagery, and surrealism's flirtation with fantastic metaphors and extravagant tropes. In *Nearer the Moon* Anaïs compares herself to Stravinsky's firebird: "I escape in space, fluid, beyond all walls, all doors—*L'Oiseau de feu*" (NM 211).

18. In her *Diary* Anaïs describes her encounter with a young grounded aviator from the Royal Air Force. He fears incipient madness provoked by the experience of peering into the eyes of the dying. Anaïs, in her role as amateur therapist, reassures him: "You're not mad. You're very hurt and frightened, and very desperate" (D 4:161).

19. For further discussion of Anaïs Nin's own perplexed relationship with her father, Joaquín Nin y Castellanos, see chapter 3 of my *Shattered*

Subjects, "Anaïs Nin's Interior Cities." In the first volume of her *Diary,* Anaïs confesses to her therapist Dr. Allendy that she has long suffered symptoms of psychic fragmentation, precipitated by "the first and ineffaceable pain of . . . Father's abandonment." She describes a "distorted, morbid, neurotic fear" of rejection and explains: "I feel that an initial shock has shattered my wholeness, that I am like a shattered mirror" (*D* 1:103).

20. In *Incest* Nin represents June Miller metaphorically as "the mandrake, a Eurasian plant (*Mandragora*) with purple flowers and a branched root resembling the human body, from which a narcotic was prepared. The mandrake of *Genesis* was—and still is—believed to have magical properties" (*I* 30). "June was telling me how much she loved the name of the mandrake plant in German, and it is to be my name for her: *Alraune*" (*I* 31).

21. "Is real love possessive?" Anaïs asks in *Fire.* "I live on a hundred planes at once," she confesses. "Desiring unity but incapable of it. Playing a million roles" (*F* 24). Yet throughout her journals Nin expresses faith that the individual, through psychoanalysis and scriptotherapy, can overcome "the malady which makes our lives a drama of compulsion instead of freedom" (*D* 4:143).

22. *Homeopathic Remedies* describes *Pulsatilla Nigricans* or Wood Flower as a remedy "often best suited to women and children with blond or sandy hair and blue eyes; mild, gentle, timid, yielding and easily moved to laughter and tears, or men with similar characteristics. The *Pulsatilla* person craves sympathy and the company of others; moods changeable and fickle. . . . Symptoms are erratic, change frequently. . . . Fever without thirst despite dry mouth" (Anderson, Buegel, and Chernin 133). In *Incest* Nin confesses to her own tendency to weep at music when feeling psychologically vulnerable and unhinged: "The turmoil is so intense that music makes me weep. . . . There is a fissure in my vision, in my body, in my desires, a fissure for all time, and madness will always push in and out" (*I* 21).

23. Franklin and Schneider watch Sabina "dissolve in her own tears as though returning to a prenatal existence" and conclude that since "she finally possesses the facts of her situation" through the aegis of Djuna and the Lie Detector, Sabina might awaken to become "a mature and loving woman" (128). Bettina Knapp interprets Sabina's tears as curative, "a baptism into a new sphere of being, a fresh beginning" (138). Sharon Spencer believes that this psychic collapse "provides an opportunity for renewal" merely because Sabina "has been brave enough to confront her own basic hollowness" (85). The evolution of *Cities of the Interior,* Nin explained, would be "from subjectivity and neurosis to objectivity, expansion, fulfillment" (*D* 4:25).

24. Oliver Evans argues that because *Spy* is a "novel of character in which the level of action is negligible," it offers the reader climax,

illumination, and narrative culmination, rather than "resolution in the ordinary sense" (159). In *A Woman Speaks,* Anaïs describes the magical power of storytelling as an "anti-toxin" that provides a sanctuary "in which to reconstruct ourselves after shattering experiences" (*WS* 182).

WORKS CITED

Anderson, David, Dale Buegel, and Dennis Chernin. *Homeopathic Remedies.* Honesdale, Pa.: Himalayan International Institute, 1978.

Bair, Deirdre. *Anaïs Nin: A Biography.* New York: Putnam, 1995.

Balakian, Anna. "'. . . and the pursuit of happiness': *The Scarlet Letter* and *A Spy in the House of Love.*" *The World of Anaïs Nin.* Ed. Evelyn J. Hinz and Wayne Fraser, 163–70. Winnipeg: University of Manitoba Press, 1978.

DeKoven, Marianne. *Rich and Strange: Gender, History, Modernism.* Princeton: Princeton University Press, 1991.

Fitch, Noël Riley. *Anaïs: The Erotic Life of Anaïs Nin.* Boston: Little, Brown, 1993.

Franklin, Benjamin, V, and Duane Schneider. *Anaïs Nin: An Introduction.* Athens: Ohio University Press, 1979.

Freud, Sigmund. *The Standard Edition of the Complete Psychological Works of Sigmund Freud.* 24 vols. Ed. and trans. James Strachey. London: Hogarth Press, 1953–74. Cited as *SE* with volume number.

Henke, Suzette A. *Shattered Subjects: Trauma and Testimony in Women's Life-Writing.* New York: St. Martin's Press, 1998.

Hinz, Evelyn J. *The Mirror and the Garden: Realism and Reality in the Writings of Anaïs Nin.* 1971. New York: Harcourt Brace Jovanovich, 1973.

Hinz, Evelyn J., and Wayne Fraser, eds. *The World of Anaïs Nin: Critical and Cultural Perspectives.* Winnipeg: University of Manitoba Press, 1978.

Irigaray, Luce. *This Sex Which Is Not One.* Trans. Catherine Porter with Carolyn Burke. Ithaca: Cornell University Press, 1985.

Knapp, Bettina. *Anaïs Nin.* New York: Frederick Ungar, 1978.

Moi, Toril. *Sexual/Textual Politics: Feminist Literary Theory.* London: Methuen, 1985.

Nin, Anaïs. *Cities of the Interior.* 1959. Chicago: Swallow Press, 1974. Cited by page number only.

———. *The Diary of Anaïs Nin.* 7 Vols. Ed. Gunther Stuhlmann. New York: Swallow Press/Harcourt Brace Jovanovich, 1966–80. Cited as *Diary* with volume number.

———. *Fire: From "A Journal of Love": The Unexpurgated Diary of Anaïs Nin, 1934–1937.* New York: Harcourt Brace Jovanovich, 1986. Cited as *F.*

———. *Incest: From "A Journal of Love": The Unexpurgated Diary of Anaïs Nin, 1932–1934.* New York: Harcourt Brace Jovanovich, 1992. Cited as *I.*

———. *Nearer the Moon: From "A Journal of Love": The Unexpurgated Diary of Anaïs Nin, 1937–1939.* New York: Harcourt Brace, 1996. Cited as *NM.*

———. *A Woman Speaks: The Lectures, Seminars, and Interviews of Anaïs Nin.* Ed. Evelyn J. Hinz. Chicago: Swallow Press, 1975. Cited as *WS.*

Spencer, Sharon. *Collage of Dreams: The Writings of Anaïs Nin*. Chicago: Swallow Press, 1977.

Waugh, Patricia. *Metafiction: The Theory and Practice of Self-Conscious Fiction*. London: Methuen, 1984.

Weedon, Chris. *Feminist Practice and Poststructuralist Theory*. Oxford: Basil Blackwell, 1987.

Zaller, Robert, ed. *A Casebook on Anaïs Nin*. New York: New American Library, 1974.

CHAPTER 4

Sex with Father

The Incest Metaphor in Anaïs Nin

Ellen G. Friedman

In the 1986 *Henry and June*—posthumously published excerpts culled from Nin's unexpurgated diary, 1931–32, having to do with her affair with Henry Miller and her obsession with his wife, June—incest is the name Nin gives to her alliance with male values and male power, particularly in regard to the traditionally male domains of creativity and mysticism: "I have remained the woman who loves incest. I still practice the most incestuous crimes with a sacred religious fervor. I am the most corrupt of all women. . . . With a madonna face, I still swallow God and sperm, and my orgasm resembles a mystical climax" (246). She articulates this alliance with male domains as choosing her father's values and negating her mother's: "A volcanic life hunger . . . a sensual potency that automatically negates my mother's values" (245–46).

Up until *Incest*, published in 1992 and consisting of unexpurgated sections of her diary, 1932–34, critics could only speculate whether she really did or did not have sex with her father. The evidence that she did lends an authority to the metaphor of incest in her work that few writers achieve with extreme metaphors. For instance, Sylvia Plath's use of Nazi metaphors has often been criticized for trivializing the Holocaust, an accusation critics do not make of writers who in some way experienced the Holocaust firsthand. Thus Nin, with the publication of *Incest*, commands a kind of scandalized respect for her artistic use of this metaphor.

The theme of incest has a full and complex development in Nin's writings. Incest in Nin's works, then, speaks literally of her affair with her father. It also speaks to woman's relationship to man. In addition, and what will concern me here, it speaks to the woman artist's relationship to traditional forms of expression and to the patriarchy in general. This idea is reinforced by the fact that after intimacy began between them, Nin referred to her father simply as HIM in her diary (Bair 177).[1]

Nin's presentation of the incest theme before the publication of *Incest* is forthright and also resonant: "I talked [to Allendy] about my father's passion for photography and how he was always photographing me. He liked to take photos of me while I bathed. He always wanted me naked" (*Diary* 1:87). Yet the lasciviousness of the scene is not the point. Rather, it is the fact that her father's attention is mediated by the camera and his glasses: "All his admiration came by way of the camera. His eyes were partly concealed by heavy glasses (he was myopic) and then by the camera lens. Lovely. Lovely. How many times, in how many places, until he left us, did I sit for him for countless pictures. And it was the only time we spent together" (1:87). With the camera, Nin suggests, her father's naked eye does not confront the actual daughter. Instead, through the two lenses he transforms the daughter he had called "ugly" into an object shaped to his desire. This perception has many transplantings into her fiction. Of the movie actress in "Stella" Nin writes, "They courted the face on the screen, the face of translucence, the face of wax on which men found it possible to imprint the image of their fantasy" (9).

In *House of Incest,* Nin's first published work of fiction and also the work in which she transforms her affair with her father into art, incest is a trope for a constellation of ideas having to do with structures enforcing patriarchal values. Incest is a form of self-love, a narcissistic desire for one's double: "If only we could all escape from this house of incest, where we only love ourselves in the other" (70). The incestuous relationship also blocks creativity, allows no seams through which the new can emerge. The incestuous desire is suffocating and destructive: "In the house of incest there was a room which could not be found, a room without window, the fortress of their love, a room without window where the mind and blood coalesced in a union without orgasm and rootless. . . . Their love like the ink of squids, a banquet of poisons" (52).

Here the imagery of incest suggests limitation, artistic and other, imposed by the father, who allows only repetitions of himself and the world he has constructed in his own image: "I borrowed your visibility and it was through you I made my imprint on the world. I praised my own flame in you" (28). The father also represents cultural constraint. Incest is a strategy to keep the daughter imprisoned in the father's world. It serves the daughter as well in that incest allies her with the father's power, yet it prevents her from choosing any objects of desire outside of the father, who represents the dominant culture, represents law and patriarchy. As the term is developed by Nin, one implication of "incest" for the artist is conforming to conventional modes; escaping the father would allow innovation, the formulating of new modes.

In a richly evocative passage, Nin presents images of the double (also an incest image) in which the two "selves" are in lacerating tension. The secret self is described as a repressed self, as "Other," while the speaking "I" describes herself as manipulated by outside forces as a "marionette": "I am ill with the obstinacy of images, reflections in cracked mirrors. I am a woman with Siamese cat eyes smiling always behind my gravest words, mocking my own intensity. I smile because I listen to the OTHER and I believe the OTHER. I am a marionette pulled by unskilled fingers, pulled apart, inharmoniously dislocated; one arm dead, the other rhapsodizing in midair" (29–30).

Her emotions are not engaged by the external self but by a hidden self, not by the manifestations of convention but by her sensing of and attraction to the repressed, not by the "talk" obligated by living in society but by its "undercurrents": "I laugh, not when it fits into my talk, but when it fits into the undercurrents of my talk. I want to know what is running underneath thus punctuated by bitter upheavals. The two currents do not meet" (30). The selves are helplessly bound together, but each struggles to free herself from the other: "I see two women in me freakishly bound together, like circus twins. I see them tearing away from each other" (30). One half of the double suggests a woman constructed by society, obedient to her father; the other half suggests a woman suppressed in this construction and by such obedience.

Incest suggests the uneasy relationship between the woman and the father who, as society, as convention, as patriarchy, is protective of her, but only of those qualities that reflect himself. Nin links the suppressed to madness: "There is a fissure in my vision and madness will always rush through." But madness, being outside a normality calibrated by the father, means freedom: "Lean over me, at the bedside of my madness, and let me stand without crutches" (39).

The images of freedom associated with escape from the house of incest increase as the narrative moves to a close, and culminate in the image of a dancer who "was listening to a music we could not hear, moved by hallucinations we could not see" (71). Yet the narrative issues are not resolved in this image of freedom. Rather, the last two paragraphs delineate the impasse that marks most of Nin's writing: the "I" who says "all movement choked me with anguish" stands watching her double who is "dancing towards daylight." This impasse is variously articulated throughout Nin's work. In "Stella," later collected in *Winter of Artifice* but written at the same time as *House of Incest,* Nin describes an actress whose movie character is able to move according to a script although she herself is immobilized: "The woman on the screen went continually forward, carried by her story, led by the plot loaned to her. But Stella, Stella herself was blocked over and over again by inner obstacles" (9). In the *Diary* for 1939–44 Nin writes, "All my life, it seems, first with my father, . . . I admired form and discipline and rejected them as interfering with life and nature" (3:8). She both identified with and could not accommodate herself to the various authorities— particularly artistic and psychoanalytic—with whom she sought her liberation.

The impasse that affects Nin's protagonists and her sense of herself as a writer was nurtured by the series of father figures with whom she associated. Although brilliant men, they based their judgments on available paradigms. Since Nin's writerly instincts drew her toward modes that were outside these paradigms, her relations to these men and the various establishments they represented, particularly the psychoanalytic and the literary avant-garde, were problematic. Ultimately, her struggle was to assert her difference as a woman artist while at the same time winning approval from a patriarchy either hostile to or dismissive of that difference. Although Hugh Guiler gave her financial support, Nin sought approval for her art, as well as emotional support, from men who were insensitive to the vision she put forward. Several of them, including Edmund Wilson, who wanted to marry Nin, offered to teach her how to write (*Diary* 4:89). Wilson, whom she identified with the "full tyranny of the father, the wall of misunderstanding and lack of intuition of the father," sent her a set of Jane Austen, "hoping," as she noted, "I would learn how to write a novel from reading her!" (4:88–89).

René Allendy, Otto Rank, Henry Miller, and Edmund Wilson, men on whom she depended for a sense of self-worth, ultimately used her to forward their own goals. Nin twice began presses, Siana ("Anaïs" spelled backwards) in the 1930s and Gemor Press in the 1940s, in order to publish her own works, which had been rejected by commercial houses, and those of her friends. Both times she put in a great deal of cash and physical labor and ironically sacrificed her own writing in order to nurture the presses and the people depending on them. Siana was planned jointly with Miller and his writer friend Michael Fraenkel, who drew up a list of works the press was to publish and excluded Nin. In the case of Gemor, Gonzalo More, the Peruvian coffeehouse revolutionary and bohemian who was to run the press, abandoned it despite the fact that one of Nin's motives in setting up the press was to provide him with a job (*Diary* 2:46). Relationships with all of them generally deteriorated to that of mother-son. In the *Diary* she describes the burdens associated with what she calls her "mothering complex": "The five flights of stairs I have to climb every day when I get home seem to represent my difficulties. Somehow, on these stairs I climb after leaving the press, the fatigue and discouragement of the whole day attacks me. It catches me on the very first step of the worn brown rug. As I climb I think that Gonzalo needs new glasses, where will I get the money? Jacobson's bill for the care of Helba [Gonzalo's wife] is overdue. Henry has to see the ear doctor. He also needs eighteen dollars for new glasses" (3:205).

Otto Rank, who was Freud's assistant for twenty years before he broke with Freud, believed, according to Nin, that women could not be artists. Nin quotes him in her *Diary*: "When the neurotic woman gets cured, she becomes a woman. When the neurotic man gets cured, he becomes an artist. . . . For the moment, you need to be a woman" (1:291). He insisted that she stop writing her diaries, which he viewed as a Scheherazade phenomenon and as the "last defense against analysis," preventing a cure (1:284). His Scheherazade metaphor equated successful analysis with death and reveals his desire to see the death of Nin of the Diary, the aspect she withheld from him. The *Diary* became a major issue in the nine months of therapy she underwent with him during the 1930s. *House of Incest* and *Winter of Artifice* were written at least partially to satisfy Otto Rank's and also Henry Miller's sense that the diary was not a literary form. To be a writer she would have to write "fiction." But she was not content with just fictionalizing, for as she wrote in her *Diary*, she was inscribing herself, something that the very form of fiction prevents: "*It is the woman who has to speak*. And it is not only the woman Anaïs who has to speak, but I who have to speak for many women. As I discover myself, I feel I am merely one of many, a symbol. . . . The mute ones of the past, the inarticulate, who took refuge behind wordless intuitions; and the women of today, all action, and copies of men. And I, in between. Here [in the *Diary*] lies the personal overflow, the personal and feminine overfulness. Feelings that are not for books, not for fiction, not for art" (1:289).

Otto Rank fell in love with Nin, and persuaded her to come with him to New York, which she did in December 1934; she became his assistant and developed her own successful practice as a lay analyst (Bair 204, 207–10). In fact, Henry Miller joined her in New York and also practiced lay analysis. However, the pressures of her practice and Rank's demand that she translate his numerous works made her flee back to France a year later. She missed her writing. She sums up her relationship to Rank in this way: "I went to Rank to solve my conflict with my father, and only added another father to my life, and another loss" (1:354).

Even the men of the literary avant-garde wanted her to solve the "problem" of her diary. Lawrence Durrell advised, "You must make the leap outside of the womb, destroy your connections" (2:232). He urged that she rewrite *Hamlet,* a story that is an exemplary representation of the loyalty owed to the father and thus an absurd recommendation to a writer trying to excavate woman's consciousness in a patriarchal society and literary tradition. Durrell and Miller's concept of art was predicated on the artist's bold declaration "I am God." In answer Nin wrote: "Woman never had direct communication with God anyway, but only through man, the priest. She never created directly except through man, was never able to create as a woman. But what neither Larry nor Henry understands is that woman's creation far from being like man's must be exactly like her creation of children, that is it must come out of her own blood, englobed by her womb, nourished with her own milk. It must be a human creation, it must be different from man's abstractions" (2:233).

Yet, as her story "Birth" intimates, she lacked full confidence in the productions of the womb because of the inadequacy of fathers. "Birth," collected in *Under a Glass Bell* (1944), is based on Nin's experience of aborting a six-month fetus, an event that she disguises as a miscarriage in the August 1934 *Diary* entry. In an extraordinary passage, she wishes her child dead because there are no "real" fathers. The account of the incident begins and ends with statements against fathers.[2] Early in the entry she tells her fetus, "You ought to die in warmth and darkness. You ought to die because in the world there are no real fathers, not in heaven or on earth" (1:338). After the birth she writes, "I do not believe in man as father. I do not trust man as father. When I wished this child to die, it was because I felt it would experience the same lack" (1:346).

The story based on this entry raises the experience to the level of myth. It is a myth of the woman artist who gives birth to a creation of her body, her consciousness, but knows this creation can only be stillborn. The story opens, in fact, with the doctor—a father figure—announcing to the protagonist, "The child . . . is dead," with an authority analogous to those who decreed Nin's diaries unworthy. The dead fetus cannot be born, so the doctor, who has told her she is not made for childbearing, thrusts a "long instrument" into her which "paralyzes" her with pain. The painful, and obviously phallic, implement is ineffective, and the doctor would like to use a more radical method—the knife. However, the protagonist reclaims the birth process and through ritual-like, soft, circular drumming on her belly, she succeeds: "It is a little girl. It has long eyelashes on its closed eyes, it is perfectly made, and all glistening with the waters of the womb" (101). It is an extraordinarily poignant and tragic story using a woman's most powerful metaphor through which to grieve the loss when a woman fails, in the arena of patriarchy, to give life to her expressly womanly imagination. In the story, her creation is female, "perfectly made" and "glistening with the waters of the womb" but dead, a condition Nin has related to the limitations of fathers.

There is a similar theme developed in *Ladders to Fire,* in which the character Lillian, who is pregnant, tells her fetus that it should die because "You will not find a father who will lull you and cover you with his greatness and his warmth" (78). Lillian has a miscarriage in her sixth month.

Her vocabulary for masculine and feminine writing is occasionally uncanny, presaging the revisionist Freudian language currently used by feminist literary critics. Traditional writing, she asserts in the *Diary,* is constructed by the phallus: "Henry and Larry tried to lure me out of the womb. They call it objectivity. . . . Man today is like a tree that is withering at the roots. And most women painted and wrote nothing but imitations of phalluses. The world was filled with phalluses, like totem poles, and no womb anywhere" (2:235). Her description of womb writing anticipates the language of those feminists who have called on women to "write the female body."[3] Her tenure in psychoanalysis, both as patient and as practitioner, gave her the vocabulary to describe the forces denying her the forms and expression that would accommodate her imagination. She used Freudian insights against the systems that validated these insights: "Man invented a woman to suit his needs. He disposed of her by identifying her with nature and then paraded his contemptuous domination of nature. But woman is not nature only. She is the mermaid with her fish-tail dipped in the unconscious. Her creation will be to make articulate this obscure world which dominates man, which he denies being dominated by, but which asserts its domination in destructive proofs of its presence, madness" (2:235–36). Here again, Nin pictures madness as the fissure through which the repressed, which Nin codes as feminine, makes its return.[4] Her unique task as a writer, she implies, is to rescue the repressed feminine.

Rank, Durrell, and Miller eventually allowed that Nin was writing in a new style, a "woman's" style, but the admission, though presented as a revelation, had the effect of a dismissal. She convinced them of her uniqueness, but their acceptance of this argument meant she was no longer in their domain; she functioned outside their realm, and her work was therefore not equal to their definitions of the "literary." They implied that if she would not adopt incestuous literary practices, she could not enter their sacred brotherhood, but would inhabit a lesser position as "woman" writer. She rejected their definition of woman writer and with courage and energy redefined the category and occupied it with genius.

AUTHOR'S NOTE

This essay is an expanded, updated version of "Escaping from the *House of Incest*," published in *Anaïs: An International Journal* 10 (1992): 39–45.

NOTES

1. Bair entitles an entire chapter in her biography of Nin "HIM." Nin also referred to other lovers as HIM—for instance, Otto Rank (Bair 203). For discussion of the father figure in Nin, see also Sharon Spencer's "'Musique Ancienne': The Ultimate Seduction in 'Winter of Artifice'" in this volume.
2. Readers should see Bair's account of the actual abortion (198–203), which differs dramatically from Nin's published *Diary* entry and the story "Birth."
3. See Spencer.
4. See Cixous and Clément.

WORKS CITED

Bair, Deirdre. *Anaïs Nin: A Biography.* New York: Putnam, 1995.

Cixous, Hélène, and Catherine Clément. *The Newly Born Woman.* Trans. Betsy Wing. Minneapolis: University of Minnesota Press, 1986.

Nin, Anaïs. *The Diary of Anaïs Nin* (1931–74). Ed. Gunther Stuhlmann. 7 vols. San Diego: Harcourt Brace Jovanovich, 1966–80.

———. *Henry and June: From the Unexpurgated Diary of Anaïs Nin.* New York: Harcourt Brace Jovanovich, 1986.

———. *House of Incest.* Chicago: Swallow Press, 1958.

———. *Incest: From "A Journal of Love": The Unexpurgated Diary of Anaïs Nin, 1932–1934.* New York: Harcourt Brace Jovanovich, 1992.

———. *Ladders to Fire.* Chicago: Swallow Press, 1959.

———. *Under a Glass Bell.* New York: Gemor Press, 1942.

———. *Winter of Artifice: Three Novelettes.* Chicago: Swallow Press, 1961.

Spencer, Sharon. "The Music of the Womb: Anaïs Nin's 'Feminine' Writing." *Breaking the Sequence: Women's Experimental Fiction.* Ed. Ellen G. Friedman and Miriam Fuchs, 161–73. Princeton: Princeton University Press, 1989.

Transference, Mourning, and Narrative Recovery in House of Incest

Diane Richard-Allerdyce

The effects of incest, like the effects of radiation, are insidious, long term, and transmitted through generations. They lie harbored in the victim until they later erupt into disease or disorder, just as toxic and radioactive waste lies 'safely buried' until it leaches out into the environment and affects all life-forms. Some of the long-term effects of incest include fear, anxiety, anger, and hostility; eating disorders; allergies and asthma; shame; low self-esteem; guilt; depression; inability to trust or to establish relationships; phobias; multiple personality disorder; sexual dysfunction; a tendency toward revictimization through participating in such activities as prostitution, drug addition, alcoholism, self-mutilation, and suicide.

Jane Caputi[1]

The word she cannot utter against her father, she shouts in the title of her first book.

Noël Riley Fitch[2]

Don't Forget to Remember: Writing as Mourning

In his discussion about Paul de Man's status as object of transference for his followers,[3] Dominick LaCapra has written on the importance of recognizing the work of mourning in texts: "Melancholy may be necessary for mourning, but it blocks Trauerarbeit (the work of mourning) insofar as the melancholic disavows loss, remains narcissistically identified with the loved other and is unable to affirm, empathize with and, in certain respects, take leave of the other as other" (213). I believe that Nin's prose poem

House of Incest (1936) represents the author's movement out of the melancholy of her childhood toward a recognition that a partnership between the artistic and psychoanalytic processes might provide a way of acknowledging and working through, rather than repressing and acting out, early issues around trauma, particularly her relationship to what in Lacan's thought is known as the paternal signifier.[4]

Although it was not published until 1936, Nin began writing *House of Incest* in 1931, the same year that she met Henry and June Miller and began psychoanalysis with René Allendy, followed the next year by her *D. H. Lawrence: An Unprofessional Study* published by Edward Titus. Coinciding with Nin's awakened sexuality and her recognition, in part through her work on Lawrence, of literature's therapeutic potential, *House of Incest* represents a narrative entrance to the psychoanalytic moment in which one can begin to do the work of mourning—to recognize narcissistic attachment and begin to make distinctions that, when carried over into behavior, can result in a healthier relationship with oneself and the world.[5] In its treatment of unresolved sexual attachments between kin—and between two women whose identities become enmeshed through the narrator's fantasies of identificatory fusion—the prose poem addresses the effects of both psychological and actual incest, portraying subjects trapped by their inability to move beyond what Lacanian critic Ellie Ragland has called "the family novel," or the destructive family myths that have structured the subject ("Dora" 219). Nin's diaries, perhaps especially the parts published posthumously as unexpurgated, show us the particularity of her own family novel.

In the late 1980s as I was completing my dissertation on Anaïs Nin, I interpreted *House of Incest* as a book about the maiming effects of psychological fusion with others and the difficulty in moving beyond such fusion to a healthy perspective. Writing from a Lacanian and feminist perspective, I was amazed and excited to discover layer upon layer of significance in the book that one critic, Bettina Knapp, had called "an alchemical drama." I interpretively peeled each layer of this drama to reveal what I took to be Nin's intuitive understanding of what Lacan had proved clinically about the nature of paternal metaphor—language in the father's name—and its role as agent of differentiation interrupting the unity of the mother-infant dyad, an interruption through which consciousness and identity are structured in humans. Nin, I wrote, had embedded in her prose poem not only the theme of breaking free from the binding strictures of psychological fusion but an insightful perspective of psychological and linguistic structure. In addition, the work resonated with emotional power which must come from a source outside language—from experience, from a deeply embedded attachment to her father. Little did I know the full import of this attachment.[6]

Nin's account of her incestuous relationship with her father as told in *Incest: From "A Journal of Love"* (1992), the volumes of Nin's diary from the period 1932–1934 that were published posthumously as unexpurgated, strengthens this interpretation of *House of Incest*. More important, it exposes the traumatic effects of literal and psychological betrayal. For me, the fuller awareness of what it was that Nin was creatively mourning sheds new light on the book's themes of struggle and hope, of psychological imprisonment and potential freedom, of mourning and creativity.

In this essay, then, I want to address from a Lacanian perspective the ways that *House of Incest* shows Nin's attempts to come to terms, in literary form, with past trauma.[7] Her first book of fiction embodies the themes of mourning, remembering, and moving through the residual effects of previously unresolved material in her psyche in a way that highlights the psychoanalytic process of transference and reconstruction as well as the materiality of language-the palpable, Real texture of language that she saw embodied in literary texts such as D. H. Lawrence's novels.[8] Both the theme (moving out of paralyzing effects of early trauma) and form (a fluid, disparate structure) of *House of Incest* speak to Nin's readiness to find a voice with which to begin pursuing what was to become her lifelong goal of creating, out of her writing, a livable life.[9] An understanding of the Lacanian concept of the name(s)-of-the-father and its link to both hysteria and the material fluidity of the type of poetic language employed in Nin's *House of Incest* is helpful in tracing the process by which Nin pursued her artistic and psychoanalytic aims.

Lacan's Name(s)-of-the-Father

In Lacan's formulation, the name(s)-of-the-father refers to the first signifier of difference or separation. Language (naming) functions as the medium of difference as the child learns to differentiate between his or her own body and another's. While the other person from whom a child must identify itself might be of either gender, Lacan taught that linguistic differentiation has always operated through the *function* of maleness, regardless of gender;

thus unconscious structure or ordering builds up around the Imaginary and Symbolic fathers. As the "no" of the Symbolic father's name interrupts the seeming unity the infant may sense in the mother-infant dyad, language becomes an alienating force. Language, then, is paradoxically both unifying and alienating. Internal unification and external alienation function through the intervention of a "third term" on the side of culture—language in the father's name. Its function as signifier is opposed to the signifier for the natural and corporal, the mother.

In cases where a child has not internalized an adequate identification with the paternal signifier, such as in cases of trauma or wounding in relation to the father signifier, clear identity borders are not established and the child often grows up to have difficulty in distinguishing between self and others. The sense of identificatory fragmentation, weak self-esteem, and relational chaos experienced by many adult survivors of childhood trauma may be linked to a traumatic disruption in their identification with whoever has the "name-of-the-father."[10] Since one of the functions of the father is to "lay down the law"—ideally, to establish clear boundaries within which subjects can live safely and free from betrayal—a violation by the person signifying that function may be particularly traumatic.[11] In his early work on hysteria, Freud linked the suffering of patients who exhibited its symptoms to early sexual experiences that had been repressed. Fitch links this point, despite Freud's later revision of the "seduction theory," to Nin's own traumatic childhood relationship with her father (Fitch 151–52). Throughout this essay, I shall take into account both the Freudian and the Lacanian usages of the term "hysteria" to refer to the identity structure in which such a wounding has taken place in terms of the father signifier.[12]

Hysteria, Psychological Structure, and Literary Form

The "hysterical" discourse of many creative artists[13] may be understood as the embodiment in language of a sense of primordial fragmentation as well as a discourse style whose form accommodates, through sensory effect, the elements of experience that are inarticulable. Potentially both a blessing and a curse, such permeability allows for the stylistic fluidity often associated with the dream state and with poetic consciousness; it also can leave the hysterically structured subject more open to a stream of Real effects—anxiety, a sense of chaos—than another whose ego is more tightly constructed against lack, owing to identification with the phallus and with the name-of-the-father, the principle of differentiation by which one leaves the unity of the mother-infant dyad and enters the Symbolic order. The elements that Lacan saw as characteristic of hysterical structure include low levels of *méconnaissance* resulting in disavowal, a laxity of repression, fluidity of ego boundaries, and a lived level of unconscious desire; all can be recognized in the most intensely surreal depictions of the dream life Nin portrays in *House of Incest* and elsewhere. In Lacanian theory, the propensity to this structure is determined by one's relation to the phallic (limiting and differentiation) signifier by which, early in life, one leaves the sense of fusion with (m)other and enters the Symbolic order. As I shall explicate in more detail in my reading of *House of Incest*, this point is particularly relevant in Nin's case because of the way the themes of fusion, separation, and affective pain are embodied in both her life and her art.

While the structure underlying and making possible the material affectivity of poetic language may be hysterical in the sense that it gives voice to the unconscious (and its other, the Real), an important distinction must be made between the hysteric-as-artist and the hysteric-as-neurotic. Taking seriously the latter's suffering, Lacan believed that the way toward freedom from slavery to unconscious patterns earned early on in identificatory patterns and reinforced by cultural discourse systems was to help the hysterically structured subject to create her own desire, a process I see Nin beginning in 1931.[14] Lacan believed that the first step in helping a hysteric to articulate her own desire was "getting her to speak" (*Four Fundamental Concepts* 11).

Finding a Voice: The Feminist and Psychoanalytic Goals

In "Dora and the Name-of-the Father: The Structure of Hysteria," Ragland explains how an hysteric's body becomes a signifier of a repressed desire, as symptoms are given body through fantasies. For example, one of the symptoms exhibited by Ida Bauer, Freud's "Dora," was loss of voice, which may be seen as a "loss of a link to the social world" ("Dora" 3). For Lacan, the voice is a primordial desired object, an organ through which one can connect with others and experience language in a sensory, masterful way. But since language functions as a substitute for the unity it fails—and pretends—to create, there is always in language a drive by which the unconscious pushes through grammar and syntax to speak the speaker. That is, since language is based on the repression of inherent lack, that lack tries to push through to consciousness. As

Ragland puts it: "Because a primary sense of void and chaos lies at the beginning of life, Lacan (after Freud) postulated a dialectic of memory, language and desire that winds and threads through grammar and being in a paradoxical attempt to complete a lack to which it simultaneously refers" ("Dora" 211). While "void material" is, for Lacan, a universal condition of human existence, it is the hysterics—whose identities are structured loosely around the name-of-the-father—who are particularly vulnerable to a sense of chaos, to the Real (the order of consciousness that resists symbolization but is nonetheless palpable). Acutely aware of the existence of unsayable realms of experience, an hysteric may respond to trauma with a refusal to speak at all, to name even that which can be named.

In the psychoanalytic clinic, a person's inability to speak is often found to be related to something from the past considered unsayable. From the title of *House of Incest* onward, however, this unsayable is given voice in Nin's first book of fiction. It is given voice through a process that is, according to the narrator, known to writers as well as, she intimates, to those who play the quena, a flutelike instrument originally made by an Indian lover out of the bones of his dead mistress. The difference between that flutist and Nin's narrator, we are told, is that the narrator does not "wait for [her] love to die" before making the instrument out of human bones with which to impart story/song.

The book begins with the narrator's account of having a choking sensation on the morning she awoke to write the book. Something is in her throat. It turns out to be her heart. She pulls it out of her throat and begins to write her story. Here Nin gives poetic body to the concept of grief as a lump in the throat; she opens the work with a dislodging of this grief, a willingness to pull it out as in analysis a narrative thread will be pulled from behind an analysand's discourse.[15] As if to emphasize what in Lacanian theory would be called the inscription of the Real (the palpably inarticulable) within language, Nin's narrator tells the story of embodied trauma (the way that one physically carries effects from the past) and its relation to psychological structure. In the telling, we can hear Nin's own story—that of patriarchy's wounded daughter striving for relief from the hysterical suffering born of that position.

House of Incest portrays this step in the artistic as well as the psychoanalytic process from its prefatory chapter. From the start, the theme of finding a voice (spitting out her heart so she can speak) is linked with language's inscription on the body, particularly in the subsequent image of a musical instrument made of human bones. There is also a corresponding inscription of the Real upon the artist's words when the narrator tells us that in the process of spitting out her heart she was conscious that it was the same process as writing.

Unlike Ida Bauer, who lived a life of acute suffering until her death in her eighties, Nin devoted her life, first, to finding a voice and, later, to encouraging others, especially young women as well as artists of both genders, to do so. During a lecture she gave in 1973, Nin said that it was only writing that had taught her to speak. Acknowledging her audience's possible disbelief, she spoke of having been nearly mute at the age of twenty and of an aunt's having told her mother that she was subnormal. Even at the age of thirty she had been extremely shy, she said. "So I taught myself to talk, and I owe to writing the fact that we can talk together now" (*A Woman Speaks* 80).

The beginning of *House of Incest* represents not only the narrative opening of the prose poem but also, in the clearing of the narrator's throat, an entrance to the psychoanalytic process of acknowledging one's transferential desire in order to mourn what has been lost, as well as to "affirm, empathize with and, in certain respects, take leave of the other as other" (LaCapra, quoted above).

Nin's case demonstrates with certainty one of the certain respects in which one must for her own benefit take leave of an other. The struggling with issues of fusion and separation in *House of Incest* indicates not only the narrator's traumatization by a lack of ego boundaries but also the author's similar traumatization. A Lacanian reading elucidates both levels: (1) the images of Imaginary fusion replete in *House of Incest* indicate the pain and frustration inherent in symbiotic relation with another in which otherness is not given its due, and (2) Nin's affair with her father during the writing of *House of Incest*[16] shows her efforts to work through and move beyond Imaginary sense of fusion with her father by enacting her fusionary fantasies beyond the boundaries of cultural (Symbolic) prohibition (the incest taboo). An extreme enactment, to say the least, Nin's seduction of her father in the summer of 1933 may be seen as part of the process of facing and taking hold of a past trauma in order to take leave of it, a process central to *House of Incest*.[17] Her early fiction shows her struggle, at best probably only partially successful, to move out of her role as seduced and seducing daughter, a role that Jane Gallop argues traps female subjects in a vicious cycle of enticement by and of a "father" presumed to know the answers and to possess authority (70–71).

Delving into the Past: Art and the Psychoanalytic Opening

Throughout *House of Incest,* scenes of womb imagery compete and alternate with the narrator's desire to differentiate herself from a symbiotic state. This conflict parallels Nin's own efforts to work through psychoanalytic processes to distinguish herself from her father's image. In Lacanian terms, she must distinguish between the imaginary father and the role she has unconsciously granted him as a master signifier. After making that distinction, she can choose a new relation to his image. Nin's prose poem is but a first step in this process, for she would spend much of her life pursuing this goal.

First, before she can learn to take leave of the past, she must delve into a realm of suppressed memory. She does this in part through her narrator who, after the prefatory chapter of *House,* enters the narrative proper with a "first vision" that links womb imagery to a process of later submersion. The narrator's first observation is that she is surrounded by "water veiled" (15). The images throughout the first section evoke the womb. The narrator's emphasis, however, is less on a primary sense of union with a (m)other than on a process of submersion itself. This was the process by which Nin, having already recorded in her *Diary* and reported to Otto Rank the incestuous relationship with her father, was beginning to delve within herself to look at the past.

In the next sentence, she emphasizes both a sense of separation from the past and the way events have been interpreted through the process of memory and reconstruction of the initial experience. When the narrator remembers her "first birth," she distinguishes her origins from subsequent "births" she will experience as she reconstructs the past. Whether Nin intended her narrator to represent a person recovering from actual incest or a person simply suffering from a psychological habit of seeking a symbiotic womblike state, the narrator's grasping for something that lies beyond conscious memory reflects the theories Nin had put forth in her first book. Lawrence, according to Nin, was fearfully sensitive to the body's vision and was able to capture in language something beyond the immediate surface. Similarly, the speaker of *House* intensely feels a textured memory and strives to give it body. Her description of that birth is itself overlaid with longing, as the narrator feels herself afloat without an adequate anchor in a watery realm, listening with all her might for "distant sounds, sounds beyond the reach of human ears" (15). She looks as well as listens beyond her immediate surroundings, burdened with uneasy memories of something lost that she cannot quite pinpoint but that she feels drawn to seek.

The title of Nin's prose poem makes a reading of her narrator as incest victim at least plausible. From this perspective, the Real realm that in Lacanian thought lies beyond everyone's consciousness is made more palpable by a process Jane Caputi has highlighted as typical in cases of incest. In excluding traumatic memory from the surface of consciousness, Caputi writes, both incest victim and victimizer are "aided by psychological responses of denial, numbing, and splitting" (118). However, the narrator now stands on a threshold ready to begin a process of remembering, mourning, and reconstructing the past.

Nin's use of Lawrence's dream imagery as a way to access an unconscious connection among perception, memory, and bodily sensation anticipated her own use of dream in this work. For example, the lack of boundaries that throughout Nin's work point to psychological disruption and an absence of protective law is evident in this realm of rooms without walls and intermingling colors. Other passages combine a surrealist appreciation of unconscious fluidity with a welcoming of protective blindness, as the narrator floats unhampered by physical obstructions through a riverlike labyrinth.

In this early section, Nin's prose reads like the speech of an analysand beginning to surrender into free association. Images of peace, comfort, and effortless movement abound, such as those characteristic of guided visualization, dreaming, and (we might imagine) the womb. Subsequent paragraphs portray the narrator's entrance into the voiceless realm of a dream, where, instead of a comforting sense of fluidity or womblike security, she confronts horrific and terrifying images of crimes committed "in the silence of slidings and brushings" (16). An ostensibly comforting image of a watery blanket is predicated on a disruption of expectation that lies oppressively over everything, "stifling the voice" (16). Laden with images of potential bedtime comfort, the blanket becomes an item of suppression as if to suggest the "cult of secrecy" that Caputi says surrounds actual incest victims. That is, Nin conflates an image suggesting an incest survivor's actual memory with psychological principles by which the unconscious can present an image and its disruption.

This disruption, rather than an actual memory, is what is wanted in psychoanalysis so that the analysand can achieve realignment to images from the past, including those that are most traumatic. In Nin's case, even as she and her narrator refuse to keep them buried, Nin uses narrative structure to acknowledge remembered images as symbolic and subject to the fictionalizing tendencies of memory itself. In this sense, she develops an analytic goal more in keeping with Lacanian thought in its emphasis on the fictions of the psyche than on a more literal interpretation of suppressed memory typical of ego psychology. In the last paragraph of the section, the narrator relates that she awoke to find herself deposited upon a rock like "the skeleton of a ship choked in its own sails" (17). An image to which the author would return again and again in both her dreams and her fiction, the grounded ship connotes the stifling effects of an early trauma that causes one not to flow. The choking image echoes the narrator's choking on her heart in the book's prefatory chapter and reflects the moment in the psychoanalytic treatment when an analyst can progress toward the goal of helping a victim to confront trauma by speaking only with the victim's willingness to "pull out her heart." That willingness is the decision to delve into the painful memories of the past, to face, embrace, and take leave of them in order to move forward toward a healthier life, to free the ship and put it back into the current.

Fragmentation and Fusion: The Psyche's Response to Trauma

The next section opens with the narrator surrounded by night. Like trauma victims who lose contact with parts of their lives through denial and partial amnesia, we lose a day between the psychoanalytic awakening of the last section's closing and the opening of this one. Similarly, incest victims "seek refuge in numbing, denial and massive repression" and prevent themselves from remembering their "worst secret" because it is so unthinkable (Caputi 132). Fortunately, the lapse of memory represented by the losing of a day in this part of the prose poem is temporary, and the narrator, like Nin, eventually moves toward confrontation.

This section's initial images reflect the sense of the culturally endorsed "psychic fissioning" and fragmentation that Caputi cites as characteristic of incest survivors (131). A photograph comes loose from its frame, the lining of a coat splits open like an oyster, and the narrator feels as if she is falling into a fissure between day and night. Immediately following this we meet Sabina, clearly based on June Miller, another woman for whom the themes of fragmentation and psychic chaos had prevailed.[18]

Ironically, as a step toward embracing her own subjectivity as opposed to fleeing it in return-to-the-womb fantasies, the narrator seeks relief from her pain in a love affair with Sabina. She does so believing that this union will be immune to the human incompleteness from which heterosexual relations provide only temporary respite. She finds out otherwise. In Sabina, the narrator recognizes herself. She strives to achieve an end to her own sense of fragmentation by collecting all of the pieces of Sabina's personality and presenting them to her as a coherent mirror image. "I AM THE OTHER FACE OF YOU," she shouts (*House* 28). The problem with the narrator's approach, of course, is that one cannot establish clear identity borders through fusion with another.

By contrast, a movement toward a healthier perspective depends on one's willingness and ability to name the trauma. She must establish her own direction and, as the Lacanian critic Mark Bracher puts it, articulate a set of master signifiers apart from the Other's desire. In Nin's case, the Other was her father, whose image she had internalized as the main pole of her being. In her effort to separate from her father's image, Nin allows her narrator to see that, in retrospect, her effort to fuse with Sabina was futile. Despite the women's efforts to form a unifying bond, they find themselves straining for individuality. The narrator realizes that they have passed beyond the possibility of merger. The narrator enjoys contact with Sabina's exclusively female gestures and ways, but she feels she is being drawn into dissolution, a paradoxical realm in which fragmentation gives birth to madness. She soon decides that her relation to Sabina is a false one that has created an infinitely regressive mirror image: "One woman within another eternally, in a far-reaching procession, shattering my mind into fragments, into quarter tones which no orchestral baton can ever make whole again" (22). This image represents the absence of a secure identity such as Nin saw in June. It also portrays the unhealthy wish to literally return to the womb, where one would be, ostensibly, safe from disruptive forces.

While all humans may experience disruption to a degree, Nin's title resonates in this image to emphasize the way universal anxiety can be intensified into traumatic fissuring for one who has experienced incest. That person, after all, has been betrayed by the very person(s) who should provide safety. Research has shown that one of the effects of such betrayal is a psychological splitting; hence the "far-reaching procession" of subjective splits the narrator sees in Sabina, the image "shattering [her] mind into fragments." The narrator is sickened by a barrage of images that appear as "reflections in cracked mirrors" (29). Hinz, in *The Mirror and the Garden,* sees mirror symbolism in Nin's work as highlighting a superficial world of imposed realism, rather than the organic and natural mode of perception Hinz saw as healthy. A Lacanian reading of Nin's mirror imagery complements Hinz's by showing the illusory and fictional nature of the image of wholeness that the narrator seeks in her relationship with Sabina. The narrator cannot deny the threat of separation and differentiation that she tried to escape through relationship with a woman.

The failure of the sexual relation to reestablish harmony descends upon the narrator with the full force of early sexual wounding and its border-erasing effects. The pain she feels is as if she is carrying a sharp blade between her legs when she walks. In the same passage, images of external precipitation converge with those of bodily fluids to create a sensory overload and to suggest that the narrator has lost, at least temporarily, all ability to distinguish self from other. A dog's barking, her own laughter, and her lover's pain swirl together in her mind as if to suggest a psychotic breakdown. Her sensory porousness is but the extreme of that typical among adult survivors of childhood trauma.

As the passage continues, perceived sources of threat converge in the body with real force, illustrating the sense of fragmentation and openness to the flow of traumatic memories that the analytic process in the author has set into motion. Nin demonstrates the painful effort to articulate this process when her narrator's desire to speak causes "each nerve . . . to break separately, continuously, making incisions" (32). Nin anticipates her own later theories about the ability of art to create a transpersonal realm when she has her narrator connect the pain of acid running into raw wounds with an attempt to "melt the pain into a cauldron of words for everyone to dip into, everyone who sought words for their own pain . . . words bitter enough to burn all bitterness" (32).

Alone in her quest to confront a singular past in language by speaking up for herself, the narrator strives to give collective voice to a pain that must be spoken one voice at a time. This is less a contradiction than it is a creative counterpart to the idea, which

Nin had expressed in her study of Lawrence, that singular concrete experience can lead to the universal through textured literary language. The concreteness of the experience anchors her in bodily trauma and holds a body-based language as a source of reconstruction. The paradox that the words must be bitter enough to burn all bitterness reflects Nin's idea about opposites' functioning to lead into each other, a version of the psychoanalytic idea that is shared by mystics. For Nin, the only way out of the labyrinth is the way in. Her narrator must, in a sense, experience trial by fire. She must descend into the unconscious realm—as a metaphor for the process the author was engaged in at the time of writing *House of Incest,* a time when insights alternated with bouts of depression and sometimes nearly suicidal thoughts. As Nin worked in psychoanalysis to formulate her relation to truth, in part by acknowledging its dependence on culture and language in order to restructure a relationship to her personal truth, the narrator experiences her own crisis of belief, which sends her into another state of psychic dissolution.

Reliving the Wound

Again, the narrator senses and laments that she is seeking something irretrievably lost but unforgettable. This time, she is involved in a process she realizes is a reconstructive one. Much as the texture of Lawrence's writing captured for Nin the sense that something palpable, but not rememberable, lies outside language and can be reconstructed through literature, Nin shows the narrator's desire for health as the reconstruction of an unconscious pattern. Using the metaphor of a bedridden patient determined to walk without crutches, she cries out her desire that someone witness her madness and her efforts toward autonomy. Once again, she describes her psychological wound in terms of a bodily inhibition.

Nin returns to the body as a basis for reconstruction because the body represents a real grounding, rather than cultural systems of power and denial based on less primary connections to the real. The connection between physical lameness and psychological wounding, appears in several references to an actual or metaphorical sexual violation. In another section a character named Jeanne feels excruciating physical and emotional pain on her wedding night because she is in love with her brother and therefore cannot love her husband. Her mental torment takes the form of an endless ringing of bells. The connection Nin draws between Jeanne's bodily and psychic suffering finds further substance in the ending section of the chapter she appears in, where numerous additional images of bodily disintegration merge with an acknowledgment that the sexual love between siblings is like the love of shadows, forever split from themselves, each other, and reality. Another example of the connection of body and consciousness appears toward the end of the book, when the narrator experiences the passing of time as "[h]ours like tall ebony women with gongs between their legs" (55). This image reiterates the link between a physical violation between one's legs and its psychic counterpart in the clanging of gongs.

When, in the early section, the narrator says that she wants "absolution" from the "lies" in which she has enmeshed herself but feels that she "cannot tell the truth because I have felt the heads of men in my womb" (40), Nin uses her narrator's status as a resident of the house of incest to suggest that her own proclivity for lying is an effect of a boundary violation. The causal link drawn by Nin's narrator between not being able to tell the truth and the experience of having men's heads in her womb suggests a sexual violation in that among the effects of such violation are psychic fragmentation, splitting, denial, and lying—all characteristics of Nin's behavior as she responded to early trauma. Simultaneously, she attributes her inability to maintain a single role to her role as creative artist. Besides its sexual connotation, having men's heads in her womb refers to Nin's belief that, whereas male artists create from their intellects, women writers create from their wombs. This is a theme that runs throughout her diaries and much of her other writing.[19]

A related theme of Nin's theoretical explorations into the nature of sexual difference and creativity continues to link her narrator's need to find absolution for lying to a boundary wound. When the narrator says her lies are like costumes, the comparison parallels a similar idea in Nin's *Diary*. It is a rationalization that may partially exonerate the teller of lies but cannot heal the pain behind their construction. The narrator sees her own lies as a way of warding off painful images. Without them, she feels herself falling into darkness and is confronted with "a face which stares at me like the glance of a cross-eyed man" (40).

Here again is an image suggesting a remembered violation restructured as art: the man's eyes—like those in the Cubist paintings Nin would later use as a visual counterpart to what she was trying to achieve in writing—appear skewed. As a signifier of either actual or metaphorical incest, he is literally too close. His physical presence is an unwanted, inappropriate intrusion. His relationship to the victim is familial and his violation is at cross-purposes with his role as protector.

As if to avoid pursuing this image, the narrative jumps to an alchemical image that captures the chilling effect of her memory even as it replicates the movement in a liar's speech from one version of truth to another. Nin reconstructs that movement as creative rather than pathological: "I remember the cold on Jupiter freezing ammonia and out of ammonia crystals came the angels" (40). The angels that can be born out of the transformative effect of delving into chilling memory through the psychoanalytic and artistic processes are the narrator's emerging abilities to provide protection and comfort for herself through art. In addition to their role as message bearers, the angels in this passage indicate the narrator's movement through re-memory toward a reconstructed future.

Nin repeats the image of the cross-eyed man near the end of the prose poem, in a passage that also addresses her stance toward truth and toward fictionalizing her version of truth as fairy tales. Rather than using repetition as a compulsion, Nin uses it creatively to represent change. For her, repeating the image at the end of *House* constitutes the next step in the analytic process, by which the analysand may return to an image in order to recognize its position in her trajectory and to reconstruct its significance in a way more in keeping with her own desire.

Stasis and Stagnation as Symbolic Resistance

Incest, the failure of human family "law" and of the father-protector function, perpetuates the wounded daughter's inability to incorporate appropriate boundaries.[20] Nin explores the theme of the psychological stagnation that can result from a lack of boundaries represented by the narrator's clinging to a fantasy of womblike safety and symbiotic union. The sibling incest of the next chapter and the stasis of the section that follows provide variations on the theme of psychic symbiosis and its corrective in the narrator's and author's increased ability to make distinctions. By contrast, the house's inhabitants have cut themselves off from all flow and remained trapped in a "mineral fixity," an extreme rigidity that the narrator acknowledges as fear of both life and death. Each is stuck in a separate experience, unrelated to the others. For them, as for the narrator when she participates in their stagnation, language itself has lost its fluidity and thus all creative potential. The characters' unspoken words and curses have "turned into magnetic iron ore, into . . . blood calcinated, . . . the mineral glow of . . . exhausted suns in the forest of dead trees and dead desires" (60).

This passage reflects the symbolic castration that occurs through language, which is intensified to the extreme for victims of paternal abuse. The narrator encounters such a situation when she discovers Lot calmly fondling his daughter's breast while the city burns behind them. Both father and daughter in this image are immobile as the city cracks open and falls into the sea. In a passage replete with images reminiscent of the nuclearism cited by Caputi as accompanying accounts of incest since the mid-twentieth century[21]—which *House of Incest* predates—Nin portrays the earth-shattering effects of incest upon the consciousness of those whose lives are blasted to numbness by this "horror of obscenity" (55).

But Nin projects an attitude of hope. The momentum of the work strives for freedom from the "dead letter office" of a permanently incestuous realm. After witnessing this scene between Lot and his daughter, the narrator looks at a clock to orient herself to the truth, a construction that reflects her effort to reenter a realm of temporality as opposed to the stasis of an eternal wounding.

Part of the process is to put into movement, though speech, the static attachments that have become a trap. In the next paragraph, the narrator comes across a forest of mutilated trees that look like the tortured and fragmented bodies of massacred slaves. The narrator feels the forest's bitter, rebellious trembling and anguished cries of loss, reflecting a "failure of transmutation" (56). Both the dead figures and the grief in this passage imply the narrator's and the author's outcry against a violation. The trees' wailing and its counterpart in the narrative show that real mourning is taking place, the kind of mourning that can, potentially, lead to recovery. It is at this point in the narrative that real progress is made in the narrator's journey out of the house of incest: after entering still another forest, this one of white plaster eggs representing the potential of finding "hope without breaking," the narrator sees a felled tree sprouting a "green live branch that laugh[s] at the sculptor" (56). This image embodies the wounded daughter's ability to come back to life, despite the violation experienced at the hands of the knife-wielding perpetrator of suffering. Nin's message of struggle and hope, of psychological imprisonment and potential freedom, of mourning and creativity, prevails throughout the passage.

The images of the next chapter are full of leave-taking as the narrator witnesses Jeanne's becoming stuck for several years at the juncture between the time she became separated from her brother and the moment she "looked at the facade of the house of incest" (61). At this point the narrator decides to leave Jeanne and to find her own way out. Meanwhile Jeanne determines to account for all the windows of the house and, in this way, to find the room where her brother is hiding from her. Asking the inhabitants to hang clothes or other items out of the windows near them, she discovers "one window without light like a dead eye" (60) and knows her brother is in that place of stasis and dead letters. She finds him sleeping among paintings of her and engages him in a reciprocal worshiping of each other's likenesses.

A Leave-Taking

At the opening of the following chapter, the narrator leaves the place she has been and seeks peace by walking into her own book. The idea of physically entering her book highlights the process the author is engaged in—creating her own story apart from patriarchal identification, a story in which she creates herself as a character in order to do the hard work of mourning required for healing. Aware of the painful necessities of this journey, Nin's narrator attributes her pain to "this seeing too much," which causes her to "carry white sponges of knowledge on strings of nerves" (62). Highlighting the way that language and awareness are inscribed on identity, this passage accounts for the material basis of psychological pain that she feels in the body through re-memorization: "As I move within my book I am cut by pointed glass and broken bottles in which there is still the odor of sperm and perfume" (62). From within this reconstructed space, the narrator converges with the author to realize how much the deterioration of human relationships appearing throughout *House of Incest* functions through attachment to the dead letters of the past. The possibility of freedom lies in its inhabitants' retaining awareness of something beyond the walls of their isolation.[22]

The narrator thus reenters the house of incest—by way of her book—in order to discover what lies beyond its walls. Inside, she enters the room of a paralyzed man who does not do the painful work of mourning and reconstructing the past in terms of the present and who remains uncreative and stuck. This would-be artist sits with an untouched paint box in front of piles of books, perhaps a thousand of them, with uncut pages. He tells her his problem, in many of the same words the narrator used to relate her own dilemma, asserting that his inability to tell the truth rests on his multiple perspectives on the overtones and undertones of that truth. Rather than work with the multiplicitous nature of truth, he does not express himself at all through his art. He is as blocked as a writer who rejects the limitations of language and as the hysteric who refuses to speak. Nin, in turn, refuses this refusal. As the paralytic sits motionless, surrounded by pieces of blank paper, a new character, the "modern Christ," begins telling the narrator and Sabina and Jeanne the ordeal of his crucifixion "by his own nerves, for all our neurotic sins" (68). "Born without skin," he also suffers from a lack of boundaries that would provide a stay against pain. Even people's voices cause his whole body to ripple with pain when they speak. The paralytic voices his envy of the modern Christ's ability to feel. Between these extremes, the narrator states her wish to escape the house of incest, "where we only love ourselves in the other" (70). Feeling alone provides no salvation.

Although the narrator says they cannot make the journey out of the darkness of this house, fearing that the tunnel that would be their escape route might close in around them and trap them in further suffocation, they know there is daylight beyond the house even though, as yet, none of them can walk toward it.

Suddenly they notice a dancer at the center of the room, armless in punishment for her clinging, and dancing as if "isolated and separated from music and from [the others] and from the room and from life" (70). Yet she dances "all for herself. She danced her fears" (71), showing the possibility of embracing—however paradoxical it might be to embrace without arms—one's own wounding.

In the process, the dancer's arms are restored to her, without narrative explanation but with the implication that dancing one's fears—as metaphor for the creative process of mourning enacted in this text—has a healing potential. Like the wounded daughter who reaches the point where she can take leave of a wounding other, the dancer opens her newly restored hands in a gesture of abandonment, release, and forgiveness. Far from a submission to her violation, this gesture represents the narrative process of "taking leave" made possible through the willingness to mourn, rather than to repress and deny and suppress, the past. The narrator, watching, realizes that she has been trapped by her inability to "bear the passing of things," and the dancer's movement chokes her with anguish. But the book ends with motion: "And she danced; she danced with the music and with the rhythm of earth's circles; she turned with the earth turning, like a disk, turning all faces to light and to darkness evenly, dancing towards daylight" (72). Although it is not the narrator who is doing the dancing, this ending demonstrates the narrator's acknowledgment that such movement is possible. Previously unable to summon the courage to enter the tunnel leading outside, the narrator and her companions within the house of incest can, by story's end, at least see their way out.

Conclusion

Writing her first published book of fiction helped Nin begin inscribing her psyche with the formal boundaries she would use to begin healing. *House of Incest* constitutes a narrative opening to the process of analytic inquiry and a corresponding action-taking in Nin's own life, as she embarked on a journey to confront her traumatic past in order to deal with its effects and allow herself to live more creatively, freer from the affective pain that tormented her. Her own difficulty in facing the past is acknowledged and confronted in her prose poem. Along with its representation of cyclic patterns of sleeping and waking, dream and reality, night and day, death and life, *House of Incest* parallels in form and content the delving into and drawing back from painful past that is characteristic of an analysand's guided confrontation of unconscious traumatic memory.

We do not know whether Nin was sexually abused by her father as a child. Nin's work implies that the nature of the abuse was secondary. Her later "continuous novel" indicates that she believed it is one's interpretation of the past, rather than any particular event in itself, that continues to wound. What we do know is that Nin's lifelong writings show the effects of severe traumatization around the issue of the paternal, and she suffered throughout her life from these effects. Her prose poem's title and its thematic unity around the issue of incest make especially viable a reading that takes particular account of the effects of an early psychosexual violation and of a process of confronting, mourning, and reconstructing the past through art and analysis. With her first book of fiction, Nin was suggesting to herself that one does not have to remain captive to a neurotic unconscious structure. She also demonstrated that an artistic embodiment of language could be used to help a wounded daughter find a voice with which to create new structures away from patriarchal violation and desire, not by taking shelter in a separate realm of language and experience but by acknowledging and working through her grief through writing.

AUTHOR'S NOTE

Portions of this article have appeared earlier in my book *Anais Nin and the Remaking of Self: Gender, Modernism, and Narrative Identity* (DeKalb: Northern Illinois University Press, 1998).

NOTES

1. In *Gossips, Gorgons, and Crones: The Fates of the Earth,* Jane Caputi draws a convincing argument connecting incest and nuclear development. See her chapter "Unthinkable Fathering" (117–40).
2. In the introduction to *Anaïs: The Erotic Life of Anaïs Nin,* Noël Riley Fitch writes: "The title of her first novel, *The House of Incest,* and scenes in four pieces of fiction say it all. Senor Joaquin Nin y Castellanos . . . seduced his daughter. This fact is impossible to prove conclusively, but it is borne out by her subsequent behavior" (3). The four pieces of fiction are three stories from the erotica and a scene in *Children of the Albatross* in which Djuna, abused as a child, describes "'a shattering blow' to her body." See also note 6 below.
3. According to LaCapra, the students of Paul de Man and others who reacted defensively to the posthumous discovery of de Man's proNazi writings in France during the war may not have analyzed their own transference to de Man. LaCapra argues that several apologists for de Man fall into the trap of unconsciously distorting or misapplying deconstructive theory to justify de Man's failure to acknowledge or account for these writings.
4. According to Fitch, Nin was never fully successful in maintaining a clear sense of identity or in overcoming the violation of the young Nin by her father. For Fitch, Nin's adult incestuous relationship with her father, her continuing to take a series of father figures as lovers, and her returning again and again to the father theme in her literature show Nin's failure to resolve her conflicts around the issue of her early abuse. My emphasis, in some contrast, is on the literary manifestation of Nin's implicit understanding of psychological structure and its relation to form, and on the elements of healing that she did accomplish through her fiction: to confront the past, to deal with trauma in ways that show the human spirit's ability to persevere through and within the also quite human tendency to repress and disavow, and to assert one's right and ability to speak. While complete healing from trauma may be never fully accomplished, and while Nin continued to battle all her life for emotional equilibrium, we can see in her works, particularly those dating from the early 1930s, an effort to move beyond a melancholic disavowal of loss and beyond a neurotic tendency to cling to the past in ways that reinforce the hysterical silence with which women have historically been marginalized.
5. Mark Bracher's *Lacan, Discourse, and Social Change* (1993) suggests that learning to analyze and to articulate on one's own terms a set of

master-signifiers (ideals around which identity is structured) is the key to maintaining a more healthy interface with the world.

6. According to the second volume of those published as "unexpurgated," Nin became lovers with her father in July 1933, when she was thirty. Fitch's assertion that her writing shows evidence of early abuse is, however, conjectural and interpretive.

7. I am far from the first to suggest that the artistic process was therapeutic for Nin. In *Anaïs Nin* (1978) Bettina Knapp writes: "*House of Incest* was the outcome in large measure of Nin the patient and the psychotherapeutic sessions working in conjunction with Nin the artist" (44). The psychoanalytic critic Suzette Henke's *Shattered Subjects* (1998) contains an excellent chapter on Nin's use of the process of writing to heal from past trauma. A Lacanian interpretation builds on this understanding with the added link to the effect of the signifier on unconscious structure and the ways that structure is given voice in the text.

8. In my article "*L'écriture féminine* and Its Discontents: Anaïs Nin's Response to D. H. Lawrence," I argue that Nin's Lawrence book, far from essentialist, rests on her understanding of the texture of Lawrence's language. This texture may be understood as an aspect of language that Lacan called its materiality; its presence in Lawrence's work indicates that his psychological structuring around the paternal (differentiating) signifier involves a porousness of identity by which affect can slip through the communicative aspects of language to be felt as a palpable presence in the work. The structuring of identity in terms of the paternal signifier is an especially relevant strain of the present essay, specifically because it is in relationship with the imaginary father (fused with the symbolic) that Nin confronts the trauma of her past.

9. Nin, of course, had much earlier begun creating a life through writing, when she started a letter to her father on board the ship that carried the eleven-year-old girl with her mother and brothers away from her father's country to New York. There Anaïs, forbidden by her mother to send the letter and still apparently believing her father's absence was temporary, continued the letter as the now-famous *Diary.* The difference between these early writings and those published in the 1930s and afterward, however, lies in Nin's increased ability to overcome not only a literal silencing of the past but also the silencing that occurs when discourse is used to avoid confronting trauma rather than to give it voice. The adolescent romanticism and melancholic sentimentality of the early diaries is not wholly abandoned either in Nin's adult diaries or in some of the adult fiction, but, as I shall demonstrate in this essay, the degree of self-questioning is markedly increased.

10. In a technical sense, the name-of-the-father is gender-neutral. Ellie Ragland has explained that one of the names of the father is "mother"

("Lacan's Seminars" 74). In other words, both male and female persons can and do function as signifiers of law and differentiation.

11. From a Lacanian perspective, we can see that the law-of-the-father, in its technical sense, is a function: the upholder of the boundaries (law) within which the family can live safely. Hence a violation of this function subjects the child not only to physical danger but also to an often lifelong internalization of a sense of danger, inscribed on the psyche through its link with the name-of-the-father as essential signifier.

12. For Lacan, hysteria is an identificatory structure rather than an illness. The effects of such a structure on one's identity are lifelong; relief of the symptoms of hysteria's neurotic manifestations depends on the subject's moving toward articulating one's own desire.

13. Examples of artists who have been considered to have "hysterical" discourse structures are James Joyce (see Ragland's "Lacan's Seminars") and D. H. Lawrence (see note 8 above).

14. Nin's decision to begin publishing her *Diary* with the 1931 entries makes sense, in my mind, from this perspective.

15. Caputi links the importance of finding a voice with which to outcry incest with that of revealing the betrayals of trust at the heart of nuclearism: "making genocidal bombs isn't taboo, but speaking out against them is. So, too, as many observers note, incest is not really taboo in our culture, but speaking out against it is. . . . Indeed, in order to thwart both child sexual abuse and nuclearism, we must gossip, or in the phrase commonly used by survivors, 'break silence'" (130–31).

16. Nin began *House of Incest* in 1931 and published in 1936. It was during the middle of this process, in July 1933, that Nin's "seduction" of her father took place.

17. That Nin rejected her father's influence shortly after their affair shows her "taking leave." This is not to say, however, that she achieves total freedom from the effects of her father-neurosis. On the contrary, her lifelong struggle to combat this neurosis highlights the traumatizing effects on a child of an adult's abuse and/or neglect. At the same time, Nin's rejection of many cultural norms—role of mother, monogamy, deference to husband—may be seen as a rejection of patriarchy itself.

18. Both Nin's first-published *Diary* and *Henry and June* portray fragmentation, disunities of selves, the need for narrative invention, and both her own and June Miller's reliance on imagination as a way to piece together the disparate elements of the psyche. Whether or not her depiction is accurate, Nin believed that the difference between June and herself was that June remained unconscious of the role of self-construction through tale-telling, while Nin herself was self-consciously embracing the role of inventor/creator (*Diary* 1:22).

19. This reading would make sense in that Nin believed that she could give birth not only to works of art of her own making but also, in the sense of midwiving, nurturing, and inspiring others' writing, to those con-

ceived in "men's heads." By "mothering" these male artists, she would participate in the birth of their brainchildren—their works of art.

20. Again, I use the father function in the Lacanian sense of a differentiating principle through which language and law occur at the intervention of symbiosis. Thus, "father" is not necessarily a male person but one who carries out and represents this function.

21. Caputi's point is that the violation of trust and function of the incestuous father is linked in the popular imagination to images of destruction and the violation of public trust that accompany the development and acceptance of nuclear weapons.

22. Correspondingly, Lacan taught that the possibility of freedom from neurosis lies in the subject's "effort to overcome its own internal, libidinal alienation" (Ragland, *Philosophy* 63).

WORKS CITED

Bracher, Mark. *Lacan, Discourse, and Social Change: A Psychoanalytic Cultural Criticism.* Ithaca: Cornell University Press, 1993.

Caputi, Jane. *Gossips, Gorgons, and Crones: The Fates of the Earth.* Santa Fe, N.M.: Bear, 1993.

Fitch, Noël Riley. *Anaïs: The Erotic Life of Anaïs Nin.* Boston: Little, Brown, 1993.

Gallop, Jane. *The Daughter's Seduction: Feminism and Psychoanalysis.* Ithaca: Cornell University Press, 1982.

Henke, Suzette. *Shattered Subjects: Trauma and Testimony in Women's Life-Writing.* New York: St. Martin's Press, 1998.

Knapp, Bettina L. *Anaïs Nin.* New York: Frederick Ungar, 1978.

Lacan, Jacques. *Écrits: A Selection.* Trans. Alan Sheridan. New York: Norton, 1977.

———. *Feminine Sexuality: Jacques Lacan and the école freudienne.* Ed. Juliet Mitchell and Jacqueline Rose. Trans. Jacqueline Rose. New York: Norton, 1982.

———. *The Four Fundamental Concepts of Psychoanalysis.* Ed. Jacques-Alain Miller. Trans. Alan Sheridan. New York: Norton, 1978.

LaCapra, Dominick. *Representing the Holocaust: History, Theory, Trauma.* Ithaca: Cornell University Press, 1994.

Nin, Anaïs. *Children of the Albatross.* London: Peter Owen, 1959.

———. *D. H. Lawrence: An Unprofessional Study.* Introd. Harry T. Moore. Denver: Swallow Press, 1964.

———. *The Diary of Anaïs Nin.* Vol. 1 (1931–1934); vol. 2 (1934–1939). Ed. Gunther Stuhlmann. San Diego: Swallow Press/Harcourt, Brace & World, 1966–67.

———. *Henry and June: From the Unexpurgated Diary of Anaïs Nin.* San Diego: Harcourt Brace Jovanovich, 1986.

———. *House of Incest.* Chicago: Swallow Press, 1958.

———. *Incest: From "A Journal of Love": The Unexpurgated Diary of Anaïs Nin, 1932–1934.* San Diego: Harcourt Brace Jovanovich, 1992.

————. *A Woman Speaks: The Lectures, Seminars, and Interviews of Anaïs Nin.* Ed. Evelyn J. Hinz. Chicago: Swallow Press, 1975.

Ragland, Ellie. "Dora and the Name-of-the-Father: The Structure of Hysteria." *Discontented Discourses.* Ed. Marleen S. Barr and Richard Feldstein, 208–40. Urbana: University of Illinois Press, 1986.

————. *Jacques Lacan and the Philosophy of Psychoanalysis.* Urbana: University of Illinois Press, 1986.

————. "Lacan's Seminars on James Joyce: Writing as 'Singular Solution.'" *Compromise Formations: Current Directions in Psychoanalytic Criticism.* Ed. Vera J. Camden. Kent, Ohio: Kent State University Press, 1989.

Richard-Allerdyce, Diane. "The Feminine Creativity of Anaïs Nin: A Lacanian View." Ph.D. diss., University of Florida, 1988.

————. "*L'écriture féminine* and Its Discontents: Anaïs Nin's Response to D. H. Lawrence." *D. H. Lawrence Review* 26.1–3 (1995–96): 197–226.

CHAPTER 6

"Musique Ancienne"
The Ultimate Seduction in "Winter of Artifice"

Sharon Spencer

Not separateness but oneness was music.

Anaïs Nin, "Winter of Artifice"

At an early age Anaïs Nin chose her lifelong dedication to art. At twelve she was visited in a prophetic dream by a "great lady" dressed in black velvet and diamonds. This muse in the form of a goddess or a fairy godmother offered the young girl a choice of expressive mediums: music, painting, or writing. As Anaïs walked toward her desk—an adult's desk, the gift of her mother—she decided on writing. To her delight, Anaïs's muse reassured her: "Write, I shall guide you" (*Linotte* 50–51).

It was natural that Anaïs grew up passionately loving art and admiring artists. Both her parents were musicians: her mother, Rosa Culmell, was a singer, her father a composer and pianist who performed in the major cities of Europe. Her surviving brother, Joaquín Nin-Culmell, is a distinguished composer whose works are performed in Europe and the United States. Anaïs tells readers that until her mother and father separated, their family life was characterized by an "atmosphere of music and books." The intensely charged significance of music for the developing girl is aptly depicted in "Winter of Artifice." She was eleven when she

113

and her mother and brothers arrived in New York, after her mother's decision to remove the family from Joaquín Nin in Europe. "She remembers vividly how she clung to her brother's violin case. She wanted everybody to know that she was an artist" (61). Anaïs was "always constructing, creating, writing, drawing, inventing plays, acting in them, writing a diary, living in created dreams as inside a cocoon" (*Diary* 1:56–57). Writing poems and stories from earliest adolescence, Anaïs visited the public library to research methods of publishing her works. At sixteen she submitted some of them to *La France* (she had not yet transferred her language preference to English). This is certainly prophetic of the tenacity and dedication she was later to display throughout her writing life.

Early on, Anaïs also discovered her dissatisfaction with the Anglo-Saxon ideal of writing "realistically." Discouraged by all who read her idiosyncratic writings, she persisted nonetheless. She invented and experimented all of her life. The essence of her unceasing search was the musicalization of her prose. Having been deeply influenced by Rimbaud, she followed the inspiration of the French symbolists, who aspired to transform poetry into music: especially Verlaine with his liquid harmonies of sounds and Mallarmé with his mysterious poetic structures that concealed their musical inspirations. Perhaps no better description of her idealization of music can be cited than that expressed by Schopenhauer: "The unutterable depth of all music by virtue of which it floats through our consciousness as the vision of a paradise firmly believed in yet ever distant from us, and by which also it is so fully understood and yet so inapplicable, rests on the fact that it restores to us all the emotions of our inmost nature, but entirely without reality and far removed from their pain" (275).

In writing prose it is a heroic challenge to orchestrate words that are as vital, as sensuous and as immediately affecting as musical notes. Nin searched for "another kind of language, the inspirational, which is the one that *penetrates our unconscious directly* and doesn't need to be analyzed or interpreted in a cerebral way. It penetrates us in the way music does, through the senses" (*A Woman Speaks* 129, italics mine). To this end Nin borrowed whatever she wished from the other arts: "My only structure is based on three forms of art—painting, dancing, music—because they correspond to the senses I find atrophied in literature today" (*Diary* 4:150). Anaïs yearned to "write as the birds sing. As the primitive dance their rituals" (*Diary* 5:150).

And she succeeded. A novella of daring content and equally daring literary ingenuity, "Winter of Artifice" is one of many works that emerged from Nin's ambition to "write as the birds sing" and "as the primitive dance their rituals." It is rich thematically, offering at least three interpretive perspectives: "Winter of Artifice" can be read as a psychological cardiogram of *any* love in which fearful vulnerability endlessly debates with an impulse toward passionate surrender; as a poetically wrought fantasy of the "orchestration of love" (74) between an adult daughter and her father; or as a wrenching probe of "acted out" mutually seductive incest between a father and his daughter, he a ruthless and reflexively self-serving philanderer of the most unscrupulous sort, she a young woman who has learned his skills only too well.

An inescapably ingenious characteristic of "Winter of Artifice" is its subversive nature. The novella's complex seductions are impressive: while readers are participating in the mutual seduction of daughter and father, an ancient story, as Nin reminds us, the narrative depends heavily upon Nin's own seduction of the reader through the lullaby of richly imagistic and insistently rhythmic prose. As in all "poetic" prose, lyricism depends upon artful recurrences of words, inversions, and time-honored devices of assonance and alliteration. Because the novella is a ballet of words and because its music and movement are subtly interwoven, even a perceptive reader may be aware of its general musicality without understanding *how* (s)he is being lured or hypnotized by it. This unperceived influence is so subversive that readers are drawn into the incestuous romance subliminally. Many very likely do not even recognize the shocking and tabooed nature of the personal drama the novella weaves with its "musique ancienne." Its ensorcelling musical prose encapsulates a story that the reader may not choose to participate in, but (s)he does so nonetheless without conscious awareness of being engaged in a *participation mystique.*

"Winter of Artifice"[1] was begun in 1933 and finished in 1939 (besides the *Diary,* Nin was working on other manuscripts at the same time). A critical year in her life, 1933 brought "acted out" or perhaps imaginary incestuous relations with her father in the summer, a break with him in September (or so one speculates after reading *Incest*), and in November the start of psychotherapy with Otto Rank. (In the summer of 1934 Nin experienced the stillbirth that is recorded in the story "Birth" as well as in her diaries for the period.) This timing is significant both to Nin's life and to the projected persona of "Winter of Artifice." Eventually, the love-famished daughter exorcises her father from her life and, more important, from her psyche. Impelled by the momentum of liberty, she runs away from him and rushes forward to embrace her own life.

The sixty-four pages of the novella are structured in thirteen movements or short passages of varying lengths. These are set off from one another by a visual device of four asterisks.[2] As usual in Nin's fiction, there are no chronological guides. Not the passage of time but the sequence of events and the individualized patterns endow the characters and their involvement with meaning. The daughter's recollections and observations alternate with passages of dialogue in present time, so that the motion in time is both backward and forward. Except for a relatively long reflective section, which occurs after the rhapsodic crisis in the sixth part, the novella's segments grow briefer as the emotional entanglement tightens, as insights gather, and as the daughter eventually flees the finally nude and unmasked father. The heightening and acceleration of the rhythm intensify the excitement and exuberance that arise in the attentive reader with the gradually growing certainty of the young woman's approaching liberation.

The symphonic narrative begins in the middle of the "action." The anxiety-tormented yet exhilarated unnamed daughter is waiting for a visit from her father, who abandoned his wife and children twenty years earlier. This account describes the history of a disturbed and torn family and, naturally, raises the question why a rejected and emotionally abused child would want to be reunited with such an irresponsible and offensive man. Indeed, at their reunion, her nervousness is so intense that this usually poised woman "leaned backwards, pushing the crystal bowl against the wall. It cracked and the water gushed forth as from a fountain, splashing all over the floor. The glass ship could no longer sail away—it was lying on its side, on the rock-crystal stones.[3] . . . 'Perhaps I've arrived at my port at last,' she said. 'Perhaps I've come to the end of my wanderings. I have found you'" (69).

The second part of "Winter of Artifice" continues the traditional narrative in a flashback that chronicles the family's arrival and life in New York, sans Papa, and ends in the projected continuous present with the approaching footsteps of the father. The closing of part 2 circles back to the beginning: "Twenty years have passed. He is coming today" (60). Apprehensive yet yearning for reunion, the daughter easily falls prey to her father's accomplished seductiveness. He is, after all, an experienced, poised, and debonair Don Juan, a youthful and glamorous figure, an artist, and she has been deprived of a girl's normal relationship with him. Her concept of her father is grossly inflated; this is a traditional characteristic of the incest theme in myth and literature. Naturally, the more she has lionized her father, he becomes a more formidable object of conquest. To submit and to conquer cannot but wage war in her heart.

In the third section Nin introduces one of the novella's dominant images, one that, although not expressly musical, is related to musical performance: the mask. She identifies it as "Greek" (70). Astutely alluding to her father's incessant playacting, as in their soon-to-come pretense of being fiancés, she evokes our remembrance that performers in classical Greek drama, as in traditional Japanese Kabuki, wear stylized masks to impersonate the characters they are representing. It is important to observe the implications of the mask as a disguise in the portrayal of gender. In both classical Greek and Kabuki drama, men play the roles of women. Toward the end of "Winter of Artifice," the daughter perceives her father as incarnating significant but, in her opinion, negative "feminine" characteristics. This perception adds to her accumulating resentment at his "theft" of her foot. It is this resentment that in great part enables her to distinguish herself from him and to create a separate and independent identity.

Part 4 introduces a startling change of locale from Paris to the south of France. Here the duo tease themselves, inflaming their ardor by pretending to be fiancés. It is now clear that to the daughter her father represents an idealized lover, an all-powerful and therefore protective father, and finally—perhaps because of his artist stature—a hero, a god. Coincidentally or not, Otto Rank, Nin's therapist in 1933, had written a monograph on incest in myth and literature in which he argues that incest is the privilege of royalty.[4] Hence the daughter's need to transform her father into a hero, even a god. Sadly, however, to the father his daughter is just another woman to be seduced, conquered, and attached to him, submissive to his every need. Ominously, even though sensitive and penetrating readers now understand that it is the daughter who has summoned her father to their enticing and dangerous reunion, he refers to her as "my betrothed" (75). Thoroughly seduced by now, the daughter revises and discredits her own memories of neglect and abuse, masking her resentment with apologies and rationalizations to explain his crass, self-focused pretense at parenting. In love, she has now become her cruel father's advocate, at the same time mounting and maintaining a slight self-protective reserve. His insistence that she is an "Amazon" (80–81) arouses her distrust and gives birth to an intuition that, once again, she will be devastated by a truth she hoped to evade:

Protection was a rhythm. They could exchange roles. But this
phrase from a father was different . . . A father.

All through the world . . . looking for a father . . . looking naively
for a father . . . falling in love with gray hairs . . . the symbol . . .
every symbol of the father . . . all through the world . . . an
orphan . . . in need of man the leader . . . to be made woman . . . and
again to be asked . . . to be the mother . . . always the mother . . .
always to draw the strength she had, but never to know where to
rest, where to lay down her head and find new strength . . . always
to draw it out of herself . . . from herself . . . strength . . . to pour out
love . . . all through the world seeking a father . . . loving the
father . . . awaiting the father . . . and finding the child. (82)

The apotheosis of "Winter of Artifice" occurs in the sixth, central
section, which opens with the father temporarily paralyzed by
"lumbago," or rheumatism. The prosaic descriptive sentences soon
are replaced and overwhelmed by "the orchestration of love" (74),
a lengthy italicized passage of dense and intensely wrought musical images evoking the daughter's fantasy of a mystical marriage.
In her imagination a mosquito net is "hung like an ancient bridal
canopy" (88).

Sitting on her father's bed, presumably to comfort him in his illness, she creates a fantasy of union, or reunion, cast in hypnotic
seductive prose: "Between each two of these phrases there was a
long silence. A great simplicity of tone. They looked at each other
as if they were listening to music, not as if he were saying words.
Inside both their heads, as they sat there, he leaning against a pil-
low and she against the foot of the bed, there was a concert going
on. Two boxes filled with the resonances of an orchestra. A hundred instruments playing all at once" (84).

After the introductory sentences, lyrical phrases describe the
"concert" for more than four pages of artfully sustained poetic
prose. Some of the images are extremely daring: a violin bow is
described as an instrument of self-pleasure, causing the gratified
woman to "foam" (85). There are occasional surreal images: "the
carpet of notes mourn with voices of black lace and dice on tele-
graph wires" (85). There are suggestive references to "boxes" (Nin
must have known the sexual connotation of this word in English):
"piano box" and "the boxes of their heads" (85–86). References to
wood and ivory are also frequent, though by this time readers do
not need to be reminded that the father is a pianist: "They danced
because they were sad, they danced all through their life, and the
golden top dancing inside them made the notes turn, the white
and the black, the words they wanted to hear, the new faces of the

world turning black and white, ascending and descending, up and down askew stairways from the bellies of the cello full of salted tears, the water rising slowly, a sea of forgetfulness" (86).

Among the most alluring passages in this virtuoso performance is this one:

> Yesterday ringing through the bells and castanets, and today a single note all alone, like their fear of solitude, quarreling, the orchestra taking their whole being together and lifting them clear out of the earth where pain is a long, smooth song that does not cut through the flesh, where love is one long smooth note like the wind at night, no blood-shedding knife to its touch of music from distance far beyond the orchestra which answered the harp, the flute, the cello, the violins, the echoes on the roof, the taste on the roof of their palates, music in the tongue, in the fingers when the fingers seek the flesh, the red pistil of desire in the fingers on the violin cords, their cries rising and falling, borne on the wings of the orchestra, hurt and wounded by its knowledge of her, for thus they cried and thus they laughed, like the bells and the castanets, thus they rolled from black to white stairways, and dreaming spirals of desire. (86–87)

Turning yet another variation on the musical theme, the text now depends on the five lines of the musical staff: thoughts; reveries; emotions; the unknown self; the giant self (their combined shadow, monstrous because unbalanced and unnatural). This extended metaphor closes with the capitalized leitmotiv of the novella: MUSIQUE ANCIENNE (88). Finally, the ecstatic yet despairing coda of this section concludes with a sexually provocative question whose answer has no doubt been predicted by sensitive readers: *"Can we live in rhythm, my father? Can we feel in rhythm, my father? Can we think in rhythm, my father? Rhythm—rhythm—rhythm"* (88).

From this peak, the work subsides into a slower pace and a more melancholy tone that expresses unavoidable loss. The long, complex formal dance that has brought the daughter and her father together, sometimes moving in tandem, sometimes separately, but always tentatively circling, attracted but wary, now moves definitely toward the daughter's exit.

After her crisis of fantasized union, the daughter attempts a solo performance. To portray this Nin uses a series of interconnected metaphors and one critical incident involving dance. In the seventh movement, the two are again in Paris. The daughter remembers that she gave a performance when she was sixteen at which, so she imagined, her neglectful father was present. In her fantasy he is proud, approving, and admiring. When she questions him about this, he insists that he was not there. "He answered that not only was he not there but that if he had had the power he would have prevented her from dancing because he did not want his daughter on the stage" (99). He is a rigid, old-fashioned snob. He wants his daughter to be a "lady." He continues to struggle to imprison her with senseless restrictions representing the outdated etiquette of his own youth.

Not surprisingly, after such ecstasy comes reflection, then panic. The daughter walks "away from his room, . . . her shadow on the carpets" (88). When she opens the door to her own room, the violent wind breaks a window, recalling her breaking of the crystal bowl with a glass ship in it soon after her father's arrival for their reunion (69). In both instances of glass breakage the daughter is attempting to move away or to back off from her father, unconsciously attempting to reject a narcissistic reflection of identification with him that is extremely threatening. Her intuition, expressed in spontaneous physical responses to danger, is more accurate, more self-protective than her earlier emotional impulse to find in this father "Her true God. . . . At communion it was her father she received, and not God. She closed her eyes and swallowed the white bread with blissful tremors. She embraced her father in holy communion. Her exaltation fused into a semblance of holiness. She aspired to saintliness in order to conceal the secret love which she guarded so jealously in her diary. The voluptuous tears at night when she prayed to God, the joy without name when she stood in his presence, the inexplicable bliss at communion, because then she talked with her father and she kissed him" (65).[5] It is not surprising, considering the ecstasy of this "secret love," that as she begins to examine the attachment more critically, she tries to run away from it. At last she understands that it was an "inhuman love" (90).

The daughter's conflict is very clear. On the one hand, she wants truth between herself and her father (because she feels compelled to lie to her other loves); on the other hand, she wants to hurt him, as he has hurt her, by deceiving him: "there were moments when she experienced dark, strange pleasure at the thought of deceiving him. She knew how deceptive he was. She felt deep down that he was incapable of truth, that sooner or later he would lie to her, fail her. And she wanted to deceive him first, in a deeper way. It gave her joy to be so far ahead of her father who was almost a professional deceiver" (89).

In the seventh part of "Winter of Artifice" the daughter's conflict is richly embroidered. "I need absolution!" she exclaims (88).[6]

After asserting that she is "the mystical bride of her father" (89), she rapidly gathers insights that profoundly alter her idealization of him. Abandoning her need for a father "god," which she now realizes represents serious confusion, she totally ravishes his meticulously constructed and painted mask of himself: "This constant yearning for the man behind the mask, this disregard of the mask, was also a disregard of the harm which the wearing of a mask inevitably produced. It was difficult for her to believe, as others did, that the mask tainted the blood, that the colors of the mask could run into the colors of nature and poison it" (97–98).

The daughter's rapidly accelerating psychological dash for independence and liberty continues in the eighth part. Flashbacks highlight, and predictably exaggerate, his unrelenting critical attitudes toward her. As always, music becomes her deliverer, her sanctuary and solace. And yet to embrace the salvation of music she is obliged symbolically to dissociate her ever-rigid father from its luminous joys: "Her father was the musician, but in life he arrested music. Music melts all the separate parts of our bodies together" (99).

Part 9 commands a unique and absorbing position, an emotional torment emanating from the alternating axes of yearning and despair. It is an invocation, a prayer to the father she has long struggled to transform into a god. Extending and expanding the fused themes of music and silence, the daughter pleads: "*Father, let me walk alone into the music of my faith. When I am with you the world is still and silent*" (100). And yet it is movement, specifically flight, that captivates her. And again she is compelled to castigate her father, the consummate musician, in musical metaphors: "*You held the conductor's baton, but no music could come from the orchestra because of your severity. As soon as you left my heart beat in great disorder. Everything melted into music, and I could dance through the streets singing, without an orchestra leader. I could dance and sing*" (100). No real music could come from the father because of his narcissistic rigidity, his basic fear of life which has caused him to freeze himself into an icon. It is naturalness the daughter treasures, above all, a music that is spontaneous, unpredictable, free-flowing. Her exuberance expresses her fiercely earned freedom from obsession, her new sense of autonomy.

The increasingly acute self-awareness of the daughter both deepens significantly and expands in the tenth section of "Winter of Artifice." One of the most tender moments in all of Nin's fiction occurs here: the daughter is led toward forgiveness of her selfish

father by a memory of her mother singing Schumann's "J'ai pardonné." The young woman reflects: "Strange how her mother,
who had never forgiven her father, could sing that song more
movingly than anything else she sang" (100). The daughter
becomes a medium for feeling; her unconscious wish presents a
memory as spiritual instruction. Walking toward her father's
house, she herself begins to sing "J'ai pardonné." This act of forgiveness is necessary not only for the father, whose weaknesses
invite redemption, but even more urgently for the daughter, who
needs to be freed from guilt in order to pursue her own growth.

The daughter has, perhaps temporarily, integrated a prominent
aspect of *his* behavior toward her when she was a child, his consistent negative critical stance, and she is in the process of turning
her own coldly analytical criticisms against him. Now it is the
father who urges that they "look for light and clarity" (84), while
she wants to "disentangle their two selves" (92): "There is no distance for her to traverse; it chokes inside of her, like the coils of
self-love, and she cannot feel any love for this sore foot because
that love leaps back into her like a perpetually coiled snake, and
she wants always to leap outside of herself. She wants to flow
out. . . . To leap out freely beyond the self, love must flow out and
beyond this wall of confused identities. Now she is all confused in
her boundaries. She doesn't know where her father begins, where
she begins, where it is he ends, what is the difference between
them" (92).

Knowing what she must do to separate from him, to "kill" him
symbolically, the daughter does not know *how* to do this except by
using the destructive psychological strategies she has learned from
him. Intelligent, analytical, and necessarily cold and aloof, she now
engages in a harshly negative analysis of her father's life and personal habits. The rejection of his narcissism and faithlessness are
effective in transforming her formerly grandiose heroic images of
him not, simply as the Count of Monte Cristo (66) or a "Spanish
grandee" (76) but even as God, into a helpless and hysterical
"trapped bird" (113). Seeing a bird inadvertently kill itself after flying into an enclosed space is an experience of terror that is not easily forgotten.[7] For the narrator's father, death is the ultimate terror.
And as the daughter observes, her father's incessant efforts to wage
war against aging and death, his energetic attempts to deny, to
postpone, and even to evade death are themselves aspects of his
living death: "everything about him was fluttering like a bird that
had flown into a room by mistake, flying recklessly and blindly in

utter terror. . . . And he was bruising himself against walls and furniture while she stood there mute and compassionate. His terror so great that he did not sense her pity, and when she moved to open the window to allow him to escape he interpreted the gesture as a menace. To run away from his own terror he flew wildly against the window and crushed his feathers. *Don't flutter so blindly, my father!"* (113)

When she is able to recognize her father's patterns of flight as evasion and escape and to "own" this as her truth, she discovers a different kind of motion in flight: running toward a positive aspiration. When she notes how "feminine-looking" her father's foot is, she imagines that he has stolen her foot. And now she understands that, whether consciously or not, he wants to appropriate her mobility for himself. But he suffers from a crippling condition, lumbago. Realizing that she is "tired of his ballet dancing" (113)—strictly choreographed, predictable movements—the daughter reclaims her image of her foot and with it her ability to escape: "As soon as she left her father she heard music again. It was falling from the trees, pouring from throats, twinkling from the street lamps, sliding down the gutter. It was her faith in the world which danced again. It was the expectation of miracles which made every misery sound like part of a symphony. Not separateness but oneness was music" (99).

A hazardous gambit for the reader as well as the daughter protagonist, "Winter of Artifice" poses risks, tempting with the lure of incest, the MUSIQUE ANCIENNE, yet liberating with the art that is the golden face of artifice. At the end of the novella, adventurous readers will have been seduced and enthralled like bevies of sleeping beauties by Nin's intensely felt and magnetically crafted poetry: *"Music runs and I run with it. Faith makes music come out of the trees, out of wood, out of ivory"* (100).

NOTES

1. Nin's earlier titles for "Winter of Artifice" include "The Double," "Father Story," and "Lilith."

2. Part 1 contains twelve pages; 2, seven; 3, eight; 4, four; 5, three; 6, six; 7, ten; 8, one; 9, one-half; 10, five; 11, five; 12, one; 13, six.

3. The breaking of the bowl containing the glass ship is especially rich with associations when one recalls that Rosa Culmell-Nin's removal of herself and her children to the United States from Barcelona (and Joaquín Nin) was accomplished by a sea voyage. Most persons who have followed Nin's writings have seen the often reprinted photo of the family, Anaïs holding the basket that contained her diary.

4. Interested readers may wish to pursue Rank's *Das Inzest-Motiv in Dichtung und Sage*, Lieberman's "Anaïs Nin," and Spencer's "The Ambiguities of Incest in Lawrence Durrell's Heraldic Universe: A Rankian Interpretation" and "The Enduring Love of Anaïs Nin for Otto Rank."

5. Suzette Henke also discusses Anaïs's father worship, noting that she "apotheosized the figure of the absent parent, transforming him into an imaginary God of judgment and devotion" (122).

6. "Absolution," a highly charged concept for Nin, may have meant different things at different periods of her life. It may be that in "Winter of Artifice" the guilt generated by the daughter's "illicit" love of her father gives rise, just before she proclaims herself "the mystical bride of her father," to her outcry *I need absolution!* Nin herself referred to Otto Rank as the magical person who could "absolve" her. And yet there is no evidence that she even confided to Rank her alleged incestuous relations with her father. Reading *Incest: From "A Journal of Love,"* I conclude that Nin's intimacy with her father occurred in August of 1933 and ended in September of the same year. In November she began psychotherapy with Rank.

7. As a child of about ten or eleven I was alone at home when a bird accidentally flew into the dining room. Overwhelmed by panic, the bird wildly crashed into the walls and the woodwork, killing itself. A similar incident is powerfully recounted in Ben Okri's highly acclaimed novel *The Famished Road*. That Nin envisions her father in this utterly helpless and inadvertently suicidal frenzy conveys both her pity and, in a more subdued way, her contempt.

WORKS CITED

Henke, Suzette. "Anaïs Nin's *Journal of Love:* Father-Loss and Incestuous Desire." *Anaïs Nin: Literary Perspectives.* Ed. Suzanne Nalbantian, 120–35. New York: St. Martin's Press, 1997.

Lieberman, E. James. "Anaïs Nin." *Acts of Will: The Life and Work of Otto Rank,* 327–53. New York: Macmillan, 1985.

Nin, Anaïs. *The Diary of Anaïs Nin* (1931–74). Ed. Gunther Stuhlmann. 7 vols. San Diego: Harcourt Brace Jovanovich, 1966–80.

———. *Incest: From "A Journal of Love": The Unexpurgated Diary of Anaïs Nin, 1932–1934.* New York: Harcourt Brace Jovanovich, 1992.

———. *Linotte: The Early Diary of Anaïs Nin, 1914–1920.* Trans. Jean L. Sherman. New York: Harcourt Brace Jovanovich, 1978.

———. "Proceed from the Dream." *A Woman Speaks: The Lectures, Seminars, and Interviews of Anaïs Nin,* 115–47. Ed. Evelyn J. Hinz. Chicago: Swallow Press, 1975.

———. "Winter of Artifice." 1939. *Winter of Artifice: Three Novelettes.* Chicago: Swallow Press, 1961.

Rank, Otto. *Das Inzest-Motiv in Dichtung und Sage.* Leipzig: Deuticke, 1912. 2d ed., 1926, rpt. Darmstadt: Wissenschaftliche Buchgesellschaft,

1974. Ms. of 3d German edition in the Rank Collection, Columbia University Library.

Schopenhauer, Arthur. *The World as Will and Idea.* Trans. R. B. Haldane and J. Kemp. 1883. Garden City, N.Y.: Doubleday, 1961.

Spencer, Sharon. "The Ambiguities of Incest in Lawrence Durrell's Heraldic Universe: A Rankian Interpretation." *Twentieth Century Literature* 33, no. 4 (1987): 436–48.

———. "Beyond Therapy: The Enduring Love of Anaïs Nin for Otto Rank." *Anaïs Nin: Literary Perspectives.* Ed. Suzanne Nalbantian, 97–111. New York: St. Martin's Press, 1997.

CHAPTER 7

Trying to Tell Her Story

Mothering Scripts and the Counternarrative in Nin's Diary and Cities of the Interior

Anne T. Salvatore

With your milk, Mother, I swallowed ice. And here I am now, my insides frozen. And I walk with even more difficulty than you do, and I move even less. You flowed into me, and that hot liquid became poison, paralyzing me. My blood no longer circulates to my feet or my hands, or as far as my head. It is immobilized, thickened by the cold. Obstructed by icy chunks which resist its flow. My blood coagulates, remains in and near my heart.

Luce Irigaray, "And the One Doesn't Stir Without the Other"

Luce Irigaray's metaphorical description of many women's emotional paralysis, rendered in striking body images, suggests the torturous relationship between traditional maternal behavior and these women's efforts to reach freedom and individual subjectivity. Behind the stunning images lie a patriarchal society's dictates for women's lives, or what psychoanalysts Omer and Strenger refer to as the "scripts" of our personal narratives. They explain: "Scripts are blueprints for life situations, which tell us what to expect and how to respond in them. Scripts are usually tacit knowledge, learned through repetition. . . . They are the daily organizers of routine interactions, as the self-narrative is the lifelong organizer of events" (254). By its very nature unchanging and mechanical, a script entices its user with the seeming comfort of a stable paradigm that can provide a safe refuge from a confusing, chaotic life situation in which frightening choices abound. In Anaïs Nin's published self-narratives (her diaries), the "script" she envisions for mothers as well as for daughters-in-training-for-motherhood limits them to what many feminists now view as "traditional" concepts of maternity.[1] Reacting first to the "good mother" and later to the "bad mother" paradigms, a troubled diary voice uses narrative to struggle with continuing tensions that arise between society's script and her own feelings and desires.

Nin's fiction often highlights similar conflicts in the obsessions of certain characters. Unlike the conflicted diary voice and the fictional characters' voices, however, the voice of the more self-assured, omniscient narrator in the novels offers a far different, more liberating perspective. These psychologically astute narrative voices subvert the dominant culture through a counternarrative commentary designed to question the values of a system that, as Irigaray suggests ("And the One Doesn't Stir" 60), imprisons mothers in a paralyzing, often deadening script. Designed to shatter readers' complacency, Nin's pioneering fictional narrators contribute new tonal qualities to the novels; moreover, they destabilize the static vision of traditional maternity inherent in the characters' performances, and offer readers the opportunity for curing paralysis through a self-consciousness that permits dynamic change in the self-narrative. With this emphasis on psychological understanding, Nin also underscores what she sees as the value of the psychoanalytic process and its potential for effecting a healthy movement in women's fiction as well as in their lives. Equally important, Nin's use of this technique serves to centralize in the plot maternal figures who, as Marianne Hirsch notes in a general observation about such figures, are generally "submerged in traditional plot structures" (3). "Mothers," Hirsch states, are "the ones who are not singular, who did succumb to convention inasmuch as they are mothers" (11). Nin's focus on the internal emotional dilemmas of these mother figures undermines a traditional emphasis on the external adventures of many male heroes in conventional novels.

Scripts in the Diaries

A scripted pattern is often handed down from previous generations. Not surprisingly, we find references in the *Diary* to Nin's mother, Rosa, who "had mothered all her three brothers and three

Anaïs Nin with the original diary volumes in a vault in Brooklyn, New York, 1966.

sisters when her mother ran away" (1:104). Images emerging from
the childhood diary show a pattern of idealization of Rosa as the
"good mother" that psychologists and sociologists have defined as
the one who accepts suffering as a joy of motherhood, is devoted
to her children, finds pleasure in this devotion, sacrifices to
achieve it, and is continually present to her child (Badinter
273–76, 285).[2] Nin's eleven-year-old persona rhapsodizes: "she is
devoted to us, more than any other mother in the world. Maman
has a heart of gold, the kindness of her glance says so. . . . My dear
Maman does everything to give us pleasure, all her sacrifices are
for us, she works only to assure the future for all of us. When I was
sick, she was at my bedside day and night. Anything she could do
to please me, she did, with never a second to herself" (*Linotte* 10).
In the *Diary*, even though by now the adult Nin begins to recognize
some of the self-serving motives and negative effects of her
mother's attempt to accumulate a "sense of debt" in her children,
the persona still reinforces a vision of Mother as "florid, natural,
warm . . . sexless . . . heroic, battling for her children, working, sacrificing" (1:243). While appearing to be morally commendable,
strong, and courageous, such mothers, as Nancy Chodorow points
out, are actually powerless under a patriarchal system (*Feminism*
83)—one that relegates them to one sphere of living and denies
them both their sexuality and the humanness of a less-than-
perfect being.

As Rosa's daughter-in-training, the "Nin" character in the childhood diary becomes a "substitute mother" (*Linotte* 61) whose
domestic tasks must precede, if not preclude, her other interests
(212, 297). When at times she ever so briefly allows those other
interests—reading, writing—to intervene, the result is a deeply felt
guilt that generally impels her to complete a task she loathes, like
darning socks (466). She reveals later that at this early age she
"was the perfect daughter": "I submerged my personality into the
personality of my mother. She chose my dresses, and kept me at
home when other young women were out working. I was lost in
my submission to her" (*Diary* 5:184). The child/persona thus
retreats from the frightening conflict between society's mothering
script and her own feelings. While the good daughter feels
momentarily safe—that is, still loved—the conflict is not resolved.

As the inherited script forces its presence into the earlier adult
diaries, the persona broadens the maternal response to include
nearly everyone she knows. Building on material from the *Diary*,
biographer Noël Riley Fitch gives examples of Nin's vicarious

mothering: "Dudley (the young painter and teller of tall tales) expects her to find an apartment for him, Duncan asks for money, Gonzalo needs rent or a hearing aid for Helba. With her first hundred dollars from the pornography 'collector' she pays Gonzalo's dentist and buys a mirror for Helba's dancing" (238). In addition, the diaries often record her "mothering" of Henry Miller, Antonin Artaud, Edmund Wilson—indeed most of her friends—even when they are able to stand on their own.

The persona's behavioral adherence to the traditional mothering script was never total, of course, as the conflicted-child image described above demonstrates. But perhaps the most compelling episode signaling the unresolved struggle in the narrative between her feelings and the script is the "stillbirth" of the persona's own daughter—an event that the later publication of *Incest* has revealed as a late-term abortion (382). As she lies on the operating table, suffering horribly, yet unable to deliver the dead child, she articulates the terrible conflict: "All of me which chose to keep, to lull, to embrace, to love, all of me which carried, preserved, and protected, all of me which imprisoned the whole world in its passionate tenderness, this part of me would not thrust the child out" (377). After the delivery, though, she calls the abortion "the abdication of one kind of motherhood for the sake of a higher one . . . the sacrifice to other forms of creation" (382).

Repeatedly the persona finds herself torn, as well she might in a social atmosphere that idealized mothers. Ann Dally notes: "The thirty years following World War II, and in America the thirty years before that, could be described as the age of idealization of motherhood. One way in which this is shown is in the extent to which our society emphasizes the importance of the family, of mother love, mother-infant attachment and constant mother care, while at the same time making life increasingly difficult for mothers"(92).[3] Such idealization, Dally continues, represses the mixed emotions women may experience, such as feelings of both love and hate (93); the idealization becomes "a defense against the consequences of recognizing ambivalence and purchases freedom from guilt and depression at the cost of loss of self-esteem" (94). The difficult, static social paradigm with which Nin's persona contends, then, may be one important cause of her internal war. And the result of her battle, she finds, is total mental and physical exhaustion: "I don't know what day I felt: *No puedo más* (I can't bear any more). But it came with such violence that I broke down. First came an extreme weakness, so extreme I could not climb the

stairs to my home. I had to take them like mountain climbing, rest-
ing between each step. Then came the weeping. Uncontrollable
weeping. It seemed to me that I was broken for good, physically
and spiritually" (*Diary* 3:239). This traumatic episode seems to
function as a turning point: the repetitive, compulsive qualities of
the script are brought to the persona's attention by her analyst, Dr.
Martha Jaeger, who offers a sympathetic counternarrative to Nin's
story: "Woman communicates with the cosmos, the cosmic,
through the earth, through her maternal self. So you became the
all-mother, giving out endlessly. You attempted to take care of
everyone. You attempted the infinite with a finite human body"
(*Diary* 3:240).

   In the diaries that follow, the persona's obsession shifts more
decidedly to the opposite extreme. That is, she transforms the good
mother into its fairy-tale opposite—the bad mother, or one who,
whatever her conscious intentions and behavior, ultimately
wreaks quite negative effects on her child by dominating the child's
life, effacing its self-image, and preventing its full development
into a mature, independent ego. Chodorow describes in general
such a "bad mother" image and its adverse effect: it is the conception of an "all-powerful mother who, because she is totally responsible for how her children turn out, is blamed for everything from
her daughter's limitations to the crisis of human existence" (*Feminism* 80).[4] Thus, Rosa, previously revered as the strong, heroic, natural earth-mother, now is portrayed as the "overpowering" mother
with "an indomitable will" (*Diary* 4:129), a woman who, when she
was alive, the persona asserts, "closed the door on me the day I
sought an independent life from her" (5:177); she "threatened my
aspiration to escape the servitudes of women" (5:182). Contending
that a mother's power continues even beyond the grave, the Nin
persona records—between anxiety attacks—the difficulties she
experiences while trying to write *Solar Barque;* she claims that she
has been "reliving the death of [her] mother and even obeying her
in not being able to write" (6:47). Despite this metaknowledge of
her own life narrative, Nin's diary voice maintains that ultimately
she "lost the battle" against her mother's influence: "I am a woman
who takes care of others on the same level my mother did"
(5:199). She finds herself reverting to her role in the earlier script
as "substitute mother," taking her brother Joaquín's pain upon
herself (5:181), even washing and ironing his shirts (5:183); in
short, "becoming my mother" after her death (5:183).

In the *Diary,* then, the good mother eventually becomes a bad mother in the persona's eyes. Yet the Nin character as daughter is perhaps so involved with her personal struggle that she does not see beyond the plight of her mother, who is herself caught in the same paralyzing script. Nor can the daughter reason with psychoanalytic principles that what appears to be her mother's monstrous ego results from Rosa's defensive seeking for the very selfhood that her daughter desires. Moreover, by envisioning a falsely dichotomous relationship between good and bad mothering, and by placing responsibility for her ambivalent "regression" upon her mother's posthumous influence, Nin's persona in the *Diary* ironically reinforces the patriarchal status quo that she appears to be struggling against. Chodorow notes that not only do such assumptions about women's—or specifically mothers'—power cause in men a fear of women; these attitudes also reinforce "the division of the social world into unequally valued domestic and public spheres, each the province of people of a different gender" (*Reproduction* 219). While the *Diary* does present a female protagonist aspiring to the predominantly male public world of art and sex, she can enter that world only by accepting it in its existing state. It is, as Ehrenreich and English point out, a public sphere "as men have defined it" (19); further, when Nin's persona enters this world, she continues, even after her breakdown, to act as the good mother toward her adult and usually male children, providing for them a refuge from the "savage scramble of the Market" (21) where too often they fail. Perceiving women as their refuge, they force the persona once again into what Ehrenreich and English term the "fatal moral compromise of sexual romanticism": rather than use their own creativity to "remake the world," these men demand instead "that women make up for it" (283). Thus, not only does the good-mother script persist in the *Diary* in spite of the bad-mother label now envisioned by the persona, but the entire social context remains a static entity, confirming once more the existing—limiting—social paradigms for women.

Significantly, though, the *Diary* does reveal some psychological and social progress in the persona's life story: by exploring first her ideal of good motherhood and then her disillusionment with its more subtle implications, Nin's persona exposes society's vision of both the good and the bad mother as social-psychological constructs disguising a multiplicity of negative effects, and she does so at a time when few people, even psychoanalysts, fully appreciated or dealt with the overwhelming nature of those effects. Further, the *Diary* persona dramatizes the struggles many women experience in attempting to articulate their life narratives in ways that validate the full range of their emotional background.

Narrative Techniques: Psychoanalysis and Folk Culture

The telling and retelling of life stories is an essential technique in the psychoanalytic process. Roy Schafer, professor of clinical psychology and psychiatry at Cornell University Medical College, explains how the voices of the analyst and the patient are juxtaposed during these two narrative processes: "People going through psychoanalysis—analysands—tell the analyst about themselves and others in the past and present. In making interpretations, the analyst retells these stories. In the retelling, certain features are accentuated while others are placed in parentheses; certain features are related to others in new ways or for the first time; some features are developed further, perhaps at great length. This retelling is done along psychoanalytic lines" (31).

A similar type of interpretive juxtaposing can be used as a literary/artistic technique; in fact, it has appeared as an important "strategy of coding" in women's folk culture, as Joan Radner and Susan Lanser have pointed out: "Because interpretation is a contextual activity, the ironic arrangement of texts, artifacts, or performances can constitute a powerful strategy for coding. An item that in one environment seems unremarkable or unambiguous may develop quite tendentious levels of meaning in another. . . . In written literature, juxtaposition may be effected through titles, epigraphs, the placement of stanzas, voices, or paragraphs" (13–14).

Through this technique of ironic juxtaposition, Nin's fiction often creates a modified replication of the psychoanalytic process in the following ways:

(1) the "maternal" characters (who are not always biological mothers) become in effect analysands who follow obsessively their scripted patterns in the novels;

(2) imprisoned in these static behavioral patterns, the characters are generally unable to tell their repressed stories;

(3) a partially omniscient narrator or sometimes another character becomes in effect the "analyst" who retells the characters' performed narrative interpretively, constructing a counternarrative "along psychoanalytic lines";

(4) in the text, the voice of this "analyst" is continually juxtaposed with the characters' inner voices (reported
thoughts), outer voices (dialogue), and compulsive behaviors ("performances")[5] as the characters' past and present
are reinterpreted;

(5) readers become privileged voyeurs to this unfolding and
mesmerizing psychoanalytic process which, by suggesting
chilling parallels with our own scripted "stories," may arouse
our deepest emotions in reaction to the text, and may prompt
our own interpretive counternarratives.

This narrative/psychoanalytical technique seems appropriate both
to Nin's immediate purposes and to her long-term goals in writing
fiction. In *The Novel of the Future* she asserts that she sought in her
novels "to have passionate experience and interpretation in a
dynamic relationship" (175). Through this blending of narrative
and counternarrative, Nin hopes to achieve her ultimate mission
for the novelist: that is, not just "to depict man as he is but also as
he might be. [The novelist] is there to give an example of the freedom of choice, freedom to transcend his destiny and his surroundings, master his limitations and restrictions" (174); the novelist
"point[s] the way to all the *potentialities* of life" (169). By sensing
the irony in the juxtaposed stories, the observing reader is encouraged to move beyond mere voyeurism; Nin's method invites us "to
participate" (168)—to become engaged emotionally—both in the
paralysis of these mother figures who follow a scripted pattern and
in the potentially saving knowledge that the pattern exists, that it
can be understood, that it can be mastered. Another important
function of this technique is to highlight the importance of the
psychoanalytic method itself—a process that Nin not only had
undergone herself as a patient but also had practiced as a lay analyst with Otto Rank.

To replicate portions of the psychoanalytic process is not necessarily to substitute a case study for a novel, however. In September
1945 Nin strongly objected to such an accusation from Diana
Trilling who, says Nin, "assumed because I had studied psychology
I was writing case histories" instead of novels (*Diary* 4:82). The alle-
gation resurfaced about two decades later when Daisy Aldan,
responding to Nin's draft of *Collages,* replied: "This is psychology and
analysis, not literature" (Fitch 365). Granted, similarities can be
noted between the guiding voices in certain case histories and Nin's
third-person, partially omniscient narrators. The general goal is the

same: helping someone to build a viable self through developing insights into the past and present. In both situations, the reader becomes aware of a variety of "symptoms" displayed by the "characters"; in both, some sort of "diagnostic" commentary appears either along with the narration of the symptoms or afterward.

But the differences between the voice of the professional analyst and the voices of Nin's analyst/narrators are substantial and, I think, important to the establishment of Anaïs Nin as a mainstream writer who, among her many achievements, brings to fiction a deep respect for psychological methods, but adapts them creatively for her own use. One difference is that many analysts use the first person, not the third, in their case studies. More significant, as they retell their patients' stories, they generally infuse them with a clinical jargon; they may employ professional conventions of discourse such as alluding to parallel cases and professional colleagues, discussing methods or questions used, and/or referring to abstract psychological theories. In his famous case "The Woman Who Felt Persecuted" (1915), Sigmund Freud refers to the subject's "paranoid delusion" (35) and her "psychical inertia" and "fixation" (37); he alludes to Otto Rank and Carl Jung (34, 36); he describes theoretically the progression of the illness, and mentions the difficulties involved in methods used (36). A later example with similar discourse properties is "The Angry Adolescent" (1942), which Carl Rogers narrates. Here the analyst details the psychoanalytic process itself: "There was further conversation along this same line" (213); discusses the theoretical context for the case (211); and records many of the counselor's actual questions and comments during the interviews (211–15). In these and similar cases, the voice used at least purports to be objective, distant, and scholarly.

In contrast, Nin's fictional narrators seem natural and intuitive rather than formally professional. Though the voices often diagnose a character's psychological problems, the narrators do so contextually, not categorically,[6] and the voices speak entirely in lay terms without professional jargon. In keeping with Nin's purpose for the novel, the voices try to "rectify failures" by pointing out the maternal characters' misapprehensions; the narrators may realign relationship boundaries; they may revise the characters' sense of the past. Unlike the voices in the professional case study, who generally address a specialized reader with the primary intent of informing theoretically, Nin's fictional narrators address the lay reader with the paramount goal of helping him or her to question society's maternal script.

Besides these differences from psychological case studies, the voices of Nin's fictional narrators also demonstrate innovative qualities that distinguish them from the voices of more traditional omniscient narrators. For instance, Henry Fielding's godlike narrator in the eighteenth-century novel *Tom Jones* not only possesses a nearly total omniscience but also wields power by deliberately withholding information from readers; moreover, Fielding's narrator generalizes extensively on moral, religious, political, and literary topics. Another traditional example is Nathaniel Hawthorne's *The Scarlet Letter*, written in the nineteenth century and featuring a narrator with the ability to fathom a character's deepest motives, to judge the validity of a character's conclusions, and to proselytize abstractly on the basis of a character's actions. While Nin's fictional narrative voices carry authority, they are neither authoritarian nor didactic nor bombastic.[7] Rarely are they abstract or godlike; they have no magic answers. Rather, the voices are simple yet eloquent, poetic, concrete, contextual; they tend to be problem-posing, not problem-solving. Unlike more formal and intellectualizing traditional narrative voices, Nin's narrators use fragments, diction laden with emotional overtones, colorful images, long series of nouns or phrases, and explosive verbs to awaken readers to the immobilizing, self-destroying, patriarchal script of traditional motherhood that Irigaray later described (60), which effectively denies to women the possibility of defining their own subjectivity.

Responses to the Scripts: Juxtaposed Voices in *Cities of the Interior*

In *Fictions of Authority: Women Writers and Narrative Voice*, Susan Sniader Lanser distinguishes between "voice" as a narratological term, referring to "specific forms of textual practice," and "voice" as feminist ideology (5). In investigating the narrators' voices in *Cities* and their relation to the voices or behaviors of the characters, I mean to exploit both of these aspects of voice in order to deal with the following issues: In what sense does the counternarrative by one or more juxtaposed voices retell the character's story? What power issues does each character's voice (or lack of voice) raise for the women in Nin's fiction who function as biological or psychological "mothers," or as outsiders to, yet compulsive onlookers at, the motherhood script? I hope to demonstrate that the "analyst's" voice, spoken by the partially omniscient narrator or another character (or both), becomes what Lanser calls a "site of crisis, contradiction, or challenge" (7) for all three of the major women characters in *Cities*. Set in ironic juxtaposition to the characters' scripted maternal roles, this omniscient analyst's voice suggests a new perspective, one that will enable women readers to break their often self-imposed silences through an understanding of past and present events that relate to their scripted roles.

Cities of the Interior is Nin's collection of five "continuous" novels: *Ladders to Fire, Children of the Albatross, The Four-Chambered Heart, A Spy in the House of Love,* and *Seduction of the Minotaur.* Although each can be read and appreciated separately, the collection becomes significantly more powerful when considered as a whole. Sharon Spencer has described the "organic structure" of the novels, noting that the protagonists "appear and reappear" as each acts variously as the protagonist ("The Music of the Womb" 166). But it is only through these reappearances in several of the novels that the entire psychological "story" of each character unfolds and can be understood. Moreover, while an "analyst" voice of some sort offers continual commentary through every novel, by the last novel, *Seduction,* this analyzing voice tends more and more to merge philosophically with the maternal character's inner voice; at least one woman, Lillian, begins to view her struggle with motherhood from a different perspective as she works toward discovering selfhood.

Of the three major characters in *Cities*—Lillian, Djuna, and Sabina—only Lillian is a biological mother, who at first blindly accepts the good-mother role and later rebels against it; Djuna has no actual children, but she lives out the maternal experience by playing an even more exaggerated good mother to adult "children"; Sabina appears to reject motherhood entirely, electing instead the dual role of child-wife and seductive adulteress, yet feels overwhelmed with guilt when she doesn't practice mothering rites. Lillian's story, featured in the first novel, *Ladders to Fire,* and again in the last novel, *Seduction of the Minotaur,* forms in the end a natural, womblike enclosure for the stories of the other, less successful characters. All three characters, actual mothers or not, struggle with the motherhood script. In their often blind and futile attempts to rise above the script, all suffer intense frustrations, all find that their ladders "lead to fire."

Sabina

When we first meet her, Sabina seems to have refused the traditional maternal pattern, or at least she has not had any actual children. In her brief appearance in *Children of the Albatross,* she is presented as one who sees herself as "always breaking the molds which life formed around her" (201). Yet the narrator/analyst's voice soon undermines Sabina's assumption by noting her ignorance of her own story: "She herself did not know what she was preserving from detection, what mystery she was defending" (201). Indeed, this brief introduction to her conflicted behavior in *Children* suggests that she, like the other characters in this novel, is burdened with the albatross of society's script for women—and for men too, in this case, since they often appear in these stories as victims of incompetent mothering. Sabina's appearance in this novel also helps to prepare readers for a more detailed rendering of her conflict in *A Spy in the House of Love*, where she is the featured character.

In *Spy*, Sabina is married to a fatherly man, Alan, who apparently does not know, or at least does not wish to know, that his child-wife continually deceives him by pretending to have a career as an actress when in reality she is conducting a series of affairs with men whom she seduces. Unlike the traditional mother figure, Sabina appears to be neither sexless nor selfless. Rather, men notice her "inviting eyes," her "provocative behavior" (381); she lives "myriad lives and loves"; she follows "immense and luxurious detours as the courtesan depositor of multiple desires" (390). While her husband waits faithfully, she has liaisons with many men—Philip, Mambo, John, Donald; she thinks about Jay. Behaving like her definition of a man, she attempts to enjoy sex for its own sake. During her exploits she seems, with some exceptions, to take care mainly of herself. Because her various acting roles contrast markedly with the kind of "natural" role that society associates with motherhood, Sabina appears to be seeking escape from a confining good-mother role; instead, she looks for power and authority in a different, public realm.

But the narrator warns us early in the novel that Sabina's "ladder" leads "to fire" (362), a symbol used traditionally in this context to suggest destruction. Her attempt to climb away from society's traditional maternal script for women seems at least as damaging to her psyche as the other characters' more obvious imprisonment in the script. Even more important, she is hindered both by her paralyzing inability to articulate a coherent "story" of her own and by her unawareness of that story's direct connection to the mothering script. Anthony Paul Kerby, basing his concept on Paul Ricoeur's fusion of narrative and identity, maintains that "the self . . . is essentially a being of reflexivity, coming to itself in its own narrational acts" (41). Lacking such narrative cohesion, the individual will fail to achieve an integrated self, and will remain indefinitely in a state of chaos in which multiple identities confuse the would-be subject and undermine any real sense of power. From the very beginning of *Spy*, Sabina shares with all humankind "the desire to make the inchoate intelligible" (Kerby 45) through narrating. For Sabina, this desire takes the form of an overwhelming need to confess, a need externalized in the character of the Lie Detector whose presence opens, closes, and otherwise punctuates the novel, offering Sabina an opportunity to tell her story. Nevertheless, in spite of her persistent and strong desire to confess, she cannot do so.

What precisely does she need to confess? Nancy Scholar suggests that Sabina flees from the guilt of loving illicitly or not loving at all; Scholar notes that the character wishes to escape "awareness of the meaning of [her] actions" (123). These assumptions seem valid, yet insufficient to explain why Sabina continues to pursue the illicit affairs, which clearly fail to contribute to her happiness. Franklin and Schneider briefly mention Sabina's connection with motherhood (124), but do not link it to her need to confess. More recently, biographer Noël Riley Fitch describes Sabina's promiscuous behavior as a compensation for "some 'shock' from a cruel father" which prompted her to "become a mistress and assume her father's role as a seducer in order not to be betrayed" (37). Deirdre Bair believes Sabina is "racked by guilt over the havoc caused by her total irresponsibility" (366).

But it is her compulsive fascination with precisely those maternal patterns she has been trying to escape that signals her most deep-seated feelings of guilt and that renders her powerless to tell a credible story. Indeed, her constant guilt can be relieved only when she "mothers" some of her men, even though the affairs continue during these episodes. Perhaps these brief intervals when she at least minimally recognizes that the maternal pattern exists, and the fleeting minutes when she feels the compulsion to adhere to it, afford her a momentary—but not permanent—relief from guilt. Such moments, if gathered together, would help her form a story she could confess.

That Nin herself felt the need for confessional narrative is clear, not only from her entire *Diary* opus, but specifically from her reiterative stories of her own late-term abortion, which of course is a more obvious, physical rejection of motherhood. As noted earlier, one of the most dramatic of these stories about Nin's dead child appears in *Incest*. Suzette Henke explains how the narration of the experience helps Nin: "Nin's late-term abortion provoked psychological dysporia and haunting flashbacks expressed in a compulsive need to narrate the tale of her birth experience over and over again—to relive the pain of pregnancy loss in compulsive aesthetic frameworks until the trauma could be revised and reiterated, mitigated, sanitized, and made acceptable to a tormented consciousness" (76–77). In contrast, Sabina offers only pseudostories, reversing herself whenever expedience dictates. She recalls, for example, her response to Jay when, as she is telling him a story about Lillian, she suddenly realizes the story would be painful for him because Sabina's own "seduction of Jay in Paris had been in part responsible for Lillian's desertion of him" (*Spy* 448). She quickly "reversed her story, and it was Jay who wondered whether he was not hearing right" (448). Nin uses the image of a "giant sponge" to convey the deceptive method her character repeatedly employs to try one false story, then another. The sponge had power: it "erased all she had said by an absolute denial" (450), hiding Sabina's truth and identity from everyone, including herself. Such power is illusory, however. Her "repressed story" (Kerby 88), the truly empowering one, is never told.

Sabina comes tantalizingly close to her repressed narrative, though, through her relationship with Donald, in which she tries to replace his notion of a "bad" mother, a mother "always preoccupied with people of no importance, while he wept with loneliness and fought the incubus of nightmares alone" (*Spy* 428). During such times, Sabina briefly takes on the expected characteristics of the traditional "good" mother, replacing Donald's "corrosive" mother by giving "full attentiveness to his secret wishes, not dancing with others, not flirting, never whining, focussing the full search-light of her heart upon him" (428–29). Confirming the pattern with more maternal imagery, the narrator describes also Sabina's "protective embrace" of Donald; Sabina becomes "the dispenser of food, of fulfilled promises, of mendings and knitting, comforts and solaces, of blankets and reassurances, of heaters, medicines, potions and scaffolds"; her breasts "flowed with nourishment" (432). In this realm, where self-effacement and goodness become her virtues, Sabina finds "a moment's surcease from guilt" (433). She perceives an absolute dichotomy: she can be either the mythological self-sacrificing mother, or the rebellious, seductive "firebird" (437). There appears to be no middle ground for a human life story.

While Sabina's performative story emphasizes her inability to compose her own narrative in *Spy*, the juxtaposed, competent voices of two other characters do offer at least the potential power

of articulation through the substitution of apparently truthful narratives for Sabina's fabrications. Djuna, a major character in *Cities
of the Interior* whose own voice is often maddeningly silent in *The
Four-Chambered Heart* (see below), ironically assumes the role of
the analyst in *Spy,* composing a credible story for Sabina to consider. For instance, Djuna corrects Sabina's fairy-tale story of Alan
as her "father": "'That's not a man's love you are describing, and
not even a father's love. It's a fantasy-father, an idealized father
once invented by a needy child'" (458–59). The other authoritative voice, at once shattering Sabina's pseudonarrative and offering
in its stead the potential power of a truthful narrative, is the voice
of the Lie Detector, the figure haunting the character throughout
the novel. In the beginning, after she telephones him anonymously, Sabina chooses to silence him. His direct generalizations
about her problems frighten her. He asserts, "You wouldn't have
called me if you were innocent. Guilt is the one burden human
beings can't bear alone. As soon as a crime is committed, there is a
telephone call, or a confession to strangers" (*Spy* 361). When he
claims that "we are more severe judges of our own acts than professional judges" (362), she hangs up on him—the counternarrative contains precisely the truth she wants to avoid. At the end of
the novel, however, she at least listens to his version of her life
narrative; admitting that her attempts to escape have failed, she
agrees to follow him. The novel ends with a tearful Sabina experiencing an apparent catharsis. Although she still cannot tell her
own story, she feels emotion through the music of Beethoven, and
she has not yet refused the inviting hands of the Lie Detector who,
most strongly suggesting now the role of a psychoanalyst, offers a
"graceful dance of sorrow" (462) or a painful but truthful narrative
of her life. It is this narrative that Sabina wants and doesn't want.
If, as Kerby notes, the end result of psychoanalysis is "a narrative
account of the analysand's life wherein the analysand finds him or
herself adequately reflected and can accept this representation as
biographical and, perhaps, more fruitfully, as a basis for future
action" (86), then Sabina may be standing on the brink of discovery. The novel closes, however, before any such discovery is
expressed by Sabina herself, freezing her in an interim state in
which her fierce attempt to escape the maternal script, without
truly understanding the powerful forces that both attract and repel
her, results ironically in the complete loss of identity she had
feared in the script itself. In *Spy,* then, the voices of authenticity
remain outside the struggling character. But the power of narrative

articulation is offered to readers as an effective strategy in the achievement of genuine subjectivity for women.

Djuna

More than any other character in *Cities*, Djuna dramatically illustrates the paralysis that can result from an inherited motherhood script of the sort that Irigaray describes with such passion in "And the One Doesn't Stir." Through Djuna's appearances in four of the five novels in *Cities*, but especially through her featured role in *The Four-Chambered Heart*, the complexities of her background and of her present relationships are examined in detail, as Nin presents readers with a troubling mosaic of the conflicted, neurotic character whose inner struggles perhaps most closely resemble problems that Nin herself experienced. Ironically, although Djuna shows at times brilliant insight into other characters' problems, she experiences considerable difficulty in looking at her own interior landscape.

Though *Ladders to Fire*, the first novel in *Cities*, is mainly Lillian's story, it does introduce us briefly to Djuna and reveal her significant past. Born into poverty, she had a consumptive mother who spent much of her time in bed and a father who squandered his money on drink. Like the Anaïs character in the *Diary* whose father had physically deserted the family, Djuna, faced with ineffectual parents, was forced into a maternal role herself. Early in the novel, Nin connects her with what might have been a positive image of a "mother madonna holding the child and nourishing it" (14). In the very next phrase, however, the image is compromised, as Nin hints at Djuna's future problem: the "haunting mother image forever holding a small child" (14). After the death of her mother, Djuna was sent to an orphanage where her social activities were severely restricted and where, as *Children of the Albatross* later hints through a reference to the powerful watchman who stares at her breasts (138), she may even have been sexually abused. One effect of this horrifying childhood, Nin suggests, is a hunger for someone who loves and nourishes. Concepts of hunger and nourishment, in fact, form the two chapter titles in *Ladders*: "This Hunger" and "Bread and the Wafer." Another effect of her past which seems particularly valid psychologically is Djuna's inclination to satisfy that hunger by becoming an almost universal provider of the love and care that were absent from her own life: "Whatever was missing she became: she became mother, father, cousin, brother, friend, confidant, guide, companion to all" (28). Her relationship with Lillian in *Ladders* introduces us to this pattern. As Lillian bemoans Jay's inability to "create" her, Djuna feels her own familiar response to others' predicaments: "She wanted to take Lillian's hand and . . . raise her above the pain and confusion" (111). Thus, while Djuna did not like real children, she did construct a good-mother version of the "maternal experience" through these adult relationships (34).

The unnaturalness resulting from this adoption of society's scripted role is symbolically suggested through the imagery surrounding her in the window scene near the end of the "Hunger" section of *Ladders*. Pitting the naturalness of the garden against the artificiality of the salon, the narrator's knowing voice highlights nature's peacefulness and appealing sensuality. The juxtaposed categories subtly present the analyst's corrective vision: "the grass was drinking, there was a sensual humidity as if leaves, trees, grass and wind were all in a state of caress. . . . Nature flowered, caressed, spilled, relaxed, slept" while, the same analytic voice tells us, "the salon was gilded, the people were costumed for false roles, the lights and the faces were attenuated, the gestures were starched" (66–67).

The negative view of the artificial social role is reinforced by the ending of *Ladders,* where a metaphor of patriarchal society's enforced role for women unfolds. A chess game is under way. But instead of being a player with control over the wooden game pieces, Djuna is herself one of the pieces, which of course have no power except as they are moved by the Chess Player. When Djuna attempts to slip off her square, the Chess Player insists that she remain on it. Later, in spite of her astonishment at the thought of being forcibly rescued, she is carried away against her will by a male who places her on "a gold chair with a red brocade top" (127). The metaphor is apt: echoing the artificiality of the "gilded salon," the gold chair represents society's enforced, unnatural enthronement of women in scripted roles (such as motherhood) which imprison them within their type (on their square) and which eliminate any possibility of developing their human subjectivity. Djuna's impotent cry during this episode, "I want my dress torn and stained!" (127), dramatizes the raging conflict between, on the one hand, her desperate need to experience the reality of her past and present and, on the other, the scripted social acts she obsessively performs as she continues her neurotic mothering.

Neurosis, Nin points out in her pamphlet "On Writing,"[8] is "a form of protest against an unnatural life" (45). But what does Nin mean by "an unnatural life"? Although she does not explain in the pamphlet how this concept plays out in an individual's life, her description of "naturalness" in relation to diary writing seems applicable to a life situation. Elements of a diary narrative that contribute to the "vitality" of writing, she says, include "spontaneity" and "freedom of selection" and writing only of "what interested [the diarist] genuinely." Nin developed through the *Diary* "a love of the living moment, of the immediate emotional reaction to experience"; the *Diary* exposed "the relation between the past and present"; it noted "the repetitions of themes, developed the sense of the totality of personality"; it was a "tale without beginning or end, which encloses all things, and relates all things" (47). In short, though Nin does not label these characteristics, they would seem to be the necessary and appropriate ones for the discovery of individual subjectivity—particularly the openness to truthful emotions and the willingness and competence to build a life narrative that takes account of recurrent themes as well as the relationship between the past and the present. Djuna's failure either to explore her emotions thoroughly or to build a cohesive self-narrative that accounts for her past and present leads her into an unnatural, artificial role as "mother" to a world that joins her in denying her natural subjectivity, even as it purports to enthrone her, as in the chair scene. As Nin points out in another pamphlet, adopting such a scripted role leads ultimately to a frustrating inability to act and a feeling of total powerlessness: "While we refuse to organize the confusions within us we will never have an objective understanding of what is happening outside. We will not be able to relate to it, to choose sides, to evaluate historically, and consequently we will be incapacitated for action" ("Realism" 39).

In *Children of the Albatross,* Nin examines more deeply the emotional and behavioral effects of a woman's journey into powerlessness through obsessive "mothering,"[9] a journey that begins with Djuna's attempts to grasp power to compensate for the control she lacks as a prisoner of the script. The narrator/analyst's voice explains that Djuna habitually separated herself from her emotions as a way to "master sorrow" (138). Indeed, her self-imprisonment in her own "sealed room" (a chapter title in *Children*) probably arises through this effort to distance herself from a childhood in which she remained the helpless victim of "absolute authority" (139). The repression of these emotions, though, leads Djuna through a pattern of seeking childlike men to mother—Michael, Lawrence, and Paul in *Children,* later Rango in *Heart.* As Nin chronicles Djuna's repetitive behavior, the narrative itself takes on what Shlomith Rimmon-Kenan has called in a different context a "textual neurosis, an issueless re-enactment of the traumatic events it narrates and conceals" (178).[10] By repeatedly seeking "man the son, carving, painting, dancing, dreaming, and always beginning" (*Children* 168), Djuna searches for someone she can exert power over—male figures who are too youthful, too inexperienced, or too irresponsible to wield any overt sexual or psychological power over her. For instance, Michael's youth and vulnerability attract her (149–50), causing her maternal qualities of "natural warmth" and "aching breasts" (153) to emerge. With Paul, a forerunner of Rango in *Heart,* Djuna becomes even more obviously the good substitute for his evil mother who forced him to kill his pet guinea pig (162). Djuna views him as a "boy" who is "lost" (163); he has the "skin of a child" (170); when he worries that his parents have forbidden him to go to her, a maternal protectiveness emerges in her insistence, "We'll all take care of you" (171); still assuming her ability to control him, she later regrets that "she had opened him to love too soon. He was not ready" (181). Because she represses her past, she dooms herself to these repetitive acts of mothering. In psychoanalysis, according to J. M. Bernstein, "past events . . . are partially constitutive of the self"; in fact, "their redescription entails a reconstitution of the self" (70). Djuna's refusal to confront her past sorrows prevents that reconstitution.

The Four-Chambered Heart, the novel at the heart of *Cities of the Interior,* emphatically demystifies the good-mother syndrome by centralizing a woman's long-term struggle and dramatizing the resulting paralysis in her life. Presented as an overresponsible "angel" in this novel, Djuna plays third party to an empty marriage between Rango and his pseudoinvalid wife, Zora. Unlike conventional love triangles, though, this one casts Djuna not only as frustrated "mother" to the immature, jobless guitar player Rango but also as "friend," companion, and maternal caregiver to her lover's mad wife. In one extreme instance, Djuna even gives up her own clothes to Zora, only to discover later that Zora keeps many items of fine apparel unused in a trunk (316). Compulsively, Djuna gets herself caught in the role of one who answers prayers, consoles, carries palliatives, lessens pain (293), and remains silent about her plight, even while she is aware that such a role annihilates her "other selves" (293). Because this type of behavior is repeatedly described and is continued over many years and many text pages, the reader is made to feel increasingly irritated by the character's inertia.

The narrative countervoice, however, explodes this model of mothering by showing its exhausting and devastating results.

Instead of Djuna's compulsive narrative, the voice suggests a story that differentiates between the real and the pseudo-ideal, between responsibility and overresponsibility, between sainthood and sickness, between authentic selfhood and crippling oppression. This voice explains Djuna's dilemma in her relationship with Rango, not by establishing yet another abstract and static script for "good" behavior, but rather by describing contextually the character's conflicting feelings: "She was invited to bring her good self only, in which Rango believed utterly, and yet she felt a rebellion against this good self which was too often called upon, was too often invited, to the detriment of other selves who were now like numerous wallflowers!" (289, 291).

Although progress might follow such a revelation in an actual therapeutic situation, here the narrative interpreter does not solve Djuna's problems; in fact, her scripted good-mother behavior continues to haunt her through most of the novel. Though the character does gradually become aware of her own neurotic behavior, she still feels "like a puppet" as she continues ministering to Zora and Rango even after years have passed. What does change is the quality and depth of the reader's understanding of the good-mother phenomenon. From the narrative countervoice we learn more about the ways Djuna's past has helped create her script. For instance, her parents had threatened to withdraw their "love" if she did not perform as they expected (292). Nin's readers also must confront the realization that following the script cannot solve the problems either of mother-women with their need for power or of their child-men: "those who threw themselves into palliating the obvious symptoms assumed an endless task, a task without hope of cure" (274). This enhanced knowledge about the characters suggests another function of the juxtaposed voices: to increase the distance between the characters and the reader, thus serving to underscore the characters' obsessions.

In addition to centralizing problems of the good-mother figure, *The Four-Chambered Heart* questions patriarchal values by demonstrating the negative effects of the maternal script on adult males who are mothered. The "masculine" male begins as a romantic icon but ends as an infantile neurotic, as compulsive as the "mother" he finds attractive. When Djuna meets Rango, he seems the epitome of stereotypical "maleness." Creative artist of the guitar and the "idol of the night clubs" (241), he is characterized by his "sensual swing," his rough-and-tumble mattress of black horsehair, the superman who hurls himself against the captain's door, breaking it down (254–55). With his proclivity to wander, he appears to possess something Djuna lacks—freedom. But the countervoice of the analyst soon hints that Rango is a child in disguise: "He rubbed his face . . . with his fists closed as children do" (250). Much later he is described similarly: "Rango . . . fell asleep almost instantly in the pose of a big child, with his fists tightly closed, his arms over his head" (352); even at the end of the story, he exhibits the "total despair" common to "children and adolescents" (358). Indeed, on a deeper level, he refuses maturity by avoiding responsibility for his troubles with Zora: "The world was to blame for her undernourishment, her ill health, her precocious marriage, her troubles. The doctors were to blame for her not getting well. The public was to blame for not understanding her dances. The house owner should have let them off without paying rent. The grocer had no right to claim his due. They were poor and had a right to mercy" (279). The scripted narrative performed by the mother figure in turn enables the child to persist in his immature, irresponsible story.

The countervoice also serves to complicate issues that may appear simple, as at the conclusion of the story. While Oliver Evans's assessment of the ending suggests an orderly denouement in which Djuna reaches self-knowledge and kills her child-self that refused to compromise "in the face of reality" (140), the outcome of the novel, I think, is not so tidy. Evans's analysis seems based on what Ellen Friedman and Miriam Fuchs refer to as patriarchal assumptions about narrative; one such assumption involves a "plot linearity that implies a story's purposeful forward movement"; another is "the movement to closure" (4). Like other experimental narratives by women, however, Nin's fiction often subverts these structures. While it is true that Djuna's eventual recognition of the gamelike quality of their lives may seem to suggest some forward movement toward a reconstitution of the self, the backward thrust of the counternarrative should not be overlooked. Djuna's awareness of the "other face of Rango," her realization that he is a "child lodged in a big man's body by a merry freak" (356), occurs during a relatively long dreamlike passage containing Djuna's own ruminations about her need to accept reality. She does not accept "reality" fully, though, as the counternarrative shows. Prior to the dreamlike segment, the narrator/analyst presents the image of a halo created by spreading hair from "all the women [Djuna] had been" (352); this image is repeated at the end of the story, but now the hair surrounds "a doll who had committed suicide during the night. The water had washed off its features" (358). Through an apparent decision to mend her life not by understanding her past but solely by focusing on the future—"countries she had not yet seen . . . [and] loves she had not yet encountered" (354)—Djuna once again effaces (kills) an important part of her self, "the broken doll of her childhood" (354). Narrative closure does not seem possible, then, in the face of two overwhelming obstacles. First, the woman herself again fails to recognize in her past a crucial component of her own subjectivity, and is thus unable to tell her story fully. Second, society, in the guise of the fisherman who "catches" the dead doll, persists in its objectifying and trivializing gaze toward women. To the fisherman, the doll-woman is a laughable item of curiosity; he reveals neither understanding of nor sympathy for the symbol he has "caught." That society as well as the woman still sanctifies the faceless (self-lacking) image is also evident in the halo surrounding the doll's face: "Her hair aureoled her face with crystalline glow" (358). In the last line, the countervoice offers a final correction to Djuna's story by referring once more to Djuna's boat as Noah's Ark, a vessel whose raison d'être is to save the world, corresponding to the traditional maternal urge to save the child (Rango). When the countervoice notes in the end that the Ark has "survived the flood" (358), the import is negative for women, forecasting a continuation of the endless, repetitive struggle between women's subjectivity and the external social code for mothering. Unlike Sabina in *Spy*, who cannot even begin to confess her story, though, Djuna can at least construct a part of her life narrative. But she remains unable to articulate it completely, depending instead on the voice of the narrator/analyst.

In the overall context of women's fiction, Nin's strategic use of narrative and counternarrative in *Heart* is significant. Friedman and Fuchs point out that the act of "subverting closure" is a way of unhinging a fixed, authoritarian point of view (7). Besides reinforcing the centralization of the mother figure's conflicts, Nin's ending also displaces the dominant culture's "marriage plot" by leaving readers with ambiguous cues and a complex situation composed of individual psyches grappling—perhaps indefinitely—with fixed social codes as well as with one another.

Lillian

Beginning in *Ladders to Fire* as society's traditional good mother, Lillian soon becomes what a patriarchal society would view as a bad mother who rebels against the maternal script by abandoning her biological children and husband; eventually, in *Seduction of the Minotaur*, she evolves into the woman in *Cities* who is most able to extrapolate and articulate her story. In *Seduction*, as the character gains the courage to examine her past, the counternarrative gradually merges with the thoughts and feelings that become Lillian's story, a narrative that illustrates Nin's belief in women's potential not only to escape from society's imprisoning scripts but also to retain and use their unique gift of motherhood in positive ways.

Nin reveals the complexities masked by society's traditional assumptions about good mothering early in *Ladders* through Lillian's ambivalence toward domestic pursuits. Although she tries to uphold the good-mother mystique through her meticulous caring for her family's home, for instance, she stops short of accepting her role emotionally. The narrative voice, reflecting the character's consciousness, explains: "The strength, the fervor, the care Lillian spent in the house, on her husband and children came from some part of her being that was not the deepest Lillian. It was as if every element but her own nature had contributed to create this life. Who had made the marriage? Who had desired the children? . . . it had not been made out of the deeper elements of her nature, and she was a stranger in it" (17–18).

Lillian's seemingly traditional good mothering behavior, then, is not really part of what Marshall Edelson terms her "master story" (104), referring to the psychoanalytic narrative she tells herself. Her powerlessness to pursue "her" story against a seemingly intractable social code leads Lillian to pursue a monstrous exaggeration of selfhood. Using subversive strategies that she does not clearly understand to escape the good-mother syndrome, she pursues power by forcing herself upon others, both women and men. Showering Djuna with perfume, jewelry, and clothes, she exerts a pressure "to fix and to hold" (*Ladders* 31). Predictably, Djuna recoils, suspecting a potentially hurtful demon hidden in such gifts (32). The countervoice explains that "Lillian became the mother who wanted to dress her child out of her own substance" (31). One of Lillian's lovers, Gerard, describes a similar type of overpowering mother image when during their relationship the dominating personality of his own mother merges with the equally overwhelming aggressiveness of Lillian. Recalling the portrait of Nin's own mother, Rosa Culmell, in volume 4 of the *Diary*, Gerard's depiction of his mother and Lillian shows two women who lived through him: "his mother and Lillian (in the nightmare they were confused and indistinguishable), instead of living out their own thoughts, occupying their own hands, . . . put all their strength, wishes, desires, their wills on him" (7). The force of the two women's combined maternal power saps Gerard's strength, causing him, like Djuna, to withdraw from Lillian in fear. Nin implies that the sacrificial good-mother script can lead to a subversive grasp for power by women who cannot narrate their repressed stories; moreover, the use of this power is perceived as malevolent by others, further damaging the ability of these women to forge satisfying relationships.

Lillian's attempts to live vicariously sometimes reveal her efforts to free herself from the script and progress toward selfhood, though. When she offers advice to Nanny, the "old nurse who took care of them all with inexhaustible maternal warmth" (18) and who becomes torn by her wish to get married and her simultaneous desire to remain with the family she "mothers," Lillian speaks from the deepest part of herself: "Nanny, it is time that you thought of yourself. You have lived for others all your life. Get married" (23). Despite Lillian's apparent inclination to advise against the futile sacrifice usually attached to motherhood, however, her advice to Nanny ignores the possibility that Nanny's marriage may lead her into precisely the same sacrificial trap that Lillian struggles against.

Her vicarious rebellion seems to shift to an actual one when she suddenly terminates what she views as her static relationship with her husband, Larry, and what she vaguely realizes is a stultifying script requiring daily care of children and home. She tries to construct a different narrative for herself by abandoning her husband and children and living with her new lover, Jay. Her conscious narrative then erases all references to her biological children. But the countervoice in *Ladders* reveals that Lillian's abrupt shift to what society would view as a bad mothering act of selfish abandonment is, for her at least, more apparent than real: In her new relationship with Jay, she continues to follow the traditional good-mother pattern, a tactic that gives a woman a sense of power when, like Djuna, Lillian displaces her maternal caretaking onto a child-man: "she carried [Jay's] head on her breast, she carried his body. . . . She felt immense, and strong, and illimitable, the boundless mother" (44). Moreover, she unwittingly reinforces the script by sacrificing her own artistic career as a pianist at least temporarily to support him when he seems chronically unable to earn a living. The social code impels her to divide her world into two oppositional spheres: the world of the professional creative artist

versus the world of the (surrogate) mother. For Lillian, choosing
one entails sacrificing the other. In a social context that enthrones
maternal sacrifice, it is an easy "choice" for a woman to adopt
some form of mothering behavior; hence, Lillian "chooses" to
mother the "adult" man, as did Djuna and Sabina. The artistic and
psychological damage resulting from Lillian's sacrifice is symbolized grotesquely in the image of the two pianos left by movers to
be ruined in the pouring rain when Jay fails to manage their care
as agreed. While the pianos actually belong to Jay's neighbor,
Lillian views the incident as an indication of his indifference to her
own potential musical career: "It was her piano Jay had left out in
the rain, to be ruined" (52). The silencing of Lillian's music at this
point suggests the patriarchal disparagement of many women
artists in an early-twentieth-century culture; the incident records
the resulting inability of these women to communicate their emotions and constitute their selfhood. The use of two pianos may
indicate the concomitant damage to the male perpetrators as well.
Nin's emphasis in *Ladders,* the first novel in *Cities,* on the importance of art to help these women find truth and fulfillment in their
narratives thus precedes and predicates every novel in *Cities.*
Equally important, the incident highlights women's own complicity in the psychologically damaging sacrifices made in service of
the social code.

To refuse sacrifice, however, is not necessarily to achieve freedom, as the character of Helen suggests in *Ladders.* The externaliza-
tion of Lillian's own pseudorebellion against the script, Helen is
Lillian's doppelgänger who has moved on to another stage. She too
has abandoned her husband and children. She tells Lillian, "I
didn't want to be a mother. . . . In my marriage I was buried alive"
(59). But after running away, she admits that her apparent escape
brought no true freedom: "Every night I dream the same dream of
prisons and struggles to escape. . . as if only my body escaped, and
not my feelings. . . . Part of my being remained with my children,
imprisoned in the past. Now I have to liberate myself wholly, body
and soul, and I don't know how. . . . How can one liquidate the
past?" (59). Closer to truthful narrative than Lillian, Helen poses
the crucial question by seeking to deal with the past. As we saw
from the example of Djuna, Nin here reaffirms a basic assumption
of modern psychoanalysis by emphasizing through her women
characters the need to articulate their entire story—including their
past—in order to progress toward liberty and self-constitution. As
Kerby points out, "It is as a character in our (and other people's)
narratives that we achieve an identity" (40). The failure to under-

stand clearly her entire scripted story, the engagement in futile and frustrating sacrifice, and the appropriation of negative kinds of power behaviors, Nin demonstrates, result in the undermining of women's attempts to escape, condemning them at least temporarily to continuance of the script.

Nin's choice of the title *Seduction of the Minotaur* for the last novel of *Cities* confirms that sacrifice and the subversive use of a pseudopower have been very seductive for women, ensnaring them in a labyrinth of psychological entanglements from which it is quite difficult to emerge. John Forrester, explaining Jean Baudrillard's philosophy of seduction, asserts that seduction is in stark contrast with (real) power because "seduction is a mastery of signs" while power "is mastery of the real"; seduction is "a play on the appearance of things, but it does not try to dispel appearance for the sake of a reality beyond"; seduction thus undermines "all discourses aimed at truth, aimed at piercing through the veil of illusion and dissemblance to appropriate truth (identified with what is real)" (85). By accepting a patriarchal script for motherhood consisting of sacrifice and pseudopower, women in Nin's fiction become seduced objects, unwittingly participating in their own imprisonment and weaving a tangled web of psychological defense mechanisms that help them avoid their own realities while giving them a perception of power. In mythology the minotaur of Nin's title, with its body of a man and head of a bull, signifies this concept of illusory power. While the bull in traditional symbolism has fecundating power (Cirlot 33), and while the minotaur at first exerts a deathly power over all who approach it, the creature is eventually stripped of all power when slain by Theseus, whose own power came from a woman: Ariadne had provided him with a sword and a thread, which he used to retrace his way out of the labyrinth. Real empowerment, Nin suggests, arises not from an acceptance of the scripted patriarchal ideal for women and motherhood, but rather from women's ability to find the way out of the maze by rediscovering their beginnings, by reconstructing the narrative of their lives.

In *Seduction* Doctor Hernandez acts as the lay therapist who asks Lillian questions to help her confront her seducer—a patriarchal society that has discounted her true narrative and impelled her instead either to accept the script without question or to rebel against it while remaining blind to its continued mastery over her life. Throughout *Cities* she has fled from her past, from her husband and children and, more remotely, from the memory of a cold, disciplined mother with critical eyes (540). Because Hernandez refuses "to dispense [the drug of] dangerous forgetfulness" (548), he is shot and killed by the natives of Golconda, who are externalizations of Lillian's earlier, highly scripted self. Metaphorically, Lillian has now received sufficient support from the doctor to turn toward remembering on her own. She moves toward retrieving a buried past that includes conflicting impressions: on the one hand her fear of her mother's antiseptic formality, and on the other her dream of being rescued by her mother when she was lost in the sewer (528). Remembering, Lillian is able to recognize and analyze her own psychological defenses—her love for her children expressed through loving and caring for Edward's children (509); her adoption of Jay's enthusiasms (569); her similarities to her husband (558); the myth of her own courage (558); the repetition of the same (scripted) stories (558).

For the first time in the continuous novel, in *Seduction* truth can be rendered in discourse by the character as subject. Notably, the counternarrative voice now sheds much of its ironic, oppositional posture toward the "maternal" character, blending instead with the character's own narrative. Rather than showing the negative effects of the character's attitudes or behavior, the analyst's voice offers positive support through suggestive questions and even indicates the achievement of real progress beyond the superficiality that seduction had induced: "Was it possible to begin one's life anew with a knowledge of what lay behind the charades one had created? Would she circumvent the masks they had donned, those she had pinned upon the face of Larry? She now knew her responsibility in the symbolic drama of their marriage. Lillian was journeying homeward" (564–65).

The blended voices, in fact, become more and more pronounced, and sometimes extend over many text pages.[11] Previously "narrated from a third-person perspective" (Kerby 6), Lillian thus shows signs of real transformation; that is, she has gained what Kerby calls "the competence for self-narration" (6). Accordingly, self in *Cities* is not "a pre-linguistic given that merely employs language"; rather, in what amounts to a postmodern assertion, self becomes for Nin what Kerby terms "a product of language" (Kerby 4). Thanks to this increasing competence, Lillian becomes more natural, able to reclaim the artistry she sacrificed in *Ladders;* she is able to embrace jazz, to experience "the music of the body," a metaphor suggesting selfhood (*Seduction* 478). Equally important, along with her performing art, she can still be "mother" to her husband's emerging sense of selfhood (588–89), but this time not with a subversive use of damaging power that maintains the man's adult-child status, but with an enabling process that helps him, too, account for his past and make substantive progress toward a mature relationship. Becoming a real subject through her own narrative, Lillian then takes on the role previously played by the third-person omniscient analyst/narrator, understanding the psychological complexity behind appearances, commenting on her own problems, and shifting her perspective. Through the real power of the character's unfolding narrative, motherhood receives a new definition as a positive, creative force that promotes, rather than prevents, a woman's subjectivity.

The apparently definitive ending of *Seduction* may, however, raise a question for some readers concerning the implied feminism of Nin's narrative techniques. As noted earlier, Friedman and Fuchs have suggested that the avoidance of closure in women's fiction is a subversive tactic that helps "undermine patriarchal forms" (7). In the other four novels in *Cities*, Nin does avoid closure and, in this and other ways, does question patriarchal assumptions about women's lives, as we have seen. And avoidance of closure is thematically appropriate for all three women in these earlier novels, since Sabina, Djuna, and even Lillian remain tortured by their emotional dilemmas. But by the end of *Seduction*, the relative closure arising from Lillian's movement "homeward" toward subjectivity seems equally appropriate and, in more than one way, feminist as well. First, intellectual and emotional knowledge of her story has taught this woman that embracing ambiguity will allow her to move toward definition and resolution of her conflicts—a movement the text should encompass. Second, Nin suggests the thematic point that strategies of subversiveness, though useful as temporary devices to deal with the patriarchal culture, may in the end reinforce women's secondary status if they are used indiscriminately and merely as defensive reactions to conventional assumptions about linear narrative. More important to Nin is an ending befitting her belief in women's potential for authentic selfhood. Integration, she implies in the continuous novel, is a laudable and perhaps attainable goal that we may approach if we are able to tolerate chaos and ambiguity as necessary correlatives of subjectivity.

Conclusion

Nin never disparages motherhood. Rather, her concern with it suggests its crucial importance in women's lives. In the *Diary* the Nin character fights endless battles with her conflicting feelings about motherhood and selfhood. In *Cities* the three major characters agonize, consciously or unconsciously, over the "desubjectivized social role" of motherhood that Irigaray would later reject ("Body" 18). Nin presents readers of *Cities* with two dramatic examples of desubjectivized women who continue to be prisoners of the maternal script, and with at least one woman who makes substantial progress toward subjectivity. Offering courageous statements for her time, Nin's diaries and novels anticipate Irigaray's feminist philosophy in calling for women's selfhood in conjunction with their motherhood.

Nin does not designate men solely as scapegoats in a scripted society, either. In the *Diary* and in *Cities*, she suggests that many men also become victims of the motherhood script, suffering both from ill-conceived acts of their neurotic mothers and from a lack of understanding of their childlike status in relationships. But most comprehensively, Nin highlights women's own foibles; in her fiction she insists that they accept responsibility for creating a new narrative for themselves.

By revealing the importance of articulated narratives for women as a necessary step toward selfhood, and by using the analyst's counternarrative voice to demonstrate women's collusion[12] with the patriarchal script, Nin also celebrates the psychoanalytic process in *Cities*. She feminizes that process by centralizing women's subjectivity, by detailing their complexity, by using a counternarrative voice that gives women interpretive and negotiating power, and by displacing what in her time was the male authority to comment on society[13] through her strong focus on women's scripted lives. Nin's characters suggest that these lives are often fraught with potentially crippling social and psychological hazards that cause many women to follow a slow and torturous path toward narrative consciousness. Using a continual process of psychoanalysis, however, the individual woman, Nin asserts, may develop the knowledge and real power to disturb the stasis of the dominant script and create a space for herself in which she can move more freely to construct a story that recognizes the validity of her emotions.

In a sense, then, Nin has written a narrative about the importance of narrative in women's lives.[14] She has shown women the need to dissolve the motherhood-versus-selfhood dichotomy. She has also shown women a way to reenvision and reinterpret their past, rendering their histories not static but interpretive and dynamic through the conscious articulation of their stories. Nin's diaries and fiction render the patriarchal script invalid for women's subjective lives. Her work invites a complacent social world to respond more sensitively to the agonized cry of a daughter to a mother in Irigaray's prose poem "And the One Doesn't Stir": "When the one of us comes into the world, the other goes underground. When the one carries life, the other dies. And what I wanted from you, Mother, was this: that in giving me life, you still remain alive" (67).

NOTES

1. Critics who have commented on Nin's maternal imagery include Sharon Spencer, who offers a detailed discussion of Nin's equation of motherhood with selfhood in the diaries and fiction in *Collage of Dreams: The Writings of Anaïs Nin;* see also Diane Richard-Allerdyce's "Anaïs Nin's Mothering Metaphor: Toward a Lacanian Theory of Feminine Creativity," in which she proposes that Nin moves in her work from "the traditional models of femininity based on motherhood" to a new use of the maternal metaphors "to refer to the artistic process" (87).

2. Badinter bases her definition of the good mother on the writings of psychoanalyst Helene Deutsch, a disciple of Sigmund Freud.

3. In *For Her Own Good: 150 Years of the Experts' Advice to Women,* Barbara Ehrenreich and Deirdre English describe a similar process of idealization and ensuing conflict in mothers (199–203).

4. Chodorow also discusses the power of the mother as a negative force in *The Reproduction of Mothering: Psychoanalysis and the Sociology of Gender.*

5. Shlomith Rimmon-Kenan distinguishes between "narration-as-reporting and narration-as-performance" in the psychoanalytic process. Nin's fictional characters do both through their speech and actions, but Nin devotes most of her text space to performance.

6. Rachel Blau Du Plessis points out that the voices of many women writers (Dorothy Richardson, for example) tend to comment in this manner—that is, "contextually rather than categorically" (153).

7. The voices of Nin's narrator/analysts also differ from the voice of Sigmund Freud in his patriarchal reconstruction of the female "hysteric's" narrative in the famous case of "Dora." Elaine Showalter asserts that if Freud can be considered an unreliable narrator, then Dora becomes a victim of his need "to dominate and control her" (27). Indeed, Freud's insistence on judging his client to be hysterical, on arrogantly filling the gaps in the "hysteric's own story" and on overcoming "her resistance to his narrative interpretations" (Showalter 26) without considering her own voice does reveal the hierarchical relationship that Freud assumed between therapist and patient. Nin's countervoice, however, speaks only after the character has spoken and acted out a performative narrative that repeatedly frustrates her. Unlike Freud, with his apparent need to win a victory over his client as Showalter mentions (26), Nin's narrator/analyst seems focused on searching for reasons for the character's frustrations; no sense of "combat" is evident in Nin's prose.

8. Philip K. Jason notes that this pamphlet was originally published in 1947 in two editions: "first by the Daniel Oliver Associates at Dartmouth College . . . then as Alicat 'Outcast' chapbook Number Eleven" (31). The text under discussion here is a 1990 republication in *Anaïs: An International Journal.*

9. In "Toward Independence and Self-Creation," Suzette Henke describes Djuna's longing to "nurture the world" and the resulting "destructive patterns of altruism and self-sacrifice" she pursues in *Children of the Albatross.*

10. Rimmon-Kenan refers here to the fiction of Günter Grass.

11. See, for example, pp. 553–58, where Lillian's thoughts blend almost completely with the analyst's commentary.

12. See Roberta Hamilton's general analysis of women's collusion with the patriarchal system.

13. I wish to thank independent scholar Phyllis Wachter for her insights on Nin's social commentary.

14. See Margaret Homans's article commenting on novels that she characterizes as "narratives about narration" (3).

WORKS CITED

Badinter, Elisabeth. *Mother Love: Myth and Reality: Motherhood in Modern History.* New York: Macmillan, 1981.

Bair, Deirdre. *Anaïs Nin: A Biography.* New York: Putnam, 1995.

Bernstein, J. M. "Self-Knowledge as Praxis: Narrative and Narration in Psychoanalysis." *Narrative in Culture: The Uses of Storytelling in the Sciences, Philosophy, and Literature.* Ed. Christopher Nash, 51–77. New York: Routledge, 1990.

Chodorow, Nancy. *Feminism and Psychoanalytic Theory.* New Haven: Yale University Press, 1989.

———. *The Reproduction of Mothering: Psychoanalysis and the Sociology of Gender.* Berkeley and Los Angeles: University of California Press, 1978.

Cirlot, J. E. *A Dictionary of Symbols.* Trans. Jack Sage. New York: Philosophical Library, 1962.

Dally, Ann. *Inventing Motherhood: The Consequences of an Ideal.* New York: Schocken Books, 1983.

Du Plessis, Rachel Blau. *Writing Beyond the Ending: Narrative Strategies of Twentieth-Century Women Writers.* Bloomington: Indiana University Press, 1985.

Edelson, Marshall. "Telling and Enacting Stories in Psychoanalysis." *Interface of Psychoanalysis and Psychology.* Ed. James W. Barron, Morris N. Eagle, and David L. Wolitzky, 99–123. Washington, D.C.: American Psychological Association, 1992.

Ehrenreich, Barbara, and Deirdre English. *For Her Own Good: 150 Years of the Experts' Advice to Women.* Garden City, N.Y.: Anchor Press/Doubleday, 1978.

Evans, Oliver. *Anaïs Nin.* Carbondale: Southern Illinois University Press, 1968.

Fitch, Noël Riley. *Anaïs: The Erotic Life of Anaïs Nin.* Boston: Little, Brown, 1993.

Forrester, John. *The Seductions of Psychoanalysis: Freud, Lacan, and Derrida.* Cambridge: Cambridge University Press, 1990.

Franklin, Benjamin, V, and Duane Schneider. *Anaïs Nin: An Introduction.* Athens: Ohio University Press, 1979.

Friedman, Ellen G., and Miriam Fuchs, eds. *Breaking the Sequence: Women's Experimental Fiction.* Princeton: Princeton University Press, 1989.

Freud, Sigmund. "The Woman Who Felt Persecuted." 1915. Trans. Edward Glover. *Great Cases in Psychoanalysis.* Ed. Harold Greenwald, 27–37. New York: Jason Aronson, 1959.

Hamilton, Roberta. "The Collusion with Patriarchy." *The Politics of Diversity: Feminism, Marxism and Nationalism.* Ed. Roberta Hamilton and Michele Barrett, 385–97. London: Verso, 1986.

Henke, Suzette. "A Confessional Narrative: Maternal Anxiety and Daughter Loss in Anaïs Nin's 'Journal of Love: Incest.'" *Anaïs: An International Journal* 14 (1996): 71–77.

———. "Toward Independence and Self-Creation: A Closer Look at Anaïs Nin's *Children of the Albatross.*" *Anaïs: An International Journal* 17 (1999): 95–102.

Hirsch, Marianne. *The Mother/Daughter Plot: Narrative, Psychoanalysis, Feminism.* Bloomington: Indiana University Press, 1989.

Homans, Margaret. "Feminist Fictions and Feminist Theories of Narrative." *Narrative* 2 (1994): 3–16.

Irigaray, Luce. "And the One Doesn't Stir Without the Other." Trans. Helene Vivienne Wenzel. *Signs: Journal of Women in Culture and Society* 7 (1981): 60–67.

———. "Body Against Body: In Relation to the Mother." *Sexes and Genealogies.* Trans. Gillian C. Gill, 9–21. New York: Columbia University Press, 1993.

Jason, Philip K. "A Delicate Battle Cry." *Anaïs: An International Journal* 8 (1990): 30–34.

Kerby, Anthony Paul. *Narrative and the Self.* Bloomington: Indiana University Press, 1991.

Lanser, Susan Sniader. *Fictions of Authority: Women Writers and Narrative Voice.* Ithaca: Cornell University Press, 1992.

Nin, Anaïs. *Children of the Albatross. Cities of the Interior,* 128–238. Chicago: Swallow Press, 1959.

———. *The Diary of Anaïs Nin* (1931–74). Ed. Gunther Stuhlmann. 7 vols. San Diego: Swallow Press/Harcourt Brace Jovanovich, 1966–80.

———. *The Four-Chambered Heart. Cities of the Interior,* 241–358. Chicago: Swallow Press, 1959.

———. *Incest: From "A Journal of Love": The Unexpurgated Diary of Anaïs Nin, 1932–1934.* New York: Harcourt Brace Jovanovich, 1992.

————. *Ladders to Fire. Cities of the Interior*, 3–127. Chicago: Swallow Press, 1959.

————. *Linotte: The Early Diary of Anaïs Nin, 1914–1920*. Trans. Jean L. Sherman. New York: Harcourt Brace Jovanovich, 1978.

————. *The Novel of the Future*. Athens, Ohio: Swallow Press/Ohio University Press, 1986.

————. "On Writing." 1947. *Anaïs: An International Journal* 8 (1990): 45–50.

————. "Realism and Reality: Overcoming the Conventionality of the Contemporary Novel." 1947. *Anaïs: An International Journal* 8 (1990): 35–39.

————. *Seduction of the Minotaur. Cities of the Interior*, 465–589. Chicago: Swallow Press, 1959.

————. *A Spy in the House of Love. Cities of the Interior*, 360–462. Chicago: Swallow Press, 1959.

Omer, Haim, and Carlo Strenger. "The Pluralist Revolution: From the One True Meaning to an Infinity of Constructed Ones." *Psychotherapy* 29 (1992): 253–61.

Radner, Joan N., and Susan S. Lanser. "Strategies of Coding in Women's Cultures." *Feminist Messages: Coding in Women's Folk Culture*. Ed. Joan Newlon Radner, 1–29. Urbana: University of Illinois Press, 1993.

Richard-Allerdyce, Diane. "Anaïs Nin's Mothering Metaphor: Toward a Lacanian Theory of Feminine Creativity." *Compromise Formations: Current Directions in Psychoanalytic Criticism*. Ed. Vera J. Camden, 86–98. Kent, Ohio: Kent State University Press, 1989.

Rimmon-Kenan, Shlomith. "Narration as Repetition: the Case of Gunter Grass's Cat and Mouse." *Discourse in Psychoanalysis and Literature*. Ed. Shlomith Rimmon-Kenan, 176–87. London: Methuen, 1987.

Rogers, Carl R. "The Angry Adolescent." *Great Cases in Psychoanalysis*. Ed. Harold Greenwald, 209–16. New York: Jason Aronson, 1973.

Schafer, Roy. "Narration in the Psychoanalytic Dialogue." *On Narrative*. Ed. W.J.T. Mitchell, 25–49. Chicago: University of Chicago Press, 1981.

Scholar, Nancy. *Anaïs Nin*. Boston: Twayne, 1984.

Showalter, Elaine. "On Hysterical Narrative." *Narrative* 1 (1993): 24–35.

Spencer, Sharon. *Collage of Dreams: The Writings of Anaïs Nin*. Expanded ed. New York: Harcourt Brace Jovanovich, 1981.

————. "The Music of the Womb: Anaïs Nin's 'Feminine' Writing." *Breaking the Sequence: Women's Experimental Fiction*. Ed. Ellen G. Friedman and Miriam Fuchs, 161–73. Princeton, N.J.: Princeton University Press, 1989.

CHAPTER 8

The Artist as Character (or the Character as Artist)

Narrative and Consciousness in Anaïs Nin's Collages

Thomas M. March

There are so many kinds of drugs. One for remembering and one for forgetting. . . . We may seem to forget a person, a place, a state of being, a past life, but meanwhile what we are doing is selecting a new cast for the reproduction of the same drama, seeking the closest reproduction to the friend, the lover, or the husband we are striving to forget. And one day we open our eyes, and there we are caught in the same pattern, repeating the same story. How could it be otherwise? The design comes from within us. It is internal.

Seduction of the Minotaur

What the psychoanalyst does is what the novelist also has to do—probe deep enough until he finds where the chain broke.

The Novel of the Future

The title of Anaïs Nin's last novel, *Collages,* is simultaneously apt and meaningfully incomplete. One of the fundamental narrative principles of Nin's fiction is that the authority of the "real" lies not in that which is prescribed, offered forth by a narrative voice as static and unchanging, but rather in individual, internal experience of the external world. As we will see, the Ninian narrative is one in which the narrator's task is to provide, ostensibly firsthand, the operations of consciousness, of the dialectical encounter of the internal with the external that comprises the *real* real. In *Collages* Nin shows that experience itself is, like a collage, not linear but a collection of engagements whose logic is not static but a product of the consciousness that encounters it.

Marie-Rose Logan notes: "The adventures of Renate unfold through . . . episodes that turn the collage technique into a lifestyle" (79). But what Nin's narrative seems to reveal most strongly is that life, one's conscious engagement in and with the world, *is* a collage. *Collages* is an apt title for this collection of narratives, each one the story (or continuing story) of the construction by an individual consciousness of the collage of its own experience. However, because of the text's use of collage as a metaphor for the individual experience, the creation of a tapestry of interwoven and imaginative significance, this collection of collages is itself worthy of the name "collage." That is, the text is the narrator's own collage. In *Collage of Dreams* Sharon Spencer writes of the artist: "The fact that Varda is a collage-maker is extremely important. Collage as a concept underlies Anaïs Nin's sense of art, both in theory and as process" (4). By calling this text *Collages,* rather than *Collage,* Nin (or her narrator) deflects attention from her own role in composition and onto those compositions of experience represented therein, an act of naming that exemplifies the narrative strategy of the narrator's ostensible submission to the authority of those represented consciousnesses.

Narrative and Consciousness

The artist is the creator of beautiful things. To reveal art and conceal the artist is art's aim.

Oscar Wilde, Preface to *The Picture of Dorian Gray*

The Ninian narrative mode[1] is, indeed, one in which the artist, or narrator, is relatively concealed, in order to better reveal the "art" that is the process by which individual consciousnesses construct their internal experiences of the external. In two essays, "Realism and Reality" and "The Writer and the Symbols," Nin outlines a narrative mode in which the task of the narrator is to create a world that is more "real," a world *as experienced.*

In "Realism and Reality" Nin makes it clear that this mode is one that breaks dramatically with the "realism" of the past. The origin of this breach lies in the relevance of internal experience to representation. She criticizes the "so-called realistic novel" for its "evasions of the essential inner drama" and characterizes it as a "novel in which we are actually being constantly cheated of reality and experience" (26). This rejected narrative mode is one dominated by "reportage" in which, Nin writes, "realism is substituted for reality" (31).

Reality is located not in the external world alone, as something static and unchanging, but rather in the encounter of the internal world with the external. The result of this new approach to narration is the ability to uncover the true experience of a character and, thus, the true character himself. For, as Nin writes in "The Writer and the Symbols," the writer "must be a subtle detective of man's hidden character since we now know that all men are their own impersonators, and that the so-called realists who believed they were copying natural man were only copying man's impersonations, the protective persons by which he carefully concealed his deepest self" (47). Implied here is one of the fundamental principles of Nin's narratology, that the character exists not only as an object in and of him/herself, but as a constituting consciousness, engaged and engaging. She further notes in "Realism and Reality": "The new investigations of the unconscious have brought people nearer to poetry, for every man knows that he is continuously constructing a dream duplicate of his life in the same symbolic terms used familiarly by the poets and that he too possesses a very subtle and intricate way of dramatizing the concealed meaning of his life" (25). Characters, too, are creating, are artists. We are also reminded by the *representation* of consciousness that these characters not only *create* but *are created,* which complicates the narrator's comparatively absent stance, in a way that will be discussed after we explore a central question: What is the nature of the relationship of internality to externality? To make consciousness the substance of narration is to underscore the relationship of internality to externality in the individual creation of "reality."

The aesthetics of the Ninian collage mode involve the submission of the narrator to a new focus on consciousness's internal dialogue with, and constitution of, the external. Roland Barthes, in his essay "Myth Today," presents a semiological system of myth construction which has as its basis the multiplicity of significations available for encountered forms. Sigmund Freud's essay "Formulations Regarding the Two Principles in Mental Functioning" provides a psychoanalytic paradigm for the operations of consciousness that the semiological model implies. In the Ninian collage mode, we find characters in the act of myth construction, inspired and interrupted by the external. It is a narrative aesthetic whose implications are simultaneously semiological and psychoanalytic.

In the Barthesian mythological system, objects as such exist only insofar as they are "appropriated" and lent significance by an encountering consciousness.[2] Barthes does not limit the category "signifier" to language, of course, but allows consideration of any object as such: "even objects will become speech, if they mean something" (111). Barthes characterizes mythological construction as "*a second-order semiological system*. That which is a sign (namely the associative total of a concept and an image), becomes a mere signifier in the second" (114).[3] That is, an object taken as itself in the first system is transformed by the encountering consciousness into the signifier of a new signification: "When it becomes form, the meaning leaves its contingency behind; it empties itself, it becomes impoverished, history evaporates, only the letter remains" (117) and "this history which drains out of the form will be wholly absorbed by the concept. . . . Through the concept, it is a whole new history which is implanted in the myth" (118–19). Thus any external qualities an object may be said to possess in and of itself are dispensable in myth construction and are subject to the demands of the appropriating consciousness. Barthes also writes: "The concept closely corresponds to a function, it is defined as a tendency" (119). As will become more clear once we consider Freud, choice of object (as well as what the object will signify once chosen), is a function, in the Barthesian sense, of the consciousness, an appropriation by consciousness (or the unconscious, as inferred from this choice) for the purpose of constituting the external internally. It is chosen because of what it *can* signify.

The construction of an internal externality is an act of naturalization of the mythological signification of encountered objects.[4] Barthes explains that "for the myth-reader . . . everything happens as if the picture *naturally* conjured up the concept, as if the signifier *gave a foundation* to the signified" (129–30; his emphasis). In other words, what a Ninian narrator provides is an account of how myths are read, of the internal mythological structures of externality produced by such reading. In providing this, the narrator functions simultaneously as a Barthesian "mythologist" and as a Barthesian "producer of myths."[5] In writing these consciousnesses, the narrator *produces* myths representing the consciousnesses; this is a function of all narration not unique to the Ninian narrative mode. But because the material of the Ninian collage mode is consciousness itself, the narrator also functions as a mythologist, lay-ing bare the process by which mythological signification occurs. "Consciousness" refers to the activity of the encounter itself, not necessarily its motive factors, which may be conscious or unconscious (or readable as both).

But how does this mechanism of object encounter and appropriation operate? In *The Ego and the Id*, Sigmund Freud proposes an answer: "later on object-cathexes proceed from the id, which feels erotic trends as needs. The ego, . . . still feeble, becomes aware of the object-cathexes, and either acquiesces in them or tries to fend them off by the process of repression" (23). The *representation* of consciousness is a representation of the ego's awareness of the id's object-cathexes. For whatever reason an object is cathected by the id, its presence in consciousness precipitates a rejection or an embrace, according to its consistency with that consciousness's preferred internal mythological construction of externality.

The object already preferred is external as well as internal. Its preferred status stems from its consistency with a mythological representation of external circumstances that is already in place internally. Desire is its only impetus; no external object need be present in order to provoke conscious consideration of the object already preferred. If an object does so, it is only because, at the mythological level, its concept is equivalent to the concept already appropriated; for example, one passes a beautiful person on the street and, rather than following that person down the street with one's gaze after the encounter, one recalls *another* beautiful person already constituted in one's consciousness. In "Formulations Regarding the Two Principles in Mental Functioning," Freud distinguishes between the operations of the pleasure and reality principles,[6] and associates the pleasure principle with the operation of "phantasy-making": "With the introduction of the reality-principle one mode of thought-activity was split off . . . kept free from reality-testing and remained subordinated to the pleasure-principle alone. This is the act of phantasy-making," which, Freud points out, occurs early in children's games and is repeated later in daydreams. Such phantasy-making, then, "abandons its dependence on real objects" (24). In Freudian terms, the object already preferred, then, is the object of "phantasy." Nevertheless, the phantasy does not necessarily "abandon its dependence on real objects" but rather, as the construction of an internal mythology of the external, it constitutes them as "real" or not by this very process.

When presented with objects that ostensibly disrupt this "phantasy," consciousness either ignores, prefers, or rejects such an object as an "object inconsistent." An ignored object functions neutrally, passing before the eye and just as quickly away again. The ignored object functions as the occasionally necessary alien external does in the narrative provided by the narrative consciousness, of which this *representation* of consciousness is a part; that is, it functions as a spatial or temporal marker within a represented consciousness's narrative of itself. We can consider this mechanism as operating in relation to Freud's early comments on the "reality principle,"[7] as given in "Formulations": "A special function was instituted which had periodically to search the outer world, in order that its data might be already familiar if an urgent inner need should arise; this function was attention. Its activity meets the sense-impressions halfway, instead of awaiting their appearance" (23). It is "attention" that makes selection possible, determines the range of objects to be considered by consciousness. "Passing of judgement" is that act of selection itself: "In place of repression . . . there developed an impartial passing of judgement, which had to decide whether a particular idea was true or false, that is, was in agreement with reality or not; decision was determined by comparison with the memory-traces of reality" (23). This "passing of judgement," however, is anything but "impartial," and its being "true or false" depends on the internal mythology already in place.

Freud's statements regarding the reality principle in *Beyond the Pleasure Principle* allow us to theorize a psychoanalytic approach to this aesthetic-mythological construction that does not depend on impartiality but implies its opposite. He writes: "This [reality] principle does not abandon the intention of ultimately obtaining pleasure, but it nevertheless demands and carries into effect the postponement of satisfaction, the abandonment of a number of possibilities of gaining satisfaction and the temporary toleration of unpleasure as a step on the long indirect road to pleasure" (7). It is not that the painful cathected object is no less mythologized than the object already preferred. And it is cathected not in spite of its being painful but precisely *because* it is painful. This process provides a means by which to gain control over a painful object, as Freud's story of the "*fort-da*" game illustrates: "the child turned his experience into a game from another motive. At the outset he was in a *passive* situation—he was overpowered by the experience; but, by repeating it, unpleasurable though it was, as a game, he took on an *active* part" (15). In "Formulations" Freud asserts that in the process of passing judgment on encountered objects, consciousness "meets the sense-impressions halfway" (23). To do so is to do as the child in the *fort-da* game does, to take an "active part" in the internal digestion of their significance, regardless of whether these objects are painful. If they are rejected, it is not because they are not mythologized in cathexis—the "attention" they are given implies that they are indeed cathected—but because their significations are not consistent with the mythology already preferred. The initial cathexis of an object that is ultimately rejected occurs as a result of what it is *able* to signify, in order that it *may* be rejected, which rejection is, in effect, a consolidation of the preferred myth, the final destination of this "long indirect road to pleasure."

In *Beyond the Pleasure Principle* Freud also writes that "the replacement of the pleasure principle by the reality principle can only be made responsible for a small number, and by no means the most intense, of unpleasurable experiences" (7). But the reality principle does not necessarily replace the pleasure principle; rather, the two act in tandem. The internal mythological construction is not simply a function of a pleasure-principle "phantasy" but of the mechanisms of the reality principle as well. Furthermore, the object cathected can function as the consolidation of a preferred myth, or "phantasy," that is already painful; that is, there can be a pleasure constituted *by* the painful. We can consider object-cathexis as the rejection of a Barthesian first-order signification in order to fill that same form with a new concept, or as a selection of elements of that first-order signification as the *whole* of the signification. Rejection of the cathected object is the rejection of an alternative second-order signification that is not consistent with that which is preferred.

At the end of "Formulations" Freud points to art as providing an interesting resolution of the apparent conflict between the pleasure and reality principles that he has outlined. He characterizes the artist as someone "who turns from reality because he cannot come to terms with the demand for the renunciation of instinctual satisfaction as it is first made, and who then in phantasy-life allows full play to his erotic and ambitious wishes. . . . with his special gifts he moulds his phantasies into a new kind of reality. . . . But this he can only attain because other men feel the same dissatisfaction as he with the renunciation demanded by reality, and because this dissatisfaction, resulting from the displacement of the pleasure-principle by the reality-principle, is itself a part of reality" (26–27). For Freud, the artist's "special gifts" are special only by virtue of their ability to persuade others to endow with significance their unique vision of the external. Nin shows, however, that the act of artistic creation is not special in this way but common, in fact the necessary means by which the digestion of the external by consciousness occurs; the unconscious is left to us as readers to infer, given these consciousnesses themselves as objects. The act of mythological interpretation by consciousness is itself an act of aesthetic creation.

Nin's narrative mode not only presents us with an object to cathect (the text and the objects within it) but takes as its "stuff" the very process by which this occurs. In their perception/creation of their own mythological texts of experience, the characters cathect but reject irrelevant objects, a function of Freudian "attention," in order to present to themselves only that which enriches or confirms the structural unity of their personal myth. One effect of this collage mode is its pointing out of our own acts of reading and interpretation. We are able, as readers, not only to read an object prior to a represented consciousness's exposure to it, but to read the reactions resulting from that exposure as well. In doing so, we mythologize them, give them a place in the structure of the myth of the text that we create.[8] Reading is a collage-making enterprise.

The role of the narrator in Nin's narrative system is to expose the mythological nature of experience by representing consciousness, the actual mechanism of this experience. To do so implies the subjugation of the narrative voice by the narrative voice itself. In other words, the narrative concerns of the text will be not the narrator's own consciousness but primarily other represented consciousnesses. The world of the text is no longer exclusively the narrator's world but one peopled by diverse, and ostensibly independent, represented consciousnesses.

Of course, the narrator can never be absent, and the text and those consciousnesses represented therein are themselves mythological constructions of the narrator. Reportage is never eradicated from the text; instead, the *matter* of what is reported shifts from static objects to represented consciousness or those objects that modify it. As Nin writes in "The Writer and the Symbols": "The creation of a story is a *quest for meaning*. The objects, the incidents, the characters are always there, as they are for the painter, but the key which catalyzes is the relation between the exterior and interior drama. The significance *is* the drama" (45). The narrator provides objects independent of consciousness only when those objects are relevant to consciousness, somehow reinforce or modify its representation.

The Ninian narrator is a sympathetic narrator. That is, the narrator attempts to negate his/her own authority, and the implications of a static external world, by presenting a myth—the text—in terms of other (represented) consciousnesses. If it does not present the consciousness itself, the narration will suggest consciousness nonetheless. The presentation of objects, scenarios, or commentary other than as received by represented consciousnesses occurs in several ways:

(1) Objects are given independent of represented consciousness, but only so that they may then be encountered by that consciousness.

(2) The consciousness is not represented directly but reported by the narrator.

(3) The narrator engages in psychoanalysis of the represented consciousness.

The narrator is, of course, inescapably present. But the Ninian narrative system undermines the narrator's authority *as such* by insisting upon a narrator whose narrative practices nullify that authority. By locating the "real" in represented consciousness or, if the narrator is to speak for him/herself, in the examination/analysis of represented consciousnesses, the narrator in the Ninian system underscores the mythological nature of all constructions of experience, including that of the narrator him/herself.[9]

Nin's indictment of realist reportage continues in *The Novel of the Future*, where she asserts the importance of psychoanalysis itself in the construction of a narrative mode whose logic is that of the internal mechanisms of consciousness. She writes: "Psychoanalysis proved that dreams were the only key to our subconscious life. What the psychoanalysts stress, the relation between dream and our conscious acts, is what the poets already know. The poets walk this bridge with ease, from conscious to unconscious, physical reality to psychological reality" (5). That is, an understanding of the relation of the external and internal is what defines the writer qua writer in Nin's model. This adjustment in focus asserts the availability, in the representation of the internal, of a more *real* real, one in which we will not be "cheated of experience," as Nin claims we are in the realist novel, through its reportage, its insistence that the knowability of the text's reality exists only in static externalities. In other words, the character is to be sufficient in and of itself, the primary locus of the text's reality, simultaneously constructed by relations to the significant objects encountered in the external world and constructing the significance, the very reality of those objects. It is this that we are to see, and in seeing it, we are to come to understand the fundamental aestheticism of everyday life. Nin writes, "I give much importance to the Walter Mitty in all of us, to our dreams and fantasies, because I am convinced of their importance, their influence, and their revelatory character" (44).

Even as Nin asserts the importance of the narrator as analyst, this does not imply that the narrator must become present as such. Indeed, to do so would be to distract us from the internal operations of the characters she represents, destroying the narrative pretense that the reality of the text is their own by undermining their ability to signify a mutable, textual world whose logic is subject to their own interpretive acts. A narrator whose analytic interpolations draw our attention to her own processes of reading and interpretation grounds the epistemological authority of the novel not in the variability implied by the representation of various consciousnesses but in her own, mediating consciousness. It is here that the influence of Rank's model of the creative personality is most apparent.

In *Truth and Reality* Rank establishes a model of artistic consciousness, of the "creative will," that differentiates the mechanisms of the artist's consciousness from those of other, nonartistic types. He writes: "While the average well adjusted man can make the reality that is generally accepted as truth into his own truth, the creative searcher after truth seeks and finds his own truth which he then wants to make general—that is, real. He creates his reality, as it were, from his truth. The neurotic, on the other hand, finds his subjective truth but cannot accept it as such and destroys therewith the given reality, that is, the pleasurable relation to it, as he is neither in position to make it his truth nor to translate his truth into reality. The difference lies again in the attitude or rather in the kind of consciousness, in its relation to will. The average man has reality consciousness more strongly developed, the creative type will consciousness, the neurotic individual self-consciousness" (43). Rank presents "will consciousness," that of the artist, as an interpretive exertion at the interface of the internal and external, a tipping of the balance in favor of the internal, a balance that Nin also seeks to tip in the construction of textual reality. Rank's distinction between the various truths and realities establishes the terms according to which he can differentiate the artistic from "normal" consciousness (not to mention the neurotic). In spite of his implicit acceptance of Freud's terms that the construction of the "real" in consciousness is a dialectical one, governed not only by external stimuli but by a willingness (or need) to receive them, Rank's model denies that these differences are simply of degree, rather than of kind. That is, Rank's model does *not* allow for the fundamental aestheticism of the normal man—or, except in passing, and prior to this set of distinctions, of the neurotic.

The true uniqueness of the creative type's conscious engagement with the world, it seems, is its intensity, its manifestation of the artist's lack of satisfaction with the raw materials already available for creation provoking an urge to manufacture different ones. But an artist does not "create his reality from his truth" any differently than the other two—he is simply more aware of the process according to which this operates. Nevertheless, Rank's notion of the creative will provides a useful model for describing the motivations, and implications, of the hyperinterpretive impulse of Nin's narrator. The Rankian character of the Ninian narrator is superficially evident in the overwhelming number of characters Nin represents, throughout her novels, who are already artists. But representing a consciousness already presumed to be creative does nothing to advance the celebration of the fundamental aestheticism of everyday life (or everyday man) that Nin's writings on narrative appear to emphasize. Similarly, analytic interpolations serve as reminders of the presence of the narrator's own governing creative will, emphasizing the location of textual reality in that single consciousness, rather than in those of the characters. Thus, the represented consciousnesses of her characters, supposed to be sites of the destabilization of realist authority because of their ostensible independence, become subordinated to her own consolidating voice, seemingly obliterating the very multiplicity that would allow such a critique.

But this present, collage-making narrative voice does not necessarily undermine the project of creating textual world(s) that come into being as functions of consciousness. In "Realism and Reality" Nin discusses her narratology in terms of the unconscious: "As my books take place in the unconscious, and hardly ever outside of it, they differ from poetry not in tone, language or rhythm, but merely by the fact that they contain both the symbol and the interpretation of the symbol" (24). In other words, the sympathetic Ninian narrator provides access not only to consciousness but also to the unconscious in two ways. As readers, we can infer the unconscious, from within whatever psychoanalytic paradigm we prefer, from the mythological exigencies of the represented consciousnesses themselves. And there are also occasions on which the narrator provides

access to the unconscious by engaging in psychoanalysis—
essentially, by interpreting the text. When doing so—or making any
interpretation—the narrator offers *him/herself* as a readable consciousness or unconscious, further reminding us that the text is not
a representation of a static, undisputed "real" but the product of a
unique consciousness's mythological exigencies, just as it is an
examination of the conditions of "reality" as experienced by the
characters within it.

The Narrator Narrating: *Collages*

Before continuing to discuss how the sympathetic narrator functions in *Collages,* we must distinguish between the structure, or
form, of the narrative and its substance or that which it narrates.
In *Collage of Dreams* Sharon Spencer writes that "collage includes
two types of materials: the ones collected for the composition and
the means of fastening them together" (5). The nineteen distinct
episodes of narrated internal experience in *Collages* are the raw
materials of the collage that is the text, and the narrator's narrative
practice is the means by which the text comes to be constructed,
itself a function of the narrator's own mythological, interpretive
exigencies. It is also important to differentiate the text's "narrator"
and "author." Though we can refer to each as "Nin," the narrator is
a construction distinct from the biographical, biological entity
"Anaïs Nin." The narrator is someone—or something—read from
the text, posited from a reading of the text, independent of any
external biographical nuance ascribable to the "author." Of course
the "author" too, to a lesser degree, is no more than a readable
object, albeit one who has actually had the luxury of breathing.[10]

Though less present than a narrator unconcerned with representing experience via consciousnesses, the sympathetic narrator,
as often as possible, puts his/her presence at the service of the very
consciousnesses represented in the text. The most obvious evidence of this presence is the structure, or arrangement, of the text
itself; the logic of the text's arrangement is a logic attributable to
the narrator—though, as Fish has pointed out, this is an interpretive move made by the reader and therefore subject to the reader's
concepts of textual logic. Franklin and Schneider comment: "A few
of the nineteen brief chapters, or collages, follow logically from
their predecessors, but most often there is no transition from chapter to chapter with the expected result that the reader recalls only
highlights and has at the end no sense of the novel's wholeness"
(147–48).[11] But in the collage text, what comprises continuity and

"wholeness"? The very lack of a distinct, continuous narrative arc is what allows *Collages* not only to present each collage episode as a discrete unit (as a single emblem of myth construction) but also to signify collage-*ness* itself. That is, the assemblage of collage episodes makes the text itself a collage, one that implies the narrator's governing consciousness as collage maker. However, though the narrator is thus uncovered as collage maker, this does not imply a reversion to a claim of narrative authority but, as we will see, quite the opposite.

Furthermore, it is not that there is *no* transition between chapters but that, often, this transition is subtle.[12] Rather than subjecting the logic of transition to the narrator's governing consciousness, the narrator of *Collages* often locates it in the consciousness(es) (s)he has represented in the text. For instance, chapter 2 ends with the automobile fetishist's letter to Renate about California's "wonderful roads" (19), and chapter 3 begins with Renate's having relocated to Malibu. The movement from chapter 2 to chapter 3 is dictated by Renate, not the narrator, and in implying a connection between the letter's available myths of California and Renate's decision, it makes available a reading of Renate's unconscious. Similarly, chapter 1 ends with the story Renate's uncle tells about how his bones become hollow, and chapter 2 begins with Renate's meeting Bruce: "When Bruce first came to Vienna Renate noticed him because of his resemblance to one of the statues which smiled at her through her bedroom window" (11). Though this does not relate in any obvious way to the story of Renate's uncle, it does reflect the significance of the beginning of chapter 1, in which we learn of Renate's fascination with the Viennese statues. That is, the logic of transition from chapter 1 to chapter 2 is a movement from the establishment of Renate's fascination (and its significance) toward the continuing effect of this fascination.

Of course, these links are not always obvious and not always, necessarily, present. But can a lack of continuity, or continuity unrelated to the represented consciousnesses that are the subject of the text, be the product of a sympathetic narrator? Is the narrator still sympathetic in such circumstances? Even in cases where no apparent logic governs the transition, the default logic, as it were, is that of the narrator. The perceived lack of continuity is then ascribable to the caprice of the narrator. This intrusion of the narrator's consciousness does not undermine the narrator's status as sympathetic because the narrative consciousness thus implied is one whose actions reveal its status as collage maker. In the process the narrator is (self-)revealed as dynamic and ultimately *readable*, rather than as static or as asserting a *world* that is static, readable only once.

But it is the representation of consciousness(es) that comprises most of the activity of the sympathetic narrator. The most direct approach to such representation, of course, is to provide access to the interior itself, to present the interior speaking for itself, instead of simply describing it or the external world it encounters. This also occurs to some extent in dialogue, especially in characters' story-telling, insofar as such instances are the instantaneous products of consciousness and provide material that can come to represent the unconscious. An example is this passage from chapter 2 of *Collages:*

> As soon as she saw it she wanted a dress of that color and that intensity. That was not difficult to find in a Mexican sea town. . . . The orange cotton had almost invisible blood-red threads running though it as if the Mexicans had concocted their dyes from the coral tree flower itself.
>
> The coral tree would kill the memory of a black gnarled tree and of two figures sheltered under its grotesque branches.
>
> The coral tree would carry her into a world of festivities. An orange world.
>
> In Haiti the trees were said to walk at night. (14–15)

Here the "coral tree" appears only as a function of Renate. We first find Renate's reaction *reported* by the narrator, but the remainder of this passage is equally ascribable to Renate herself. In Nin's text, it is often difficult to determine whether such a passage is a repre-sented consciousness or a description by the narrator of the activi-ties of such a consciousness. But, again, such is not the "reportage" against which Nin rails in her essays; if it is reportage, it is at least of a variety concerned with a description not of a static externality but of the process by which that externality is constituted internally.

It is common for the narrator to provide an object independently of the consciousness represented, but only to establish its presence so that said consciousness may encounter it. *Collages* begins:

> Vienna was the city of statues. They were as numerous as the people who walked the streets. They stood on the top of the highest towers, lay down on stone tombs, sat on horseback, kneeled, prayed, fought animals and wars, danced, drank wine and read books made of stone. They adorned cornices like the fig-ureheads of old ships. They stood in the heart of fountains glis-tening with water as if they had just been born. They sat under the trees in the parks summer and winter. Some wore costumes

of other periods, and some no clothes at all. Men, women, children, kings, dwarfs, gargoyles, unicorns, lions, clowns, heroes, wise men, prophets, angels, saints and soldiers preserved for Vienna an illusion of eternity.

As a child Renate could see them from her bedroom window. (7)

The description of the statues is followed by the narrator's presentation of Renate's reaction to them. This last line is also an instance of reporting consciousness, where we are provided not with that consciousness itself but a description of it. The statues exist only in order to be encountered by Renate, or in order that Renate's encounter with them may be reported.[13] Still, one wonders if, at times during the description of the statues, it is not the narrator but Renate endowing the statues with their mythological significance, especially when we learn later, when given the reasons for her initial attraction to Bruce, that the statues do tend to have such significance for her.

In *The Mirror and the Garden* Evelyn Hinz correctly notes that "all of Nin's fiction is structured upon the principle of limited point of view" (51). She errs, however, when she claims that "Nin's characters are depicted through their musings rather than through authorial comment" (51). In Nin's texts, it is also common for the narrator actually to psychoanalyze those characters/consciousnesses represented. In chapter 6 we are introduced to Raven, a young woman who identifies with the birds who share her name. She tells Renate, "His black wings, his sharp beak, his strong claws completed me, added something I lacked, added the element of darkness" (40). Of course, these are things Raven already possesses but allows the raven to signify. If we were now to construct a case study of Raven, this would be an excellent place to start. Indeed, the narrator does so, commenting just before Raven's confession, "This dream of a fierce raven seemed to balance elements of her being" (40). If this is not a *report* of Raven's own interpretation of her behavior, it is the narrator's analysis. Even so, the interpreting, or psychoanalytic, narrator is still sympathetic, maintaining a presence whose function it is, if not to represent consciousness, then to report it or comment on the circumstances of its internal encounters with the external.

It is almost impossible, mechanically, in a third-person narration at least, to completely subdue or obliterate evidence of the narrator's presence. For example, it may be necessary to indicate who is delivering dialogue by the use of such phrases as "he said." The narrator may establish a scene, or the objects within it, in order to allow the consciousnesses represented there to cathect and react to them; those reactions in turn undermine any claims to independent "reality" that the objects or scenarios may claim in and of themselves. The narrator is never absent and can only undermine narrative authority by creating a text that calls attention to the internally mediated status of any representation of the "external." The sympathetic narrator thus enables the representation of the relationship between internality and externality, just as it depends on that representation to temper the significance of its own presence.

The Self as Collage

In *Collages* the representation of myth construction, of the internal/external dialectic, occurs primarily in two ways. In the first, the narrator reports the objects, process, and result of myth construction; this is accomplished without direct access to the consciousness in question. The second is storytelling. Characters' storytelling is the primary ostensibly *direct* indicator Nin's narrator gives of the consciousnesses of the characters represented in the text. In storytelling, characters simultaneously reveal their own myths and offer these, and consequently themselves, as objects to be embraced (appropriated) or rejected according to the mythological/interpretive demands of the listener. In the present exploration of myth construction and collage making in *Collages*, I will focus on only a few exemplary moments. Such an exploration entails the exclusion of many episodes, characters, or moments that may likewise be exemplary. This should be taken not as an assertion of the insignificance of the excluded objects but as symptomatic of critical practice which is, after all, a process of collage making as well.

A Collage of Miscellaneous Myths

Within *Collages* are numerous reports of myth construction. One of the most imaginative instances is the story of the old man who becomes enamored of living the life of a seal. He has loved the sea, associated the sea with himself and himself with the sea: "One night he slept in one of the caves. He thought to himself: Now I am a merman" (45). He appropriates the sea and all associated with it, including the seals, as "external" objects that reinforce (and create) his preferred myth of himself. Indeed, his later attempt to approximate the behavior of seals indicates that their presence in this scene has led to a subtle alteration of the myth: not only are the seals a part of what signifies *him,* but in this activity he has come to signify the seals, in a circular reinforcement of his own preferred seaside myth. Within the larger story that is the narrator's report of the old man's myth-creation process is a rare example of the narrator unequivocally presenting the internal voice of a character: "Now I am a merman."

More often, the narrator does not explicitly indicate the source of such observations, leaving us wondering whether it is the narrator speaking or the consciousness represented. In the story of the consul's wife and her obsessive acquisition of rugs, we find an instance of such narrative behavior: "The last one was so ancient that only the backing showed, and very little of the colored wool's design, but she knew what this design had been. / She even preferred to re-weave these missing fragments in her mind. It was a spiritual discipline which enabled her, sitting in her California patio, to re-weave the fragments of her life in foreign places" (86). In the most of this passage the speaker, referring to the consul's wife not as "I" but as "she," is the narrator. The opening clause of the first sentence, however, could just as easily be read as originating in the consul's wife herself, as an ostensibly unmediated observation by that consciousness.[14] This ambiguity is representative of the narrative strategy of the collage mode itself, which seeks to problematize the status of the narrator's authority just as it confirms the inescapability of the narrator's presence.

Most often, we receive these processes indirectly, as *reports* of the myth-making activity of consciousness, rather than as ostensibly independent statements by those consciousnesses themselves (which are also, necessarily, reported but whose very presence indicates a narrative attempt to obscure that status). Appropriately, the narrator describes the artistic process of Varda the collagist thus: "After his scissors had touched them, his women became flowers, plants and sea shells" (59). We are not simply told that Varda creates art, we are shown the very process itself, which is a process in which Varda embraces the objects preferred by transforming them into objects that, previously, they have only implied to him. They are preferred because they first *suggest* themselves as available, as possibly consistent with the notions of "flowers, plants and sea shells" to Varda who then, with his scissors, transforms them into, or appropriates them as, representations of those very things. The myth—of the beauty that "flowers, plants, and sea shells" can represent—is already in place, and these women, for Varda, are easily cathectable as preferred objects that reinforce that myth. Similarly, when Renate and her friends begin an arts magazine, they are swindled by a gardener who poses as a millionaire: "There was no law to jail a man who swindled one of illusions and not money. The gardener watered other people's dreams. It was not his fault that they grew so big and had to be pruned" (105). Certainly it is not his fault that those at the magazine believed so strongly in the myth of their own success that their cathexes of him admitted no contradiction of his appearance as a wealthy savior. That is, his appearance lent him credibility, allowed them to cathect him as a preferred object, yet another reinforcement of the myth of their magazine's success.

A Collage of Stories

Just as there are many peripheral *reports* of myth construction, so there are many *stories* told by characters, marginal and otherwise, dramatizing their own processes of mythologization. An early example is the story Renate's uncle tells to justify his belief that his bones are hollow: "My mother told me that she became pregnant while still nursing me. Slowly I realized that this other child, my brother, had absorbed all the nourishment away from me, thus leaving me without marrow in my bones" (10). This is the story of the appropriation of *another* story, that which his mother has told him about the circumstances surrounding her nursing him. Whether this is the "true" genesis of the uncle's myth of hollow bones or whether that myth produced this memory to reinforce it—a case of Freudian "deferred action"[15]—is irrelevant. Renate's uncle has cathected as preferred the object that is this story from his mother and has made it reinforce the myth of his hollow bones. His telling of the story makes it, and him, available to interpretation, cathectable as a representation of him, in the service of whatever myth of him—as insane, as magical—the listener, or the reader, may have. Storytelling is not always a direct account of the construction of a myth, as Renate's uncle's story is. But storytelling is always an act whose product is available to be interpreted/cathected and subsequently appropriated in the service of whatever mythological structure is required by the listener/reader.

Representations of storytelling dramatize the circumstances of all reading. We are not told whether Renate's uncle is crazy or whether Renate thinks he is. The absence of interpretation reminds us of the availability of the story to many different interpretations, once again reminding us of the absence of stability in interpretation. A conversation between Renate and the consul is also significant:

"And you'll be disappointed when I tell you I am not Jean."

"You mean, you are no longer Jean. You have become someone else."

"I never was Jean. I was the non-hero of the book, the half-
gangster, the ambiguous adventurer. The hero was the man my
mother wanted me to be. The gangster was me. The man you
came to see is the hero of the book. The world I create I leave
behind me, like an old skin." (84)

The consul assumes that Renate associates him with the character
Jean of his fiction, and he corrects her by disavowing any similarity. Unwilling to relinquish her cathexis of him as a preferred
object in the service of the myth of "Jean," Renate resists his claim,
suggesting that he can still represent "having been Jean." But the
consul denies this as well, offering his own alternative reading of
his text, offering himself as an object signifying "the gangster." He
recognizes Renate's myth when he comments that she has come to
see "Jean," and in the next sentence he implicitly confirms his
availability as a reinforcement of "Jean." In spite of his denial that
he *is* "Jean," the consul's assertion that he abandons the fictional
worlds he creates "like an old skin" is a confession of their availability to interpretations independent of his own intentions. In
effect, he has confirmed the validity of Renate's appropriation of
him as a reinforcement of "Jean" even as he disagrees with it in his
own self-cathexis as reinforcement of his own myth of himself.

Renate's and Bruce's Collage(s)

Franklin and Schneider comment that "Nin makes several exquis-
ite collages in this novel, but the artist Renate is unable to give
shape to her own life" (149). But in fact *Collages,* as we have begun
to see, documents the number of ways in which a number of characters "give shape" to their own lives. And the drama of Renate's
infatuation and disillusionment with Bruce is one of the text's
most comprehensive explorations of myth construction, or collage
making. It begins with Renate's whimsical attachment to the Viennese statues: "At night, when the white muslin curtains fluttered
out like ballooning wedding dresses, she heard them whispering
like figures which had been petrified by a spell during the day and
came alive only at night. Their silence by day taught her to read
their frozen lips as one reads the messages of deaf mutes. . . .
Renate would never allow anyone to tell her the history of the
statues, or to identify them. This would have situated them in
the past" (7). Because they are silent and assert nothing to the
contrary, Renate is free to cathect them as part of whatever

mythological paradigm she pleases. In a remarkably literal parallel of the Barthesian system, Renate refuses the history of the statues so that she can continue to cathect them in this always changing, imaginative way.

When Renate meets Bruce, her initial mythological cathexis of him stems from her earlier cathexes of the Viennese statues. Her noticing him at all occurs only because of his resemblance to the object already preferred: "When Bruce first came to Vienna Renate noticed him because of his resemblance to one of the statues which smiled at her through her bedroom window" (11). Specifically, it is the statue of the god Mercury, and all that it signifies, that "Bruce" invokes: "She recognized in Bruce the long neck, the runner's legs, the lock of hair over the forehead. / But Bruce denied this relationship to Mercury. He thought of himself as Pan. He showed Renate how long the downy hair was at the tip of his ears. / Familiarity with the agile, restless statue put her at ease with Bruce. What added to the resemblance was that Bruce talked little" (11). Renate embraces "Bruce" as the embodiment of the myth of Mercury in spite of his insistence that he bears more resemblance to Pan. For Renate the long, downy hair becomes the object rejected, though in its evocation of Pan it is the already-preferred object in Bruce's own established myth of "Bruce." The text here, like Renate, allows Bruce's presentation of evidence only to avoid further commentary on it. Instead the text returns, as does Renate, to "Bruce" as "Mercury," both signifiers of the already-preferred myth of restlessness and agility. The final line of this passage is, first, another comparison of Bruce with the statue-as-object—that is, the statue does not talk, and Bruce's taciturnity is further grounds for physical comparison. What is of greater importance is that Bruce's taciturnity provides Renate with fewer objects to cathect and reject, less evidence to contradict her already-preferred myth of, now, "Bruce"-as-"Mercury"-as-"restlessness-and-agility." What this "adds" to is not the signification itself but the *ease* of the signification; Renate, even confronted with numerous objections from Bruce, would simply reject them and cling to whatever evidence about Bruce would enable the survival of the myth.

Bruce's attempts to utilize storytelling as a means to make Renate understand him only highlight further the disparities in their respective mythological cathexes of "Bruce." After having let her read the beginning of his novel, Bruce provides Renate with some boxes, each of which contains a story about him, to be opened, Bruce says, "Whenever you get desperate with my mysteries, my ambiguities" (29). At first Renate too appreciates these stories as a means to come to know Bruce: "The time came again, when she felt she did not possess a love; that a love which was mute, elusive, and vague was not really a love" (29). When she doubts the validity of her "Bruce," she turns to these stories to quell her doubts. But what she finds there only contradicts her idea of "Bruce" or, at the very least, cannot reinforce it. After the story of Bruce's erotic flogging encounter with a Mexican boy, Renate rejects all of the stories: "Renate took the pages, folded them as tightly as they had been folded to fit into the compartment, pushed them into the opening and slipped the various slats back into place, *as if she would bury the story forever.* She walked down the hill with the box. She stood on the edge of the rock, and threw it in a wide, high arc, into the sea. Then she returned home, placed the pyramid of boxes inside the fireplace and set fire to them" (32, emphasis mine). Her attempt at burial is a rejection of these as objects that could reinforce her preferred myth of Bruce. However, they have also had the effect of establishing a new, at least equally powerful myth of Bruce, one that she rejects as inconsistent with her mythological lover. We know that Bruce can no longer signify Renate's precious myth of the lover, her precious myth of "Mercury," because she takes all of their linens to be cleaned, "stained with marks of love, dreams, nightmares, tears and kisses and quarrels, the mists that rise from bodies touching, the fogs of breathing, the dried tears" (33). She refuses to allow the objects to retain their signification of her love for Bruce, indicating that this love is no longer part of the signification of "Bruce." Disillusion is the moment of *re*-illusion, however. Renate's disillusionment with Bruce as the preferred "Bruce" occurs only when "Bruce" comes to signify something new and contradictory. That is, she can reject Bruce as the signifier of what "Bruce" has signified once "Bruce" has a new signification, in this case one that is the opposite of its original.

The Collage(s) of Dr. Mann and Judith Sands

The relationship between Dr. Mann and Judith Sands not only dramatizes the conditions of myth construction, it is consciously predicated on those conditions. We are given the following paragraph as Dr. Mann is determining how to go about bringing Judith Sands out of seclusion: "Every novelist knows that at one time or another he will be confronted with the incarnation of one of his characters. Whether that character is based on a living person or not, it will draw into its circle those who resemble it. Sooner or later the portrait will attract its twin, by the magnetism of narcissism, and the author will feel this inhabitant of his novel come to life and hear his character speaking as he had imagined. / And so, Doctor Mann . . . picked up his own story" (113–14). The words "And so" indicate that the preceding paragraph, presumably an interjection of the narrator's thoughts, is actually a report of Dr. Mann's reasoning. We are told that he "began an interminable monologue like one of the characters in her novel" (113). The purpose of his monologue is to present to Judith Sands a version of "Dr. Mann" that will evoke a character in her novel, not through physical resemblance but by means of an aesthetic similarity, a *narrative* similarity. However, he can do so only because he has already appropriated Sands's novel as an object in the service of a preferred myth of "Judith Sands—writer"; it is this that he tries to approximate, in fact *enacting* "Judith Sands—writer" in order to attract the interest of Judith Sands.

But in enacting "Judith Sands—writer," it turns out, Dr. Mann is only portraying a version of himself that the figure of Judith Sands already signifies. He tells her: "But you have been my writer self writing for me. I could talk wastefully, negligently, only because you were there preserving and containing my spirit. . . . No one should be forced to carry the unfulfilled self of another. But if you are so skilled with words and have already written *me,* in a sense you have stolen *me,* and must return what you stole" (115–16). "Judith Sands—writer" is the repository of Dr. Mann's concept of his own "writer self." Having read "Judith Sands" as his "writer self," Dr. Mann's performance outside Judith Sands's door is, in effect, an attempt to reconcile himself to his own creative power. Indeed, in the very act of courting such approval, Dr. Mann proves this power, and the statements regarding a novelist's encounter "with the incarnation of one of his characters," which initially seem to refer only to Judith Sands, are equally applicable to Dr. Mann. That is, the revelation that Dr. Mann's mythological cathexis of "Judith Sands—writer" is essentially a reinforcement of an already established and preferred myth of "Dr. Mann" asserts that every internal encounter with and interpretation/construction of the "external" is, in fact, an act no different from that of the author writing, of the narrator narrating. Judith Sands is just as much a character in Dr. Mann's fiction as he is trying to be—and is—in hers.

Further complicating a reading of Judith Sands is the ending of *Collages*. It is fitting that Judith Sands is the last major character introduced in the text. There have been other writers—the consul, his wife, Bruce—but Judith Sands is the "writer" of the text we have been reading. The novel ends with a (nearly) verbatim repetition of the first several lines of the text:[16] "Vienna was the city of statues. They were as numerous as the people who walked the streets. They stood on the tip of the highest towers, lay down on stone tombs, sat on horseback, kneeled, prayed, fought animals and wars, danced, drank wine and read books made of stone" (122). It is ironic that the text ends on the phrase "read books made of stone," for books, in the narratological universe of this text, are not made of stone, are not well *represented* by stone. We do not read books of stone but books whose significances, like those of every other object encountered in the "external" world, are subject to the demands of encountering consciousnesses. That the novel ends with a repetition of its beginning, in the "hand" of Judith Sands, indicates that this text is *her* collage, her greatest myth, a dramatization of all of her narratological principles. That she includes herself as a character not only indicates the character-ness of *everyone* in others' internal fictions, it confirms the distinction between author and narrator in which the narrator is the fictional, readable guiding voice of the text.[17] When Judith Sands, a character, is revealed as simultaneously the author/narrator of the text, the effect of this representation is the obliteration of the hierarchical distinction between "author" and "character," all of which not only reinforces the narratological principle of the "col-lage" but reminds us that we are *all* the authors of fictions in which we are also, ourselves, characters.

Conclusion

Franklin and Schneider claim that *Collages* "works best as a flawed extension of the continuous novel; it is a work in which most of the characters are frustrated and pathetic and in which Renate is merely a weak sister to Lillian, Sabina, Djuna, and even Stella" (163). In fact, *Collages* is the most logical extension of the continuous novel, as the self-conscious narratology of the collage metaphor provides a narratological framework from within which to reread those texts. But the purpose of this analysis has not been to reveal Nin's fiction as either consistent or inconsistent with the narratological principles available in readings of her essays. The latter serve as a starting point for the formulation of a reading of the collage metaphor, which subsequently informs (or *re*-forms) our reading of those essays. That is, it is not as though there is *no* reportage, *no* narrative intervention, but a moderation and redirection of those impulses in the service of new textual priorities.

When Franklin and Schneider call *Collages* "a portfolio of collages" (147), the word "portfolio" associates the text with an individual artistic entity. Indeed, the very mode that enables the representation of the process according to which each consciousness is an artist or creator in and of itself, has as its source only one consciousness, that of the narrator. But, though undeniably *present*, the narrator of the text whose terms are the operation of consciousness and the consequent instability of textual authority necessarily implies its own subjection to those same terms in the encountering consciousness of the reader. The narrator's interpolations may subordinate characters' consciousnesses, and thereby their realities, to her own, but these interruptions are represented as interpretations, not as reports of immutable external truths. Thus, even by undermining the (now unnecessary) illusion of the independence of her characters' consciousnesses, by calling attention to herself as the consciousness governing the realities of this text, Nin's narrator is able to maintain the narrative epistemology of variability that her appeal for representations of the internal has always implied. In other words, the attempt to undermine realism as the governing principle of fiction is not a disavowal of "reality" as such but the assertion of a more accurate verisimilitude. As Nin writes in *The Novel of the Future*, "It is to reach a greater *reality* (authenticity) that I abandoned realism" (45).[18]

In "The New Woman" Nin observes that "one writes because one has to create a world in which one can live" (95). The collage mode enables the documentation of the nature of such creation. Her comment in *The Novel of the Future* that "Dr. Otto Rank predicted a new structure of the personality. . . . The writer will be responsible for inventing a form of writing to contain this" (192) is available both as a call for the representation of the consciousness of the creative will or of the fundamental aestheticism of our everyday interpretive mechanisms and also, simultaneously, as an appeal for the emergence in the novel of the analytic narrator. By drawing attention to her own interpretive operations, Nin's narrator embodies our own, as well as the characters,' processes of reading the world, of making art of our encounters with the external. She thus continues to locate the logic of the text's reality in consciousness by taking on the formalities of omniscience and turning them inside out.

AUTHOR'S NOTE

Portions of this essay, including the discussion of Rank and of some of Nin's theories, were previously published, in slightly different form, as "The Storyteller as Analyst: On the Rankian Impulse of Anaïs Nin's Narrator" in *Anaïs: An International Journal* 17 (1999): 103–8. The material presented in this chapter also appears in slightly different form in chapters 1 and 3 of my dissertation, "Sympathetic Narration: The Party and the Collage in Virginia Woolf, Anaïs Nin, and Jeanette Winterson."

NOTES

1. Although the present analysis deals only with *Collages* among Nin's fiction, the "Ninian" narrative mode as formulated herein is a fundamental narrative principle in Nin's fiction. *Collages,* as we shall see, is a text in which this principle not only is in effect but is, in fact, the *subject* of the text.
2. "The fundamental character of the mythical concept is to be appropriated:. . . French imperiality must appeal to such and such a group of readers and not another" (Barthes 119).
3. That is, both of Barthes's systems, first- and second-order, are comprised of the signifier, signified, and sign; the second borrows its signifier from the sign produced in the first (Barthes 115).
4. Barthes writes that "driven to having either to unveil or to liquidate the concept, it [myth] will *naturalize* it" (129).
5. Barthes writes: "If I focus on an empty signifier, I let the concept fill the form of the myth without ambiguity, and I find myself before a simple system, where the signification becomes literal again. . . . This type of focusing is, for instance, that of the producer of myths" (128). And: "If I focus on a full signifier, in which I clearly distinguish the meaning and the form, and consequently the distortion which the one imposes on the other, I undo the signification of the myth, and I receive the latter as an imposture. . . . This type of focusing is that of the mythologist: he deciphers the myth, he understands a distortion" (128).
6. "The sovereign tendency obeyed by these primary [unconscious] processes . . . is called the pleasure-pain (Lust-Unlust) principle, or more shortly the pleasure-principle. These processes strive towards gaining pleasure; from any operation which might arouse unpleasantness ('pain') mental activity draws back (repression). Our nocturnal dreams, our waking tendency to shut out painful impressions, are remnants of the supremacy of this principle" (22).
7. "The mental apparatus had to decide to form a conception of the real circumstances in the outer world and to exert itself to alter them. A

new principle of mental functioning was thus introduced; what was conceived of was no longer that which was pleasant, but that which was real, even if it should be unpleasant" (22).

8. Stanley Fish writes in "Interpreting the *Variorum*" that "formal units are always a function of the interpretative model one brings to bear; they are not 'in' the text, and I would make the same argument for intentions" (176). He also writes: "Interpretive communities are made up of those who share interpretive strategies not for reading (in the conventional sense) but for writing texts, for constituting their properties and assigning their intentions" (182). Not only can we understand our own reading in this way, allowing a synonymy between "formal unit" and "object," but it provides a means by which to theorize the motives, unconscious or conscious, that underlie processes of represented mythologization themselves.

9. Indeed, cases in which the narrator's analysis contradicts the assertions of the consciousness analyzed blatantly beg for an interpretive act on the part of the reader, the effect of which is to undermine the narrator's status as dictator of the "real."

10. Franklin and Schneider rightly suggest a similar distinction even regarding the *Diary* when, in the preface to their book, they refer to "Nin (who shares the name of the *Diary*'s persona)."

11. What Franklin and Schneider are describing here is, essentially, the reader's act of collage making with the text, an act that defines the reader's encounter with *any* text, not just *Collages*. What they describe as the recollection of "highlights" from a text does not prohibit the construction of a reading of "wholeness" but, in fact, is the foundation of such a reading.

12. Ultimately this transition, the relevance of one chapter to those that precede and follow it, is readable for all of the chapters in *Collages*, depending on the interpretive leaps the reader is willing to make.

13. Of course, the ending of *Collages* complicates a reading of this first paragraph in ways that will be dealt with in the discussion of Judith Sands that follows.

14. This episode is, in fact, the story of *two* myth-creation processes. Within the act of imagining the design of the rug, we find a second mythmaking process, in which the consul's wife is not only recreating the rug but, in the process, creating a myth of that act itself, in a regenerative act of self-recovery.

15. See Freud, "From the History of an Infantile Neurosis" (1918), 202n.

16. The word "tip" here is "top" at the novel's beginning—perhaps because "tip" is something more closely associated with the pen, with writing, than "top"? In any event, it is a curious "error," or perhaps only a wink. Perhaps this is the humor Nin's dedication has promised.

17. Franklin and Schneider observe: "That *Collages* is cyclical and that it begins as does Sands's own unpublished novel suggests at least a parallel between Nin and Sands" (162), which is certainly true in that

Sands, as a writer having ostensibly written this very text about (all kinds of) writing, is readable as a representative of "Nin" as narrator or even—as a biological entity. But Sands is not the only representative—in effect, every character in this text actively writes.

18. Quoted in Hinz, 85.

WORKS CITED

Barthes, Roland. *Mythologies.* Trans. and ed. Annette Lavers. 1972. New York: Hill and Wang/Farrar, Straus and Giroux, 1995.

Fish, Stanley E. "Interpreting the *Variorum.*" *Reader-Response Criticism: From Formalism to Post-structuralism.* Ed. Jane P. Tompkins, 164–84. 1976. Baltimore: Johns Hopkins University Press, 1980.

Franklin, Benjamin, V, and Duane Schneider. *Anaïs Nin: An Introduction.* Athens: Ohio University Press, 1979.

Freud, Sigmund. *Beyond the Pleasure Principle.* Trans. and ed. James Strachey. Vol. 18 of *The Standard Edition of the Complete Psychological Works of Sigmund Freud.* 24 vols. New York: Norton, 1975.

———. *The Ego and the Id.* Trans. Joan Riviere. Ed. James Strachey. Vol. 19 of *The Standard Edition of the Complete Psychological Works of Sigmund Freud.* 24 vols. New York: Norton, 1989.

———. "Formulations Regarding the Two Principles in Mental Functioning." *General Psychological Theory.* Ed. Philip Rieff, 21–28. New York: Collier Books/Macmillan, 1963.

———. "From the History of an Infantile Neurosis." 1918. *Three Case Histories.* Ed. Philip Rieff, 161–280. New York: Collier Books/Macmillan, 1963.

———. "On the Mechanism of Paranoia." 1911. *General Psychological Theory.* Ed. Philip Rieff, 29–48. New York: Collier Books/Macmillan, 1963.

Hinz, Evelyn J. *The Mirror and the Garden: Realism and Reality in the Writings of Anaïs Nin.* 1971. New York: Harcourt Brace Jovanovich, 1973.

Logan, Marie-Rose. "Renate's Illusions and Delusions in *Collages.*" *Anaïs Nin: Literary Perspectives.* Ed. Suzanne Nalbantian, 79–94. New York: St. Martin's Press, 1997.

March, Thomas M. "The Storyteller as Analyst: On the Rankian Impulse of Anaïs Nin's Narrator." *Anaïs: An International Journal* 17 (1999): 103–8.

———. "Sympathetic Narration: The Party and the Collage in Virginia Woolf, Anaïs Nin, and Jeanette Winterson." Ph.D. diss., New York University, 2000.

Nin, Anaïs. *Collages.* Athens, Ohio: Swallow Press/Ohio University Press, 1964.

———. "The New Woman." 1946. *The Mystic of Sex and Other Writings.* Ed. Gunther Stuhlmann, 95–104. Santa Barbara, Calif.: Capra Press, 1995.

———. *The Novel of the Future.* 1968. Athens, Ohio: Swallow Press/Ohio University Press, 1986.

————. "Realism and Reality." 1946. *The Mystic of Sex and Other Writings*. Ed. Gunther Stuhlmann, 23–31. Santa Barbara, Calif.: Capra Press, 1995.

————. *Seduction of the Minotaur*. Chicago: Swallow Press, 1961.

————. "The Writer and the Symbols." 1986. *The Mystic of Sex and Other Writings*. Ed. Gunther Stuhlmann, 45–58. Santa Barbara, Calif.: Capra Press, 1995.

Rank, Otto. *Truth and Reality*. Trans. Jessie Taft. 1936. New York: Norton, 1978.

Spencer, Sharon. *Collage of Dreams*. Chicago: Swallow Press, 1977.

Wilde, Oscar. Preface to *The Picture of Dorian Gray*. *The Artist as Critic: Critical Writings of Oscar Wilde*. Ed. Richard Ellmann. New York: Random House, 1969; Chicago: University of Chicago Press, 1982.

CHAPTER 9

"Dismaying the Balance"

Anaïs Nin's Narrative Modernity

Philippa Christmass

The women contributing to the modernist avant-garde of the 1920s and 1930s often produced writing that diverged radically in form and content from that of their male counterparts. This essay explores the subversiveness of Anaïs Nin's determination to write uncompromisingly experimental fiction, and argues that Nin's early fiction in particular is deserving of greater recognition as part of the modernist oeuvre. Texts such as *House of Incest* and "Birth" from *Under a Glass Bell* constitute "an/other modernism" which, in the words of Violet Lang, "dismays the balance" (78) of narrative convention.

Nin found her creative freedom in her devotion to fiction, and in her refusal to write to a formula which, though bringing her closer to commercial success, would have compromised her own literary vision. Jayne E. Marek has noted: "Women's frequent rejection of conventional lifestyles and of conventional literary forms, their sense of obligation to literature and their indirect as well as direct support of it, their rejection of 'male consciousness' and concomitant development of female-centered systems of support—these are crucial aspects of women's experiences during the Modernist era. A close examination of women's aims during the growth and maturity of Modernism reveals the deeply radical nature of much of their work, breaking the 'sentence' and the 'sequence' of traditional language and literature the better to allow for women's experiences" (19).

Despite differences in approach, most feminist scholars have agreed upon one crucial aspect of women's involvement in modernism: that regardless of race, class, or sexual preference, geographic location or economic status, women artists in the modernist era were in some way or another unconventional or rebellious. "Modernism," notes Marek, "designates not only a literary phenomenon but also a period in which women were developing alternative ways of thinking and living their lives. . . . By upending conventions, Modernist women developed their literary tastes and their lives in ways that were not necessarily predicated upon the prerogatives of men" (19). While Nin openly discussed her continued reliance and complex sexual and emotional dependence on men throughout her lifetime, the clarity of her creative vision was rarely compromised by them. In this aspect of her life, Nin takes an important place alongside the other women of modernism.

I have chosen to align Anaïs Nin's experimentalism more closely with Peter Nicholls's definition of "another Modernism." In this other modernism, which is specific to a number of women writers of the era, the attempted objectivity, celebration of technological progress, and overtly political themes of the male modernist canon are replaced with explorations of intimate personal reflection, a focus on the interiorized stream of consciousness of female characters, and a narrative style that is more ambiguous, fluid, and corporeal in its use of imagery. As with the work of Virginia Woolf, Djuna Barnes, Jean Rhys, and Kay Boyle, Nin's fictions of the 1930s represent an expansion or purposeful transgression of masculinist modernism and the narrative aspects attributed to the works of the high modernist avant-garde.

Another Modernism

Discussions of the modernist era invariably trace its ancestry back to romanticism and symbolism.[1] However, agreement upon what constitutes the modern era, or the defining influence on modernist form, is notoriously elusive. As Marianne DeKoven notes in her analysis of the modernist era, "It is difficult to discuss 'modernism' or 'modernity' without adverting to vexed questions of terminology and periodization. . . . A minority of Anglo-American critics [follow] the largely Continental version of modernism (or 'modernity') that locates its starting point in the Enlightenment or in

Romanticism. Other Continentally-aligned critics, notably Alice Jardine in *Gynesis,* equate 'modernity' roughly with the twentieth century. . . . Bradbury and McFarlane, in their influential book *Modernism,* go on to establish roughly 1890 and 1930 as its temporal boundaries" (5–6).

In *The Gender of Modernity,* however, Rita Felski specifically situates the rise of the modern era in the context of preceding literary eras such as romanticism, decadence, and symbolism. Aspects of each are to be found, she argues, in modern works of the twentieth century. I would extend Bradbury and McFarlane's periodization of modernism to the late 1930s but, like Felski, would suggest that modernist art drew upon previous historical art movements, including symbolism, romanticism, and the decadent movement that immediately preceded the modernist era.

Both Felski and Nicholls explore the ways in which the modernist avant-garde either appropriated or rejected various elements of the romantic, symbolist, and decadent aesthetic. They argue that the supposedly feminine elements of romanticism and the decadent movement were vehemently rejected by the high modernist avant-garde. They also suggest that women writers of the modernist era were more likely to appropriate the aspects of these movements that were considered by male writers and critics of the period to be narcissistic, self-indulgent, or overly "feminine." Nicholls associates high modernist art with the refusal of a bodily or corporeal form of narrative identified by the male modernist avant-garde with a subjective or solipsistic femininity. He also delineates "the agonistics of this particular avant-garde, and the stress it places upon technique as mastery, for 'form' must be seen to be won through what Pound calls the 'combat of arrangement,' a 'combat' only marginally less dramatic than man as 'the phallus or spermatozoide charging, head-on, the female chaos'" (196). The phallic and militaristic implications of Pound's formulation are overtly misogynistic, leading to an "often aggressive objectification of the other" by the male modernist avant-garde. In the male modernist text, the "other" represents the feminine unconscious, which is conceptualized as chaotic, hysterical, or in some way threatening.

Nicholls argues that high modernist art can be seen as a partial rejection of preceding aesthetic trends that incorporated supposedly feminine elements of excessive subjectivity, narcissism, eroticism, and stylization. Furthermore, he suggests that the language employed in the decadent fiction of the late 1800s was, for the high modernists, "one which has become somehow 'bodily,' a condition which prevents 'objectivity' and which is quickly marked as 'feminine'" (195). DeKoven also notes: "In *The War of the Words,* Sandra Gilbert and Susan Gubar argue that male modernists, threatened by the advent of women in force into politics and literary high culture, invented modernist formal 'classicism,' with its cool, tough detachment, primarily as a move to rescue literary writing for masculinity from late-nineteenth-century 'effeminacy'" (8). In the decadent and surrealist movements, the "early modernist appropriation of the feminine was [not] necessarily in sympathy with the aims of feminism. On the contrary . . . its appropriation of an aesthetic of parody and performance in fact reinscribes more insistently those gender hierarchies which are ostensibly being called into question. . . . In other words, to assume that a male identification with the feminine is necessarily subversive of patriarchal privilege may be to assume too much" (Felski 92–93). The decadent writing of the 1890s was characterized by "ambiguous and shifting" representations of gender, but the latent homosexual undercurrent of much fin de siècle writing revealed a "misogynistic strain" in which women were parodied, ridiculed or disdained by male figures as being artificial, unnatural, or hysterical creatures.[2] Nin's own appropriation of the decadent aesthetic relates most specifically to her use of language and a concern with the symbolic and the erotic. D. H. Lawrence, Rimbaud, Baudelaire, the decadent writers of the fin de siècle, and the surrealists were certainly to have the greatest influence on Nin's aesthetic taste.

Many of the male modernist writers of the early twentieth century argued that contemporary literature must be "saved," both from the decadence of the previous decades and from the increasing numbers of women contributing to "literary high culture." In high modernism, according to Nicholls, "the absolute fixing of sexual difference, which is seen as the condition of the self's autonomy, makes the feminine a fantasized source of threat and aggression simply because of the independence which is symbolically assigned to her" (194). It is worth considering this phallocentric conceptualization of the feminine "other" in the context of the work produced by the male avant-garde during the modernist era. The interrelationship between modernism or avant-gardism and present-day theories of "feminine writing" is a field of theoretical inquiry that is rapidly gaining momentum; Nin's work is certainly worth situating at the crossroads of modernist study and feminist inquiry. Jayne E. Marek observes: "If modernist literature is indeed characterized by its 'subjective fictions' of reality, then French feminist thought not only illuminates women's language but also offers an approach for theorizing about the ways modernist subjectivity may have provoked, as well as expressed, masculine anxieties. . . . to define modernism as multifarious, diffuse, and self-conscious suggests that there may be important connections between modernist innovations that have often been seen as 'female' attributes" (16).

In defining the modernist text as multifarious and diffuse, however, critics such as Marek deviate from Nicholls's definition of the high modernist text as incorporating an aesthetic of precision and narrative control. The innovations of which Marek speaks are more closely aligned with French feminist theorists' conceptualizations of a feminine writing that is potentially more experimental, in terms of narrative structure, than the work of the canonized high modernists. In *Subversive Intent: Gender, Politics, and the Avant-Garde* Susan Rubin Suleiman explores the similarities between certain claims made in modernist or avant-garde manifestos and the aim of French feminist theorists to create an *écriture féminine*, or "feminine writing." DeKoven is another theorist who has discussed this connection, observing that "modernist form's disruptions of hierarchical syntax, of consistent, unitary point of view, of realist representation, linear time and plot [and] its formal decenteredness, indeterminacy, multiplicity, and fragmentation are very much in accord with a feminine aesthetic or Cixousian écriture féminine" (8). In *Hélène Cixous: Authorship, Autobiography, and Love,* Susan Sellers observes: "For Cixous, *écriture féminine* is the endeavor to write the other in ways which refuse to appropriate or annihilate the other's difference in order to create and glorify the self in a masculine position of mastery. In *The Newly Born Woman,* she compares the male discourse of 'classical fiction,' which she describes as 'a signifier referring always to the opposing signifier that annihilates its particular energy, puts down or stifles its very different sounds,' with a writing 'freed from the law' [which] would entail relinquishing the desire for power and approval, and attending to both the purpose and process of writing, including the impact of the body, one's sexuality and unconscious drives. . . . Abandoning the unitary subject position required by phallic authority, the feminine writer, Cixous suggests, adopts a number of places simultaneously" (11–12). Sellers identifies the main characteristics of a Cixousian écriture féminine in the above passage. First, "feminine writing" is a mode of writing in which realist constraints and conventions are subverted. Realist or classical fiction is named as masculine in its assertion of narrative mastery or control. In such narratives, there is little room for fluidity, ambiguity, or open-endedness. Realist narrative also explores the theme of otherness in a way that either denigrates, appropriates, or negates the other. By contrast, "feminine" narrative seeks to reverse these ingrained textual traditions. By exploring unconscious drives and psychological motivations, investing writing with a sense of corporeality, and inventing fresh ways to describe erotic desire, Cixous's version of *écriture féminine* abandons the unified point of view and narrative linearity in favor of shifting subject positions and a multiplicity of narrative styles and themes.

Certain aspects of this theory of *écriture féminine* are detectable in general descriptions of the modernist credo. For example, the modernist writers of the early twentieth century generally diverged from the descriptive naturalism that characterized the social realist novel. Canonized modernist texts such as Joyce's *Ulysses* explored a stream-of-consciousness technique and experimented with uses of language, incorporating open-ended narratives, fluidity of syntax, multiple points of view, and temporal inconsistency. Anaïs Nin's fictional work can be interpreted as both modernist and in some ways precursive to *écriture féminine* in its adoption of such experimental fictional techniques. As I mentioned, however, Nin's insistence on a bodily or rhythmic form of narrative is less common in the works of canonized male modernists. There are exceptions to this, of course, but Cixous's vision of a corporeal, lyrical, and eroticized narrative was less important to the male modernist elite than a mechanized and impersonal form and style that owed more to futurist manifestos than to any desire to formulate a fluid or "feminine" style of literature.

At the same time, it is difficult and dubious to characterize Nin's fiction solely as a precursor to Cixousian visions of feminine writing. Nin's roman-fleuve *Cities of the Interior* deviates in some ways from traditional modernist themes and in other ways from a feminist "writing the body." The most important aspect of Nin's writing in relation to feminism and modernism is that the texts are representative of the ways in which women artists of the period absorbed the principles of the "modernist experiment" to create literatures in which gender concerns are of central importance. In this "other modernism" we may find a counternarrative of the modern period, an investigation of those aspects of the modern condition that the male modernist avant-garde feared and negated in their own texts. In the works of Nin, Virginia Woolf, Hilda Doolittle ("H. D."), Djuna

Barnes, Kay Boyle, and others, states of subjectivity and introspection, erotic desire, and a dreamlike structural formlessness are more truly indicative of the state of modern Western consciousness than the "technical and ethical self-discipline, [the] *ascetic* refusal to collapse art into life" practiced by Eliot, Pound, or Hemingway (Nicholls 197). With their fragmented and spontaneous narratives, Nin's journals and fiction of the 1930s provide an example of the way in which women writers challenged the importance of "technical self-discipline" in modernist works of literature. In her early journals Nin makes constant reference both to her disapproval of the "traffic regulations" associated with realist fiction and to her desire to invent a "new form" freed from these regulations. Furthermore, the journal narratives constitute an embrace, rather than a refusal, of the "collapse [of] art into life." The desire for narrative detachment and the quest for a form of impersonal objectivity evident in avant-garde manifestos of the modernist era are absent not only from Nin's writing of the 1930s but also from the works of many of her female contemporaries.

In a postmodern climate, the textual and gender subversions of the decadent writers and surrealists have begun to receive more attention. In contrast, canonical modernism has come to seem reactionary and either subtly or overtly misogynistic. Women writers of the modernist movement, hitherto invisible, are increasingly being viewed as the truly radical arbiters of modernism. Many feminist historians interested in women writers of the 1920s and 1930s are not necessarily willing to place them within the traditional definition of high modernism. For these literary historians, canonized modernism is not subversive, nor does it function as a radical critique of twentieth-century culture. As Felski succinctly notes, "A text which may appear subversive and destabilizing from one political perspective becomes a bearer of dominant ideologies when read in the context of another" (27). With an increasing volume of feminist studies of the modernist era appearing over the last two decades, this paradox has become only too apparent. The high modernist's formal experimentation is accompanied by "a misogynistic strain" that has simultaneously "enabled and constrained the contestatory nature of its textual politics" (93). Feminist studies of the modernist era have cited the "other modernisms" of which Nicholls speaks as representing the truly radical and subversive edge of the modernist avant-garde, more trenchantly criticizing class, race, and gender inequalities because its practitioners are themselves writing from the margins, whether they be cultural, sexual, socioeconomic, or political. DeKoven suggests:

Despite the patrilineality of what has become the high modernist canon, the literary wombs of women writers were just as important to the birth of modernism as the seminal ink of the modernist founding fathers. James, Yeats, Pound, Eliot, and Joyce are credited not with giving birth to modernism . . . but with inventing modernism: the figure of "invention" locates modernism within the discourse of "male" technology. . . . a formal analysis looking for the right things finds powerful evidence that, in texts such as Charlotte Perkins Gilman's "The Yellow Wallpaper," 1891, Kate Chopin's *The Awakening*, 1899, and Gertrude Stein's *Three Lives*, 1903–06, previously buried texts that have become crucial to the emerging feminist canon, women writers "invented" modernist form, "discovered" it "independently," to switch to the also frequently invoked scientific metaphor, at just the same time that male writers did. (10–11)

DeKoven's observation on women writers' independent discovery of modernist form is rearticulated in Nin's recognition of her own modernist tendencies, "so sincerely arrived at" (*Journal of a Wife* 464). However, like the "other" women of modernism, Nin's fictional texts and journals of the 1930s and beyond display a resistance not only to the "traffic regulations" of realism, but also to those of the high modernist avant-garde. Themes of dehumanization, alienation, and violence are replaced with subtle evocations of personal exchange, relationship, and shifting emotional states. Nin's texts embody the corporeal, intimate, and introspective qualities that critics of modernist narrative, as well as some of the high modernists themselves, dismissed as self-indulgent, narcissistic, and "feminine." Until recently, critics have rarely acknowledged Nin's narratives as modernist experiments in form, primarily because they did not correspond, thematically or stylistically, with the great works of her male contemporaries, which were already achieving canonical status within the literary circles of Paris and beyond.

Nin viewed the social realist novel as indicative of the "rigidities and patterns made by the rational mind." The works of art that Nin came to admire most were those that attempted to transcend the formalities of logical explanation and defy rational interpretation. Nin's early works of fiction express an avant-garde understanding of the purpose of fiction as a challenge to readers' assumptions, as a vehicle for the free expression of internal sensations, and as an exploration of "new realms" of subject matter. Nin's "other modernism" is most evident in *House of Incest* and *Under a Glass Bell*, whose narratives focus on an evocation of women's interior psychological states rendered in often surrealistic and abstract imagery, and in the constant association between splintered identities and fractured bodies.

Critical Reactions to Nin's Modernism

The study of modernism has constituted a thriving literary industry in the second half of the twentieth century. Until the early 1980s, however, most scholarly appraisals of modernist art excluded or avoided any mention of women in modernism. At this juncture, feminist historians began to question the way in which the modernist movement was represented by scholars in their compilations of literary history, concluding that the almost exclusive focus on male practitioners of modernism had resulted in unjust critical neglect of their female contemporaries. Until recently, women writers and artists remained little known or invisible to the eye of the student of modernism. Pioneering works such as Shari Benstock's *Women of the Left Bank* and Gilbert and Gubar's *No Man's Land: The Place of the Woman Writer in the Twentieth Century* laid the groundwork for an enterprise that is still continuing today: to expose the works of women modernists to a new audience, and to create for them a valid and important place in the history of modernism. Such histories of the network of women artists in the modernist era are crucial to our understanding of what has previously been omitted from discussions of the period.

Feminist revisionists of modernism have often attempted to deconstruct the pejorative associations that the word "marginality" engenders, as it is this word that seems to have defined women's positions within the modernist movement. The celebration of marginality (or otherness, or difference) that is intrinsic to the French feminist theory of the late 1970s and 1980s coexists in an uneasy alliance with the American revisionist effort to lift women out of the margins and into the center of modernist study. Whichever approach is taken, feminist scholars have agreed that women modernists must be studied in a context other than that of mere supporters of the great male writers. In the literary memoirs assessing this period, women appear primarily as patrons, wives, lovers, moral supporters—artistic muses inspiring the male Genius. The process of selectivity that characterizes such milieu studies has resulted in the historical misconception that women stood permanently on the sidelines of artistic invention. Until recently it was rarely acknowledged that women were often writers, artists, editors, and publishers themselves. Shari Benstock suggests that "working definitions of Modernism—its aesthetics, politics, critical

principles, and poetic practices . . . excluded women from its concerns" (Preface x). This is not to suggest that male writers had no
difficulty in getting their work published. But the notoriety created
by a work such as Joyce's *Ulysses* differed greatly from the notoriety women writers received if they published controversial or
explicit material. Joyce's notoriety, and the difficulties he encountered in publishing his work, led to his eventual critical acceptance
and canonization. The same cannot be said for many of the
women modernists, including Nin. While certain circumstances
have prompted increased interest in the fictional works of Anaïs
Nin since the late 1960s,[3] her work is rarely situated in a specific
literary context, and her place within modernism has not been
explored in extensive detail. However, this lack of interest in
women's contributions to modernism is not uncommon. The modernist period produced many highly inventive and talented
women artists who never saw their work emerge beyond little-
magazine acceptance, much less to commercial publication stage.

In *The Gender of Modernism: A Critical Anthology* Bonnie Kime
Scott criticizes the selectivity engendered by a patriarchal institution of literary critics, reappraises early feminist contributions to
modernist studies, and gathers together essays on Djuna Barnes,
Mina Loy, Nancy Cunard, Jean Rhys, and Rebecca West, among
others. She argues that, as an art movement, modernism was
always "unconsciously gendered masculine" (2) and that women
writing in a modernist vein were rarely as visible as their male
counterparts. Until recently, only the male contributors to the
modernist "cause" were anthologized and discussed in academic
circles.[4] The American feminist project of revisionism has "brought
into question the adequacy of the previous canon" (2). Interestingly, feminist revisionists such as Gilbert and Gubar and Elaine
Showalter have tended to emphasize motifs of war and violence in
their studies of women in modernism. This is especially true of
Gilbert and Gubar, who have utilized images of the "battleground
between the sexes." Scott proposes a different way of looking at
the contributions of women to modernism, suggesting that there
exists an enormous fund of vitality and vibrancy in this body of
work. Bolstered by the experimental fervor that defined the art of
the period, women began to create their own stories of what it
meant to be a woman in that volatile time and place, with a degree
of honesty that some found unsettling or threatening but that others found enormously liberating.

In her account of women publishers in modernism, Jayne E.
Marek argues that we should not wholly accept Benstock's claim

that women formed the "underside" of modernism, or that modernism involved a raging "war of the sexes," as Gilbert and Gubar
propose (Marek 13). The approach taken by feminist scholars of
modernism has often been dualistic, and perhaps in some ways
negative, suggesting that "women's lives and art developed only in
reaction to the constrictions of prevailing social modes" (14). The
trend is to depict women in battle against or in conflict with a
monolithic patriarchy. Marek also argues against a universalist
position, noting: "Many feminist scholars have responded to masculinist histories by trying to establish a tradition of counterhege-
mony, through rediscovering women's works and placing them in a
line of female influence. This attempt can result in the urge to rein-
scribe both hierarchy and selectivity and to gloss over the uneven-
ness of the particular influences of gender" (194).[5] Scott's motifs of
vibrancy and vitality are more productive to revisionist study than
reinforced notions of conflict and struggle, which tend to place
women artists in the position of victims, often unintentionally.

Nin's recorded experiences in Paris in the 1930s both resemble
and differ from the experiences of other women modernists. It is
possible to place her as a victim of her male acquaintances and
lovers, who criticized the amount of time invested in the journal
and continually put their publication needs before her own,
despite her financial patronage. It would also be possible to dwell
upon the dubious benefits gained from her interactions with psychoanalysts, or Henry Miller's appropriation of her ideas for his
own writing. However, I would prefer to focus here on the ways in
which Nin challenged the conventions of her time, most impor-
tantly in her writing. I also wish to consider the factors that have
prevented Nin from being included in most scholarly histories of
modernism, including feminist histories.[6] It is interesting that Nin's
name is rarely mentioned in critical and biographical anthologies
of modernism. It must be noted that Benstock does place Nin within her modernist landscape, insightfully exploring the prose poem
House of Incest (1936) as a radically experimental work that distills
and reinterprets the themes of psychological fragmentation and
neurosis common to modernist literature in general.[7] However,
the groundbreaking works of Gilbert and Gubar and of Gillian Hans-
combe and Virginia Smyers make only passing reference to Nin's
oeuvre. In "Out of and Into the Labyrinth," Hoshang Merchant
explores Nin's aesthetic theories in the context of symbolism, modernism, and surrealism but does not connect his observations on
Nin's modernism to more overtly feminist interpretations of these
movements.[8]

The modernist commitment to experimentation with narrative form and thematic content was, for Nin, practically an invitation to invisibility. Nin may not have faced the economic difficulties of some of her contemporaries, such as Jean Rhys, but she did face similar criticisms of her fiction: that it was impenetrable, apolitical, or too self-indulgent. Self-indulgence and impenetrability were often accepted in the works of male modernists but regarded as unacceptable in the works of women artists whose output was often as innovative and more unorthodox, especially in their criticisms of prevailing or culturally sanctioned sexual mores.

One factor contributing to the continuing critical unpopularity of Nin's work was the widespread acceptance of realist or classical canons of literature within the academic establishment of postwar America. This preference for social realism resulted in critical discomfort with Nin's fiction. Of course, Nin was not the first writer to explore certain psychological impulses in women, such as their motivations in relationships, using an intimate and associative written style. Virginia Woolf, Dorothy Richardson, Jean Rhys, and Djuna Barnes explored similar themes in their works. But of all these writers, only Woolf has received sustained critical praise or status within the modernist canon.[9] When modernist critics have taken into account the works of, for example, Djuna Barnes or Mina Loy, they have done so at the expense of "important feminine or feminist elements in their work," preferring to concentrate on the aspects associated with high modernism (Scott 4). Women writers whose works could not be fitted neatly into the category of high modernism often suffered the fate of critical neglect. Kay Boyle, also writing in Paris in the 1930s and greatly admired by Henry Miller and Nin, is still known only to a relative few. Her short stories proved popular for a time, earning her a Guggenheim Fellowship in 1934. However, her delicately written novels of the 1930s have generated less attention. In retrospect, it is apparent that a form of gender discrimination greatly contributed to the obscurity of the women modernists. The prominent reviewers of the postwar period could often appear confusingly contradictory. In January 1944 the esteemed critic Edmund Wilson's review of Nin's work appeared in the *New Yorker*. It represented the first favorable review of her fiction by an established and highly respected critic. In the review Wilson praises *Under a Glass Bell*, published that year, comparing the stories stylistically with Virginia Woolf's fiction and expressing admiration of Nin's original use of symbolic imagery. That such a conservative critic as Wilson should praise Nin's surrealistic style in an era where surrealism was conspicuously out of fashion in America was remarkable. What proved more remarkable, perhaps, was the furiously negative review Wilson wrote in the same month of 1944 of Kay Boyle's *Avalanche*. The very quality Wilson praised in Nin's fiction, her talent as a stylist, was simultaneously denounced as a "bad romantic habit" in Boyle's. Only when Boyle turned her attention to political issues did her writing begin to merit uniform praise.

It is also worth making a comparison between male and female reviewers of women's writing in the 1940s. Some of Nin's most vehement critics were women,[10] but generally women reviewers were more likely to be sympathetic towards Nin's fiction. In a 1944 review of *Under a Glass Bell*, Isaac Rosenfeld suggests that "There are no regions of sex where a few well equipped masculine surrealists cannot penetrate, or to which, even if women be the ultimate discoverers, Freud, D. H. Lawrence and James Joyce cannot be taken as guides" (76). Even if we disregard the phallic imagery that makes this observation particularly distasteful, Rosenfeld's comment stands as a typical response to Nin's work by male reviewers in the postwar period. The dismissiveness of the review is echoed almost twenty years later by Frank Baldanza, who in 1962 criticized Nin's fiction as "banal" and "clichéd," solipsistic and erratic, and suggested that "whatever the reason for preserving this work, it has little to do with literature" (16). In a review of *Under a Glass Bell* published four years after Rosenfeld's, Violet Lang praises Nin's collection of short stories for their unsettling originality, arguing that "some part of the hostility with which Anaïs Nin has been dismissed by some readers may be attributed to betrayal of objectivity; she is embarrassing. She has discredited the importance of environment of place and time; her streets are alike in New York or in Paris; she has returned to the natural city. . . . Because these written lives are not lived in the language or seen from the perspective we are accustomed to assume, in the act of recognition, we are caught unawares. This is unsettling, and we are not used to it. . . . [Nin] dismays the balance" (77–78). Lang makes a number of interesting observations here, emphasizing the difficulty experienced by writers who do not pay heed to current literary trends and popular or academic tastes. Nin's subjective fictions were published in an era when subjectivity was deemed "embarrassing." Her deliberate challenging of the literary conventions associated with realism had become, for the conservative reader, somehow disturbing or unsettling. In their lack of detailed description of time, place, and appearance, Nin's texts operated on a more elusive, symbolic level. Nin's narrative modernity "dismays the balance" achieved by the realist text, which is concerned with an almost scientific presentation of daily life and a supposedly mimetic and objective point of view. In the novels comprising *Cities of the Interior,* Nin creates a series of ambiguous, open-ended narratives which are epiphanic and which incorporate a rotating cycle of characters, most of whom appear and disappear at irregular intervals throughout each story.

These narrative traits were interpreted negatively by the majority of Nin's male reviewers. In "Nin: The Tropic of Paris," James Korges refers to Nin's novels as a "mess of flat character sketches, trite descriptions, surreal actions, lesbian affairs, and so on. The women are all variations of the same character: neurotic but wise, artistic but motherly, curious but aloof, passionate but frustrated . . . in love with Father but searching for Love, Love, Love" (112). Most of the time, Korges argues, Nin is incapable of "rendering the relationship between two people." Instead, she reports "monologues and actions, notations copied from a diary set down for psychoanalysis." He suggests that Nin's plots are little more than "the clichés of women's magazines and of soap opera" (113). Frank Baldanza is no less scathing: Nin's stories, in his opinion, are "pointless, rambling explorations of erotic entanglements and neurotic fears. . . . The handling of characters and incidents is so erratic and baffling that one must assume the writer simply means to spill random impressions onto the page" (10). Baldanza calls Nin's plots ludicrous, her language farcical, and her imagery pretentious. In contrast, recent female reviewers of Nin's fiction are more sympathetic to her idiosyncratic style. In *Aesthetic Autobiography* Suzanne Nalbantian suggests that Nin "sought to transpose [the] fluid relativism [of her journal] to her fiction with characters continuously developing through interpersonal relations and open-ended narrative with no conclusion to circumscribe any character" (178). For Baldanza, Nin's open-ended narratives and amorphous character sketches constituted glaring structural and thematic faults. For Nalbantian, these aspects of Nin's work challenge the expectations of conventional realist fiction, forcing readers to reassess traditional understandings of plot, narrative continuity, chronology, and fictional closure.

Nin's refusal to provide conventional linear chronology, character detail, or a traditional cumulative structure to her novels frustrated a generation of staid American critics accustomed to the minutiae of social realism. Nin's characters did not have last names. They lived in a world dominated by symbolic and dream-like imagery; there was no real plot to speak of. Her novels consisted of emotional epiphanies and reveries, and made reference to unpopular psychoanalytic terminology in order to describe the characters' emotions. The characteristics that mark Nin's writing—fragmented narrative, episodic chronology, refusal of closure, exploration of subconscious desires—have since been claimed by scholars of modernism as prototypically modernist. At the time of publication, however, Nin's innovations were dismissed as passé, decadent, and neoromantic in their preoccupation with dreams, imagination, and the individual subject. Her proclamations that structure should be "flowing" or language rhythmic and tactile, a literary equivalent to music or dance, seemed absurd to the critics of the 1940s and 1950s. To anyone familiar with the work of the French feminist theorist Hélène Cixous, they would seem strikingly familiar.

Two Modernist Texts: *House of Incest* and "Birth"

By the late 1920s Nin had already established a pronounced distaste for conventional realism, which conflicted with her own propensity for symbolic imagery and elusive storytelling. The condensed form of her fictional narratives was a direct result, she argued, of the compression in her journal writing: "I know I have one quality which I owe my Journal. I discard the conventional and futile details and go straight to the center, to draw the *essence*, and only the essence, of my experience" (*Early Diary* 223). In May 1930 Nin defined her writing as "abstract and symbolical," with a tendency toward suggestiveness and evasion of concrete detail—an antithesis to the sociological minutiae that characterized the realist novels of the period. The highly symbolic, fragmented, and occasionally surrealistic nature of *House of Incest, Winter of Artifice* (1939), and certain stories in *Under a Glass Bell* renders them some of the most complex and intriguing fictional works of the late modernist period.

Without characterizing Nin's work as specifically modernist, Sharon Spencer has commented upon Nin's novelistic techniques as "imagistic and improvisatory": "To an inexperienced reader her characters may seem elusive. They have no family names. Ethnic, religious and national identity are of no consequence. Their ages are rarely noted. The duration of their relationships with one another is left to the reader's determination. Their appearances are seldom described in a comprehensive way. Instead, significant details of dress, gesture or temperament are extracted from a general

collection of traits; these are then treated metaphorically, emphasized, and sometimes repeated in a process that much more closely
resembles the composition of poetry than of fiction" (67). Referring
to the roman-fleuve *Cities of the Interior,* Spencer notes that Nin
"rejects the organizing principle embodied in plot. . . . The reader is
never allowed to decide once and for all the fate of any of Anaïs
Nin's characters, for she deliberately rejects the neat resolution of
the classically composed novel, striving instead to suggest dynamic
and unpredictable possibilities for the personages she has created
outside and beyond the situations of the novelettes" (68). The
sequence is organic, cumulative, but also reversible or interchange-
able. The five novelettes comprising *Cities of the Interior* do not necessarily have to be read in the order in which they appear in the
text.[11] The same characters appear in each, and the narrative impetus of the series is cyclical rather than linear. The collection can be
read in a rotating cycle, or from last story to first, without seriously
disrupting the reader's sense of plot progression.

Anna Balakian has commented on Nin's focus on interiority,
placing her in the symbolist tradition of Rimbaud and Mallarmé:
"The symbolist psyche was one of self-containment, introverted
self-contemplation, preoccupation with inscapes; the symbolist
eye sucked the material substance of the surrounding and turned
it into idealized, formless, fluid images all bearing the imprint of
the writer's own psyche. The language of the symbolist was a
purification of all functional connotations." This interpretation is
particularly relevant to an understanding of *House of Incest,* in
which "fluid" and symbolic imagery functions purely as an indication of the turmoil and complexity of the narrator's psyche.

The modernist text has been theorized as incorporating mon-
tage and collage techniques, thematic ambiguity, an emphasis on
subjectivity and individualism, fluctuations in narrative point of
view, a breakdown of formal sentence structure, and a concern
with the aural or rhythmic qualities of language. In this sense,
House of Incest can be viewed as representatively modernist in technique. Thematically, the text is also indicative of certain modernist
concerns. In the *Incest* journal, Nin describes the theme of *House of
Incest:* "Death. Disintegration. Perversion. Spengler's prophecies
unraveled: lesbianism, June (minor themes in connection with
June of lies, abortion, primitivism, psychism), incest . . . A thoroughly neurotic book including all the symptoms, phenomena,
description of moods, dreams, insanities, phobias, manias, hallucinations—tableau of disintegration, franker than Lawrence's
treatment of homosexuality, than Radclyffe Hall's treatment of

lesbianism" (52).[12] The description indicates some of the main themes and concerns of modernist art: death, disintegration, the surrealist interest in psychic phenomena, dreams and hallucinatory states, and the psychoanalytic exploration of "insanities, phobias, manias." However, Nin also draws attention to themes that are less commonly found elsewhere in the modernist art of the 1930s: lesbianism, incest, abortion, and neurosis. Thematically, then, Nin's earliest work of fiction differs from the high modernist text by exploring the psychological repercussions of experiences that are often specific to women or, like neurosis, have traditionally been attributed to them.

In *Modernisms: A Literary Guide* Peter Nicholls draws attention to the ways in which H. D. and Gertrude Stein sought to create a "deliberate and often polemic disturbance within the canonical version" of modernism (197). Nicholls notes that Stein "invents another version of modernism by circumventing the image altogether and by exploring precisely that self-sufficiency of language which had seemed decadent to the 'Men of 1914'" (202). Although Anaïs Nin's fiction is heavily reliant on the use of symbolic and metaphorical imagery, texts such as *House of Incest* and "Birth" also draw attention to the "self-sufficiency" of language in itself, as not necessarily referring to or representing events or places outside the mind. The repetitious language and ritualistic "drumming" of the "Birth" narrative can be seen as a parallel example to Nicholls's observations on the use of language in the works of Gertrude Stein. In both, "language is to be grasped not as a means of reference to a world of objects which can be dominated, but as a medium of consciousness" (204). Samuel Beckett's observation on the work of Joyce—that it "is not about something; it is that something itself"—has some relevance for a reading of these stories. The narrative of "Birth" is presented as a literal transcription of the protagonist's thought processes as she struggles to deliver her child: "I have to push. I have to push. That is a black fixed point in eternity. At the end of a long dark tunnel. I have to push. A voice saying: 'Push! Push! Push!' A knee on my stomach and the marble of my legs crushing me and the head so large and I have to push" (104). The entire story is narrated in the present tense, although the story is structurally cyclical, beginning at the end with the doctor's proclamation that "the child . . . is dead." The narrative then returns to the early stages of the protagonist's labor. "I am ready! The nurse presses her knee on my stomach. There is blood in my eyes. A tunnel. I push into this tunnel, I bite my lips and push. There is a fire and flesh ripping and no air. Out of the tunnel! All my blood is spilling out. Push! Push! Push! It is coming! It is coming! It is coming! I feel the slipperiness, the sudden deliverance, the weight is gone. Darkness. I hear voices. I open my eyes" (106–7).

In both *House of Incest* and "Birth," repetitive phraseology is used to draw attention to either the aural, musical, or ritualistic qualities of language. The passage above attempts to approximate the confusion of voices and commands heard by the narrator through a veil of intense pain as she labors to deliver the child: "Push! Push! Push! It is coming! It is coming! It is coming!" *House of Incest* also contains numerous lists of color, texture, and material substance in order to create a trancelike and rhythmic flow of words.[13] As Jeanne rushes into the garden of the house of incest, she trips over "lava paths, over the micha [*sic*] schist, and all the minerals on her path burned, the muscovite like a bride, the pyrite, the hydrous silica, the cinnabar, the azurite like a fragment of benefic Jupiter, the malachite, all crushed together, pressed together, melted jewels, melted planets, alchemized by air and sun and time and space, mixed into mineral fixity, the fixity of the fear of death and the fear of life" (60). This metallic and mineralized garden serves as a metaphor for what had been stamped into the ground: "the words we did not shout, the tears unshed, the curse we swallowed, the phrase we shortened, the love we killed" (60). In "Birth" certain crucial phrases connected with the birth are repeated: "push," "drum," "dying," "flesh," "blood," "out," and "darkness." As the narrator recounts her ritualistic incantation to bring forth her baby, she notes the bewilderment of the doctors and nurses: "I put my two hands on my stomach and very softly, with the tips of my fingers I drum drum drum drum drum drum on my stomach in circles. Around, around, softly, with eyes open in great serenity. The doctor comes near with amazement on his face. The nurses are silent. Drum drum drum drum drum drum in soft circles, soft quiet circles. Like a savage . . . But my hands are so weary, so weary, they will fall off. The womb is stirring and dilating. Drum drum drum drum drum" (106–7). The ritualistic "drum drum drum drum" introduces a moment of calm into an otherwise violent scenario. For a brief moment the protagonist slips into a mystical state, her softly spoken incantation signifying a rejection of the doctor's knives and instruments. The doctor's desire to "interfere" in the process with scientific equipment is thwarted by the narrator's "Struggle with nature, with myself, with my child and the meaning I put into it all . . . No instrument can help me" (106).

A recent critic, Lajos Elkan, has attempted to define the ways in which "Birth" represents a specifically female style of writing, drawing attention to the repetition of phrase and image in the story as a form of "impulsive utterance" or "ritualistic shout." Elkan characterizes Nin's use of language as visceral, chantlike, repetitious, and onomatopoeic: "Nin uses the resources of ritualistic texts characterized by a repetitious, rhythmical scansion. Her vocabulary relies on details typical of symbolist and surrealistic texts. Her language is lively and rich in graphic detail. She also succeeds in lifting the veil of mystery that used to surround birth in traditional and mystical literatures. These elements define Nin's language as poetic and make her writing specifically female" (162). In Elkan's reading, the connection made between the process of writing and the act of giving birth renders Nin's texts "specifically female." The narrator declares in the prologue to *House of Incest:* "The morning I got up to begin this book I coughed. Something was coming out of my throat: it was strangling me. I broke the thread which held it and yanked it out. I went back to bed and said: 'I have just spat out my heart.'" In "Birth" a similar image occurs: "'Push! Push! Push with all your strength!' I pushed with anger, with despair, with frenzy, with the feeling that I would die pushing, as one exhales the last breath, that I would push out everything inside of me, and my soul with all the blood around it, and the sinews with my heart inside of them choked, and that my body itself would open and smoke would rise, and I would feel the ultimate incision of death" (103). For Nin the image of bodily expulsion—the pushing out of a child, spitting out the heart—is connected to the image of a woman giving birth to a work of art. Giving birth involves the "pushing out" of "everything inside of me." In the prologue to *House of Incest,* the narrator envisages the expulsion of her heart in the process of "giving birth" to her book. Similarly, in the passage from "Birth," the narrator pushes so violently that she imagines herself ejecting a blood-soaked soul and heart. Descriptive terminology of the pain of childbirth is fused with surrealistic imagery as the narrator drifts in and out of consciousness:

> Am I pushing or dying? The light up there, the immense round blazing white light is drinking me. It drinks me slowly, inspires me into space. If I do not close my eyes it will drink all of me. I seep upwards, in long icy threads, too light, and yet inside there is a fire too, the nerves are twisted, there is no rest from this long tunnel dragging me, or am I pushing myself out of the tunnel, or is the child being pushed out of me, or is the light drinking me. Am I

dying? The ice in the veins, the cracking of the bones, this pushing in darkness, with a small shaft of light in the eyes like the edge of a knife, the feeling of a knife cutting the flesh, the flesh somewhere is tearing as if it were burned through by a flame, somewhere my flesh is tearing and the blood is spilling out. I am pushing in the darkness, in utter darkness. (105)

As with *House of Incest*, the syntax breaks down in "Birth" as the protagonist's physical and emotional turmoil increases. Broken phrases suggest a state of confusion, and images of flesh tearing and blood spilling symbolize a pain which cannot be specifically located in one part of the body: "Ice in the veins, the cracking of the bones, this pushing in darkness . . . somewhere my flesh is tearing and the blood is spilling out." An exhortation for the surrounding nurses to "Please hold my legs! Please hold my legs! Please hold my legs! PLEASE HOLD MY LEGS!" (104) is an example of what Elkan refers to as a "ritualistic shout" within the text. Elsewhere, voices are heard seemingly from afar, dislocated, repetitious, and confusing:

> The head was showing, but I had fainted. Everything was blue, then black. The instruments were gleaming before my eyes. Knives sharpened in my ears. Ice and silence. Then I heard voices, first talking too fast for me to understand. A curtain was parted, the voices still tripped over each other, falling fast like a waterfall, with sparks, and cutting into my ears. The table was rolling gently, rolling. The women were lying in the air. Heads. Heads hung where the enormous white bulbs of the lamps were hung. The doctor was still walking, the lamps moved, the heads came near, very near, and the words came more slowly. They were laughing. One nurse was saying: 'When I had my first child I was all ripped to pieces. I had to be sewn up again, and then I had another, and had to be sewn up, and then I had another . . .' The other nurse said: 'Mine passed like an envelope through a letter box. But afterwards the bag would not come out. The bag would not come out. Out. Out . . .' Why did they keep repeating themselves? And the lamps turning. And the steps of the doctor very fast, very fast. (103–4)

As the narrator recovers from a momentary loss of consciousness, she hears the conversation of the nurses surrounding her. The heads of the nurses appear to be severed, and as they float over the operating table they laugh and chatter in a mundane way about their own experiences of birth: "I was all ripped to pieces. I had to be sewn up again"; "Mine passed like an envelope through a letterbox." These ordinary and almost humorous descriptions lose their concreteness as the narrator slips in and out of consciousness, so that certain words appear to be repeated or echoed, and other words trail off: "The bag would not come out. Out. Out . . ." In this way an ordinary conversation between women becomes distorted and surrealistic. Like most of the stories in *Under a Glass Bell*, "Birth" illustrates Nin's interest in the "marriage of illusion and reality" in modern fiction, fusing realistic detail with elements of absurdism, surrealism, and irony. In a preface to a 1968 reprint of *Under a Glass Bell*, Nin suggests that "these stories [broke] a mould and used the distillation of poetry. I feel that a contemporary evaluation of them may come closer to their intention. My Journals, covering the period during which the stories were written, and giving undistilled, human and authentic characters from which they were drawn, will also throw a new light upon them. The Journals supply the key to the mythical figures and assert the reality of what once may have seemed to be purely fantasy. Such a marriage of illusion and reality—or illusion as the key to reality—is a contemporary theme" (7).

The second aspect of modern fiction to which Nin draws attention in the preface to *Under a Glass Bell* is form: "I am always reminded of the interplay between Debussy and Erik Satie: Debussy said to Satie that his compositions had no form. Satie responded by titling one: Sonata in the Form of a Pear" (7). Nin compared the form of her own fictional work to the musical compositions of Erik Satie, which Debussy regarded as essentially formless. Satie pointed out that his compositions were formless only in relation to one understanding of musical form. Like the realist novel, the standard orchestral arrangement includes an introduction, a crescendo (the dramatic peak), and a descent (closure). Satie suggested that the structure of a composition can be approached in a less formulaic manner, hence his absurdist reference to a "sonata in the form of a pear." In *The Novel of the Future* Nin classified the form of her fiction as "oceanic," an ebb and flow of movement and imagery rather than a linear and consciously directed accumulation of detail and event toward a singular dramatic climax. In the short stories, Nin's preference for condensation of imagery, dialogue, and external detail found its fullest expression.

The investigation of the effects of repetitious language represents one aspect of Nin's exploration of language as the conveyor of a female-centered consciousness. Her focus on women's relationship to their bodies, and the exploration of the body as an exterior manifestation of interior conflict, also marks the early fiction as an example of "another modernism." The textuality of

Nin's early fiction—the way in which it draws attention to language as both referential *and* ritualistic—aligns her more closely with Stein and H. D. than with her male modernist contemporaries. Nin's focus in *House of Incest* on the rendering of a woman's inner psychological state differentiates it more noticeably from the works of her immediate male contemporaries, such as Henry Miller and Lawrence Durrell, whose use of language was much less experimental and more immediately accessible. For most of the critics of the 1940s and 1950s, Nin's often esoteric use of language simply indicated excessive stylization, or pretentiousness. Today, Nin's attention to language, imagery, and repetition of phrase may be seen to be innovative and complex, an/other point along the modernist spectrum.

NOTES

1. Peter Nicholls emphasizes the plurality of "modernisms," arguing that as a literary phase or style, modernism was not hegemonic or monolithically uniform. Contemporary scholars of modernism must inevitably distinguish between different modernist avant-gardes, as Nicholls does.
2. Felski elaborates that "the aesthete's playful subversion of gender norms and adoption of feminine traits" is an attempt to "reinforce his distance from and superiority to women," who are supposedly "incapable of this kind of free-floating semiotic mobility and aesthetic sophistication" (93).
3. For example, the publication of the "unexpurgated" journals.
4. With, perhaps, just two exceptions: Virginia Woolf and Gertrude Stein.
5. It must be noted, however, that any attempt to place Nin within a hegemonic community or network of women modernists is fraught with difficulty, given her comparative isolation from other women artists; while she acknowledged the influences of a number of female contemporaries, such as Colette and Djuna Barnes, Nin did not specifically declare an intention to form part of a female literary lineage.
6. One of the few specifically feminist collections of modernist women's writing to include Anaïs Nin is Bronte Adams and Trudi Tate's anthology, *That Kind of Woman: Stories From the Left Bank and Beyond.*
7. See Benstock's chapter entitled "The City They Left."
8. Elizabeth Podnieks also discusses the influence of modernism and avant-garde movements on the work of Nin but, once again, not in a specifically feminist context.
9. Djuna Barnes has only recently begun to receive a similar amount of attention.
10. For example, Elizabeth Hardwick and Diana Trilling.

11. In the Swallow edition (1961) the order runs: *Ladders to Fire, Children of the Albatross, The Four-Chambered Heart, A Spy in the House of Love,* and *Seduction of the Minotaur.*

12. This assessment was written in November 1932.

13. This repetition of imagery and phrase is also common in the novels comprising *Cities of the Interior.*

WORKS CITED

Adams, Bronte, and Trudi Tate, eds. *That Kind of Woman: Stories from the Left Bank and Beyond.* London: Virago Press, 1991.

Bair, Deirdre. *Anaïs Nin.* London: Bloomsbury, 1996.

Balakian, Anna. "The Poetic Reality of Anaïs Nin." *A Casebook on Anaïs Nin.* Ed. Robert Zaller, 113–31. New York: New American Library, 1974.

Baldanza, Frank. "Anaïs Nin." *The Critical Response to Anaïs Nin.* Ed. Philip K. Jason, 9–16. Westport, Conn.: Greenwood Press, 1996.

Benstock, Shari. *Women of the Left Bank: Paris, 1900–1940.* Austin: University of Texas Press, 1986.

DeKoven, Marianne. *Rich and Strange: Gender, History, Modernism.* Princeton: Princeton University Press, 1991.

Elkan, Lajos. "Birth and the Linguistics of Gender: Masculine/Feminine." *Anaïs Nin: Literary Perspectives.* Ed. Suzanne Nalbantian, 151–63. New York: St. Martin's Press; London: Macmillan, 1997.

Felski, Rita. *The Gender of Modernity.* Cambridge: Harvard University Press, 1995.

Korges, James. "Nin: The Tropic of Paris." *The Critical Response to Anaïs Nin.* Ed. Philip K. Jason, 111–17. Westport, Conn.: Greenwood Press, 1996.

Lang, Violet. Review of *Under a Glass Bell.* Rpt. in *The Critical Response to Anaïs Nin.* Ed. Philip K. Jason, 77–79. Westport, Conn.: Greenwood Press, 1996.

Marek, Jayne E. *Women Editing Modernism: "Little" Magazines and Literary History.* Lexington: University Press of Kentucky, 1995.

Merchant, Hoshang. "Out of and Into the Labyrinth: Approaching the Aesthetics of Anaïs Nin." *Anaïs: An International Journal* 8 (1990): 51–59.

Nalbantian, Suzanne. *Aesthetic Autobiography: From Life to Art in Marcel Proust, James Joyce, Virginia Woolf, and Anaïs Nin.* New York: St. Martin's Press; London: Macmillan, 1994.

Nicholls, Peter. *Modernisms: A Literary Guide.* London: Macmillan; Berkeley and Los Angeles: University of California Press, 1995.

Nin, Anaïs. "Birth." *Under a Glass Bell,* 102–7. 1948. London: Penguin Books, 1978.

———. *Cities of the Interior.* 1961. Chicago: Swallow Press, 1974.

———. *The Early Diary of Anaïs Nin, 1927–1931.* New York: Harcourt Brace Jovanovich, 1985.

————. *House of Incest*. 1936. Chicago: Swallow Press, 1958.

————. *Incest: From a Journal of Love*. 1993. London: Penguin Books, 1994.

————. *Journal of a Wife: The Early Diary of Anaïs Nin, 1927–1931*. New York: Harcourt Brace Jovanovich, 1986.

Podnieks, Elizabeth. "The Theatre of 'Incest': Enacting Artaud, Mirbeau and Rimbaud in the Pages of the Diary." *Anaïs: An International Journal* 13 (1995): 39–52.

Rood, Karen Lane, ed. *American Writers in Paris, 1920–1939*. Detroit: Gale Research, 1980.

Rosenfeld, Isaac. Review of *Under a Glass Bell*. Rpt. in *The Critical Response to Anaïs Nin*. Ed. Philip K. Jason, 76–77. Westport, Conn.: Greenwood Press, 1996.

Scott, Bonnie Kime, ed. *The Gender of Modernism: A Critical Anthology*. Bloomington: Indiana University Press, 1990.

Sellers, Susan. *Hélène Cixous: Authorship, Autobiography, and Love*. Cambridge: Polity Press, 1996.

Spencer, Sharon. "Anaïs Nin's 'Continuous Novel' *Cities of the Interior*." *A Casebook on Anaïs Nin*. Ed. Robert Zaller, 65–75. New York: New American Library, 1974.

Suleiman, Susan Rubin. *Subversive Intent: Gender, Politics, and the Avant-Garde*. Cambridge: Harvard University Press, 1990.

Wilson, Edmund. "Kay Boyle and the *Saturday Evening Post*." *New Yorker*, January 15, 1944, 66, 68, 70.

CHAPTER 10

Writing the Mind in the Body

Modernism and Écriture Féminine in Anaïs Nin's
A Spy in the House of Love *and* Seduction of the Minotaur

Maxie Wells

ost readers associate modernist
literature with Ezra Pound's metaphrase "Make it new," which
describes the international movement's experimentation with
form in all creative mediums as a reaction to cultural changes
caused by such forces as the Industrial Revolution and World War
I. This analysis of *A Spy in the House of Love* and *Seduction of the Minotaur,* the last two free-standing novels in *Cities of the Interior,*[1] examines how Anaïs Nin's narrative techniques "make it new" in ways
both similar and dissimilar to the modernist linguistic aesthetics of
formal modernism and of feminist modernism (Bair xviii).[2] Formal
modernism experiments with linguistic form and subject matter
within guidelines based on tradition and logic which are outlined
in T. S. Eliot's "Tradition and the Individual Talent," in James
Joyce's *Stephen Hero* and *Portrait of the Artist as a Young Man,* and in
Pound's *Canto XXIX* and his "Translator's Postscript" to Remy de
Gourmont's *The Natural Philosophy of Love* (Eliot 4–5; Gish, "T. S.
Eliot" 139–40; Joyce 211; Pound 169–80; Bush 353, 356; Scott,
"James Joyce" 200–201). Feminist modernism takes all modernist
mediums' interest in the psychoanalytic, the subconscious, and
subjectivity into the realm of gender and creates an aesthetic of the
individual and the irrational against formal modernists' claims for

tradition and logic; the feminist modernist aesthetic is outlined in
H. D.'s (Hilda Doolittle's) *Notes on Thoughts and Visions,* in Virginia
Woolf's *A Room of Her Own,* and in Gertrude Stein's various essays
on language (Benstock 34; Elliott and Wallace 58, 60, 63, 89; S. S.
Friedman 88–89; Kaplan 10). I suggest that Nin introduces yet a
third modernist poetics, which is rooted in her practice of a particularly modernist form of *écriture féminine,* or women's writing.
Nin's modernist *écriture féminine* shares the nonlinear narrative
structure of the *écriture féminine* named and practiced by French
feminists of the 1970s such as Hélène Cixous, Luce Irigaray, and
Julia Kristeva. However, Nin's modernist *écriture féminine* differs
from the *écriture féminine* of the French feminists in focus. Where
Cixous and other practitioners of *écriture féminine* primarily explore
new linguistic ways to "write the female body," to express the multiplicity and jouissance—the feelings beyond desire and orgasm—
of female desire and sexuality, Nin focuses on developing a poetics
that seeks to express the ways in which the female body reflects
the female mind, the ways in which a woman's psychological state
is expressed in the appearance and movement of her body (Formentelli 84, 86; Papachristou 58–59, 63).[3]

These definitions of formal modernism, feminist modernism,
and *écriture féminine* are, of course, reductive and somewhat essentialist. Each of these forms of writing is complex and fluid within
itself, and the relationships between them are incredibly dynamic
and dialogic; one must be somewhat reductive and essentialist in
order to discuss them with any brevity at all. What I would like to
avoid is essentializing any modernist writer by gender. All modernist writers, both male and female, are seeking to change language in order to define the new relationships to the self, to the
other, and to the world created by the postindustrial, postwar cultural changes of the first three decades of the twentieth century.
Although formal modernists such as Hemingway and Pound
experiment mainly within the guidelines of formal modernism,
most others, such as Eliot, Joyce, William Faulkner, D. H.
Lawrence, H. D., Stein, and Woolf, frequently transverse the
boundaries of formal modernism, feminist modernism, and modernist *écriture féminine.* While the similarities between formal and
feminist modernism are fluid and overlapping, there are distinct
differences between the linguistic aesthetics, and both influence
Nin's poetics of modernist *écriture féminine.*

The symbolic representative of formal modernism is Joyce's
highly autobiographical character Stephen Dedalus, who says the

mission of the modernist "man of letters" is to record "with extreme care" the "epiphanies," the "sudden spiritual manifestations" that come to him through language (Joyce 211). To formal modernists like Joyce, Eliot, Hemingway, and Pound, the fragmentation of the modern world represents a breakdown of the old order of Western culture, and they view themselves as Dedalus-like *artist/priest* figures whose mission is to reappropriate and to reconfigure language in order to find a spiritual wholeness through which one might somewhat *transcend* the psychological and cultural wasteland of modern culture (on artist/priest figures see Benstock 158–59, Kaplan 55). Ironically, however, the aesthetics of formal modernism judge these new linguistic forms by "the standards of the past," "the ideal order" of "the mind of Europe" (dead, white, androcentric males) which privilege hegemonic, phallologocentric, past-centered form and order over "female chaos" (Benstock 25, 33; Eliot 4–5; Elliott and Wallace 5, 7; Gilbert and Gubar 156; Pound 169–80). In order to make language new, as Pound dictates, formal modernists frequently rely on recycling the old: artificial images, the abstract, tradition, and logic. Formal modernism is thus a reactive reappropriation and reconfiguration of Eurocentric male-centered language that reinforces the hierarchical, binary oppositions of Western metaphysical thought—male over female, reason over emotion, mind over body—to which the mind/body integration of Nin's modernist *écriture féminine* is antithetical (Benstock 7–8).

In contrast to formal modernism, feminist modernists see the breakdown of the Western cultural order as a positive shattering of patriarchal master narratives that prescribe not only how to speak and write but also who to be and how to live. They want not simply to reappropriate and reconfigure language to express the modern human condition but to appropriate it for the marginalized and to rejuvenate it to express what Pound calls "female chaos," the suppressed history and multiplicity of female experience (Pound 169–80). Feminist modernists rediscover many of the beliefs and ideals that characterize formal modernism, but with a focus on issues of gender and sexuality, such as exploring the nature of the feminine and of women's anxieties, sexual desires, and responsibilities for their own freedom, including reproductive freedom (Davis 209–14; Scott, "D. H. Lawrence" 219; Spencer, *Collage* 40; Spencer, "Mobile" xi-xii). Rather than artist/priests seeking spiritual wholeness to transcend the modern world, feminist modernists view themselves as *artist/activists* seeking through new linguistic forms to express a gendered/sexualized wholeness in order to *transform* the language and culture of the modern world to accommodate and express female experience. In contrast to formal modernism's emphasis on the past, feminist modernism emphasizes the possibilities of the present and future to develop new relationships to the self, to others, to the world, and to language. Feminist modernists also, like formal modernists, rely on the old to "make it new"; however, it is not the static old of artificial imagery, of the abstract, and of past ideological standards; it is a fluid old of reconstituted archetypal symbols and myths that express the collective, ceaselessly changing nature of human experience in language freed from authoritarian forms and order (Benstock 157, 163; Elliott and Wallace 71; S. S. Friedman 86–87; Schenk 317–18; Wall 170–71, 173).

While Nin's poetics of modernist *écriture féminine* has much in common with both formal modernism and feminist modernism, it differs from each in dramatic ways. In contrast to formal modernism's emphasis on tradition, logic, and binary oppositions, the poetics of modernist *écriture féminine* emphasizes an integration of mind and body that is essential to the organic physical and psychological wholeness that occupies Nin and her literary predecessor D. H. Lawrence (Franklin and Schneider 39, 11, 14; Scott, "D. H. Lawrence" 217–18). Nin "aims . . . to dissolve the modern conflict" between mind and body, which she calls the conflict between "nature and neurosis," and which she believes leads to sterility in life, in relationships, and in writing (Zinnes 36). Although Nin shares feminist modernists' interest in describing women's experience, the emphasis on gender and sexuality which becomes an organizing principle in feminist modernists' analyses of "the question of influence, the problematics of genre, the encoding of sexuality . . . and the struggle for technique" becomes in Nin's poetics a focus on how desire, the erotic, and the body express female psychology (Bair 98; Benstock 235, 250–51, 253, 286; Davis 210–11; Kaplan 9, 17; Scott, "D. H. Lawrence" 218; Scott, Introduction 13–14). Nin's exploration of how modernist *écriture féminine* can write the female mind as reflected in the female body shows interest not so much in formal modernism's traditions of the past or in feminist modernism's possibilities of the present and future as in the mythic, archetypal timelessness of nature's organic wholeness (Bair 99–100; Conn 21; Elliott and Wallace 6, 33; Karsten 36–42; MacNiven 97; Nin, "Mystic" 31–35; Nin, "To Write" 87–88, 90; Spencer, *Collage* 22). Rather than formal modernism's artist/priests seeking spiritual wholeness to transcend the modern world, or feminist modernism's artist/activists seeking a language of gendered/sexualized wholeness that can transform the modern world to accommodate female experience, Nin views herself as an *artist/healer* seeking an organic wholeness of integrated mind and body containing psychological, emotional, spiritual, and physical elements through which one *transmutes* one's relationship to self, to others, and to nature in order to live within the fragmented modern world (Formentelli 77–94; Hoy, "Poetry" 63–65; Nin, *Delta* xiii; Nin, *Seduction* 118; Paine 8–9, 72; Scott, Introduction 13; Spencer, *Collage* 25).

The differences between formal modernism, feminist modernism, and modernist *écriture féminine* could also be expressed as the differences between, respectively, "ideological, abstract values," the "psychic torments" of female experience, and "human" values (Burke 236; Hanson 301; Kaplan 47; Paine 72; Nin, "Women's Liberation" 28). In *Seduction of the Minotaur* Nin uses the long-standing "civilized"-white-man-versus-"savage"-other binary opposition to indict the past-oriented, abstract factors of formal modernism as Eliot defines them in "Tradition and the Individual Talent." As Nin extrapolates Eliot's standards for formal modernism in *Seduction,* the "[p]oor white man"—representing Eliot's civilized "mind of Europe" and "standards of the past"—always wants to abstract human beings into distancing images and symbols (4–5). In contrast, the natives of Golconda—representing the "savage" non-Western world and the present—want the closeness of actual human relationships: "The natives had not yet learned from the white man his inventions for traveling away from the present, his scientific capacity for analyzing warmth into a chemical substance, for abstracting human beings into symbols. The white man had invented . . . cameras, telescopes, spyglasses, objects which put glass between living and vision. It was the image he sought to possess, not the texture, the living warmth, the human closeness. . . . Poor white man, wandering and lost in his proud possession of a dimension in which bodies became invisible to the naked eye (7).

In its search to express the organic wholeness of mind/body integration, Nin's poetics of modern *écriture féminine* focuses not exclusively on either the abstract, transcendent spiritual self of formal modernism or on the gendered/sexualized self of feminist modernism, but on the search for the closeness of human relationships. Just as the feminine writing defined by French feminists is practiced by males like Joyce and Faulkner as well as by females, the poetics of modernist *écriture féminine* can be both practiced by and applied to men as well as women. While Nin primarily applies the poetics of *écriture feminine* to the integration of female characters' minds and bodies, the linguistic aesthetic—heavily influenced by D. H. Lawrence—also seeks to express not only an *intra*personal organic wholeness of mind connected to body but also an *inter*personal organic wholeness of self connected to nature and to others rather than the separation of human beings from each other and the world around them and the distinctions between masculine and feminine seen in formalist and feminist modernisms (Bair 99–100; Conn 21; Elliott and Wallace 6, 33; Franklin and Schneider 39, 11, 14; Hinz 5; Karsten 36–42; MacNiven, 97; Nin, "Being a Woman" 23; Nin, "Mystic" 31–35; Nin, "To Write" 87–88, 90; Nin, "Women's Liberation" 27, 29–33, 36–37; Schlesinger 26; Scott, "D. H. Lawrence" 217–24; Spencer, *Collage* 12, 22; Spencer, "Mobile" xvii–xviii).

In *A Spy in the House of Love* and *Seduction of the Minotaur,* Nin uses the poetics of modernist *écriture féminine* to experiment with style in techniques similar to that of both formal and feminist modernists. Using a narrative technique similar to those of Joyce, Djuna Barnes, H. D., Katherine Mansfield, and Jean Rhys, Nin alters linguistic form by substituting a Proustian episodic chronology of emotion and memory for the traditional cumulative, linear narrative structure of novels (S. S. Friedman 86; Hanson 302; Hinz 5; Howells 376; Hoy, "Poetry" 54, 65; Kaplan 3; Nin, *On Writing* 19; Nin, "Out of the Labyrinth" 75; Nin, "Talking About Proust" 127–34; Nin, "To Write" 88–89; Spencer, *Collage* 23; Spencer, "Mobile" xiii). Like other feminist modernists, Nin turns to marginalized genres such as the journal, psychological fiction, and poetic prose to express women's new reality (Benstock 239–40; Broe 24; Burke 230–37; DuBow xii; Elliott and Wallace 57, 71, 74, 127; Gillespie, "Dorothy Richardson" 393–94; Hanson 300; Kaplan 40, 47–48, 67; Merchant 33; Millett 6; Nin, "Interview for Sweden" 19; Nin, *On Writing* 23; Nin, "Writers at Work" 3–4; Paine 11; Sayre 45–58; Scott, Introduction 12–13; Spencer, "Mobile" xii; Spencer, "Ragpicking" 165; Zinnes 39–40).[4] For example, she experiments with linguistic techniques such as repetition, rhythm, stream-of-consciousness sentence structure, and the use of sexual language much as do Barnes, Stein, Woolf, Zora Neale Hurston, and Dorothy Richardson (Bair 110; Benstock 159–61; Burke 230; Conn 21; Durell 2; Elliott and Wallace 106–107, 163; Hoy, "Poetry" 64; Kaplan 3; Nin, *On Writing* 21; Papachristou 65; Schneider 44; Scott,

Introduction 12, 14; Spencer, *Collage* 23). In a narrative mode analogous to those of Joyce, Woolf, Kay Boyle, Richardson, Evelyn Scott, and others, Nin uses a fluid, impressionistic style suitable to her interest in surrealist and symbolist imagery (Benstock 281–82, 294; Formentelli 78; Franklin and Schneider 3, 41; Gilbert and Gubar 258–61; Gillespie, "Dorothy Richardson" 396–97; Gish, "Hugh MacDiarmid" 275–79; Henke 113; Hinz 4–5; Hoy, "Poetry" 65–66; Karsten 41; Mathieu 63–76; McNay 41; Merchant 31; Nin, *On Writing* 24; Nin, "To Write" 89, 91; Nin, "Women's Liberation" 26; Nin, "Writer and the Symbols" 129–31; Nin, "Writers at Work" 13; Schlesinger 26; Scott, Introduction 13; Scott, "James Joyce" 198; Spencer, *Collage* 19, 23). She also uses what Sharon Spencer calls "the idea of collage," which makes language new by changing types of elements, by using incomplete elements, or by combining unexpected elements in literature (*Collage* 4).

In addition to these experiments with linguistic style, Nin's poetics of modernist *écriture féminine* in *Spy* and *Seduction* shares common subject matter with the works of both formal and feminist modernists. Most of Nin's writing is engaged with psychoanalysis, the subconscious, and subjectivity, topics that interested both formal and feminist modernists such as Joyce, Lawrence, Barnes, H. D., Stein, Woolf, Mina Loy, Mansfield, and Marianne Moore (Bair xviii; Benstock 241–42; Durrell 2; Franklin and Schneider, preface; Gillespie, "May Sinclair" 437; Hoy, "Poetry" 53; Jason, "Princess" 15; Kaplan 60, 64–65; Nin, "Being a Woman" 25; Nin, *On Writing* 19, 22–23; Nin, "To Write" 91–92; Nin, "Writer and the Symbols" 131–33; Paine 8–9; Scott, "D. H. Lawrence" 219; Scott, Introduction 13; Spencer, *Collage* 2).[5] Nin's general attention to psychoanalysis and subjectivity leads to a specific absorption with fragmented, multiple, or split selves, a topic that Barnes, H. D., Mansfield, Rhys, and Stein also explore (Benstock 248; Elliott and Wallace 109; Formentelli 89–90; Franklin and Schneider 49–50; S. S. Friedman 86; Hanson 302; Henke 113; Howells 376; Hoy, "Poetry" 59, 66; Kaplan 37; Nin, "Being a Woman" 23; Nin, "Ingmar" 116; Nin, "Interview for Sweden" 15, 17–18; Nin, "On Truth" 63; Nin, "Out of the Labyrinth" 80; Nin, "To Write" 90; Spencer, *Collage* 12–18).[6] For example, *Spy* presents a detailed analysis of the psychological fragmentation experienced by Sabina, the central female character in many of Nin's novels, in her quest for self-realization through a series of unfulfilling love affairs. Likewise, *Seduction* presents the psychological anguish experienced by Lillian Beye as she seeks to create a complete self from her fragmented, competing roles as musician, wife, and mother.

In their emphasis on issues related to gender and women's experience, *Spy* and *Seduction* also demonstrate Nin's kinship to feminist modernists such as Barnes, Nella Larsen, Mansfield, Rhys, Richardson, Stein, and Woolf (Davis 210–11; Elliott and Wallace 68, 81; Nin, *On Writing* 18; Nin, "To Write" 89; Scott, Introduction 14). Many of the works by these women demonstrate feminist modernists' strategies for negotiating unequal and uneasy relationships with their male modernist counterparts, with men in general in a disintegrating society, and sometimes with each other (Elliott and Wallace 17, Formentelli 91–92, Zinnes 36). These strategies frequently shun activism in political causes in favor of "a modernism of the margins" based on private and personal experience because public and political activities often encode patriarchy and violence. Feminist modernists see their emphasis on the subjective as political in its redefinition of women's experience as a valuable framework through which to analyze the modern human condition (Benstock 31, Elliott and Wallace 153). This focus on the personal revives the domestic as a subject for literature, where in the past critics often devalued it because it is "feminine," the term used synonymously with "minor" literature (Hanson 299–300). Nin's writing has frequently been described as "female" or "feminine," a characterization that takes on positive or negative connotations depending on the evaluator's personal ideology regarding feminism (Formentelli 92; McEvilly 52–53).[7] Like other feminist modernists, Nin avoids social realism in *Spy* and *Seduction* and chooses instead to focus on the personal "psychic torments" brought about by Sabina's and Lillian's newfound social and sexual freedoms; Nin deals with the anguish of love instead of with the destruction of society (Bair 400; Elliott and Wallace 29; Hinz 4–5; Jason, "Gemor" 30; Merchant 31; Nin, "Imaginative Realism" 67; Spencer, "Mobile" xii–xvi).

Like the work of many formal and feminist modernists such as Barnes, Natalie Barney, Colette, H. D., Joyce, Rhys, Stein, and Edith Wharton, Nin's fiction is highly autobiographical (Benstock 14, 90, 233, 236; Elliott and Wallace 38; Howells 372–76). In *A Spy in the House of Love,* Sabina's multiple sexual alliances and her guilt over them reflect Nin's own varied sexual history and the enormous strain she felt in juggling her various lovers, especially Henry Miller and René Allendy, with her bigamous marriages to Hugh Guiler and Rupert Pole (Franklin and Schneider, preface, 41; Hoy, "Poetry" 85; Jason, "Dropping" 27–32; Nin, "Being a

Woman" 20–22; Nin, "To Write" 91; Secrest 33–35; Seybert 71; Struck 36–42; Zaller ix, xi).[8] Although Nin cites a newspaper article about polygraph tests as her genesis for the lie detector in *Spy*, the character's notebook is no doubt also based on the "Lie Box" Nin had to use to keep her stories to each husband straight (Bair 360–63, 376). Sabina's marriage to Alan is also heavily based on Nin's marriage to Hugh Guiler (Bair 634–35; Balakian 58–66; M. Miller 39–41; Nin, *"Journal"* 3–23). Sabina's exaggerated dress and walk seem to be based on Nin's dressing in unconventional clothes—a trait she shared with other feminist modernists—in response to the "audible cult" for her physical presence that developed as she became a celebrity in the 1960s and 1970s (Bair 144, 289, 481; Benstock 177, 253; DuBow xiii; Edmiston 43; Elliott and Wallace 20, 26–28; Evans xv; Formentelli 82–90; Herlihy 68; Hoy, "Getting" 81–85; McNay 40; Moore v; Schlesinger 24; Spencer, *Collage* 1).[9]

Seduction of the Minotaur is also modernist in its incorporation of autobiographical elements. The novel's protagonist, Lillian Beye, who also appears in *This Hunger*, is described by critics both as a fictional alter-ego for Nin and as based on her friend Thurema Sokol (Bair 228, 300; Henke 113). Lillian's fleeing to escape an unsatisfactory marriage and later rediscovering love in that relationship and returning to it is based on Nin's marriage to Guiler (Seybert 72). Lillian's watching over Jay's work, particularly her arranging his work into a portfolio, also mirrors Nin's combination sexual/professional relationships with Guiler and with Henry Miller (Bair, 289, 290–92, 296; Hugo 42–51; Nin, Foreword 41; Nin, *Seduction* 114–15; Ryan 18–19; Soteriou 17–18). The incorporation of both pain and pleasure into Lillian's relationship with her physically and emotionally abusive father is based on Nin's similar relationship to her father, although Nin's relationship with her father was also an incestuous one (Bair 16–21, 173–79, 319; Franklin and Schneider 299; Henke 122–24; Hoy, "Poetry" 56–58; McNay, 40; Rank 20–23; Schlesinger 25).[10] The exotic descriptions of Golconda can be traced to Nin's months in Cuba and to her travels in Mexico and Morocco (Bair 356, 358–59, 391, 425, 486, 499; Franklin and Schneider 238–40; Nin, "Morocco"; Nin, "My Turkish Grandmother"; Nin, "Port Vila"; Nin, "Spirit"; Nin, "Swallows").[11] Elements of the dancing scene in *Seduction* can be traced to Nin's life as a dancer, which often enters into her writing (Nin, "Writing and Dancing" 3–18; Papachristou 65). Even the detail of Lillian's journeying to the tropical bird section of a Sears, Roebuck store to experience warmth in winter is based on Nin's visit to the Sears tropical bird center in Pasadena in 1955–56 (Bair 389).

In spite of these similarities in style and subject matter, Nin's modernist *écriture féminine* differs from formal and feminist modernisms in subtle ways. While formal modernists explore new concepts of the self and of the self's relationship to the fragmented modern world based on Freud's psychoanalytic theories of the subconscious, and while feminist modernists examine both the psychology and the sexuality of the modern female self, Nin, more than other modernist writers, is self-consciously seeking a poetics to express the link between the psychological and the sexual, the connection between mind and body. For example, Nin's work shares with texts by lesbian writers such as Barnes and Stein an unusual frankness and explicitness in describing female genitalia and orgasm; in *Spy,* however, Nin uses relentlessly honest sexual language not so much to describe female sexuality as to express how the pain of Sabina's unfulfilled love and desire is written in her body (Bair 365–66; Franklin and Schneider 113–14; Hoy, "Poetry" 62). Like many formal and feminist modernists such as Barnes, Joyce, Lawrence, Mansfield, and Rhys, Nin has a fascination with surrealistic dreams, memories, myths, mood, and sense impressions (Bair 111; Burford 13–14; Evans xii; Formentelli 78; Franklin and Schneider 7, 38, 44, 261; Hoy, "Poetry" 53; Karsten 40; Merchant 29; Moore v; Paine 7; Spencer, "Mobile" xii, xiv, xvi–xvii). But where these other modernists use surrealistic images as techniques for exploring subjectivity, Nin is interested not only in how surrealistic techniques function psychologically but also in how they function as catalysts through which one might experience life directly through the body, through the senses, into the unconscious, and thus experience the ceaseless change essential to organic wholeness, which is both psychological and physical (Evans 145–47, 151, 162; Karsten 36, 38).

Like the works of both formal and feminist modernists, Nin's *A Spy in the House of Love* focuses on a character's quest for the self through the confusion of the modern world. However, Nin's description of Sabina's search for the self is developed through the narrative technique of modernist *écriture féminine* by Nin's constantly linking Sabina's mental state to her sexuality. When we encounter Sabina on page 3 of *Spy,* it is through the eyes of the lie detector, a man she has reached in a random phone call, who describes her as a woman on fire, a woman about to be consumed

by the raging fever of her sexual desire (Evans 149, 158; Papachristou 66). Using a technique similar to Stein's use of rhythmic, repetitive words and images in poems like "A Rose is a Rose is
a Rose" and "Lifting Belly," Nin uses the repetitive motif of woman
about to be consumed by the fever of desire to emphasize that the
wholeness Sabina seeks can be found only in the fusion of mind
and body, not in the separation of emotion from sex that characterizes her unfulfilling relationships with men (Evans 160–61;
Formentelli 91; Karsten 39; Nin, "Women's Liberation" 38; Nin,
"Eroticism" 3, 5).

When the lie detector tells Sabina that each individual is his or
her own worst judge, Sabina hangs up on him. He traces the call
and goes to the bar from which it was made, where he recognizes
Sabina by her voice and anonymously observes the way the conflicting emotions of desire and guilt are written in her body: She
had a "feverish breathlessness" and "sat as if she could not bear to
sit for long . . . drank hurriedly . . . smiled so swiftly that he was
not even certain it had been a smile" and "behaved like someone
who had all the symptoms of guilt: her way of looking at the door
. . . her erratic and sudden gestures." As she talks to other patrons
in the bar, the lie detector notices that in her descriptions of her
life, the fragmented quality of her relationships seems to be paral-
leled by "changes in her personal appearance" (*Spy* 3, 5).

Throughout the novel, Sabina's body continues to be "dressed"
by her emotions in this way. The morning after she first encounters
the lie detector, she attempts "to bring together body and mind" by
reassembling herself with carefully considered makeup and clothes.
Ironically, she achieves the fusion of mind and body that she seeks,
but it is the wrong kind—one of holeness rather than wholeness, as
she chooses "a dress with a hole in its sleeve," a perfect shell for her
ragged, empty emotions (*Spy* 7). When she returns home to her
husband after eight days in a hotel with a lover, "the shame" of the
illicit relationship "dresse[s] her suddenly . . . cloud[s] her beauty . . .
with a sudden opaqueness . . . an absence of quality" (*Spy* 15).

Nin's narrative technique of modernist *écriture féminine* is further
demonstrated in the way Sabina's changing emotional state is
written in the way she walks. Beneath the protective folds of her
cape, she feels free to walk with audacity and with "some swagger
of freedom denied to a woman," "a quality possessed exclusively
by man" (*Spy* 7).[12] However, when she feels the judgmental eye of
the lie detector gazing on her, the character of her walk changes
to "slightly out of rhythm" (*Spy* 8). Confidently walking to the

apartment of her lover Philip, Sabina moves with "power and vigor to her hips," with her shoulders thrown back and her breasts pushing against her dress; in contrast, heading back to the prison-like confinement of her overly protective husband's house (it is always his house, not their house), she walks with bowed shoulders (*Spy* 38). When Sabina meets her seventeen-year-old paramour John, the wartime aviator who has been grounded by malaria, she finally finds a man with whom she is "in step," but the stride they share is one not of joyous sensuality but of "guilt for living and desiring" (*Spy* 67–68, 70; Evans 154; Karsten 41). In the captivity of her strange psychological relationship with her homosexual friend Donald, Sabina's walk becomes "less animal" as she accepts Donald's "moulding" of her into a self-sacrificing motherly role that causes her to lose her eroticism as a "moulting" firebird loses its plumage (*Spy* 84–85; Evans 154–56). Setting off on her "first assignation with desire," Sabina briefly feels within her body the "vainglorious walk" of her father's unrepressed desire, but when she mentally tries to separate his being from hers, she is unable to find a separate Sabina; the mental space that she empties of his presence is quickly filled by physical images of her lovers bearing down on her, indicting her with their eyes (*Spy* 90–91).

As demonstrated in the shared, guilty stride of John and Sabina, Nin applies modernist *écriture féminine* to write the mind in the body for male characters as well as for Sabina, indicating that the wholeness achieved through the fusion of mind and body is that of the complete human being, not of the exclusively masculine or feminine. Each of Sabina's lovers wants only a singular aspect of the multiple facets of her personality; when with a lover, she represses all parts of herself but the one he seeks, and his response to that facet is written in his body. For example, Alan, Sabina's father-figure husband, to whom she can reveal only her vulnerable self, has a "rock-like center to his movements, a sense of perfect gravitation" that reflects both the security and the stasis his overprotection represents in Sabina's life (*Spy* 12).[13] Philip, her opera star lover, wants the "provocative" Sabina, "the adventuress, the huntress, the invulnerable woman," and he has the assured voice, walk, good looks, and cold impersonal gaze of a Don Juan to match that strong woman (*Spy* 21–25, Evans 151–52). Interestingly, Sabina desires only one aspect of her paramour Mambo, who caresses her with the "silken voluptuousness" of tropical seas, kisses her with lips of island spices, and makes love to her with the "island body on which no bone showed." Sabina wants only the native drummer as the exaggerated representation of physical desire, not the cerebral mathematician/artist/composer that Mambo values most in himself. At the same time, Mambo limits Sabina by his desire for her to be a woman of "single love" and undivided affection toward him (*Spy* 39, 47, 53–54, 57; Evans 153; Karsten 37–38).

However, Sabina misinterprets these signals from the men's bodies. She assumes that the desire of each of these men for a singular aspect of her represents a firm center to his personality; in contrast, she feels her multiple facets as a "constant unsureness" at the "core" of her being (*Spy* 26; Evans 145–46, 150, 156–57; Karsten 37). Nin's portrayal of Sabina's inability to define her own selfhood and to accept her multiplicity demonstrates the overlapping nature of formal and feminist modernists' concepts of the self; Sabina represents both the fragmented self of formal modernists' texts and the singular woman's multiple sexual nature that feminist modernists express. Although she is certainly fragmented in her insecurity about the multiple facets of herself, only the combination of multiple selves is the complete Sabina who cannot remain suppressed, a fact graphically demonstrated by two examples of Nin's writing the mind in the body.

Early in the novel, when Sabina returns to Alan after an affair, she takes a bath, washes off the old makeup, changes clothes, even alters the rhythm of her movement—modifies her face and body, attitudes and voice—to "become the woman Alan loves." Nevertheless, she literally and repeatedly has to cover her face and mouth with her hand and hold her breath to keep back "something," the women that are not the one he loves (*Spy* 13–17).

Close to the end of the novel, in a "confessional fever," Sabina tells partial stories about her multiple affairs to friends, especially to Jay, a former lover who understands the sexuality at the core of her essence. When she "lifts the veil" on herself, though only "slightly," the multiply-faceted Sabina of varying desires is symbolically reborn in a stream-of-consciousness sentence thirty-four lines long—the breathless rush of words gushing from Sabina's mouth like the regurgitated poison of her repressed sexuality, her "true," complete self emerging with the unrestrainable force of a woman's final push in childbirth (*Spy* 102–3).[14] In spite of this confession and further ones to her friend Djuna and the lie detector, the Sabina who has many lovers and the Sabina who feels guilty cannot coexist in Sabina's conscious mind, and at the end of the novel her "essence" dissolves in a "water veil" of tears (*Spy* 109–118).[15]

Although Nin most frequently uses *écriture féminine* in *Spy* in her expanded modernist emphasis of writing the mind in the body, she also uses *écriture féminine* in its strictly Cixousian sense. Where formal modernists focus on the abstract multiplicity of the spirit or of the universe, Nin shares with feminist modernists and the French feminists of the 1970s an interest in describing the multiplicity of female sexuality, and she does it in often graphically sensual, highly explicit terms for the early 1950s (Nin, "Eroticism" 5–6, 11). Nin alludes to oral sex in the thinly veiled metaphors of "sensual cannibalism," "a carnal banquet," and "tasting every embrace, every area of her body" (*Spy* 29, 68, 77). She describes vaginal lubrication as "honey flowing between the thighs" and mentions Sabina's feeling the need to wash away the lingering "odors" of her illicit intercourse with Philip (*Spy* 36, 43). Nin also illuminates both the erogenous and maternal nature of the female breast. First she describes male fetishization of the erogeny of the female breast in Philip's fantasy of taking a woman whose arms are bound behind her back, bondage that positions her breasts like the "twin-nippled mountains" that had first inspired his fantasy of copulation with a woman with no entrapping arms (*Spy* 40). Later, in Sabina's mother-child relationship with Donald, when her breasts become like the maternal, nourishing breasts of the mother, they lose the erogenous quality of being "tipped with fire" (*Spy* 83). Sabina also finds a kind of "musical autobiography" of her genitals in Stravinsky's *Firebird Suite;* she recognizes in it her own "crimson suspenses" and "purple vulvas of the night" (*Spy* 56; Spencer, *Collage* 20–22, 39–41).

In describing the multiple facets of Sabina's female sexuality, Nin, like other feminist modernists, appropriates myths and archetypal conventions related to the female body, such as water, flowers, and fruit; however, she is interested in these images as expressions not only of female sexuality but of organic wholeness, representing the connection of the psychological with the physical, and also humans' interconnectedness with nature (Kaplan 49; Schenk 318–19; Spencer, *Collage* 65). Nin especially brings new life to the long-established literary trope of using flower imagery to describe female sexuality and genitalia (Franklin and Schneider 11, 50; Nin, "Eroticism" 4). First she describes Sabina as scattering her sexuality like a flower "exfoliating pollen," and Sabina's mother as exuding "hothouse" charms (*Spy* 68, 77). Later Nin writes Sabina's realization that she cannot find fulfillment through sexual desire alone in the most intimate, female part of her body: Sabina begins to lose symbolic "withered leaves" from the "tropical

growth" of her desire, from the "purple-bell-shaped corolla of narcotic flesh," the "purple flower" of her genitalia (*Spy* 93, 104).

In a use of *écriture féminine* that is both modernist and Cixousian,
Nin also invokes flower imagery to counterpose female sexuality
and fertility to the hatred produced by war and to the barrenness of
war's aftermath, two favorite topics of many modernist writers
(Benstock 26–29; Cowley 3–12; Elliott and Wallace 64–65, 153; Nin,
On Writing 19–20). In seeking to replace a torn paper umbrella that
she once wore as a hair adornment, Sabina encounters a shop-
keeper who tells her to throw her umbrella in the gutter because it
was made by the Japanese. Sabina cannot bring herself to discard
the "innocent and fragile" parasol, which is "made like a flower,
lighter than war and hatred" and decorated with "tender gardens."
The parasol's torn, innocent, fragile, and floral qualities suggest a
penetrated hymen and thus female sexuality and fertility. As she
quietly folds this "fragile structure of dream," Sabina thinks she
"could not keep pace with the angry pulse of the world. She was
engaged in a smaller cycle, the one opposite war. There were truths
women had been given to protect while the men went to war. When
everything would be blown away, a paper parasol would raise its
head among the debris, and man would be reminded of peace and
tenderness" (*Spy* 88; Evans 161–62). In this passage, "cycle" evokes
menstruation and female fertility, and "the one opposite war"
evokes love and life in opposition to hatred and death. Thus, the
"truths women had been given to protect while the men went to
war" are about how to love, how to live, and how to combine the
two, which is the only avenue to "peace and tenderness" and the
only assurance of the continuation of the human race (*Spy* 88).

In these descriptions of female sexuality, Nin does not merely
litanize the damage that patriarchal culture has caused in suppressing free expression of desire, though her reiterative association of drugs and guilt with Sabina's "feverish" sexuality leaves no
doubt that, for Nin, Sabina's repressed desire has become a sickness. It is through the myriad negative examples of Sabina's and
her lovers' failures to find fulfillment in sexual desire alone that
Nin drives home the broader admonition that beats through *Spy*
with the frequency and intensity of the "drumming" of desire to
disrupt an otherwise floating, dreamlike narrative. Sabina has
sought to find self-actualization in learning to sexually enjoy a
stranger "as a man could . . . without love . . . without any warmth
of the heart" (*Spy* 40; Evans 146; Nin, "Eroticism" 3, 5; Nin,

"Women's Liberation" 38). But in seeking to find a cure for the fever of her repressed sexual desire in that desire itself, Sabina—like Nin—finds that sex represents only "a partial relationship," when what she really seeks in each of her lovers is the full human being of integrated mind and body who is capable of that "miraculous openness which takes place in whole love," "the open naked tenderness . . . the exposure of all feelings . . . that we usually reveal only to the loved one . . . the one who understands us" (*Spy* 87; Bair 413; Seybert 70–71, 74).

In *Seduction of the Minotaur* too, Nin practices *écriture féminine* in its modernist form of writing the mind in the body as well as in its Cixousian form of writing the sexuality of the female body. However, in contrast to the actions of her friend Sabina in *Spy*, Lillian Beye of *Seduction* seeks to heal the pain of her troubled soul through abandoning herself to the power of her senses rather than to her sexuality.[16] Lillian feels trapped in a "static" marriage symbolized by her recurrent dream of "a ship that could not reach the water" in spite of "her . . . great effort" to push it to the sea (*Seduction* 104, 5).[17] She has purposely taken an assignment to play the piano with a jazz orchestra at a seaside Mexican resort hotel in order to escape the "absence of mobility" in her life with her husband and children in New York and to experience life in the state of "excess" and "exaggerations" she has sought since childhood (*Seduction* 110, 16, 84). In contrast to the stasis of her old life, Lillian knows that she can find the "chaos" and the "warmth and naturalness" she seeks in the Mexican city she names Golconda (*Seduction* 84–85). In Golconda, which represents freedom, re-creation of the self, ecstasy, and illumination, "the sun paint[s] everything with gold," including "the lining of her thoughts" (*Seduction* 5; Evans 164–65; Nin, "New Woman" 12; Nin, "To Write" 87).

Like Bali and the New Hebrides as described in Nin's travel writings, Golconda has a soft sensuality, a multiplicity of sense experience, and an intensity evocative of a female body in complete touch with its senses and experiencing the jouissance of multiple orgasm; Lillian responds to those pleasures and excesses with both mind and body (Nin, "Port Vila" 148; Nin, "Spirit" 137–38). Lillian is convinced of "the deep power of the tropics to alter a character" because, as far back as the Greeks, the tropics have "signified change and turning" (*Seduction* 30, 5–6). In Golconda "the air, the scents, and the music conspired to hypnotize by softness" and to thus obliterate painful "thoughts and memories" from other lives

(*Seduction* 6). "With [Lillian's] first swallow of air, she inhaled [this] drug of forgetfulness," and she allowed herself—even the "nerves . . . of which she had always been sharply aware"—to be "metamorphosed by the light and caressing heat into a spool of silk" (*Seduction* 5–6, Henke 116–17).

In contrast to many formal modernists' emphasis on tradition and logic over natural forces, Nin infuses Golconda and its people with a primitive naturalness and even an "Oriental" aura—Nin uses such words as "Oriental" and "Japanese" and "Arabian" several times to indicate an Eastern as opposed to Western racial and cultural quality—that invoke the exotic mystery and heightened sensuality often associated (politically incorrectly) with "the other," such as Mambo in *Spy*.[18] The natives in Golconda display a "naked curiosity, naked interest," and seminaked bodies—"Clothes seemed ponderous and superfluous"—that "restored the dignity and importance of the body" (*Seduction* 6–8). Even before leaving the airport, Lillian feels already "incarnated, in full possession of her own body because the porter was in full possession of his," and "[h]er skin blossomed and breathed" in response to the pervasive guitars playing "the music of the body . . . a continuous rhythm of life" (*Seduction* 6–7, 14; Nin, "At a Journal Workshop" 101; Nin, "Morocco" 134; Nin, "Spirit" 139, 147). But this reincarnated body is not one that Lillian has always wanted to possess. She knew that "her father had wanted her to be a boy," and as a result she "did not see herself as beautiful" and "had no confidence in herself as a woman" (*Seduction* 124; Hoy, "Poetry" 59–60; Nin, "Out of the Labyrinth" 79). Lillian's feelings about her physical appearance are obviously based on Nin's early lack of confidence in her beauty caused by her father's calling her "ugly little girl" (Bair 15).

In a passage in *Seduction* that resonates with Nin's attraction to June Miller and somewhat mirrors the works of lesbian feminist modernists such as Barnes, H. D., and Stein, Lillian explores lesbian sexuality as a means of self-discovery (Bair 128, 219–20; Benstock 177; Formentelli 84–90; Hoy, "Poetry" 61–62; H. Miller 93–103; Nin, "*Je T'Aime*" 75–77; Nin, "With Henry" 3–14; Papachristou 58; Petrequin 43–57). Several years before her trip to Golconda, Lillian had a relationship with an artist, Jay, while "disconnected" from her family and fulfilling a several-month musical engagement in Paris (*Seduction* 115). During this period Sabina (from *Spy*) became a model for Jay and became intimately involved in his life with Lillian, and Lillian soon developed what she thought was a lesbian passion for Sabina. However, Lillian's and Sabina's friend Djuna helped Lillian to understand that what she really desired was not to have a sexual relationship with Sabina but to "BECOME Sabina . . . to merge with Sabina's freedom," with her irresponsibility, with "her chaotic and irresistible flow," in order to intensify "the submerged woman" in herself that "Lillian could not liberate fully" (125, 129). Lillian, "disguised as Sabina," wanted to move "out of her own body for good, to become one of the women so loved by her father" (126). Sabina, in turn, wanted Lillian's "innocence" and "her inexperience, her newness, as if [Sabina] wanted to begin her own life anew" (129, 126). Each woman, in virtually all aspects of her life, played a role—Sabina the actress of "dramatic effects, disappearances, mysteries" and Lillian the sincere person who was "dictated by her outward appearance of naturalness and honesty"— and both women "dreamed of escaping from our bodies, our moulds" (127, 129). They toyed with the exchange in a brief physical encounter where they kissed but then "realized they felt closeness but not [sexual] desire" (126). Lillian would ultimately escape her mold by liquidating the painful memories of her past and thereby becoming comfortable with her body; in contrast, Sabina would come to understand the source of her mental anguish, but she would be unable to transcend it and become comfortable either mentally or physically.

Lillian's encounter with Sabina is only one of the relationships that move her toward the self-discovery sought by virtually all characters created by modernist writers. In Golconda she encounters a man similar to Sabina's lie detector, a man "intent on penetrating the mysteries of the human labyrinth from which [Lillian] was a fugitive" (19–20). Lillian's lie detector figure is Doctor Hernandez, a Spanish–East Indian physician who had come to Golconda as an intern many years before and decided to stay. In a parallel with the lie detector's emotional mentorship of Sabina, Doctor Hernandez, who, in spite of his dark side, represents a Christlike figure sacrificed for the sins of the people of Golconda, serves as Lillian's diagnostician, father-confessor, and curative prescriber (Evans 170, Henke 121). He diagnoses Lillian as "one of the underprivileged of pleasure" and, more important, as "a fugitive from the truth" (18, 28–29). He advises Lillian that rather than using Golconda as a "drug for forgetting"—a phrase repeated many times throughout the novel—she must discover "the familiar within the unfamiliar" in order to understand and transcend the painful emotional truth about herself from which she is fleeing

(19, 103). Hernandez cautions her on three different occasions that if she does not "remember" in this way, she will be condemned to reenact the same pattern with every new relationship, and each will be a reproduction of the relationship she is "striving to forget" (19, 29, 103). He emphasizes that the therapy for emotional wholeness "could [not] be otherwise. The design comes from within us. It is internal. It is what the old mystics described as karma, repeated until the spiritual or emotional experience [is] understood, liquidated, achieved" (103).[19]

However, because Lillian has felt "new" in mind and body since arriving in Golconda, she believes that the city's "lull[ing] . . . reverie" will heal her emotional wounds (29, 16). Hernandez points out that "only the backdrop has changed," but Lillian is convinced that Golconda's "flowing" waters and its natives' "flowing" rhythm will reawaken the "flow" of life within her and set her on a "flowing" journey away from the stasis of her marriage (23–25). A canoe trip into the jungle with Doctor Hernandez and a guide, during which "the canoe and her body accomplished the magical feat of cutting smoothly through the roots and dense tangles," persuades her that she has found her "solar barque . . . flowing continuously with life . . . [into] endless discoveries" and that she has ended her dream of a ship in stasis, a ship "unable to float on the waterless routes of anxiety" and "buried in the limestone . . . voyage of memories" (22–25).

Following this "flowing" experience, Lillian prescribes herself a water cure, feeling that "the [hotel's] pool, the sea, the plants . . . were . . . charged with essences . . . like the newest drugs which altered the chemistry of the body" (30). In a passage that is a particularly good example of Nin's practice of modernist *écriture féminine*, of writing the mind in the body, Lillian assures herself that by plunging into Golconda's waters she can "wash her body of all memories" and reassemble her fractured psychological self by rejuvenating her body: "At every moment of anxiety, of probing, she would slip into the sea for rebirth. Her body would be restored to her. She would feel her face as a face, fleshy, sunburned, warm, and not as a mask concealing a flow of thoughts. She would be given back her neck as a firm, living, palpitating, warm neck, not as a support for a head heavy with fever and questions. Her whole body would be restored to her, breasts relaxed, no longer compressed by the emotions of the chest, legs restored, smooth and gleaming. All of it cool, smooth, washed of thought" (28, 83). In keeping with Nin's use of water/ocean to signify the unconscious, three of Lillian's water therapy sessions are linked to epiphanies of acute emotional truths, as are the self-discoveries of many characters wrought by both formal and feminist modernists (Bair 61; Henke 118; Hoy, "Poetry" 54; Nin, *On Writing* 22; Nin, "To Write" 87). Although one of the water cures is described as a "baptismal immersion," Lillian's emotional epiphanies should not be confused with the ur-modernist spiritual epiphanies of Joyce's Stephen Dedalus, which occur completely on an intellectual plane (*Seduction* 110). Lillian's emotions are virtually always written in her body, so the therapy must restore both mind and body and must reconcile them as well.

The first of Lillian's epiphanic water sessions is diagnostic rather than curative, but it marks the beginning of Lillian's acknowledgment that she must confront the pain of her emotional past and thus sets her on the road to recovery. Lillian is taking her pre-bedtime swim in the hotel pool perched high on a cliff—similar to the hotel Nin describes in "The Labyrinthine City of Fez"—when Doctor Hernandez makes his habitual visit (120). Because Lillian's mother's "coldness . . . always curtailed . . . Lillian's outbursts of affection," Lillian "felt an unconfessed need of receiving from some gentle source the reassurance that the world was gentle and warm, and not . . . cold and cruel" (84, 26). The hotel pool's gentle warmth provides "the lulling atmosphere she had missed when she had passed from childhood to womanhood" and also the "pulsating life in the muscles . . . the pleasure of motion" that seem to erase the stasis of her old life (26–27). Lillian leaves the pool to sit near the doctor, but when he begins the evening's conversation by speculating about her emotional state, she tries to escape his diagnosis by slipping back into the pool and even by swimming underwater. When Hernandez persists in confronting her, she once again "plunge[s] into the deep water . . . as if to wash herself of the past" (28). However, Hernandez's accurate diagnosis that she is "a fugitive from truth" causes a pressure in her chest that "compel[s] her to leave the pool" and to confess to him: "I was a woman who was so ashamed of a run in my stocking that it would prevent me from dancing all evening. . . . / I've never been able to describe or understand what I felt. I've lived so long in an impulsive world, desiring without knowing why, destroying without knowing why, losing without knowing why, being defeated, hurting myself and others. . . . All this was painful, like a jungle in which I was constantly lost. A chaos" (28–29). When Hernandez prescribes, as a cure for her anxiety, that she remember, understand, and transcend the emotional experience she wants to forget, Lillian retreats to her self-treatment, assuring both Hernandez and herself that she does feel new, that she is being reborn from Golconda's womblike warm and gentle waters (28).

Lillian's second water therapy session occurs during her visit to the primitive rural home of Hatcher, an American road and bridge engineer with whom she shared a taxi from Golconda's airport. Hatcher is the most imperialist, patriarchal, and androcentric of the several white men Lillian encounters during her three months in Golconda. Although he insists that he is happy living like a native with his Mexican wife, his "enormous" storage room belies his "umbilical ties with his native land's protectiveness": "As large as a supermarket. With shelves reaching to the ceiling. Organized, alphabetized, catalogued. / Every brand of canned food, every brand of medicine, every brand of clothing, glasses, work gloves, tools, magazines, books, hunting guns, fishing equipment. / 'Will you have cling peaches? Asparagus? Quinine?' / He was swollen with pride. 'Magazines? Newspapers?' / Lillian saw a pair of crutches on a hook at the side of the shelf. His eyes followed her glance, and he said without embarrassment: 'That's in case I should break a leg'" (79). Hatcher's "commanding" attitude and insistence on "nam[ing] all the [natural] beauties of his place" vividly personify Jacques Lacan's Law of the Father, a theory that privileges patriarchal men in the development and execution of cultural laws and moral imperatives; also, Hatcher's domineering countenance reminds Lillian of her physically and emotionally abusive father (75, 77).[20]

In sharp contrast to Hatcher, who knows exactly who he is because he unquestioningly follows the Western cultural imperative of what it means to be a patriarchal male, Lillian is gradually beginning to reassemble her fragmented self both by reshaping her thoughts and by renewing her body through a union with nature. As she goes to the sea to forget Hatcher and her father, the tropical waters engulf her painful memories and physically rejuvenate her. In this passage Nin once again, as in *Spy*, uses the feminist modernist technique of appropriating archetypal conventions such as water and flowers to express not only Lillian's reconstituted female body/sexuality but also her achieving an organic wholeness that represents the interconnectedness of mind with body and of self with nature. In a passage that evokes the sensuality of Georgia O'Keeffe's floral paintings, the tropical waters leave Lillian feeling like one of the "violet red velvety" seaside flowers and of the

"velvet . . . red hibiscus" described in Nin's travel writings about
Bali: "The sea folded its layers around her, touched her legs, her
hips, her breasts—a liquid sculptor, the warm hands of the sea all
over her body. / She closed her eyes. / When she came out and put
on her clothes she felt reborn, born anew. She had closed the eyes
of memory. She felt as though she were one of the red flowers,
that she would speak only with the texture of her skin, the tendrils
of hair at the core, remain open, feel no contractions ever again. /
She thought of the simplified life. Of cooking over a wood fire, of
swimming every day, of sleeping out of doors in a cot without
sheets, with only a Mexican wool blanket. Of sandals, and freedom
of the body in light dresses, hair washed by the sea and curled by
the air. Unpainted nails" (*Seduction* 78; Nin, "Spirit" 144). This
water treatment to wash away painful memories barely lasts pasts
dinner, however: "Hatcher's umbilical cord had stirred her own
roots. His fears had lighted up [the] intersections of memory. . . . /
The farther she traveled into unknown places, unfamiliar places,
the more precisely she could find within herself a map showing
only the cities of the interior" (*Seduction* 80).

Lillian's third water therapy session occurs on a night when she,
Doctor Hernandez, and their friends Fred, Diana, and Edward visit
Golconda's native dance halls and later swim naked at a secret
cove known only to Hernandez (104–10). By this time Lillian has
had the emotional epiphanies of her confession to Hernandez and
of Hatcher's evoking memories of her father, and also of her visit to
Michael Lomax's house in an ancient city partially buried in volcanic lava (59). Like the inhabitants of many cities Nin visited in
her travels, the Indians who populate Lomax's ancient city live on
primarily inner patios behind walls. "The immobility of the people,
the absence of the wind, gave [the city] a static quality" and a
"silence . . . so noticeable and palpable that it disturbed Lillian"
(*Seduction* 59, 61; Nin, "Morocco" 132, 134–35; Nin, "Port Vila"
164; Nin, "Spirit" 142). Lomax too has "a static quality, like that of
the ancient city itself"; Suzette Henke describes him as a ghost arising from a "symbolic landscape emblematic of a consciousness
imprisoned in an ossified past" (*Seduction* 66–67; Henke 118). He
has decided to never fall in love again, and this burial of his emotions has "caused a kind of death" which gives him his static quality (*Seduction* 66–67). Lomax's similarity to his surroundings
suggests to Lillian that the city in which each of us chooses to live
"represents our inner landscape"—the city of our interior thoughts

and emotions—and Lomax has chosen "a magnificent tomb, to live among the ruins of his past loves" (66).

Nin's use of Lomax's volcanically ruined city as a metaphor for his static emotional state is a classically modernist use of the city as a symbol for the fragmented modern psyche (Hinz 5; Nin, "Morocco" 134; Nin, "Out of the Labyrinth" 76; Spencer, "Mobile" xiii). Both formal and feminist modernists such as Eliot, Joyce, Barnes, Mansfield, Rhys, and Woolf, like the French symbolists, use the modern urban city as a symbol of the destruction of society (Benstock 241–42; Kaplan 67, 72–73, 75, 78–80). Nin, however, echoing H. D.'s and Lawrence's positing a return to nature in contrast to other modernists' emphasis on the city, chooses an ancient city populated by Indians in which the Indians represent an organically whole society, one in which humans coexist with nature (Scott, Introduction 16). The Indians' organically whole city/society has been destroyed by nature's symbolic eruption against the industrialism of modern society; thus, forces beyond their control have put the Indians into a state of static sterility. In contrast, Nin's Lomax, much like the characters of formal modernists such as Eliot and Joyce, represents the fractured, static, sterile modern psyche; he has chosen to be inorganically whole by separating his wounded emotions from the world around him. Sharon Spencer observes that the combination of the ancient and the new as Nin has used it to describe Lomax's city is an attribute of modernism in that modernism is new in its acceptance of the discoveries of modern science but old in its "insistence on the indivisibility of matter and spirit and the power of the unconscious to animate and rejuvenate" sterile modern life ("Mobile" xii). But where other modernists focus on the effects of the rupture of matter and spirit, Nin focuses on characters' achieving the repair of the rupture between body and mind. Lillian Beye's journey into the cities of her psychological interior will accomplish such a repair.

The surreal ruins of Lomax's ghost town resurrect Lillian's memories of "the city beneath the city," an uncompleted subway excavation, where she played as a child. She and her playmates had been forbidden to go there, and the secrecy of their visits to the hidden city made them even more intense. Once, Lillian ignored her mother's whistle to come home and remained in the tunnel after her playmates had left; when her candle went out and she walked into wet clay which conjured stories of "wells, sewers, and underground rivers," Lillian thought that she would die in the tunnel (*Seduction* 71). The lesson she learned from this experience was: "When you do not answer the whistle of duty and obedience . . . [w]hen you choose to play in a realm far away from the eyes of parents, you court death" (72).[21] Lillian had disobeyed not only her mother's whistle but also a Lacanian Law of the Father–type cultural imperative that civilized little American girls do not go where they are forbidden, and they most certainly do not consort with little Mexican "savages" in doing so (84). Although Lillian's fear of dying in the tunnel was more than enough punishment for a seven-year-old, Lillian's disobedience would also fall under the law of her father, whose punishment would echo through the labyrinthian tunnels of her subconscious and structure her identity for more than twenty years before it would be exorcised. Nin's use of the labyrinth as an anology for one's journey through his/her subconscious—the journey whose outcome we do not know—is a recurring theme in her work; the labyrinth analogy's emphasis on the epiphanic and spiritual nature of this journey is similar to the emphasis on the spiritual seen in the works of formal modernists such as Eliot and Joyce (Evans 169; Henke 119; Nin, "To Write" 87).

After Lillian's visits with Hatcher and with Lomax summoned disturbing images of her abusive father and her cold mother, she wondered: "Why should it be among these shadows, these furtive illuminations, these descending passageways" of her painful childhood memories "that her true self would hide?" (*Seduction* 89). By the evening of the native dance halls and the swim in Doctor Hernandez's secret cove, Lillian's three emotional epiphanies had provided the self-awareness for her to understand that "it was fear who had designed her life, and not desire or love" (109). She had feared entering the labyrinth of her soul "and meeting the Minotaur who would devour her. . . . Yet now that she had come face to face with it, the Minotaur resembled someone she knew. It was not a monster. It was a reflection upon a mirror, a masked woman, Lillian herself, the hidden masked part of herself unknown to her, who had ruled her acts. She extended her hand toward this tyrant who could no longer harm her" (111). Nin only partially extrapolates the Minotaur mythology in suggesting that a hidden part of Lillian herself is the Minotaur she has always feared facing, perhaps because Nin's interest is in the personal mythology of the subconscious more than in a strict adherence to the details of classical literature, "the standards of the past" that Eliot espouses as a criterion for modernist writing. Reading Lillian's Minotaur myth more closely against the classical Greek one offers further insight into the dynamics of Lillian's journey to self-awareness.

In Greek mythology, the Minotaur was a monster half human, half beast, the offspring of the wife of Minos, the ruler of Crete, and a beautiful bull. When the Minotaur was born, Minos did not kill him, but had the architect Daedalus build a mazelike structure called the Labyrinth to imprison him. Every nine years, seven maidens and seven youths were put into the Labyrinth, from which they could not escape, and the Minotaur devoured them. This sacrifice continued until Theseus, the strong son of the king of Athens, offered himself as one of the youths so that he might kill the Minotaur. With the help of Minos's daughter Ariadne and Daedalus, Theseus learned that he could unroll a ball of string in order to retrace his steps to the entrance of the Labyrinth. Armed with this knowledge, he went boldly into the maze, found the Minotaur asleep, and beat him to death (E. Hamilton 139–40, 149–52).

In her visits to Hatcher's and Lomax's homes, Lillian has entered the labyrinth of her memories and subconscious. Just as Theseus found the courage to boldly enter the Labyrinth with the guidance of Ariadne and Daedalus, Lillian finds the courage to enter her labyrinth with the guidance of Doctor Hernandez. But instead of relegating Lillian to the secondary role played by Ariadne in the Greek myth, Nin positions her as the central figure: a woman's subjective consciousness becomes the main issue, and the merging of mind with body becomes the primary method of self-discovery. In the labyrinth of her subconscious, Lillian encounters a very specific memory of her father's neglect and physical and emotional abuse, a passage that is undoubtedly based on Nin's relationship with her father, who fondled her and took nude photographs of her, alternately with beating her, until he abandoned the family when Nin was eleven (Bair 15–29, 41). During Lillian's childhood in Mexico, where her father's unbending will to build roads and bridges was "frustrated by enigmatic natives, and elemental cataclysms," he would "come home to the one kingdom, at least, where his will was unquestioned" (*Seduction* 111). He would listen to the mother's report of the day and perpetually find some infraction that required a spanking. Since Lillian received no other attention from him, the spanking became "the only caress she had known from her father," making her relationship with him—and her subsequent relationships with men, which developed in the same "groove"—a mixture of pain and pleasure: "Thus the real dictator, the organizer and director of her life had been this quest for a chemical compound—so many ounces of pain mixed with so many ounces of pleasure in a formula known only to the unconscious" (111–14).

When Lillian reaches this conscious, psychological epiphany in her journey through the labyrinth of her memories and subconscious, she meets her Minotaur, who is, appropriately, a multiply faceted creature like the Minotaur of Crete. Lillian's Minotaur is a "hidden masked part of herself unknown to her, who had ruled her acts," the part of herself which had unconsciously sought that mixture of pleasure and pain. However, this masked part of Lillian herself is also "a reflection upon a mirror," and this reflection emanates from the father whose abusiveness gives him a beastlike quality. Thus Lillian's Minotaur is part human and part beast: it is the human, confused child whose identity is formed by the mirrored reflection of her beastly father's abuse—"someone she knew," the child who is "not a monster," but also the father who is a "tyrant" (111).[22] Like Theseus of the Greek myth, by boldly entering the labyrinth and seeking the Minotaur, Lillian has been able to destroy it "now that she had come face to face with it. . . . She extended her hand toward this tyrant who could no longer harm her" (111).[23] At this point in Nin's extrapolation of the Greek myth into an epic modernist search for self-discovery, Lillian's organically whole self—one in which mind and body are connected—now hovers on the brink of rebirth.

By the time Lillian and her friends visit the native dance halls and swim naked in Hernandez's secret cove, "the true freedom of Golconda, its fluid, soft, flowing life," has "expose[d] [Lillian's] own imprisonment," not only the myth of her Minotaur but also "the myth of her courage, the myth of her warmth and flow . . . which had caused her to pass judgment on the static quality of Larry [her husband], concealing the static elements in herself" (104). As she dances with the natives in their hall, Lillian knows now "that it was an illusion that one lived in full possession of one's body": as long as one has unexplored labyrinths of the cities of the interior, one is not in full possession of one's mind, a prerequisite state for full possession of one's body (106). However, Lillian has exorcised enough of her personal demons: "The time was past when her body could be ravished . . . by visitations from the world of guilt," and, despite Hernandez's repeated warnings to put her shoes on, she exhibits her now organically whole self by dancing with the natives in her bare feet, feeling "no interruption between the earth and her body as if the same sap and rhythm ran through both simultaneously, gold, green, watery, or fiery when you touched the core" (105).

As Lillian and her friends swim naked at Hernandez's secret cove after the dancing is done—a scene Oliver Evans says "might have come right out of Lawrence" in its emphasis on organic whole-ness—Lillian's new state of mind, in which she has finally begun to "flow" with the natural world around her, finally produces a lasting rebirth of her body from the womblike sea of Golconda: "The fatigue and the heat of the dance were washed away. The sea swung like a hammock. One could grow a new skin over the body. The undulations of the sea were like their breathing, as if the sea and the swimmers had but one lung. / Out of the full beauty of the tropical night, the full moon, the full blooom of the stars, the full velvet of the night, a full woman might be born. No more scattered fragments of herself living separate cellular lives, living at times in the tempo-rary home of others' lives" (*Seduction* 110; Evans 171). Reborn as a "full" human being through the integration of mind and body, Lillian can journey homeward to repair her relationship with her husband, Larry. He too was betrayed by parents, and he "disap-peared behind a facade of obedience" and "detachment" until he "was truly born in [Lillian's] warmth and her conviction of his exis-tence" (*Seduction* 135–36). Now he "had to be maintained on the ground, given a body. She breathed, laughed, stirred, and was tumultuous for him. Together they moved as one living body and Larry was passionately willed into being born, this time perma-nently" (136). With Lillian's return to Larry and her children, *Seduc-tion* differs from *Spy* in that Lillian's new self-awareness "is followed by action" (Evans 163). Lillian is able to repair her relationship with Larry by doing what Nin advocates that men and women should do: emphasizing "the resemblance" between them and trying "to inte-grate the differences" between them (Nin, "Being a Woman" 23; Nin, "In Favor" 53).

In addition to modernist *écriture féminine,* Nin uses other narra-tive techniques and subject matter associated with modernism in *Seduction of the Minotaur.* Although the plot of *Seduction* is more lin-ear than that of *Spy* in order to reflect Lillian's journey toward self-awareness, the linear narrative structure is interrupted by Proustian flashbacks to Lillian's childhood and to her relationship with Jay (Evans 170). Nin's frequent allusions to and combinations of color, music, odors, tastes, and touch sensations in describing Golconda exemplify the use of surrealism associated with Barnes and the use of repetition associated with Stein (Evans 175; Henke

118; Nin, "Writer and the Symbols" 127–28). Nin also uses surreal-istic imagery in Lillian's dreams of the waterless ship, of the floating solar barques, of the giant Coca-Cola bottle in the bullring, in rep-resentations of the "nightmare figures" of beggars in Golconda, of the vulture biting Lillian's shoulder in the ancient city, and of the double-exposure photograph at the Mayan temple in which Lillian is both standing up and lying down, her head seemingly inside the jaws of a giant snake (*Seduction* 5, 23–24, 43, 45, 62–63, 80).[24] Lil-lian's journey to Golconda also represents the modern woman's restlessness in search of the self, seen in the works of feminist mod-ernists Larsen and Mansfield (Davis 211; Kaplan 70).

Sabina's and Lillian's journeys to self-awareness are in many ways typical of the search for the self seen in all modernist texts. However, where formal modernists such as Joyce seek to tran-scend the modern world through the spiritual manifestations of the mind, and feminist modernists seek to transform the modern world through an emphasis on gender and sexuality, Nin's charac-ters seek to heal the pain experienced in the modern world through transmuting the self into an organically whole human being—Sabina through dreams and sexual desire, Lillian through myths and dreams and abandonment to the senses. Both Sabina and Lillian ultimately realize that they must leave the surreal, pro-tected world of myth, dream, and emotionless sensuality and reen-ter the painful world of life in order to become complete persons; it is through this journey to an organically whole self-awareness which connects both mind to body and self to nature and to other human beings that they become artist/healer figures to themselves and, in Lillian's case, to those they love.

In her practice of modernist *écriture féminine*—in her writing how the female mind is expressed in the female body—in *A Spy in the House of Love* and *Seduction of the Minotaur,* Nin has created a new nar-rative form that incorporates many of the linguistic stylistic experi-mentations and much of the subject matter of concern to formal and feminist modernists. Perhaps more important, however, in her descriptions of Sabina's and Lillian's journeys to self-awareness, Nin has given us portraits of how to become whole human beings within the fragmentation of the modern world. She repeatedly insists that, rather than seeking to transcend the modern world through the spiritualized wholeness of the formal modernists, or to transform the modern world through the gendered/sexualized wholeness advocated by feminist modernists, one must transmute one's self into an organically whole self in which mind is connected to body and self is connected to nature and to other human beings in order to live within the modern world. Only such a complete self can remain whole within the cultural devastation described by formal modernists. Only such a complete self can respond to the multiplicity of female experience described by feminist modernists. Only such a complete self can truly experience the jouissance of sexuality, the feelings beyond orgasm and desire, described by the French feminists who named writing the female body *écriture féminine*. Only the complete self of integrated mind and body and of self integrated to nature and to others represented in Nin's modernist *écriture féminine* can truly experience the jouissance of life, the potential for ultimate pain or pleasure, the intensity that makes us fully alive.

NOTES

1. Nin published five related works, *Ladders to Fire* (1946), *Children of the Albatross* (1947), *The Four-Chambered Heart* (1950), *A Spy in the House of Love* (1954), and *Solar Barque* (1958), as individual novels. Franklin and Schneider note that shortly after the publication of *Solar Barque*, Nin "decided to conclude her continuous novel, but instead of writing a new volume she presented the text of *Solar Barque* and a lengthy, previously unpublished coda to Alan Swallow who published them together as *Seduction of the Minotaur* in 1961. This book serves now [they were writing in 1979] as both a self-contained novel and as the conclusion to the much larger whole [*Cities of the Interior*] that began in 1946 with *Ladders to Fire*" (130).

   The overlapping material in *Solar Barque* and *Seduction of the Minotaur* exemplifies what Franklin and Schneider describe as the "textual problems" of "changing and shifting contents" in much of Nin's work; see 20–21, 62–64, 83, 99, 113, 130. See also Franklin 28–31.

2. For an excellent description of the modernist literary canon, see Benstock's chapter "Women of the Left Bank," particularly 21–34. Benstock's distinction between the "center" and the "margin" of the modernist literary canon inspired my distinction between "formal" and "feminist" modernisms. The issues and writers included under each of my terms are not exactly equivalent to Benstock's, but there is significant overlap.

3. There is not a precise definition of *écriture féminine*, of what writing the female body means. One of the most frequently cited works regarding it is Cixous's "The Laugh of the Medusa," which, with a number of other works defining and demonstrating feminine writing, is found in Marks and de Courtivron's *New French Feminisms*. Jane Gallop's *The Daughter's Seduction* also defines and discusses *écriture féminine*. Irigaray's *Speculum of the Other Woman* and Monique

Wittig's *Les Guérillères* are frequently cited as examples of writing the female body.

    In her essay on Nin's "appropriation of feminine writing," Lynette Felber suggests that Nin's *Diary* and prose poem *House of Incest* exemplify and intensify Christiane Makward's description of the stylistic features of feminine writing as "open, nonlinear, unfinished, fluid, exploded, fragmented, polysemic, attempting to 'speak the body,' i.e. the unconscious, involving silence, incorporating the simultaneity of life as opposed to or clearly different from logical, nonambiguous, so-called 'transparent' or functional language" (316). For additional discussions of Nin's feminine writing, see Margaret Andersen's "Critical Approaches to Anaïs Nin," Ellen G. Friedman's "Anaïs Nin," and Sharon Spencer's "The Music of the Womb: Anaïs Nin's 'Feminine' Writing" (Felber 322). Although Bair does not use the term *écriture féminine*, she suggests that Nin theorizes women's language as writing the female body in Nin's assertion that women's language must be made of blood and flesh and must be nourished by the womb and breast milk (239–40).

4. Nin indicated in an interview with Daisy Aldan that the greatest innovation she made through her work was her use of "poetic prose" (Nin, "To Write" 86, 90, 92).

5. Julie Karsten observes that Nin's interest in the psychological was especially influenced by D. H. Lawrence (38). Nin briefly practiced psychoanalysis under the tutelage of Otto Rank in New York, but within a few months returned to Paris and her literary career (Bair 203–10, Franklin and Schneider 185–86).

6. Bair notes that Nin's self-division began with her use of multiple languages (34–35). By the time Nin was seventeen she "had begun to divide herself into what she called 'the double person in me: Miss Nin and Linotte.'" Miss Nin was her "good" public persona and Linotte her "impossible . . . secret, private self [which eventually] became her true reality and certainly the dominating part of her adult personality" (39, 42). Bair further describes this *dédoublement* in Nin's life on 83–84, 143, 207, 228–29, and 553n25. Margaret Miller also discusses the *dédoublement* in Nin's life in "Diary-Keeping and the Young Wife" (39–44).

7. Felber suggests that Nin's "choosing to cultivate the identity of a feminine writer . . . may have relegated [her] to the status of a vogue writer and contributed to her own *literary* marginality with both male critics, for whom 'feminine' is a term of denigration or conde-scension, and feminist critics, who in the 1980s and '90s often dis-miss the self-proclaimed feminine writer as essentialist" (309).

8. Bair asserts that Nin's unfaithfulness to Hugh (Hugo) Guiler began within five years of their 1923 marriage with her sex play with dance teacher Antonio Francisco (Paco) Miralles (83). Bair also suggests that Nin sometimes juggled as many as three regular lovers (including

Hugo) interspersed with one-time sexual encounters. However, as Seybert points out in her analysis of Nin's relationships with Guiler and Miller as described in *Henry and June,* Nin "does not commit adultery without scruples" but "approaches adultery from the point of view [that] it becomes a psychic necessity in her development": although she loved Hugh Guiler "tenderly," Nin "enjoyed a sexual liberation and satisfaction with Henry Miller which her husband could not provide, though, technically speaking, he was obviously quite capable" (68). Seybert further describes Nin's relationship with Guiler as *tenderness* and *love* and Nin's relationship with Miller as *blood* and *passion* (70–71, 74). Seybert also notes that *Henry and June* "shows that for a long time [Nin] hesitated to become physically intimate with Henry Miller" (68).

9. Benstock describes Nin's clothing as "femme-fatale" (177). Seybert notes that "Anaïs [knew] how to keep [Henry Miller's] interest aroused" with "constantly changing costumes—her Andalusian dress, the clanging metal bracelets she wears even in bed" (72). Gubar describes female modernists' interest in theatrical clothes as likely rooted in "escap[ing] the strictures of societally-defined femininity by appropriating the costumes they identified with freedom" (477).

10. Franklin and Schneider were among the first to note that incest became one of the basic concerns of Nin's writing (50). Djuna Barnes was also sexually abused by her father (Elliott and Wallace 163).

11. In "Interview for Sweden" Nin noted that her greatest pleasures were "friendships, relationships, and travel," and she did throw herself into all three with gusto (15).

12. The protective and freedom-invoking nature of Sabina's cape is clearly based on Nin's interest in theatrical clothes. Knapp asserts that Sabina's cape is a role-playing costume which can be either a "bed of nomads" or a "flag of adventure" (133). On Nin's wearing of capes, see Edmiston 46.

13. The concepts of *stasis* and *flow* are cornerstones of Nin's philosophies of life, human relationships, and writing. She frequently speaks of "the flow" of life and of writing and of the "fluid connections" between people, between events, between the past, present, and future, and between the conscious and the subconscious (Henke 117; Nin, "Being a Woman" 23; Nin, "Interview for Sweden" 18–19). Bair notes that Nin's concept of a "system of mobility," or flow, comes from D. H. Lawrence (100). Evans observes that Nin's characters are defined by a commitment to either movement/life or stasis/death (170–71). Interestingly, many of Nin's male characters are associated with stasis and/or death—Alan in *Spy,* and Hernandez, Hatcher, Fred, Larry, and Lomax in *Seduction* (Evans 148–49, 171).

14. I have chosen the childbirth/rebirth metaphor to describe this remarkable stream-of-consciousness sentence, but the breathless

rush of words might also be compared to an extended orgasm in which Sabina's repressed multiple sexual personae finally achieve release. Sophia Papachristou also links Nin's writing to the rhythm of a woman's experiencing intercourse (62–63).

15. Critics disagree about whether the ending of *Spy* represents Sabina's achieving self-realization, her having a breakdown, or inconclusiveness (Evans 145, 149, 158–5; Formentelli 90; Karsten 37, 39; Nin, "To Write" 90; Spencer, *Collage* 41).

16. Nin's writing often focused on the power of the five senses, and she intended it to be received through the senses (Evans xv; Nin, *On Writing* 21–22; Paine 7–8; Zinnes 37–38). Lillian's experience of the heightened response of her senses in Golconda is very similar to the heightened response of the senses seen in Nin's travel writings "Morocco" (136), "The Labyrinthine City of Fez" (119–25), and "The Spirit of Bali" (138). There is also frequently an overlap between abandonment to the senses and female sexuality in Nin's work (Hoy, "Poetry" 61; Papachristou 60–61). Although Lillian abandons herself to the sensual experience of Golconda rather than to sexual experiences with men, she always experiences the sensations with her mind as well as with her body, and those sensations have a markedly sexual quality to them.

17. Ship imagery recurs in Nin's writing in connection with the concepts of stasis and flow. Landlocked ships represent the past, memory, and stasis; moving ships represent the present and future, discovery, and flow (Evans 7–8, 166–67, 174–75, 177; Henke 116–17; Hoy, "Poetry" 65–66; Nin, "To Write" 87).

18. In his towering cultural history, Edward Said defines the significance of the Oriental to Western culture: "The Orient was almost a European invention, and had been since antiquity a place of romance, exotic beings, haunting memories and landscapes, remarkable experiences.

" . . . the French and the British—less so the Germans, Russians, Spanish, Portuguese, Italians, and Swiss—have had a long tradition of what I shall be calling *Orientalism,* a way of coming to terms with the Orient that is based on the Orient's special place in European Western experience. The Orient is not only adjacent to Europe; it is also the place of Europe's greatest and richest and oldest colonies, the source of its civilizations and languages, its cultural contestant, and one of its deepest and most recurring images of the Other. In addition, the Orient has helped to define Europe (or the West) as its contrasting image, idea, personality, experience" (1–2).

Nin uses a similar concept of the Orient in *Seduction,* not only in her description of Golconda, but also to define the role of the artist through the character Jay: "I'm finding my own world. . . . Something between the will of the European and the Karma of the oriental. I want just the joy of illumination, the joy of what I see in the world. . . . That was always the role of the artist, to reveal the joy, the ecstasy" (118).

Like natives of several of the countries Nin visited, the people of Golconda also have a primitive simplicity, harmony of life, and hospitality in comparison to tourists and colonial oppressors (Evans 173–74; Nin, "Labyrinthine City" 129, 133; Nin, "Port Vila" 148; Nin, "Spirit" 139, 141, 147). Nin introduces this primitive-savage-versus-civilized-man dichotomy in the first few pages of *Seduction* by juxtaposing various "other[s]" to the three predominantly white men with whom Lillian shares a cab from the airport (9, 14). The American road and bridge engineer Hatcher and the Austrian Hansen, who owns the Black Pearl nightclub where Lillian will perform, represent the worst of androcentric imperialism in their attempts to "conquer" rather than submit to the tropics (*Seduction* 10). Doctor Hernandez, who is mixed "other"—Eastern Indian and Western Spanish—has come to "love" the people and place of Golconda, but nevertheless seeks to exert imperialistic control over illness in the hospital he has "created" and over local culture by controlling the drug traffic (*Seduction* 13, 20–21). In contrast to these patriarchal Western males, the "other," female Lillian is willing to be "metamorphosed," to be "changed and turned," by the "Oriental" (Nin uses the word twice in one page) landscape and people of the tropical Golconda (*Seduction* 6, 13).

19. Several critics contend that Lillian is a classic Freudian neurotic doomed to repeat the relationships of the past (Evans 169; Henke 114, 117; Hoy, "Poetry" 57). This concept of reenacting the same pattern with every new relationship seems to be based on Nin's adulterous sexual relationships with Henry Miller and with one of her therapists, René Allendy. Through her analysis with Allendy, Nin realized that both men "represent[ed] father figures . . . whom she must seduce in order not to lose them" (Seybert 71–73). In his preface to the early *Diary,* Otto Rank suggests that Nin's reproduction of seeking her father in her relationships with men is also a reproduction of a "mythological motif" of incest as "handed down in legends and fairy tales" (21–23). Similarly, Henke and McEvilly discuss Lillian's confronting her Minotaur as a "quest to 'slay the father'" which has epic, archetypal connotations. Sabina is similarly reenacting a pattern in *Spy,* although she is seeking to gain a "perfect love," which is the "fusion of mind and flesh," rather than to not lose a father (Seybert 71–73).

20. Hatcher's annoyance with the tourists of Golconda echoes Nin's annoyance with the French tourists in "Morocco" (135). Evans notes Hatcher's "appurtenances of civilization" and Lillian's wondering if there is any similarity between Hatcher's situation of *thinking* he has freed himself in Golconda and her similarly seeking escape there (168–69). Regarding the trappings of civilization in primitive locations, Nin notes that in Bali, which is clearly a model for Golconda in the various references noted above, "you are not judged by your

possessions . . . [but] by your manner and your hierarchy in the spiritual and artistic world" ("Spirit" 144).

21. Henke suggests that Lillian's childhood search for autonomy is a pattern repeated in Lillian's adult life: "The woman who rejects the call
of duty and obedience [to her husband and children, whom she has
left], who chooses artistic creativity over traditional roles prescribed
by society, invites personal catastrophe. The search for autonomy is
perilous indeed" (119).

22. In "The New Woman" Nin connects a troubled childhood with development as an artist; she states that she learned from Baudelaire "that
in each one of us there is a man, a woman, and a child—and the
child is always in trouble. . . . So the poet said we have three personalities, and one was the child fantasy which remained in the adult
and which, in a way, makes the artist" (13–14).

23. Henke suggests that, in confronting her Minotaur, "Lillian plays the
role of the epic hero described by Freud. On a psychological level,
she acts out the primordial heroic myth of a quest to 'slay the father'"
(115–17, 120, 122–23). McEvilly also gives the confrontation mythic
proportions based on Jung's process of individuation: "that moment,
crucial, heightened with archetypal significance, of the meeting with
the minotaur of one's own self" (1).

24. Nin mentions the bullring or bullfighter three times in *Seduction*.
Papachristou contends that when Nin writes erotically, she "dips into
her Spanish blood, and into the memory of Spanish culture" and that
"[t]oreador and bull are constantly evoked" (64, 66). In *Seduction* Nin
uses the toreador and bull to evoke the erotic. When traveling by bus
to Hatcher's remote home, Lillian meets a young bullfighter named
Miguelito on the bus. He is sullen because, in his fight the previous
Sunday, the bull had "torn his pants with its horns, had undressed
him in public." Nin suggests that this "small patch of flesh showing
through the turquoise brocaded pants . . . had made the scene with
the bull more like a sensual scene, a duel between aggressor and victim, and the tension had seemed less that of a symbolic ritual
between animal strength and male strength than that of a sexual
encounter" (*Seduction* 68). This link between the bullfight and the
sexual foreshadows Lillian's encounter with her personal Minotaur,
one that will also be a symbolic ritual between aggressor and victim
with decidedly sexual overtones.

WORKS CITED

Aldan, Daisy. *See* Nin, Anaïs, "To Write Is to Love Again."

Andersen, Margaret L. "Critical Approaches to Anaïs Nin." *Canadian
Review of American Studies* 10.2 (1979): 263.

Bair, Deirdre. *Anaïs Nin: A Biography.* New York: Putnam, 1995.

Balakian, Anna. "A Tale of Two People: Feminism and Anaïs Nin's 'Diary
of a Wife.'" *Anaïs: An International Journal* 6 (1988): 58–66.

Benstock, Shari. *Women of the Left Bank: Paris, 1900–1940.* Austin: University of Texas Press, 1986.

Broe, Mary Lynn. "Djuna Barnes." *The Gender of Modernism.* Ed. Bonnie Kime Scott, 19–29. Bloomington: Indiana University Press, 1990.

Burford, William. "The Art of Anaïs Nin." Introduction to *On Writing,* by Anaïs Nin, 5–14. Yonkers, N.Y.: Alicat Bookshop, 1947.

Burke, Carolyn. "Mina Loy." *The Gender of Modernism.* Ed. Bonnie Kime Scott, 230–37. Bloomington: Indiana University Press, 1990.

Bush, Ronald. "Ezra Pound." *The Gender of Modernism.* Ed. Bonnie Kime Scott, 353–59. Bloomington: Indiana University Press, 1990.

Cixous, Hélène. "The Laugh of the Medusa." Trans. Keith Cohen and Paula Cohen. *The Signs Reader: Women, Gender, and Scholarship.* Ed. Elizabeth Abel and Emily K. Abel, 279–97. Chicago: University of Chicago Press, 1983.

Cixous, Hélène, and Catherine Clement. *The Newly Born Woman.* Trans. Betsy Wing. Foreword by Sandra M. Gilbert. Minneapolis: University of Minnesota Press, 1986.

Conn, Jeanne. "Anaïs Nin and the Beats." *Kerouac Connection* 21 (1991): 20–21.

Cowley, Malcolm. *Exile's Return: A Literary Odyssey of the 1920s.* 1934. New York: Penguin, 1976.

Davis, Thadious M. "Nella Larsen." *The Gender of Modernism.* Ed. Bonnie Kime Scott, 209–14. Bloomington: Indiana University Press, 1990.

DuBow, Wendy M. Introduction. *Conversations with Anaïs Nin,* ix–xx. Jackson: University Press of Mississippi, 1994.

Durrell, Lawrence. "Preface to *Children of the Albatross.*" *A Casebook on Anaïs Nin.* Ed. Robert Zaller, 2. New York: New American Library, 1974.

Edmiston, Susan. "Portrait of Anaïs Nin." 1970. *Conversations with Anaïs Nin.* Ed. Wendy M. DuBow, 43–51. Jackson: University Press of Mississippi, 1994.

Ekberg, Kent. "Studio 28: The Influence of the Surrealist Cinema on the Early Fiction of Anaïs Nin and Henry Miller." *Deus Loci: Lawrence Durrell Newsletter* 4.3 (1981): 3–12.

Eliot, T. S. "Tradition and the Individual Talent." 1919. *Selected Essays,* 4–5. New York: Harcourt, Brace, 1950.

Elliott, Bridget, and Jo-Ann Wallace. *Women Artists and Writers: Modernist (im)positionings.* New York: Routledge, 1994.

Evans, Oliver. *Anaïs Nin.* Carbondale: Southern Illinois University Press, 1968.

Felber, Lynette. "The Three Faces of June: Anaïs Nin's Appropriation of Feminine Writing." *Tulsa Studies in Women's Literature* 14.2 (1995): 309–24.

Formentelli, Beatrice. "The Difficulty of the Real: A French Perspective." Trans. Frank S. Alberti. *Anaïs: An International Journal* 2 (1984): 77–94.

Franklin, Benjamin, V. "Anaïs Nin: A Bibliographical Essay." *A Casebook on Anaïs Nin.* Ed. Robert Zaller, 25–33. New York: New American Library, 1974.

Franklin, Benjamin, V, and Duane Schneider. *Anaïs Nin: An Introduction.* Athens: Ohio University Press, 1979.

Friedman, Ellen G. "Anaïs Nin." *Modern American Women Writers.* Ed. Elaine Showalter, Lea Baechler, and A. Walton Litz, 339–51. New York: Scribner's, 1991.

Friedman, Susan Stanford. "H. D." *The Gender of Modernism.* Ed. Bonnie Kime Scott, 85–92. Bloomington: Indiana University Press, 1990.

Gallop, Jane. *The Daughter's Seduction: Feminism and Psychoanalysis.* Ithaca: Cornell University Press, 1982.

Gilbert, Sandra M., and Susan Gubar. *The War of the Words.* New Haven: Yale University Press, 1988.

Gillespie, Diane F. "Dorothy Richardson." *The Gender of Modernism.* Ed. Bonnie Kime Scott, 393–99. Bloomington: Indiana University Press, 1990.

———. "May Sinclair." *The Gender of Modernism.* Ed. Bonnie Kime Scott, 435–42. Bloomington: Indiana University Press, 1990.

Gish, Nancy K. "Hugh MacDiarmid." *The Gender of Modernism.* Ed. Bonnie Kime Scott, 275–79. Bloomington: Indiana University Press, 1990.

———. "T. S. Eliot." *The Gender of Modernism.* Ed. Bonnie Kime Scott, 139–43. Bloomington: Indiana University Press, 1990.

Gubar, Susan. "Blessings in Disguise: Cross-Dressing as Re-Dressing for Female Modernists." *Massachusetts Review* 22 (1981): 477–508.

Hamilton, Dran. *See* Herlihy, James Leo.

Hamilton, Edith. *Mythology: Timeless Tales of Gods and Heroes.* 1940. New York: New American Library, 1963.

Hanson, Clare. "Katherine Mansfield." *The Gender of Modernism.* Ed. Bonnie Kime Scott, 298–305. Bloomington: Indiana University Press, 1990.

Henke, Suzette A. "Lillian Beye's Labyrinth: A Freudian Exploration of *Cities of the Interior.*" *Anaïs: An International Journal* 2 (1984): 113–26.

Herlihy, James Leo. "I Want You Here With Me." Interview by Dran Hamilton. *Anaïs: An International Journal* 1 (1983): 68.

Hinz, Evelyn J. *The Mirror and the Garden: Realism and Reality in the Writings of Anaïs Nin.* 1971. New York: Harcourt Brace Jovanovich, 1973.

Howells, Coral Ann. "Jean Rhys." *The Gender of Modernism.* Ed. Bonnie Kime Scott, 372–77. Bloomington: Indiana University Press, 1990.

Hoy, Nancy Jo. "Getting to Know Anaïs Nin." *Anaïs: An International Journal* 1 (1983): 81–85.

———. "The Poetry of Experience: How to Be a Woman and an Artist." *Anaïs: An International Journal* 4 (1986): 52–66.

Hugo, Ian. "On the Art of Engraving." *Anaïs: An International Journal* 1 (1983): 42–51.

Irigaray, Luce. *Speculum of the Other Woman.* 1974. Trans. Gillian C. Gill. Ithaca: Cornell University Press, 1985.

Jason, Philip K. "Dropping Another Veil." *Anaïs: An International Journal* 6 (1988): 27–32.

———. "The Gemor Press." *Anaïs: An International Journal* 2 (1984): 24–36.

———. "The Princess and the Frog: Anaïs Nin and Otto Rank." *Anaïs, Art and Artists: A Collection of Essays.* Ed. Sharon Spencer, 13–22. Greenwood, Fla.: Penkevill, 1986.

Joyce, James. *Stephen Hero.* Ed. John J. Slocum and Herbert Cahoon. New York: New Directions, 1963.

Kaplan, Sydney Janet. *Katherine Mansfield and the Origins of Modernist Fiction.* Ithaca: Cornell University Press, 1991.

Karsten, Julie A. "Self-Realization and Intimacy: The Influence of D. H. Lawrence on Anaïs Nin." *Anaïs: An International Journal* 4 (1986): 36–42.

Knapp, Bettina L. *Anaïs Nin.* New York: Frederick Ungar, 1978.

MacNiven, Ian S. "Criticism and Personality: Lawrence Durrell—Anaïs Nin." *Anaïs: An International Journal* 2 (1984): 95–100.

Marks, Elaine, and Isabelle de Courtivron, eds. *New French Feminisms: An Anthology.* New York: Schocken, 1981.

Mathieu, Bertrand. "On the Trail of Eurydice: From the Prospectus for a Booklength Study." *Anaïs: An International Journal* 10 (1992): 63–76.

McEvilly, Wayne. Afterword. *Seduction of the Minotaur,* by Anaïs Nin. Athens: Swallow Press/Ohio University Press, 1969.

McNay, Michael. "Non-belligerent in the Sex War." 1970. *Conversations with Anaïs Nin.* Ed. Wendy M. DuBow, 40–42. Jackson: University Press of Mississippi, 1994.

Merchant, Hoshang D. "The Aesthetics of Anaïs Nin: Ariadne Within the Echo Chamber." *Panjab University Research Bulletin: (Arts)* 17 (1986): 29–39.

Miller, Henry. "About the 'Mona' Pages." *Anaïs: An International Journal* 6 (1988): 93–103.

Miller, Margaret. "Diary-Keeping and the Young Wife." *Anaïs: An International Journal* 3 (1985): 39–41.

Millett, Kate. "Anaïs—A Mother to Us All: The Birth of the Artist as a Woman." *Anaïs: An International Journal* 9 (1991): 3–8.

Moore, Harry T. Preface. *Anaïs Nin,* by Oliver Evans. Carbondale: Southern Illinois University Press, 1968.

Nin, Anaïs. "Anaïs Nin on Women's Liberation." Interview by Clare Loeb. 1970. *Conversations with Anaïs Nin.* Ed. Wendy M. DuBow, 27–39. Jackson: University Press of Mississippi, 1994.

———. "Anaïs Nin Talks about Being a Woman." 1971. *In Favor of the Sensitive Man and Other Essays,* 20–26. New York: Harcourt Brace Jovanovich, 1976.

———. "At a Journal Workshop." Review of *At a Journal Workshop,* by Ira Progoff. 1975. *In Favor of the Sensitive Man and Other Essays,* 98–104. New York: Harcourt Brace Jovanovich, 1976.

———. *Delta of Venus: Erotica.* 1941. New York: Harcourt Brace Jovanovich, 1977.

———. "Eroticism in Women." 1974. *In Favor of the Sensitive Man and Other Essays,* 3–11. New York: Harcourt Brace Jovanovich, 1976.

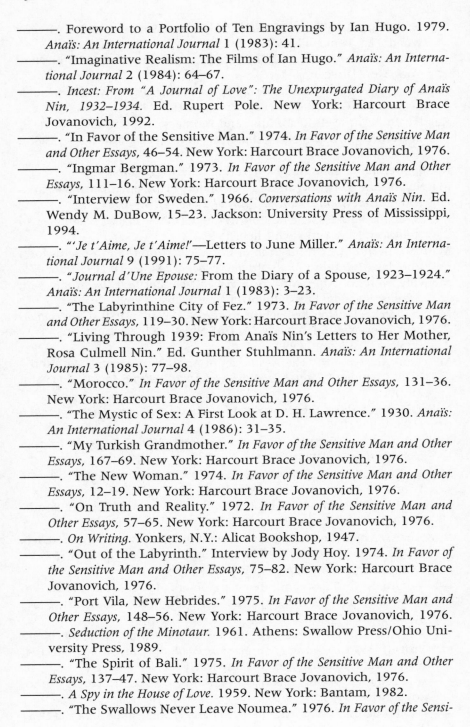

———. Foreword to a Portfolio of Ten Engravings by Ian Hugo. 1979. *Anaïs: An International Journal* 1 (1983): 41.

———. "Imaginative Realism: The Films of Ian Hugo." *Anaïs: An International Journal* 2 (1984): 64–67.

———. *Incest: From "A Journal of Love": The Unexpurgated Diary of Anaïs Nin, 1932–1934.* Ed. Rupert Pole. New York: Harcourt Brace Jovanovich, 1992.

———. "In Favor of the Sensitive Man." 1974. *In Favor of the Sensitive Man and Other Essays*, 46–54. New York: Harcourt Brace Jovanovich, 1976.

———. "Ingmar Bergman." 1973. *In Favor of the Sensitive Man and Other Essays*, 111–16. New York: Harcourt Brace Jovanovich, 1976.

———. "Interview for Sweden." 1966. *Conversations with Anaïs Nin.* Ed. Wendy M. DuBow, 15–23. Jackson: University Press of Mississippi, 1994.

———. "'Je t'Aime, Je t'Aime!'—Letters to June Miller." *Anaïs: An International Journal* 9 (1991): 75–77.

———. "*Journal d'Une Epouse:* From the Diary of a Spouse, 1923–1924." *Anaïs: An International Journal* 1 (1983): 3–23.

———. "The Labyrinthine City of Fez." 1973. *In Favor of the Sensitive Man and Other Essays*, 119–30. New York: Harcourt Brace Jovanovich, 1976.

———. "Living Through 1939: From Anaïs Nin's Letters to Her Mother, Rosa Culmell Nin." Ed. Gunther Stuhlmann. *Anaïs: An International Journal* 3 (1985): 77–98.

———. "Morocco." *In Favor of the Sensitive Man and Other Essays*, 131–36. New York: Harcourt Brace Jovanovich, 1976.

———. "The Mystic of Sex: A First Look at D. H. Lawrence." 1930. *Anaïs: An International Journal* 4 (1986): 31–35.

———. "My Turkish Grandmother." *In Favor of the Sensitive Man and Other Essays*, 167–69. New York: Harcourt Brace Jovanovich, 1976.

———. "The New Woman." 1974. *In Favor of the Sensitive Man and Other Essays*, 12–19. New York: Harcourt Brace Jovanovich, 1976.

———. "On Truth and Reality." 1972. *In Favor of the Sensitive Man and Other Essays*, 57–65. New York: Harcourt Brace Jovanovich, 1976.

———. *On Writing.* Yonkers, N.Y.: Alicat Bookshop, 1947.

———. "Out of the Labyrinth." Interview by Jody Hoy. 1974. *In Favor of the Sensitive Man and Other Essays*, 75–82. New York: Harcourt Brace Jovanovich, 1976.

———. "Port Vila, New Hebrides." 1975. *In Favor of the Sensitive Man and Other Essays*, 148–56. New York: Harcourt Brace Jovanovich, 1976.

———. *Seduction of the Minotaur.* 1961. Athens: Swallow Press/Ohio University Press, 1989.

———. "The Spirit of Bali." 1975. *In Favor of the Sensitive Man and Other Essays*, 137–47. New York: Harcourt Brace Jovanovich, 1976.

———. *A Spy in the House of Love.* 1959. New York: Bantam, 1982.

———. "The Swallows Never Leave Noumea." 1976. *In Favor of the Sensi-

tive Man and Other Essays, 157–66. New York: Harcourt Brace Jovanovich, 1976.

———. "Talking About Proust." Interview by Frank S. Alberti. 1976. *Anaïs: An International Journal* 2 (1984): 127–34.

———. "To Write Is to Love Again." Interview by Daisy Aldan. 1969. *Anaïs: An International Journal* 6 (1988): 86–92.

———. "With Henry and June—From the Original, Unedited *Diary,* November, 1932." *Anaïs: An International Journal* 5 (1987): 3–14.

———. "The Writer and the Symbols." 1959. *Anaïs: An International Journal* 4 (1986): 127–133.

———. "Writers at Work: Anaïs Nin Talks with Frank Roberts." 1965. *Conversations with Anaïs Nin.* Ed. Wendy M. DuBow, 3–14. Jackson: University Press of Mississippi, 1994.

———. "Writing and Dancing: From the Unpublished *Mon Journal* and *Note Book,* 1930." *Anaïs: An International Journal* 2 (1984): 3–18.

Paine, Sylvia. *Beckett, Nabokov, Nin: Motives and Modernism.* Port Washington, N.Y.: Kennikat, 1981.

Papachristou, Sophia. "The Body in the Diary: On Anaïs Nin's First Erotic Writings." *Anaïs: An International Journal* 9 (1991): 58–66.

Petrequin, Marie-Line. "The Magic Spell of June Miller: On the Literary Creation of Female Identity in Anaïs Nin's *Diary.*" *Anaïs: An International Journal* 6 (1988): 43–57.

Pound, Ezra. Translator's Postscript. *The Natural Philosophy of Love,* by Remy de Gourmont, 169–80. 1932. New York: Willey, 1940.

Rank, Otto. "On the Early Diary: A Preface." 1935. *Anaïs: An International Journal* 2 (1984): 20–23.

Ryan, Mary. "The Heritage of Atelier 17: Some Thoughts on Ian Hugo—Printmaker." *Anaïs: An International Journal* 4 (1986): 18–19.

Said, Edward W. *Orientalism.* New York: Pantheon, 1978.

Sayre, Gary. "*House of Incest:* Two Interpretations." *Anaïs, Art and Artists: A Collection of Essays.* Ed. Sharon Spencer, 45–58. Greenwood, Fla.: Penkevill, 1986.

Schenck, Celeste M. "Charlotte Mew." *The Gender of Modernism.* Ed. Bonnie Kime Scott, 316–21. Bloomington: Indiana University Press, 1990.

Schlesinger, Marian C. "Anaïs Nin: An Era Recalled." 1969. *Conversations with Anaïs Nin.* Ed. Wendy M. DuBow, 24–26. Jackson: University Press of Mississippi, 1994.

Schneider, Duane. "The Art of Anaïs Nin." *A Casebook on Anaïs Nin.* Ed. Robert Zaller, 43–50. New York: New American Library, 1974.

Scott, Bonnie Kime. "D. H. Lawrence." *The Gender of Modernism,* 217–24. Bloomington: Indiana University Press, 1990.

———. Introduction. *The Gender of Modernism,* 1–18. Bloomington: Indiana University Press, 1990.

———. "James Joyce." *The Gender of Modernism,* 196–204. Bloomington: Indiana University Press, 1990.

Secrest, Meryle. "Economics and The Need for Revenge." *Anaïs: An International Journal* 6 (1988): 33–35.

Seybert, Gislinde. "Between Love and Passion: Some Notes on the Physical in 'Henry and June.'" Trans. Gunther Stuhlmann. *Anaïs: An International Journal* 9 (1991): 67–74.

Soteriou, Alexandra. "A Door to the Inner Self: Ian Hugo's Unconscious Drawings in Copper." *Anaïs: An International Journal* 4 (1986): 17–18.

Spencer, Sharon. "The Art of Ragpicking." *Anaïs, Art and Artists: A Collection of Essays*, 155–75. Greenwood, Fla.: Penkevill, 1986.

———. *Collage of Dreams: The Writings of Anaïs Nin*. Chicago: Swallow Press, 1977.

———. "The Music of the Womb: Anaïs Nin's 'Feminine' Writing." *Breaking the Sequence: Women's Experimental Fiction*. Ed. Ellen G. Friedman and Miriam Fuchs, 161–73. Princeton: Princeton University Press, 1989.

———. "The Novel as Mobile in Space." Introduction to *Cities of the Interior*, by Anaïs Nin, vii–xx. Chicago: Swallow Press, 1974.

Struck, Karin. "Logbook of a Liberation." *Anaïs: An International Journal* 6 (1988): 36–42.

Wall, Cheryl A. "Zora Neale Hurston." *The Gender of Modernism*. Ed. Bonnie Kime Scott, 170–75. Bloomington: Indiana University Press, 1990.

Wittig, Monique. *Les Guérillères*. 1969. Trans. David Le Vay. New York: Viking, 1971; Boston: Beacon, 1985.

Woolf, Virginia. *A Room of One's Own*. 1929. New York: Harcourt Brace Jovanovich, 1957.

Zaller, Robert. Introduction. *A Casebook on Anaïs Nin*, ix–xvi. New York: New American Library, 1974.

Zinnes, Harriet. "The Fiction of Anaïs Nin." *A Casebook on Anaïs Nin*. Ed. Robert Zaller, 35–41. New York: New American Library, 1974.

CHAPTER II

Anaïs Nin's Rhizomatic Diary

Mai Al-Nakib

There are many ways to read a diary. A few of the ways diaries have been read within literary studies include: as not quite autobiography (Gusdorf 35; Pascal 3), as detailed expressions of the quotidian (Juhasz 221–37), as distinctly feminine in form (Hogan 95–107), and as postmodern in their fragmentary conception of "self" (Nussbaum 128–40). Anaïs Nin's *Diary*, the first volume of which was published in 1966, has been read in some of these ways. In the late 1960s and early 1970s liberationist feminists like Kate Millett embraced Nin's *Diary* as revolutionary and antipatriarchal. But as early as 1978 some feminist critics, among them Estelle C. Jelinek, began to question Nin's essentializing of the "feminine," her apoliticism, her elitism, and her sexism (Jelinek 320). By the 1980s and 1990s, it is fair to say, feminist focus on Nin's work had become far more critical and perhaps even waned. While unexpurgated versions of Nin's *Diary* continue to be published, her texts remain visibly absent from university reading lists. Transformations in feminist criticism, along with the prevalence of poststructuralism and cultural criticism in the American academy over the last three decades, have much to do with wavering academic interest in Anaïs Nin.[1] But this need not always be the case. Nin's overly stratified critical reception can be shaken up in ways that might regenerate interest in her work.[2] Reading Nin's *Diary* through some of the theories of Gilles Deleuze

and Félix Guattari could be one way to reactivate the radical feminist potential of her texts.[3]

Deleuze and Guattari's term "rhizome" is somewhat difficult to
define. The difficulty stems in part from the fact that a rhizome
cannot be gauged in terms of what it *is* but, rather, in terms of
what it *does*. To define is to plot a point or to fix an order, which is
precisely what a rhizome does not do (*Thousand Plateaus* 7). Since
it is perhaps better to demonstrate than to define a rhizome, I will
attempt to read Anaïs Nin's *Diary* as one. I would like to suggest
that, as a rhizome, Nin's *Diary* ceases to be a qualitatively narcissistic, subjective form. Instead, as a secretly proliferating rhizome,
Nin's *Diary* can be understood as part of a collectivizing process
whose effects are imperceptible and untimely because they remain
as yet unexplored. Reading Nin through Deleuze and Guattari
makes possible a reconceptualization of her work as both unessen-
tialistically feminist and unexpectedly political.

Deleuze and Guattari suggest that, against the normative hierarchical, arborescent, or tree logic that has dominated Western thinking and institutional organization, there exists the possibility of the
rhizome (*Thousand Plateaus* 3–25).[4] The rhizome is constantly in
motion, always in between things, and never identic. It is a multiplicity, a web of relations, linkages, and assemblages. As Deleuze
puts it, in a rhizome "what counts are not the terms or the elements, but what there is 'between'" (*Dialogues* viii). Nin's *Diary* was
generated in between an unsent letter to her father and her novelettes. Additionally, like the rhizome, everything about Nin's *Diary*
implies perpetual motion. But what is perhaps most intriguing
about Nin's rhizomatic *Diary* is its paradoxical secrecy.

Deleuze and Guattari argue that a secret is almost always rhizomatic. According to "arborescent" (we might say binary) logic, a
secret is normally understood within the following opposition:
"hidden secret" versus "disclosure of secret." On a rhizomatic
understanding, however, a secret cannot be contained within this
type of opposition. Deleuze and Guattari suggest that a secret "has a
way of spreading that is in turn shrouded in secrecy. The secret as
secretion. The secret must sneak, insert, or introduce itself into the
arena of public forms; it must pressure them and prod known subjects into action" (*Thousand Plateaus* 287). In a counterintuitive way,
a secret is always already secreted into the "outside." Perception by
others is the very condition of the secret's possibility. What is seemingly the most private, the most isolated, the most hidden turns out
to be a collective or public assemblage (*Thousand Plateaus* 287).

Nin says that the *Diary* "was really written for someone else and, then, because my mother didn't let me mail it, it became a secret" (*Woman Speaks* 149). Nin's *Diary* is a secret that contains its own discovery within itself rather than in opposition to itself. This is unlike the novelette or novella as a literary genre; there, according to Deleuze and Guattari, "[e]verything is organized around the question, 'What happened?'" (*Thousand Plateaus* 192). Nin's novelettes fall into the oppositional "What happened?" genre. Novelettes follow arborescent logic because their structures are implicitly teleological: a novelette invites a reader to interpret signs or traces toward answering the question "What happened?" This static, closed structure is everything a "rhizome-book" is not. Yet Deleuze and Guattari do seem to suggest that a rhizome has just as much to do with habits of reading as with generic classifications. For example, they say that they "will never ask what a book means, as signified or signifier" nor will they "look for anything to understand in it"; instead, they say they "will ask what it functions with, in connection with what other things it does or does not transmit intensities, in which other multiplicities its own are inserted and metamorphosed" (*Thousand Plateaus* 4). This seems to suggest that a novelette might potentially be read rhizomatically. However, the tendency, as Deleuze and Guattari point out, is to read it from beginning to end with the objective of finding the hidden key to some riddle. Reading other less conventional forms such as a diary could destabilize rigid reading habits and might, in turn, encourage new ways of experiencing texts. For Deleuze and Guattari, any secret holds this potential.

If the *Diary* became a secret for Nin, it was paradoxically a secret that oozed into the outside. In fact, the diary form, presumably the most private and individualistic genre of all, becomes, as a rhizomatic secret, the most collective. Deleuze and Guattari suggest that the secret "was invented by society; it is a sociological or social notion. Every secret is a collective assemblage" (*Thousand Plateaus* 287). If an assemblage is the "increase in the dimensions of a multiplicity that necessarily changes in nature as it expands its connections," and connections are made by the "deterritorializing" movement of a rhizome, then a collective assemblage can occur through the rhizomatic movement of a secret (*Thousand Plateaus* 8).[5] Nin herself comes to recognize the seeming contradiction of the diary form as both a secret and a collective genre when she says in *A Woman Speaks* that "the discovery that I made when I

relinquished the diary, which was my secret . . . [was] that it
belonged to everybody, and not only to me" (162).

What makes a secret part of a collective assemblage is its constant movement. A secret is always in the process of becoming
something else. Incest, for example, is a private secret that cannot
help but disrupt social hierarchies because it implicitly subverts the
normative consolidation of gender identity. Judith Butler has
argued that the incest taboo is one of the "generative [construc-
tivist] moments of gender identity" and that breaking the taboo
can be a way of subverting the "heterosexual construction and
regulation of sexuality within the reproductive domain" (135). In
other words, physically disrupting this social (but not essential)
taboo or law problematizes the "naturalness" of gender consolidation and can point to gender as a fabrication disguised as nature, a
fiction made invisible by its semblance of necessity (136). By "performing" incest as a consenting adult instead of enacting the pro-
hibitions aligned with the incest taboo, Nin effectively reveals the
contingency of the taboo itself and, thus, the fiction of a "true"
gender identity consolidated *by* the incest taboo. Nin subverts the
law within the law itself. She states, "It is by thinking about taboos
that we have become aware of their foolishness. When we began
to do some healthy thinking about morality, we discovered it was
ordained by fashions, no higher dictate than that, and when we
began to think about 'abnormal' acts, we realized we could not say
they were against 'nature' because nature gave us a million examples of worse abnormalities than we ever invented for ourselves. It
is *thinking* which shows us that the *feelings* we have against certain
acts have been acquired" (*Literate Passion* 76). Nin's incest or, more
accurately, Nin's writing (up) of the incest in her *Diary* disrupts the
supposedly natural continuum of sex, gender, desire, and sexual
practice. Because she does not continue to miss, or to "lose," her
father, she stops internalizing, in Butler's performative sense, her
desire for men only. Against Freud's theory of mourning, this
means that there is no lack in her desire, and if there is no internalization of the lost object of desire (the father), then there is also
no deflection of the desire onto other men.[6] All of which implies
that heterosexuality itself, with its attendant social laws, is a constructed, and therefore contingent, form of desire. (This short
digression has served, I hope, to demonstrate one way in which
the private—a secret incestuous relationship—becomes, moves
into, or can affect public structures of organization, if not instru-
mentally, then at least theoretically. Whether Nin herself was

homosexual or bisexual doesn't matter one way or the other, for what her texts demonstrate is that desire itself need not be essentialized or naturalized in socially restrictive and prohibitive ways.)

Nin's *Diary*, a secret series born of the letter to her father, is always in the process of becoming something other than a private form. In her *Diary* Nin portrays her life as being in ceaseless motion. She presents this picture in sharp opposition to patriarchal institutions like psychoanalysis which try to block her flow. She calls her life "the great tumultuous flow" (*Incest* 132) and that is what she constantly seeks: "Flow. Evolution. Movement" (224). She is always critical of her own attempt to limit movement, as if in self-conscious chastisement of her effort to follow arborescent logic. She declares, "The effort I make to outline, chisel, demarcate, separate, simplify, is idiotic. I must *let myself flow multilaterally*" (21). Her husband, Hugh Guiler, asks in amazement, "Do you realize what a live force you are, just to speak of you in the abstract? I feel like a machine that has lost its motor. You represent everything that is vital, live, moving, rising, flying, soaring" (*Henry and June* 39). In fact, in the terms of Deleuze and Guattari, Hugh is experiencing his "Body without Organs" (*Anti-Oedipus* 9–16).[7] His body is being deterritorialized by Nin's movement and, by connecting with her intensities, with her multilateral flows, he is becoming part of a new rhizomatic "machine" (1–8).[8] This is not the standard machine *with* a motor but the Deleuzian machine, quite distinct from "mechanism"; it is a machine as the "condition as well as the effect of any making, any producing" (Grosz, *Volatile Bodies* 168). A description of a day in Nin's life demonstrates these active, rhizomatic flows and is worth quoting at length:

> Taxis are my wings. I cannot wait for anything. Wonderful to step off the little train at 3:25 in the smoke and noise and crowd of the city, to run downstairs, to ride dreaming through the city, to arrive at Allendy's just when he is about to pull open the black Chinese curtain. To run out again to the café where Henry is sitting with friends. The taxi is the magic chariot, passing without pain from one plane to another, a smooth course through the pearl-grey city, the opal that is Paris, answering my mother about the dyed sheets while I am still, on another line of the musical score, repeating in myself the fragments of my talk with Allendy. My mother is saying, "Fifille, do you like the binding for your last journal? It only cost twenty francs." I love my mother deeply now, her humanity, her goodness, her energy, her buoyancy. Joaquin says, "You are so quiet, are you ill?" He catches me smiling at myself, at the overfullness of my life: the music holder filled with books I have no time to read, George

Grosz's caricatures, a book by Antonin Artaud, unanswered letters,
a wealth of stuff. (*Diary* 1:183)

She is connected to the texture and movement of Paris, to Henry,
to Allendy, to her mother, to her brother, to books that cannot yet
be read but are important enough to mention, to music (and her
father?), to her journal, and so on.

Nin is not unaware of how this kind of overflowing and movement opposes patriarchy. For example, about her cousin Eduardo's
effect on his sister, Ana Maria, she says, "People like Eduardo who
cannot *move* or *live* become the great sterilizers, the great blockers
in others' lives. Eduardo wants to paralyze Ana Maria. He is frantic
that he cannot exert his *negative protection* while I am exerting a
positive influence of a sort" (*Incest* 17–18). She is especially wary of
the blockage to movement represented by psychoanalysis, even as
she appears to be drawn deeper and deeper into it. She says, "I am
afraid that I am going to be at war with Allendy's superwisdom. It
blocks my great desire to move on, to disperse myself in passion, to
spread myself by the loss of myself; it blocks the adventures
desired by my imagination—dangers" (18). Nin is suggesting, as
Deleuze and Guattari do, that psychoanalysis often leads only to
dead ends, or blocks exits.[9] Psychoanalysis tries to stop the spreading of the secret (the *Diary*) and, further, tries to prevent her dis-
persal or her "becoming-imperceptible" (a concept I shall return to
later). That Nin might be anything but enthusiastic about psychoanalysis is a little hard to imagine, given her ardent involvement
with it. Nonetheless, in her *Diary* she says: "It is while cooking,
gardening, walking, or love-making that I remember my childhood, and not while reading Freud's 'Preface to a Little Girl's Journal'" (1:155). Similarly, Deleuze argues that the "Freudian formula
must be reversed. You have to produce the unconscious. It is not at
all a matter of repressed memories or even of phantasms. You
don't produce childhood memories, you produce blocs of child-
becoming with *blocs of childhood* which are always in the present"
(*Dialogues* 78).

Psychoanalysis is like the novelette form which can only ask and
answer the question "What happened?" Novelettes have a static,
arborescently organized, beginning-to-end structure. For example,
in "Winter of Artifice," one of three novelettes in a collection of
the same name, Nin writes about incest symbolically as a musical
composition. There is a dirty little secret just waiting to be discovered behind the clues and traces left in italics. In this novelette Nin

follows the conventions of what Deleuze and Guattari call a
"major" literature, an inevitably male-dominated literature, and as
a result neutralizes her story's revolutionary content.[10] The novelette remains stuck in a form/content opposition parallel to the
secret/disclosure opposition. There can only ever be one response
to the question "What happened?" either in a psychoanalysis
dominated by the law of the father or in a literary tradition dominated by the phallogocentric law of genre (Derrida 221–52). That
response is the Oedipal triangle.[11]

"Winter of Artifice" falls into the Oedipal trap because of its conventional literary form. By a sort of double reversal, Nin writes
about incest as a musical composition likened to sex:

> They looked at each other as if they were listening to music, not as if he were
> saying words. Inside both their heads, as they sat there, he leaning against a
> pillow and she against the foot of the bed, there was a concert going on. . . .
> Two long spools of flutethreads interweaving between his past and hers, the
> strings of the violin constantly trembling like the strings inside their bodies,
> the nerves never still, the heavy poundings on the drum like the heavy
> pounding of sex. . . . The orchestra all in one voice now, for an instant, in love,
> in love with the harp singing god and the violins shaking their hair and she
> passing the violin bow gently between her legs, drawing music out of her
> body, her body foaming, the harp singing god, the drum beating . . . (84–85)

While interpreting the symbol (musical composition symbolizing
incest) is easy after the publication of *Incest*, her initial attempt to
aesthetically mask the incest was her way of disguising her real-
life (and *Diary*'s) escape from the incest taboo. "Winter of Artifice"
is a story about the Oedipal triangle: a girl's obsession with the
father who had abandoned his family, her reunion with him, and
her escape from her obsession with him. The escape, however, is
reterritorialized by the form in which it is expressed. She explodes
the image of the father but does not, or cannot, accept the personal or social implications of such a destabilization. Nin retreats
into the security of a stable identity and the closure of the novelette form. The unnamed narrator reflects, "Now that the world
was standing on its head and the figure of her father had become
immense, like the figure of a myth, now that from thinking too
much about him she had lost the sound of his voice, she wanted
to open her eyes again and make sure that all this had not killed
the light, the steadiness of the earth, the bloom of the flowers, and
the warmth of her other loves (91). The narrator goes on, "Now
she is all confused in her boundaries. She doesn't know where her

father begins, where she begins, where it is he ends, what is the difference between them" and "She must know wherein she is not like him. She must disentangle their two selves" (92). The narrator wants to separate from her father because he arrests movement, and she realizes that without movement there can be no "multilateral" flows. Addressing the father directly, she pleads:

> *Father, let me walk alone into the music of my faith. When I am with you the world is still and silent.*
>
> *You give the command for stillness, and life stops like a clock that has fallen. You draw geometric lines around liquid forms, and what you extract from the chaos is already crystallized.*
>
> *As soon as I leave you everything fixed falls into waves, tides, is transformed into water and flows. I hear my heart beating again with disorder. I hear the music of my gestures, and my feet begin to run as music runs and leaps. (100)*

But the desire for separation from the father inadvertently ends up reconsolidating the incest taboo. While seeking to escape the "geometric lines," or what Deleuze and Guattari call the Oedipal triangle, Nin ends up, through her symbolic portrayal of the incest episode, enclosing the experience in "geometric lines" of her own and blocking her potential flight. This flight or escape is blocked by the form of the short novel itself. Deleuze and Guattari suggest that a "major, or established, literature follows a vector that goes from content to expression. Since content is presented in a given form of the content, one must find, discover, or see the form of expression that goes with it. That which conceptualizes well expresses itself. But a minor, or revolutionary, literature begins by expressing itself and doesn't conceptualize until afterward. . . . Expression must break forms, encourage ruptures and new sproutings. When a form is broken, one must reconstruct the content that will necessarily be part of a rupture in the order of things" (*Kafka* 28). In her novelettes, Nin follows the male-dominated literary traditions of a major literature and moves from content to expression. Despite the revolutionary content, despite its anti-Oedipal implications, the novelette form of "Winter of Artifice"—which still answers the question "What happened?"—blocks its disruptive, radical potential.

However, by its movement, by its proliferation of the secret, the *Diary* manages to sidestep this question by revealing its absurdity while, in the process, annihilating the form (novelette or psychoanalysis itself) that posed the question to begin with. Nin writes that "living is the constant motion towards unraveling, a dynamic movement from mystery to mystery; otherwise one remains faced with a single one (mystery of the origin of fire, for instance). And such a static mystery becomes a restriction. Mystery born of ignorance, of taboos, fear, ignorance" (1:291). Nin escapes interpreting secrets (or mysteries) as symptoms of hidden origins or motivations and thus flees patriarchy's Platonic enslavement to forms; that is to say, she escapes the redundant psychoanalytic issue of discovering the cause of problems or neuroses, inevitably traced back to Oedipal anxiety. As Deleuze and Guattari put it, "When the question 'What happened?' attains this infinite virile form, the answer is necessarily that nothing happened, and both form and content are destroyed. The news travels fast that the secret of men is nothing, in truth nothing at all. Oedipus, the phallus, castration, 'the splinter in the flesh'—that was the secret? It is enough to make women, children, lunatics, and molecules laugh" (*Thousand Plateaus* 289).

In fact, Nin favors the rhizomatics of the secret. She does not simply see the secret as being in opposition to its disclosure, which is why the *Diary* does not reproduce the "What happened?" structure of the novelettes. Instead, the secret *Diary* expands and flows. Whereas in "Winter of Artifice" escape or subversion is reduced to the predictable overcoming of the father in the Oedipal sense, the rhizomatic form of the *Diary* establishes "lines of flight" out of the (patriarchal) law of genre that are expressions of rupture.[12] The "diary" makes its appearance in the novelette (Nin uses events taken from her *Diary* in the story), but it is, like the Oedipal triangle, content rather than expression. In the novelettes, the "diary" is a limited character like any other, cut off from its own proliferating capacities. Deleuze and Guattari write about Kafka's novels as an endless series that never stops proliferating (*Kafka* 53). The same can be said of Nin's *Diary*. As a proliferating series, Nin's diaries create "lines of flight" that are impossible with the novelettes.

Nin's novelettes stop short of allowing any kind of rhizomatic movement. In "Winter of Artifice" Nin writes about the incestuous affair with her father as a sort of fall-from-grace narrative triangle (having the father, losing the father, regaining the father). As I have suggested, it remains trapped by literary conventions which also form a triangle (deterritorializing incest, patriarchal law of genre, incest reterritorialized). But the *Diary* is not enclosed by any of the triangles that limit the novelettes. Nin's writing in the *Diary* is not limited to the Oedipal conflict, nor is it limited by genre.

In Nin's *Diary*, as in Kafka's novels, "the doubles and the triangles that remain . . . show up only at the beginning . . . and from the start, they are so vacillating, so supple and transformable, that they are ready to open onto series that break their form and explode their terms" (*Kafka* 54). Not only does the rhizomatic *Diary* have the potential to explode literary forms, it also has the capacity to derail certain patriarchal forms of organization.[13]

Specifically, Nin's *Diary* expresses ways of escape out of the Oedipal trap with the father, psychoanalysis, and even modernism as represented by Henry Miller and others. In her *Diary* Nin does not separate father from psychoanalysts or from Henry Miller. In fact, more often than not, she creates parallels between the four men: Joaquín Nin, René Allendy, Otto Rank, and Henry Miller.[14] For example, she writes about their eyes, focusing on the similarities without making overt comparisons. About her father, she recollects his cold, blue eyes staring at her from behind the camera lens as a child: "he was always photographing me. He liked to take photos of me while I bathed. He always wanted me naked. All his admiration came by way of the camera. His eyes were partly concealed by heavy glasses (he was myopic) and then by the camera lens. Lovely. Lovely. How many times, in how many places, until he left us, did I sit for him for countless pictures" (1:87). About Miller she states that "his blue eyes are cool and observant" (1:8) and that she is "aware at times, while he speaks in a mellow way to others, of that small, round, hard photographic lens in his blue eyes" (1:258). Allendy has fascinating "strange blue" eyes (*Henry and June* 249), "crystal-gazer eyes" (*Diary* 1:159). And with Rank, she shifts focus away from his "short, dark-skinned" face and onto his eyes, "which were large, fiery, and dark" (1:271). The differences between the four men are de-emphasized by Nin's focusing on their eyes and by positing herself as the object of their respective gazes. Furthermore, she notes that all four men feel somehow threatened by her *Diary*. All four ask Nin, at one time or another, to stop writing in it. Miller tells her, "Lock up the journal, and swim. What I would like you to do is live without the journal, you would write other things" (1:158). Rank also wants to free her of the "compulsion to write everything in the diary, and so little in the novels" (1:301). "Father, too," Nin notes, "is jealous of my journal. 'My only rival,' he says" (1:215). "All of them," she is aware, "would slay the journal if they could" (1:215). But she is equally aware that it is through the journal that she can not only deflect the gazes of these four, symbolically powerful, men but also control what they see. The *Diary*'s proliferation enables Nin to escape these limiting patriarchal influences.

Nin's affair with her father can be interpreted as an almost helpless act of surrender to a patriarch who victimizes his daughter the way patriarchal society victimizes all women.[15] Earlier I argued that Nin's incest can be interpreted as a performatively subversive act. Additionally, her writing about the incest in the *Diary* becomes a way of escaping by way of proliferation. Nin is, needless to say, tied to her father both emotionally and sexually. Her reunion with Joaquín Nin after a twenty-year separation can be read as a surrender to the Oedipal crisis. Nin's style in the novelettes masks the incestuous act behind a tapestry of symbolic writing. But her writing about the incest in the *Diary* has implications far beyond the mere call for interpretation set up by the surrealistic novelettes. By using a form that is traditionally expected to tell the "truth," Nin openly expresses what has happened between her and her father without recourse to "content" first. "Because expression precedes content and draws it along . . . living and writing, art and life, are opposed only from the point of view of a major literature" (Deleuze and Guattari, *Kafka* 41). However, from the point of view of a minor, rhizomatic literature like Nin's *Diary*, the opposition between life and writing is collapsed or displaced. Nin writes about the experience with her father in the *Diary* even though he specifically asks her not to: "I had wanted the journal to die with the confession of a love I could not make. I had wanted at least my incestuous love to remain unwritten. I had promised Father utter secrecy. But one night here in the hotel, when I realized there was *no one* I could tell about my Father, I felt suffocated. I began to write again. . . . It all stifles me. I need air, I need liberation. I must achieve liberation again, and this time alone. No one can teach me to enjoy my tragic incest-love, to shed the last chains of guilt" (*Incest* 216–17). Nor does Nin stop writing about the incest when she switches subjects. When she writes about Allendy, Rank, or Miller, she is not necessarily moving away from the father. It is this expansion of Oedipus from father to psychoanalysis to modernism (or literary conventions generally) that makes the patriarchal series proliferate, a process that ultimately enables Nin to escape.

Nin's relationship with Allendy can be read as a repetition of her relationship with her father. She needs a father figure to satisfy her desire for the missing father (and on this reading desire is negative rather than productive). However, Nin is not content with having Allendy as her analyst. In fact, she finds his tight formulaic responses limited, one-dimensional, and in sharp contrast to the way she sees herself. Nin writes herself as multiple and always in motion. She laments, "How can I accept a limited definable self when I feel, in me, all possibilities? Allendy may have said: 'This is the core,' but I never feel the four walls around the substance of the self, the core. I feel only space. Illimitable space. The effect of analysis is wearing off in this way. . . . I have accepted a self which is unlimited" (*Diary* 1:200). She is not content with the Oedipal explanations given by Allendy about her relationships with men. She is skeptical about psychoanalysis: "More and more, it seems to me, the generative, fruitful principles of analysis which lay in the reconstitution and re-enacting of the individual's drama, were overshadowed by the eagerness to find the diagnosis and classifi-ableness, in order to maintain an intellectual control over them. Each time the artificial process of the drama's reconstruction was done with less respect for the drama, and a greater respect for the pattern of the drama, then the fruitful elements were diminished" (1:296). This is similar to what Deleuze and Guattari state about psychoanalysis as a possible way to enter the rhizome but never as an end in itself.[16] In fact, Nin seems to be suggesting that psycho-analysis ends up by blocking the possibility of multiplicity and explaining (away) everything as a repetition of the Same.

As quoted earlier, Nin expresses concern about Allendy's "superwisdom." She worries that he will try to "block my desire to move on, to disperse myself" (1:139). Nin reverses the analyst-analysand relationship by playing his role. "I began our session by making Allendy sit in the patient's armchair and by analyzing his 'omens'. . . . He laughed. I used all his formulas and his lingo on him" (1:165). But the reversal does not stop there. The relation-ship develops into a short love affair. Nin takes all of Allendy's explanations about how she is repeating the Oedipal crisis (the separation from her father) over and over again with the other men in her life and manages not only to play them out before his very eyes but to coax him into participation. It is never clear whether or not Allendy sees himself acting the role of the father, perhaps imagining that he is somehow helping her break her pat-tern by repeating it once again. But Nin's "seduction" of Allendy, or at least her participation in the affair, as well as her refusal to lock herself into his facile psychoanalytic explanations, can be read as a sort of subversion of the patriarchal theorization of desire as lack and, thus, woman as man's other. By knowingly repeating the so-called Oedipal crisis or by breaking the incest taboo once again, this time with a father figure rather than the actual father, Nin is expanding Oedipus beyond the father to include the institution of psychoanalysis. She escapes the Oedipal trap, not necessarily by performing the act itself—which could actually be seen as a fall *into* the trap—but, rather, by writing her way out of it in the pages of the *Diary*. She writes, "And then I felt the need to leave, the need I always have, to leave. . . . Flight. I always look for the exit" (1:238). Although in this particular quote she is talking about her father, her desire for flight is part of her relationships with all four men, including Allendy.

A similar kind of reversal or subversion occurs with Otto Rank, the Austrian psychoanalyst considered Freud's "son" or protégé. The publication of his work *The Trauma of Birth* prompted a break with Freud, and Rank moved from Vienna to Paris, where Nin went to see him in November of 1933. He took her on as a patient hoping to "cure" her of her neurosis and free her either to become a fulfilled woman or to become an artist. According to Nin, he pronounced: "When the neurotic woman gets cured, she becomes a woman. When the neurotic man gets cured, he becomes an artist. Let us see whether the woman or the artist will win out. For the moment you need to become a woman" (*Incest* 301). But once again, according to the *Diary,* the analyst-analysand relationship is reversed and, eventually, turns sexual. In the *Diary* Nin expresses her line of flight out of the institution of psychoanalysis—and, by extension, the institution of patriarchy. It is not she who succumbs to the psychoanalytic explanations but the psychoanalysts themselves who seem to want to emulate her escape. In fact, with Rank being Freud's one-time "son," Nin is virtually undoing Oedipus with Oedipus himself! It doesn't matter whether the *Diary* account is "true" or exaggerated. Either way, the result of her expression is a line of flight, an unblocking of the impasse left by the Oedipal triangle. She writes: "I rather enjoy seeing that he is destroying his own creation (undermining psychoanalysis, from which he lives). . . . Rank wants to live. I am joy, the body, expansion, and danger, movement, color. He craves a kind of suicide after having seen the ultimate error of all philosophies and systems of ideas. He is afraid of the truths he has discovered. They do not help to live. He has met me and he has lost his head" (*Incest* 357). She is not sleeping with Rank as a substitute for or repetition of sleeping with her father. "Writing the sex" with Rank, like the sex with Allendy and even the sex with Joaquín Nin, becomes Nin's way out. What she says about her escape from Henry and his wife June applies equally to her escape from Rank, Allendy, and her father: "It is then I become fluid, dissolved, *fuyante* [fleeting, elusive]. I fly from the torture which awaits me like a gigantic blood squeezer, pressing my flesh. . . . From this I escape by superhuman effort—to avoid self-destruction and madness" (*Incest* 6). Nin does not accept the Oedipal structure and then struggle to escape it; rather, she manages to transform the structure itself—at least in the *Diary*—and open the situation to change.

Nin met Miller in the winter of 1931. They had an affair that lasted a decade and a friendship that continued long after that. They encouraged each other's writing, wrote long letters to each other, and helped edit each other's work for eventual publication. But throughout the *Diary* Nin expresses her struggle to escape Miller, not necessarily as a lover, but certainly as a father figure and as a dominant influence on her writing. As with her portrayal of her position in relation to her father, Allendy, and Rank, Nin's portrayal of herself with Miller is as one who refuses to repeat the Oedipal triangle even while superficially seeming to do so. Nin writes about an episode with Henry that begins to hint at her need for flight: "Henry was telling me about a book I had not read. It was Arthur Machen's *Hill of Dreams*. I was listening, and suddenly he said, 'I am talking almost paternally to you.' At that moment I knew Henry had perceived the part of me that is half child, the part of me who likes to be amazed, to be taught, to be guided. I became a child listening to Henry, and he became paternal. The haunting image of an erudite, literary father reasserted itself, and the woman became a child again. I felt as if he had discovered a shameful secret. I ran away from Clichy" (1:80). While Nin might seem somewhat accepting of the Oedipal repetition of Henry as missing father, this does not remain the case for long. Henry argues against her journal writing, insisting that she create "art"— making the distinction between art and life that her published *Diary* ended up blurring—and then goes on to use much of her journal material in his own texts. She writes, "Henry has asked the impossible of me. I have to nourish his conception of June and feed his book. As each page of it reaches me, in which he does more and more justice to her, I feel it is my vision he has borrowed. Certainly no woman was ever asked so much. . . . Today I begin to think of an escape" (1:128–29). She seems able, despite the odds, to escape Miller's influence: she does not write the "art" he wants; she writes the *Diary*. She escapes the limits of form that he, despite his experimental style, remains bound to. She, like Deleuze and Guattari's Kafka and unlike Miller, does not "oppose life and writing," nor does she take "refuge in writing out of some sort of lack, weakness, impotence, in front of life. A rhizome, a burrow, yes—but not an ivory tower. A line of escape, yes—but not a refuge. The creative line of escape vacuums up in its movement all politics, all economy, all bureaucracy, all judiciary: it sucks them like a vampire in order to make them render still unknown sounds that come from the near future" (*Kafka* 41). Nin records that Miller sees the diary-writing as an evasion or a circumvention of the "big task of my art," as an "escape from my art problem," and as a substitute for what she "lack[s] in communication with others" (*Incest* 79), yet a rhizomatic reading of her *Diary* emphasizes its line of flight out of the Platonic life/art opposition and, therefore, a line of flight out of a patriarchal tradition. She is fluid in a way that eludes Miller, who tells her: "I still feel in you an immense yielding, so that one feels there is no *limit* to you, to what you might be or do—that is decadence—an absence of boundary— a perverse yielding, limitless in experience" (*Incest* 149). In her *Diary* Nin manages to subvert and even escape patriarchal traditions (the father, psychoanalysis, and modernism) while seemingly remaining tied to them.[17]

While both Nin and Miller were relatively unknown at the time they met, as early as 1934 Miller had received recognition for *Tropic of Cancer* from T. S. Eliot and Ezra Pound. Although Miller was not to have his books officially published in the United States until the early 1960s, after his publisher won the censorship cases in court, by that time he was already fairly well established as a writer. Nin, on the other hand, was not. By the early 1960s she was known mainly as a cult figure in the literary underground, a writer of surrealistic novels, and the friend of famous male writers like Miller, Lawrence Durrell, and Gore Vidal. She couldn't find a publisher for her by-then-gigantic *Diary*. Once she did find willing publishers in Harcourt, she had to deal with privacy issues. Many of the people she wrote about in her diaries did not want to see themselves in the published version. Her publishers insisted that she get written permission from every person she wrote about, or they would not include that person in the *Diary*. Nin's husband, Hugh, notably refused to appear in the published version, so Nin had to cut or rewrite huge chunks of the seven expurgated volumes of *The Diary of Anaïs Nin*. Nin's uphill struggle to get published in an inhospitable and male-dominated publishing world makes it hard to see her as the "elitist" writer some feminists have accused her of being. Deleuze and Guattari argue that a minor literature is a "literature that produces an active solidarity in spite of skepticism; and if the writer is in the margins or completely outside his or her fragile community, this situation allows the writer all the more possibility to express another possible community and to forge the means for another consciousness and another sensibility" (*Kafka* 17). Both the expurgated and unexpurgated versions of Nin's *Diary* do just that. They were troublesome at the time to publishers who did not want to deal with potential lawsuits from people unhappy with their portrayal, and they were (and are) troublesome to feminists who did not like Nin's supposed emulation of the male writers she was associated with.

I suggest that Nin is not the writer of surrealist (modernist) texts, nor is her *Diary* a mere extension or complementary part of that literary tradition. She is not Miller's female counterpart, nor is she an elitist, apolitical antifeminist. Nin is the writer of a "minor literature," a literature that uses a minor language. She sets up a minor practice of a major language from within; she ruptures the language used by the male writers around her in order to move in a different direction. About how to use a minor language, Deleuze and Guattari state: "Go always further in the direction of deterritorialization, to the point of sobriety. Since the language is arid, make it vibrate with a new intensity. Oppose a purely intensive usage of language to all symbolic or even significant or simply signifying usages of it. Arrive at a perfect and unformed expression, a materially intense expression" (*Kafka* 19). Nin manages to do this in her diaries as they grow out of her more molar, striated novelettes. The *Diary* uses the English language, a major language, intensively. "Even when major, a language is open to an intensive utilization that makes it take flight along creative lines of escape which, no matter how slowly, no matter how cautiously, can now form an absolute deterritorialization" (*Kafka* 26). Nin, who was respected by Miller but constantly told by him that she needed to brush up on her usage of English and that he would help her "master" the language, remained unknown as a literary figure until the publication of her *Diary,* a proliferating, rhizomatic form. Her *Diary* has made her a marginal literary figure at best; she is still eschewed by feminists and known more for her relationships with famous men than for her writing. However, it is important to realize that her marginality is not the fault of her rhizome (her *Diary*) but, rather, the fault of the arborescent nature of literary canonization. Her *Diary* manages to deterritorialize language and create a line of flight that still remains unrecognized for its potential to offer alternative intensities and values.

Yet even in the *Diary* Nin often makes statements like "I can turn away from reality into the reflections and dreams [the diary] projects" (1:333) which get her into trouble with feminists who read this as an apolitical and elitist turning away or escape from the "real" world. Statements of this kind make it seem that, in fact, Nin's secret is completely unrhizomatic, that it is absolutely private, introverted, and subjective. However, Nin's escape from life through writing is not necessarily a turning away from reality. "In reality," Deleuze suggests, *"writing does not have its end in itself, precisely because life is not something personal."* Or rather, the aim of writing is to carry life to the state of a non-personal power. In doing this it renounces claim to any territory, any end which would reside in itself" (*Dialogues* 50). As a rhizome, Nin's *Diary* becomes a line of flight out of patriarchal institutions. A line of flight is not a renunciation of action. On the contrary, "nothing is more active than a flight. It is the opposite of the imaginary. It is also to put to flight—not necessarily others, but to put something to flight, to put a system to flight" (*Dialogues* 36). Not only does the rhizomatic *Diary's* line of flight derail patriarchy by, among other things, rupturing the law of the father by writing about incest and breaking the law of genre by using an uncontainable and ever-expanding form, it also derails a collective common sense characterized by the unnecessary tendency to reduce life to an Oedipal narrative. Nin's rhizome is written as an escape: "[M]y struggle was against every trap, every entrapment of experience, every limitation, every restriction, either by the poverty which I experienced in my childhood or by being uprooted and not speaking the language of my new country. I had to find immediately the way out" (*Woman Speaks* 223). Instead of being an escape from reality, Nin's *Diary* can be read as the embodiment of a reality or a collectivity yet to come. After all, as Nin puts it, "one does not need to remain in bondage to the first wax imprint made on childhood sensibilities. One need not be branded by the first pattern" (*Diary* 1:105).

The *Diary* expands against the objections of her father, Allendy, Rank, and even Miller. By allowing the *Diary* to proliferate, to expand, despite the men's objections, Nin creates a line of flight out of limiting patriarchal influences, first, for herself and, second, for a future collectivity. By disrupting the foundations of psychoanalysis (by breaking the incest taboo) and of modernism (by inadvertently breaking with its formal conventions), Nin manages to produce something unexpected with her *Diary*. Her line of flight, rather than escaping reality, deterritorializes or transforms reality itself. Or at least it has the potential to do so.

But the *Diary*'s line of flight—its explosion of form, its oozing of the secret from private into public—becomes "imperceptible."[18] According to Deleuze and Guattari, becoming-imperceptible is what happens when a rhizomatic line takes flight and, paradoxically, becomes invisible to the collective common sense while nonetheless sweeping that majority itself into a "becoming." It is a process of becoming-minor within the major. It is a process that shatters reactive, often oppressive, notions of identity toward an untimely becoming that has the potential to transform dominant affects or at least to reveal their contingency. A secret attains imperceptibility not when it is fixed and hidden from view but when it becomes "nonlocalizable," when its form can no longer contain it (*Thousand Plateaus* 288). Nin's secret goes from being a personal childhood diversion to a multivolume published text. The more her secret proliferates, the more its form dissolves.

But Nin's becoming-imperceptible does not just begin with the publication of her *Diary*. For her, secrecy was not simply a matter of hiding her diary but of hiding her "core self." Of course, she is perfectly aware of the fictional aspect of the notion of a core self, but that doesn't stop her from trying to dupe those around her into believing that she actually does believe in a fixed identity. After all, she seems to be sharing it with whomever she happens to be with at the time. As early as 1928 Nin writes, "I was tempted today to keep a double journal, one for things which do happen, and one for imaginary incidents which pass through my head as a result of some insignificant happening on which I embroider. I live *doubly*. I'll write *doubly*" (*Early Diary* 56). By 1932 the imaginary diary has become necessary to keep her identities from stepping on each other's toes. She creates a "false" diary exclusively for Hugh so that he will not realize she is having an affair with Miller. She writes, "I tell Hugo about my *imaginary* journal of a possessed woman, which fortifies him in his attitude that everything is make-believe except our love" (*Henry and June* 75). Lying—about herself, about her diary, about her relationships—to the various people with whom she is involved encourages all of them to believe that they know the "true" Nin. In fact, only she knows that the secret of her "identity," if it can be called that, is its multiplicity or proliferation. She declares, "I enlarge and expand my self; I do not like to be just one Anaïs, whole, familiar, contained. As soon as someone defines me . . . I seek escape from the confinements of definition" (*Diary* 1:29). But what is it that she is seeking through her disguises? She writes, "I am against my Father because he is all mind and reason.

I want to live alone in unknown hotel rooms. Lose my identity. My memory. My home and husband and lovers" (*Incest* 261). This desire to lose identity, to escape the ties to patriarchy in all its various forms—father, memory, bourgeois home, husband, psychoanalysts, and modernist writer/lover—is exactly what she manages to accomplish through her rhizomatic *Diary*. Her lines of flight release her from and reveal the gratuitousness of the various "necessities" of patriarchal institutions. In addition, the constant editing, transforming, and reshaping of the *Diary*, which preclude its ever being called definitive, is aligned with Nin's desire to lose her identity, to become-imperceptible.

Why can't the *Diary*, as it is presented to the public, be called definitive? The first seven volumes of the *Diary* were published after undergoing major editing and cuts. Some critics have found this troubling since, to say the least, it muddies the distinction between "true" autobiography and "false" fiction. As Sharon Spencer states, "Precisely because, as she herself said, there is 'no separation' between her life and her work, because she succeeded in blending the form of her art with the form of her life and because she rejects 'artificial patterns,' Nin inadvertently presents a problem for traditionally oriented readers. They do not know *what* she is writing: poetry; prose; memoirs; autobiography. Unable to fit her books into historical literary categories, too many readers and even critics dismiss them as inept" (156). Yet not only does Nin have no qualms about editing her diaries before publication, she also doesn't mind lying about or distorting the nature of the editing process itself. In a 1972 interview she says, "I must be very careful not to cheat. I mustn't cheat because that would ruin it completely" (Freeman 187). But "cheat" she did, as the more recently published "unexpurgated" versions make clear. In fact, the unexpurgated versions have themselves been edited, as Deirdre Bair has noted: "All this shaping of [Nin's] original text, from initial selection to correction of her grammar, punctuation, and spelling, and even in many instances of her actual language, has resulted in something different in many cases from what she actually wrote" (518). The *Diary*'s multiple transformations are absolutely in line with Nin's own desire to multiply, to proliferate, and even, in a sense, to lose her identity—that is, to become imperceptible.

"There is always betrayal in a line of flight," Deleuze states, and one who betrays is automatically a traitor (*Dialogues* 40). Furthermore, "it is difficult to be a traitor; it is to create. One has to lose one's identity, one's face, in it. One has to disappear, to become unknown" (45). Nin's line of flight out of patriarchy certainly involves betrayal; in fact, many would read her promiscuity, her lies in life, and her self-proclaimed embellishment of the *Diary* as betrayals. Yet as a traitor, Nin creates. From the betrayals, from the lies, grows the *Diary*. And from between the pages of the *Diary* comes the dismantling of identity. Deleuze is suggesting that with the sharing of the creation, with the disclosure of the secret, "identity" disappears altogether. When "we no longer have any secrets, we no longer have anything to hide. It is we who have become a secret, it is we who are hidden, even though we do all openly, in broad daylight" (46). This is certainly the case with Nin's self-representation. For who is the "real" Anaïs Nin? Is it the Nin of the *Early Diaries,* of the seven edited volumes, of the unexpurgated versions? Is it Hugh's Nin, Miller's Nin, Joaquín's Nin, Allendy's Nin, Rank's Nin, or Rupert Pole's Nin?[19] Disclosing the "truth" about her "self" displaces the very notions of "truth" and "self" by sheer proliferation. Nin is aware of the implications of multiplicity when she states, "I want to be a writer who reminds others . . . that there is infinite space, infinite meaning, infinite dimension" (*Diary* 1:5). In her betrayal, she creates; in sharing with others, she becomes imperceptible, a secret.

About the secret's move into imperceptibility Deleuze says, "Influence by rays, and doubling by flight or echo, are what now give the secret its infinite form, in which perceptions as well as actions pass into imperceptibility" (*Thousand Plateaus* 289). In a lecture, Nin similarly likens the publication of the *Diary* to being struck by an overwhelming ray: "[J]ust before I published the diary I had a frightening dream. I dreamt that I opened my front door and was struck by lethal radiation" (*Woman Speaks* 149).[20] She goes on, "Instead of that, however, I opened my front door and found a sense of union with the world and communication with other women. Instead of finding myself destroyed, I found the beginning of communion with the whole world" (*Woman Speaks* 149). Although a "communion with the whole world" might have seemed within reach in the late 1960s and early 1970s, it certainly isn't the case now and especially not in feminist academic circles. As Ellen G. Friedman puts it, "feminist literary criticism has not yet embraced her" (349). It seems that Nin's becoming imperceptible has not led to a new collectivity. In fact, Nin herself voiced concern about her state of fragmentation; she did not always feel like celebrating the condition of her multiple identities. She wrote, "I can no longer put my mosaics together. I just cry and laugh" (*Henry and June* 58). As Sidonie Smith warns, "Any autobiographical practice that promotes endless fragmentation and a reified multiplicity might be counterproductive since the autobiographical subject would have to split itself beyond usefulness to be truly nonexclusionary. It is hard to coalesce a call to political action around a constantly deferred point of departure" (188).

Similarly, the problem with becoming-imperceptible, as numerous feminists have pointed out, is that it seems countereffectual to feminist political agency. For example, Alice Jardine has argued that Deleuze and Guattari's terminology depoliticizes feminist struggle because the process of becoming-imperceptible seems to imply "women becoming obsolete" (54). However, Elizabeth Grosz has demonstrated that this is not necessarily the case. In fact, becoming-imperceptible does not mean the obliteration of all characteristics but instead "implies the demassification of the categories of sex, class, race, and sexual preference, so that even within these categories a whole range of forces is always in play" (*Volatile Bodies* 181). This understanding suggests that the rhizomatic process of becoming-imperceptible might enable what Diana Fuss has called a "more mature identity politics" since it does not attempt to level differences for strategic political practices (104). Nin's becoming-imperceptible can be understood as a collectivizing line of flight that might renew feminist interest in her work. Grosz states that rhizomatics "is concerned with what can be done; how texts, concepts and subjects can be put to work, made to do things, make new linkages" ("Thousand Tiny Sexes" 200). With that in mind, a rhizomatic reading of Nin's rhizomatic texts might hint at assemblages or "machines," to use Deleuze and Guattari's term, that are implicitly or virtually collective and political.

As a rhizome, Nin's *Diary* must be understood as a productive "desiring machine." In Deleuze and Guattari, desiring-machine is another name for an assemblage or a linking of singularities. It can be equated with Spinoza's *conatus* and Nietzsche's will to power (Massumi 82). Contrary to Freudian or Lacanian understandings of desire, in Deleuze and Guattari, desire is not based on lack. It is not subjectivist or essentialist. Instead, desire is what it produces, what it connects with; in short, desire is the rhizome itself. Nin's *Diary* as rhizomatic writing, like the body and as a body, is affective. Deleuze and Guattari's theory of the affective body develops out of both Spinoza and Nietzsche; the term they use, the "Body without Organs" or BwO, comes from Antonin Artaud. The BwO is a body without organization, "without a psychical interior, without internal cohesion or latent significance" (Grosz, "Thousand Tiny Sexes" 201). In the *Diary,* Nin's own body becomes a series of flows connecting with other bodies, both organic and nonorganic. She writes, "I am like a person turned inside out, flowering to the utmost, through my senses, mind, emotions. . . . I discover a whole forest of strange new flowers. No ideologies. The realm of pure senses. . . . The woman is turned inside out, and all this wealth that was once a secret is pouring out. I have an immense hunger for life. I would like to be in so many places. I would like to be traveling and roaming and vagabonding. I would like to be writing. I would like to be dancing somewhere in the South. . . . I would like to meet the whole world at once" (1:329). Nin's emphasis on the body as a site of circulating intensities, as well as her focus on the body's myriad affective capacities, points to the productivity of desire itself. The *Diary* produces in singular ways that interrupt its readers' habits of mind. These singularities—for example, Nin's active dismantling of the incest taboo and her destabilizing of identity—can produce new desires, values, and affects in those who read her texts, thus making Nin's readers part of the rhizomatic assemblage. In contrast to psychoanalysis and to psychoanalytic readings of Nin which tend to block the body's affective capacities at the Oedipal impasse, Nin's body and her *Diary* as a BwO are always affective and always already linked to a collective and social reality.

Nin's collective BwO occurs by way of the rhizomatics of the *Diary* and the assemblages the *Diary* forms with other desiring-machines. She tells "Countess Lucie" (actually Nellie, the comtesse de Vogüé, as we learn in the unexpurgated version), "I can only tell you that my surroundings are *me.* Everything is me because I have rejected all conventions, the opinion of the world, all its laws" (1:185–86)—which would include the Lacanian law of the father, the law that defines desire as lack. Nin's focus on the body's ability to connect multilaterally with various intensities both organic and nonorganic, as well as her shattering of the notion of identity by way of her imperceptibility, are all elements of her becoming-minor or -molecular; she is minor within a major or molar collectivity that, as of yet, does not have the ears to hear the changes in sensibility her diaries announce. Becoming-minor in a major collectivity—that is, within the prevailing common sense— means that untimely seeds are planted which prepare the conditions for a different collectivity, a different way for people to view, as well as sense, the world. Instead of "a conception of truth determined by unthinking subjection to an acquired habit" (Nietzsche 172), the body, as a productive desiring-machine, overcomes its reactivity and becomes active (Deleuze, *Nietzsche* 39–72).

Nin's rhizomatic *Diary* has this affective potential. If Nin is read as antifeminist, as essentialistic, as overly elitist, as she often is, it is not simply because her texts situate her as such; rather, it is because reactive readers reterritorialize her lines of flight. Nin's self-proliferation has often been interpreted as ineffectual for feminist identity politics. However, it is also possible to read Nin's becoming-imperceptible as a move toward the creation of an alternative collective common sense. For example, the present collectivity is one in which the father's word is law; the incest taboo is strictly upheld, thereby privileging the heterosexual norm. But an alternative collective common sense—one that emerges from or, more accurately, assembles with Nin's rhizome—might be characterized by its recognition of the contingency of the incest taboo and by its acknowledgment of the fiction of gender "necessities" and supposedly "natural" heterosexual desires. By writing about her evasion of certain patriarchal institutions—the absolute authority of the father, the Oedipal constraints of psychoanalysis, and conventional literary genres—Nin's *Diary* suggests that these kinds of "minor" effects always constitute dominant systems of organization despite any dominant collectivity's attempt to deny or ignore this. As Nin herself puts it, "Each artist has to struggle not to conform to the culture but to add to the culture, to create the future" (*Woman Speaks* 193).

I would like to end with two quotes. Nin proclaims, "I must constantly renounce and sublimate. When I am most deeply rooted, I feel the wildest desire to uproot myself" (*Henry and June* 262). And Deleuze and Guattari warn, "Never send down roots, or plant them, however difficult it may be to avoid reverting to the old procedures" (*Thousand Plateaus* 23). In this essay I have tried to show that as a rhizome Nin's *Diary* manages to avoid reverting to at least some of the "old procedures." What begins as a secret goes on to explode into imperceptibility while paradoxically embodying a virtual or potential collectivity. It is all too easy to read Nin's texts in psychoanalytic terms. It is even easier to argue that her brand of feminism is too essentializing and apolitical for our constructivist and politically exigent tendencies. It is perhaps time to uproot Nin's reactive critical reception and to recognize how Nin's *Diary* actively constructs the conditions for progressive change.

NOTES

This essay is a revised and expanded version of "A Secret Proliferation: Anaïs Nin's 'Diary' as Deleuzian Rhizome," published in *Anaïs:
An International Journal* 17 (1999): 78–86.

1. Originary notions of selfhood, sexuality, individualism, and the autonomy of art form part of Nin's textual apparatus as it has been commonly received. Poststructuralists like Jacques Derrida, Michel
   Foucault, and Gilles Deleuze have problematized these very notions in
   ways that call into question some of Nin's essentializing assumptions
   about femininity and creativity. This has, I would argue, complicated
   and transformed critical responses to her work in recent times.
   Philippa Christmass gives an account of how changes in feminist theory have affected Nin's critical reception. She raises questions about
   the appropriateness of Nin's texts to feminism in the 1990s. She states,
   "In the 1960s, Nin's journals were viewed by many as feminist simply
   because they focused on a woman's personal history. Thirty years later,
   definitions of what constitutes a feminist text have, in many ways,
   changed. What was radical in the 1960s may seem less so now" (36).
2. Diane Richard-Allerdyce's recent Lacanian study of Nin's texts
   demonstrates how Nin's critical reception can be complicated in
   ways informed by more contemporary critical theories.
3. For the purposes of this essay, I shall be focusing primarily on the
   years 1931–34. In *Diary* terms this means: *The Diary of Anaïs Nin, Volume I, 1931–1934; Henry and June: From the Unexpurgated Diary of Anaïs
   Nin;* and *Incest: From "A Journal of Love": The Unexpurgated Diary of
   Anaïs Nin, 1932–1934*. I shall also be looking at Nin's novelette entitled "Winter of Artifice," from her three-novelette collection of the
   same name, since it is a fictionalized version of the events of 1933.
4. "Deleuze and Guattari argue that the Western tradition has a second
   major metaphor [after the metaphor of the mirror], that of the tree,
   whereby the mind organizes its knowledge of reality (provided by
   the mirror) in systematic and hierarchical principles (branches of
   knowledge) which are grounded in firm foundations (roots). These
   allow arborescent culture to build vast conceptual systems that are
   centered, unified, hierarchical, and grounded in a self-transparent,
   self-identical, representing subject" (Best and Kellner 98–99).
5. Deleuze and Guattari describe "deterritorialization" as a process of
   destabilizing, disrupting, or even displacing any arborescent category
   or code of organization (identity, capitalism, patriarchy, psychoanalysis, family, modernism, etc.). Any territorialized form of organization contains within it the possibility of being deterritorialized.
   Further, any deterritorialized "body" (used in a broad sense to
   include both organic and nonorganic bodies) is in constant danger of
   being "reterritorialized" (*Thousand Plateaus* 9–12).

6. For Deleuze and Guattari, unlike Freud and Lacan, desire "has absolutely nothing to do with lack or with the 'law'" (Deleuze and Parnet 95). Instead, desire is understood as productive and affirmative. As Elizabeth Grosz explains, "Desire is what produces, what makes things, forges connections, creates relations, produces machinic alignments. Instead of aligning desire with fantasy and opposing it to the real, as psychoanalysis does, for Deleuze, desire is what produces the real; instead of a yearning, desire is an actualization" ("Thousand Tiny Sexes" 195). In *Volatile Bodies* Grosz argues, "Such a notion of desire cannot but be of interest to feminist theory insofar as women have been the traditional repositories and guardians of the lack constitutive of desire, and insofar as the opposition between presence and absence, reality and fantasy, has traditionally defined and constrained woman to inhabit the place of man's other. . . . Any model of desire that dispenses with the primacy of lack in conceiving desire seems to be a positive step forward" (165).

7. In Deleuze and Guattari's terms, any deterritorialized body is called a "Body without Organs" (BwO). The BwO is not a body without any organs but, rather, a body without organization. It is a body (organic or nonorganic) that "breaks free from its socially articulated, disciplined, semioticized, and subjectified states (as an 'organism'), to become disarticulated, dismantled, and deterritorialized, and hence able to be reconstituted in new ways" (Best and Kellner 90–91). This term will be discussed in relation to Nin's *Diary* shortly.

8. Deleuze and Guattari use the term "machine" to explain their productive notion of desire. On Deleuze and Guattari's understanding, "machine" should not be confused with "mechanical" or "technological." Both organic and nonorganic bodies can be "machinic" when they are in a process of becoming or of deterritorialization. More on machines will soon follow.

9. Nin's flows do not merely represent an alternative to the Oedipalizing tendencies of psychoanalysis in a way that is covertly ideological. That is, her promiscuity does not have to be read as a *necessary* alternative to defining woman as man's other and woman's desire as lack. On the contrary, Nin's flows, her connections to all aspects of life— personal, social, political—by way of her incestuous affair with her father and her relationships with Allendy, Rank, and Miller demonstrate just how contingent any ideology is. Her rhizomatic *Diary* is not a manifesto proclaiming the merits of narcissistic and promiscuous living, nor does it advertise the validity of "reading" a life as an Oedipal psychonarrative, as some would argue. Instead, the *Diary* is part of a deterritorialization (or a "becoming-minor") that disrupts the inevitability of the prevailing common sense while remaining within it. Nin connects with her father while simultaneously subverting the "Father," thereby undermining any appearance of stability and

necessity. But her "lines of flight" or escapes are certainly not the only ones possible.

10. For Deleuze and Guattari, "major" and "minor" literatures are not qualitatively opposed. To "become-minor" always implies to "crack up" the major within the major itself. There are three main characteristics of a minor literature. First, language in a minor literature deterritorializes majoritarian language practices. Second, everything in a minor literature is political. Third, everything in it takes on a collective value. In this essay I am suggesting that Nin's literature can be read in "minor" ways just as Deleuze and Guattari in *Kafka* (16–27) read his literature as minor.

11. The Oedipal triangle of father-mother-child is one that a minor literature explodes. This explosion or exaggeration unblocks the psychoanalytic impasse within which everything is caught. Instead of an individual psychology, which is often what modernist writers are criticized for focusing on to the exclusion of the political realm, there is a whole world—political, economic, and social (Deleuze and Guattari, *Kafka* 9–15).

12. For Deleuze and Guattari, a "line of flight" is a deterritorializing movement away from rigid or "molar" identities and other systems of organization. A "molecular" line disrupts or even subverts "molar" lines, but it is the "line of flight" that expresses or creates a shift in (whatever) order. Whereas subversion is mere reversal with the terms kept intact, escape transforms the terminology itself—and, potentially, the embodiment of that terminology (*Thousand Plateaus* 3–25 and 192–207).

13. I am not suggesting that Nin's novelettes are "bad" in any evaluative sense, simply that her *Diary* is radical in a way that they are not. I am quite certain rhizomatic readings of Nin's fiction that could challenge my claim are possible. However, I would argue that it would be necessary to base such readings on what she accomplishes in the *Diary*. The *Diary*, on the other hand, does not *need* the novelettes in order to be rhizomatic.

14. I have chosen not to discuss Hugh Guiler, not because Nin's representation of him in the unexpurgated versions of her *Diary* does not warrant analysis, but only because it goes beyond the scope of this essay. Nin's negotiation of her complex marital circumstances over the years as expressed in her *Diary* deserves special attention. Suffice it to say that I think it is far too easy to claim that, simply because she was financially dependent on Hugh, all her escapes are reterritorialized. In fact, I would argue that her financial dependence on Hugh, before, during, and after the years I am specifically dealing with here, might have been the very condition of possibility for her textual expressions of escape—expressions that, in Deleuze and Guattari's sense, do not reflect some deep, hidden subjectivity but instead occur because of the material conditions of a body's existence.

15. This is exactly the way Ellen G. Friedman reads it. She argues that Nin must escape her father and the incest taboo in order to truly escape the law of the father and patriarchy. She states that the "imagery of incest suggests limitation, artistic and other, imposed by the father who allows only repetitions of himself and the world he has constructed in his own image. . . . Thus the father also represents cultural constraint. Incest is a strategy to keep the daughter imprisoned in the father's world. It serves the daughter as well in that incest allies her with the father's power, yet it prevents her from choosing other objects of desire—those outside of the father, who represents the dominant culture, represents law and patriarchy. As the term is developed by Nin, one implication of 'incest' for the artist is conformity to conventional modes; escaping the father would allow innovation, the formulating of new modes" (343). Though I would agree with Friedman's last statement, I disagree with her formulation of "escape." Friedman argues that escaping the father in Nin's case means accepting the incest taboo in order to be able to choose other "objects of desire." However, as Butler has argued and as I mentioned earlier, accepting (and naturalizing) the incest taboo means accepting (and naturalizing) the heterosexual norm. This in turn means that those "objects of desire" can only ever be other men. Additionally, escaping the father by escaping incest means entering an already patriarchally and heterosexually constructed world. I would like to argue that Nin's breaking of the incest taboo and her proliferation of this transgression in her relationships with other men and in her *Diary* create a different kind of escape.

16. In *A Thousand Plateaus* Deleuze and Guattari state: "If it is true that it is of the essence of the map or rhizome to have multiple entryways, then it is plausible that one could even enter them through tracings or the root-tree assuming the necessary precautions are taken. . . . It is even possible for psychoanalysis to serve as a foothold, in spite of itself" (14–15).

17. Julia Casterton makes a similar claim. Casterton states, "The act of confession implies a confessor, an eye that sees, an intelligence that approves or condemns—and the 'art' of the Journals involves a series of flights *towards and away from* such a figure. The diary describes a struggle, away from the father, away from the analyst who seeks to force her to cease keeping a diary, away from the consuming demands of close male artist friends" (Molyneux and Casterton 96, emphasis added).

18. "Becoming-imperceptible" is one degree of "becoming" theorized by Deleuze and Guattari. "Becoming-animal," "becoming-woman," and "becoming-child" are other forms of deterritorialization they discuss (*Thousand Plateaus* 232–309).

19. I mention Rupert Pole here because, of course, he has been the "editor" of the recent unexpurgated versions of Nin's *Diary*.

20. Her dream eerily foreshadows the radiation treatments Nin would have to undergo to treat her cancer in—according to Deirdre Bair's biography—1970.

WORKS CITED

Bair, Deirdre. *Anaïs Nin: A Biography.* New York: Putnam, 1995.

Best, Steven, and Douglas Kellner. *Postmodern Theory: Critical Interrogations.* New York: Guilford Press, 1991.

Butler, Judith. *Gender Trouble: Feminism and the Subversion of Identity.* New York: Routledge, 1990.

Christmass, Philippa. "A Mother to Us All? Feminism and *The Diary of Anaïs Nin*—Thirty Years Later." *Anaïs: An International Journal* 14 (1996): 35–41.

Deleuze, Gilles. *Nietzsche and Philosophy.* Trans. Hugh Tomlinson. New York: Columbia University Press, 1983.

Deleuze, Gilles, and Félix Guattari. *Anti-Oedipus: Capitalism and Schizophrenia.* Trans. Robert Hurley, Mark Seem, and Helen R. Lane. New York: Viking, 1977; rpt. Minneapolis: University of Minnesota Press, 1983.

———. *Kafka: Toward a Minor Literature.* Trans. Dana Polan. Minneapolis: University of Minnesota Press, 1986.

———. *A Thousand Plateaus: Capitalism and Schizophrenia.* Trans. Brian Massumi. Minneapolis: University of Minnesota Press, 1987.

Deleuze, Gilles, and Claire Parnet. *Dialogues.* Trans. Hugh Tomlinson and Barbara Habberjam. New York: Columbia University Press, 1987.

Derrida, Jacques. "The Law of Genre." *Acts of Literature.* Ed. Derek Attridge, 221–52. New York: Routledge, 1992.

Freeman, Barbara. "A Dialogue with Anaïs Nin." *Conversations with Anaïs Nin.* Ed. Wendy M. DuBow, 186–94. Jackson: University Press of Mississippi, 1994.

Friedman, Ellen G. "Anaïs Nin." *Modern American Women Writers.* Ed. Elaine Showalter, Lea Baechler, and A. Walton Litz, 339–51. New York: Scribner, 1991.

Fuss, Diana. *Essentially Speaking: Feminism, Nature and Difference.* New York: Routledge, 1989.

Grosz, Elizabeth. "A Thousand Tiny Sexes: Feminism and Rhizomatics." *Gilles Deleuze and the Theater of Philosophy.* Ed. Constantin V. Boundas and Dorothea Olkowski, 187–210. New York: Routledge, 1994.

———. *Volatile Bodies: Toward a Corporeal Feminism.* Bloomington: Indiana University Press, 1994.

Gusdorf, Georges. "Conditions and Limits of Autobiography." Trans. James Olney. *Autobiography: Essays Theoretical and Critical.* Ed. James Olney, 28–48. Princeton: Princeton University Press, 1980.

Hogan, Rebecca. "Engendered Autobiographies: The Diary as a Feminine Form." *Autobiography and Questions of Gender.* Ed. Shirley Neuman, 95–107. London: Frank Cass, 1991.

Jardine, Alice. "Woman in Limbo: Deleuze and His Br(others)." *SubStance* 44/45 (1984): 46–60.

Jelinek, Estelle C. "Anaïs Nin: A Critical Evaluation." *Feminist Criticism: Essays in Theory, Poetry, and Prose.* Ed. Cheryl L. Brown and Karen Olson, 312–23. Metuchen, N.J.: Scarecrow Press, 1978.

Juhasz, Suzanne. "Towards a Theory of Form in Feminist Autobiography: Kate Millet's *Flying* and *Sita;* Maxine Hong Kingston's *The Woman Warrior.*" *Women's Autobiography: Essays in Criticism.* Ed. Estelle C. Jelinek, 221–37. Bloomington: Indiana University Press, 1980.

Massumi, Brian. *A User's Guide to Capitalism and Schizophrenia: Deviations from Deleuze and Guattari.* Cambridge: MIT Press, 1992.

Molyneux, Maxine, and Julia Casterton. "Looking Again at Anaïs Nin." *Minnesota Review* 18 (1982): 86–101.

Nietzsche, Friedrich. *Untimely Meditations.* Trans. R. J. Hollingdale. Cambridge: Cambridge University Press, 1983.

Nin, Anaïs. *The Diary of Anaïs Nin, Volume I, 1931–1934.* Ed. Gunther Stuhlmann. San Diego: Swallow Press and Harcourt Brace Jovanovich, 1966.

———. *The Early Diary of Anaïs Nin, Volume Four, 1927–1931.* Ed. Rupert Pole. San Diego: Harcourt Brace Jovanovich, 1985.

———. *Henry and June: From the Unexpurgated Diary of Anaïs Nin.* Ed. Rupert Pole. San Diego: Harcourt Brace Jovanovich, 1986.

———. *Incest: From "A Journal of Love": The Unexpurgated Diary of Anaïs Nin, 1932–1934.* Ed. Rupert Pole. New York: Harcourt Brace Jovanovich, 1992.

———. "Winter of Artifice." 1942. *Winter of Artifice: Three Novelettes,* 55–119. Denver: Alan Swallow, 1961.

———. *A Woman Speaks: The Lectures, Seminars, and Interviews of Anaïs Nin.* Ed. Evelyn J. Hinz. Chicago: Swallow Press, 1975.

Nin, Anaïs, and Henry Miller. *A Literate Passion: Letters of Anaïs Nin and Henry Miller, 1932–1953.* Ed. Gunther Stuhlmann. San Diego: Harcourt Brace Jovanovich, 1987.

Nussbaum, Felicity A. "Toward Conceptualizing Diary." *Studies in Autobiography.* Ed. James Olney, 128–40. New York: Oxford University Press, 1988.

Pascal, Roy. *Design and Truth in Autobiography.* London: Routledge & Kegan Paul; Cambridge: Harvard University Press, 1960.

Richard-Allerdyce, Diane. *Anaïs Nin and the Remaking of Self: Gender, Modernism, and Narrative Identity.* DeKalb, Ill.: Northern Illinois University Press, 1998.

Smith, Sidonie. "The Autobiographical Manifesto: Identities, Temporalities, Politics." *Autobiography and Questions of Gender.* Ed. Shirley Neuman, 186–212. London: Frank Cass, 1991.

Spencer, Sharon. "The Art of Ragpicking." *Anaïs, Art and Artists: A Collection of Essays.* Ed. Sharon Spencer, 155–74. Greenwood, Fla.: Penkevill, 1986.

Contributors

Mai Al-Nakib, a Ph.D. candidate in the English Department at Brown University, is working on a revision of contemporary critical rhetorics within modernist and postcolonial studies from the perspective of Deleuze and Guattari. She has previously published on Anaïs Nin's work in *Anaïs: An International Journal*.

Philippa Christmass has published articles on Nin in *Anaïs: An International Journal* and in the Australian feminist journal *Outskirts*. Interested in popular culture and surrealism, she completed her Ph.D. thesis on Anaïs Nin at the University of Western Australia in 1999.

Marion N. Fay is an instructor of English at the College of Alameda, California, where she also produces a cultural events series for the college and community. She has published articles on Anaïs Nin in *Anaïs: An International Journal* and in *Anaïs Nin: A Book of Mirrors*. Her essay on Willa Cather will appear in the forthcoming book *Literature and Music*.

Ellen G. Friedman is professor of English and director of Women's and Gender Studies at The College of New Jersey. Author of numerous articles on feminism and contemporary culture, she has also written, with Corinne Squire, *Morality USA* and edited, with Miriam Fuchs, *Breaking the Sequence: Women's Experimental Fiction*.

Suzette Henke is Thruston B. Morton, Sr., professor of Literary Studies at the University of Louisville and author of numerous articles and books, especially on twentieth-century writers. Among her most recent publications are *Shattered Subjects: Trauma and Testimony in Women's Life-Writing* and *James Joyce and the Politics of Desire*.

Thomas M. March completed his Ph.D. at New York University in May 2000. He has written essays on the work of Anaïs Nin, George Orwell, Virginia Woolf, Edmund Wilson, Saki, and Bessie Head. His interests include twentieth-century British and American literature, with special emphasis on the novel, psychoanalysis, and the representation of consciousness.

Diane Richard-Allerdyce has published *Anaïs Nin and the Remaking of Self: Gender, Modernism, and Narrative Identity* as well as several essays on Nin's work. She is professor of English, department chair, and co-director of the honors program at Lynn University in Boca Raton, Florida.

Anne T. Salvatore is professor of English and associate director of Writing Across the Curriculum at Rider University, New Jersey. Specializing in twentieth-century prose narratives and writing theory, she is the author of *Greene and Kierkegaard: The Discourse of Belief* and editor, with Robert Reilly, of *Knowing and Writing: New Perspectives on Classical Questions.*

Sharon Spencer has published both fiction and literary criticism. Her works devoted to Nin include *Collage of Dreams: The Writings of Anaïs Nin* and more than two dozen articles and review essays; she also edited *Anais, Art and Artists: A Collections of Essays.* She is retired professor of Comparative Literature at Montclair State University.

Maxie Wells is assistant professor of English at Baton Rouge Community College in Baton Rouge, Louisiana. She specializes in nineteenth- and twentieth-century American and southern literature, particularly literature by women.